Ethnography and the
Historical Imagination

Studies in the Ethnographic Imagination

John Comaroff, Pierre Bourdieu, and Maurice Bloch, *Series Editors*

Ethnography and the Historical Imagination

John & Jean Comaroff

First Interview with the Chief of the Bachapins

WESTVIEW PRESS

Boulder • San Francisco • Oxford

Studies in the Ethnographic Imagination

Shown on the cover is William J. Burchell's 1812 drawing of his first interview with Mothibi [Mattivi], chief of the Batlhaping [Bachapīns], at Dithakong [Litākun].

Published in 1992 in the United States of America by Westview Press, Inc., 5500 Central Avenue, Boulder, Colorado 80301-2847, and in the United Kingdom by Westview Press, 36 Lonsdale Road, Summertown, Oxford OX2 7EW

Library of Congress Cataloging-in-Publication Data
Comaroff, John L., 1945–
    Ethnography and the historical imagination / John and Jean
Comaroff.
    p.   cm. — (Studies in the ethnographic imagination)
Includes bibliographical references and index.
ISBN 0-8133-1304-X. — ISBN 0-8133-1305-8 (pbk.)
    1. Ethnology—Philosophy.   2. Ethnology—Methodology.
I. Comaroff, Jean.   II. Title.   III. Series.
GN345.C64   1992
305.8′001—dc20   91-45642
                                                                                          CIP

Printed and bound in the United States of America

∞   The paper used in this publication meets the requirements
      of the American National Standard for Permanence of Paper
      for Printed Library Materials Z39.48-1984.

10   9   8   7   6   5   4   3   2   1

Contents

Preface

ONE OF OUR SENIOR COLLEAGUES recently reflected, somewhat ruefully, that anthropology has lost control over its two most basic terms, *culture* and *ethnography;* that, in the age of deconstruction and critical postmodernism, we have entered a conceptual free-for-all in which our disciplinary quest has no terrain of its own any more. Our tropes have been taken over, our signs seized. Even the exotic, the world of cultures unambiguously other, is no longer a secure refuge. After all, literary criticism has also, to borrow Torgovnick's aphorism, "gone primitive" (1990). And cultural studies devote themselves increasingly to the "subcultures" of those who inhabit the margins of the modern world order. Nice ontological debates between, say, anthropological structuralists and theorists of practice, materialists and meaning-mongers, slip into insignificance next to the danger of death by dispossession.

We shall have to wait and see whether this new academic angst is justified; over its relatively short life, anthropology has been prone to periodic attacks of epistemological ennui (see, e.g., Leach 1961; Hymes 1969; Banaji 1970; Worsley 1970; Murphy 1971; Ardener 1971; Crick 1976). In the meantime, the present volume argues for the continuing value of a historical anthropology in which ethnography and culture remain vital—indeed, are even revitalized. In specifying what this anthropology may entail, amidst the intellectual turbulence of the late twentieth century, we shall suggest that the discipline is best distinguished by its method—in the European sense of "theoretically informed practice"—rather than by its current theories, its repertoire of terms, or its subject matter. This, of course, echoes Geertz's (1973) stress on "doing ethnography." As will become clear, however, our sense of "doing" is quite different from his. The method of which we speak is emphatically *neo*modern. It seeks to construct imaginative sociologies of terrains both near and far, more or less complex, familiar and strange, local and global—accounts at once social and cultural, both imaginative in their grasp of the interior worlds of others and yet, to paraphrase Thorburn (1990:x), respectful of the real. In this we keep close to the essential pulse of anthropology while simultaneously straying into the territory of social history and literary studies. But no matter. More than disciplinary proprieties, what counts here is a shared spirit of inquiry.

Before we speak further of neomodernist anthropology—its substance is the subject of Chapter 1—let us say something of the provenance of the essays themselves. Written between 1982 and 1990, they were produced in a climate, perhaps already "postdated," in which the social sciences at large were suffering an acute bout of distrust and doubt. Established assumptions and powerful paradigms appeared, at least to some, to be caving in, undermined by forces that were also dissolving meaningful differences in human experience. Developments such as the rise of global communications and mass media, the internationalization of the division of labor, the revolution in worldwide patterns of consumption, the commoditization of popular culture, and the dissolving of neat political and ideological boundaries around societies and cultures (accompanied by a renaissance of nationalism and ethnicity) had severely taxed the trusty old analytic toolkit, not to mention, with apologies to C. Wright Mills (1961), the sociological imagination. To be sure, if African villagers now found their heroes in American soap operas rather than in primordial myths, if their rituals had come to be as much about shopping as making sacrifices, if their music was mingling with ours to yield a ubiquitous "world beat," wherein lay the cultural contrasts, the practices of "otherness," that we had hitherto spent so much time analyzing—and squabbling about? Cultural anthropology, for which these contrasts had always been a major stock-in-trade, was probably more destabilized by these processes than were the other social sciences. By the end of the 1980s, many of the bluff certainties with which the decade had begun seemed to have evaporated.

For some, the growing awareness of past naïveté, real or imagined, was paralyzing; others went on doing the same as they always had done, reassuring themselves that the crisis would pass. Amidst all this, however, were signs of the emergence of a new generation of anthropologists—intellectual, that is, not chronological—that made virtue of necessity and began in earnest to study mass culture and social movements, rapidly changing societies and state formations, nationalism and ethnicity, colonialism and other global processes. In other words, to do ethnography in, and ethnographies of, the contemporary world order. This shift in focus promised, in principle, to save the discipline from some forms of deconstructionist distrust, postmodern pique, and, perhaps most important, the censure of those "natives" who were formerly the object of study. But, inevitably, analytic questions presented themselves more quickly than did persuasive solutions; notwithstanding various piecemeal efforts, many of them highly creative, we remained heavily dependent on the observer's omniscient eye. And badly in need of a methodological apparatus to extend its range.

All of our essays were written to address this need in one or another form. All sought, in practical terms, to expand upon received techniques of interrogating particular social phenomena. All bear the imprint of contemporary debates, of assumptions and claims profoundly questioned, of the impossibility of ironic detachment. But they also assert a faith that the human world, post-anything and -everything, remains the product of discernible social and cultural processes: processes partially indeterminate yet, in some measure, systematically determined; ambiguous and polyvalent, yet never utterly incoherent or meaningless; open to multiple constructions and contest, yet never entirely free of order—or the reality of power and constraint. It is in this sense that we affirm, by prefix and predilection, our commitment to *neo*modern anthropology. And to the conviction that, far from being opposed to (or detachable from) theory, ethnography is instrumental in its creation—and hence is indispensable to the production of knowledge about all manner of social phenomena.

Indeed, we would argue that no humanist account of the past or present can (or does) go very far without the kind of understanding that the ethnographic gaze presupposes. To the extent that historiography is concerned with the recovery of meaningful worlds, with the interplay of the collective and the subjective, it cannot but rely on the tools of the ethnographer. It must, as the likes of Thompson (1978a), Darnton (1985), Samuel (1989), and Hobsbawm (1990) have suggested, be more than a little bit anthropological. By the same token, however, no ethnography can ever hope to penetrate beyond the surface planes of everyday life, to plumb its invisible forms, unless it is informed by the historical imagination—the imagination, that is, of both those who make history and those who write it.

Two further things are to be said about the essays. First, we have deliberately selected, from among our recent writings, a number of studies whose themes converge and complement each other, studies that share a body of ethnographic and historical material; each, of course, was written to advance a particular line of argument or methodological exploration. As a result, some repetition is to be found in them. We have not attempted to eliminate this, for in each case the passages concerned are integral to an unfolding narrative. We beg the indulgence of the reader, hoping that, in return, each essay may stand on its own, to be read alone as well as part of a coherent discourse.

Second, the immediate circumstances that stimulated the essays may have passed by, but debts remain to those who posed the original questions and insisted on answers. All were written at the University of Chicago, where colleagues in Anthropology, the African Studies Workshop, and the Committee on Critical Practice continue to engage us in energetic debate over the relationship of anthropology to history and to explore with us the "crisis of representation" in the human sciences. We are grateful, in particular, to Nancy Munn and Beth Helsinger for their acute and constructive readings of the title essay and to Amy Stambach for her concerned and effective research assistance. The National Science Foundation, National Endowment for the Humanities, Lichtstern Fund of the Department of Anthropology at the University of Chicago, Spencer Foundation, and American Bar Foundation have all extended welcome support. Dean Birkenkamp and Kellie Masterson at Westview Press, models of editorial enlightenment both, persist in offering cheerful encouragement and advice. And our children, Josh and Jane, with us perforce on yet another authorial adventure, contrive to show kindly tolerance and healthy skepticism in roughly equal measure. But, above all else, a cohort of gifted and generous students—many non-American—have shared with us the excitement of their intellectual journeys and faced us with the demand for an anthropology worthy of their age. It is their uncompromising challenge that has elicited this book and forced us to reflect on the place of ethnography in the world they will inherit.

John and Jean Comaroff

Editorial Note

SOME OF THE WRITINGS INCLUDED here have been published, others not. Chapter 1 has been prepared specially for this volume. It sets out our present concerns and serves as the axis—*pinagare*, Tswana would say, the center-pole—around which the other essays revolve. Chapter 2, drafted first in 1982, appeared under the title "Of Totemism and Ethnicity: Consciousness, Practice, and the Signs of Inequality" in *Ethnos* 52(1987):301–323. An earlier version of Chapter 3, "Bodily Reform as Historical Practice: The Semantics of Resistance in Modern South Africa," is to be found in the *International Journal of Psychology* 19(1985):541–567; it has, however, been heavily revised. Chapter 4 was intended for a book that never saw the light of day. Produced in 1983 to fit the subject and style of that project, its genre is one with which we are no longer comfortable. But because it contains our most condensed account of the workings of an African social system, we offer it here in its original form.

Chapters 5–7 are reproduced by courtesy of the *American Ethnologist*: "Goodly Beasts, Beastly Goods: Cattle and Commodities in a South African Context" came out in 1990(17:195–216); "The Madman and the Migrant: Work and Labor in the Historical Consciousness of a South African People" in 1987(14:191–209); and "Images of Empire, Contests of Conscience: Models of Colonial Domination in South Africa" in 1989(16:661–685). Chapter 8, published here for the first time, will also appear in M. Lock and S. Lindenbaum (eds.), *Analysis in Medical Anthropology*. Chapter 9, with a slightly different title, appeared in *Economy and Society* 18(1989):267–296. Finally, an abridged version of Chapter 10 will be published in K. Hansen (ed.), *African Encounters with Domesticity*, currently in preparation. Chapters 1, 4, 5, 6, 9, and 10 are coauthored; 3 and 8 are by Jean Comaroff; 2 and 7 are by John Comaroff. All, however, draw on work done together. In a few places, especially in Part Three, we have used (variously amended) passages from our two-volume study, *Of Revelation and Revolution: Christianity, Colonialism, and Consciousness in South Africa*.

In preparing the essays for inclusion here, we have not been unduly worried about reproducing them precisely as first published; our words are hardly weighty enough to demand their original inscription. It seemed aesthetically desirable, more in keeping with the substance and spirit of the enterprise, to standardize their presentation. After all, we offer these writings not as a miscellany, but as a coherent comment on a discipline and its contemporary discourses. Hence, although no changes have been made to their content, save where we specifically say so, we have, among other things, transposed English to American spellings, altered titles and headings, rendered our notes in a single format at the end of each chapter, and deleted acknowledgments and explanations that are no longer necessary. Also, in order to save repetition, we include a general bibliography at the close of the volume.

We follow historiographic convention throughout and annotate all *primary* materials in our end-of-chapter notes; at the same time, in accordance with anthropological usage, we refer to *secondary* writings (by author and year) in parentheses in the text itself and give full publication details in the general bibliography. In most cases, archival documents are cited by author/source, place of writing, date, and storage classification (box-folder-jacket or, if applicable, just box). Note that CWM is the Council of World Mission. Its papers (which include the records of the London Missionary Society [LMS] and Wesleyan Methodist Missionary Society [WMMS]) are housed at the School of Oriental and African Studies, University of London. References to other archives and official documents, which are much less frequent, are explained as we proceed. Wherever possible, however, we have annotated published rather than primary sources on the assumption that these are more accessible to the nonspecialist, yet interested, reader.

J. & J.C.

Part One

Theory, Ethnography, Historiography

1

Ethnography and the Historical Imagination

I

"MYSTIC WARRIORS GAINING GROUND IN MOZAMBIQUE WAR." The head-line was exotic enough to make the front page of the *Chicago Tribune* one Sunday.[1]

"Call it one of the mysteries of Africa," the report began. "In the battle-ravaged regions of northern Mozambique, in remote straw hut villages where the modern world has scarcely penetrated, supernatural spirits and magic potions are suddenly winning a civil war that machine guns, mortars and grenades could not." The account went on to describe an army of several thousand men and boys, sporting red headbands and brandishing spears. Named after their leader, Naparama—who is said to have been resurrected from the dead—they display on their chests the scars of a "vaccination" against bullets. Their terrain is the battle-scarred province of Zambesia, where a civil war, with South African support, has been raging for some fifteen years. Now heavily armed rebels flee at the sight of the Naparama, and government troops appear equally awed. Western diplomats and analysts, the report recounts, "can only scratch their heads in amazement." The piece ends in a tone of arch authority: "Much of Naparama's effectiveness can be explained by the predominance of super-stitious beliefs throughout Mozambique, a country where city markets always have stalls selling potions, amulets and monkey hands and ostrich feet to ward off evil spirits."

Faced with such evidence, anthropologists might be forgiven for doubt-ing that they have made any impact at all on Western consciousness. It is more than fifty years since Evans-Pritchard (1937) showed, in the plainest prose, that Zande magic was an affair of practical reason, that "primitive mentality" is a fiction of the modern mind; more than fifty years of writing

3

in an effort to contextualize the curious. Yet we have not routed the reflex that makes "superstitious" most aptly qualify African belief. No, the straw huts and magic potions are as secure in this text as in any early nineteenth century traveler's tale. There is even the whiff of a traffic in flesh (the monkey *hands*; the ostrich *feet*). No matter that these wayward warriors are in fact the victims of a thoroughly modern conflict, that they wear civilian clothes and file into combat singing Christian songs. In the popular imagination they are fully fledged signs of the primitive, alibis for an evolutionism that puts them—and their fascinating forays—across an irretrievable gulf from ourselves.

These sensationalized savages, thrust across our threshold one snowy Sunday, served to focus our concerns about the place of anthropology in the contemporary world. For the "report" told less of the Mozambican soldiers than of the culture that had conjured them up as its inverted self-image. Despite the claim that meaning has lost its moorings in the late capitalist world, there was a banal predictability about this piece. It relied on the old opposition between secular mundanity and spectral mystery, European modernism and African primitivism.[2] What is more, the contrast implied a telos, an all too familiar vision of History as an epic passage from past to present. The rise of the West, our cosmology tells us, is accompanied, paradoxically, by a Fall: The cost of rational advance has been our eternal exile from the sacred garden, from its enchanted ways of knowing and being. Only natural man, unreconstructed by the Midas touch of modernity, may bask in its beguiling certainties.

The myth is as old as the hills. But it has had an enduring impact on post-Enlightenment thought in general and, in particular, on the social sciences. Whether they be classical or critical, a celebration of modernity or a denunciation of its iron cage, these "sciences" have, at least until recently, shared the premise of disenchantment—of the movement of mankind from religious speculation to secular reflection, from theodicy to theory, from culture to practical reason (Sahlins 1976a; n.d.). Anthropologists, of course, have hardly ignored the effects on the discipline of the lingering legacy of evolutionism (Goody 1977; cf. Clifford 1988). Nonetheless, it remains in our bones, so to speak, with profound implications for our notions of history and our theories of meaning.

The mystic warriors underscored our own distrust of disenchantment, our reluctance to see modernity—in stark contrast to tradition—as driving a "harsh wedge between cosmology and history" (Anderson 1983:40). To be sure, we have never given any analytic credence to this ideologically freighted opposition or to any of its aliases (simple:complex; ascriptive:achievement-driven; collectivist:individualist; ritualist:rationalist; and so on). For, dressed up as pseudohistory, such dualisms feed off one another, caricaturing the empirical realities they purport to reveal. "Traditional" communities are still frequently held, for instance, to rest upon sacred certainties; modern societies, instead, to look to history to account for themselves or to assuage their sense of alienation and loss (cf. Anderson 1983:40; Keyes, Kendall, and Hardacre n.d.). What is more, these sterotypic contrasts are readily spatialized in the chasm between the West and the rest. Try as they might, the Naparama will never be more than primitive rebels, rattling their sabers, their "cultural weapons," in the prehistory of an African dawn. As Fields (1985) has noted, their "milleniary" kind are seldom attributed properly political motives, seldom credited with the rational, purposive actions in which history allegedly consists. In the event, the Western eye frequently overlooks important similarities in the ways in which societies everywhere are made and remade. And, all too often, we anthropologists have exacerbated this. For we have our own investment in preserving zones of "tradition," in stressing social reproduction over random change, cosmology over chaos (Asad 1973; Taussig 1987). Even as we expose our ethnographic islands to the crosscurrents of history, we remain fainthearted. We still separate local communities from global systems, the thick description of particular cultures from the thin narrative of world events.

The bulletproof soldiers remind us that lived realities defy easy dualisms, that worlds everywhere are complex fusions of what *we* like to call modernity and magicality, rationality and ritual, history and the here and now. In fact, our studies of the Southern Tswana have long proved to us that none of these were opposed in the first place—except perhaps in the colonizing imagination and in ideologies, like apartheid, that have sprung from it. If we allow that historical consciousness and representation may take very different forms from those of the West, people everywhere turn out to have had history all along.

As it has become commonplace to point out, then, European colonizers did not, in an act of heroism worthy of Carlyle (1842), bring Universal History to people without it. Ironically, they brought histories in particular, histories far less predictable than we have been inclined to think. For, despite the claims of modernization theory, Marxist *dependistas,* or "modes of production" models, global forces played into local forms and conditions in unexpected ways, changing known structures into strange hybrids. Our own evidence shows that the incorporation of black South Africans into a world economy did not simply erode difference or spawn rationalized, homogeneous worlds. Money and commodities, literacy and Christendom challenged local symbols, threatening to convert them into a universal currency. But precisely because the cross, the book, and the coin were such saturated signs, they were variously and ingeniously redeployed to bear a host of new meanings as non-Western peoples—Tswana prophets, Naparama fighters, and others—fashioned their own visions of modernity (cf.

Clifford 1988:5–6). Neither was (or is) this merely a feature of "transitional" communities, of those marginal to bourgeois reason and the commodity economy.

In our essays, as we follow colonizers of different kinds from the metropole to Africa and back, it becomes clear that the culture of capitalism has always been shot through with its own magicalities and forms of enchantment, all of which repay analysis. Like the nineteenth-century evangelists who accused the London poor of strange and savage customs (see Chapter 10), Marx insisted on understanding commodities as objects of primitive worship, as fetishes. Being social hieroglyphs rather than mere alienating objects, they describe a world of densely woven power and meaning, enchanted by a "superstitious" belief in their capacity to be fruitful and multiply. Although these curious goods are more prevalent in "modern" societies, their spirit, as Marx himself recognized, infects the politics of value everywhere. If, as Chapter 5 demonstrates, we cast our gaze beyond the horizon where the so-called first and third worlds meet, concepts like the commodity yield useful insights into the constitution of cultures usually regarded as noncapitalist. And so the dogma of disenchantment is dislodged.

Save in the assertions of our own culture, in short, assertions that have long justified the colonial impulse, there is no great gulf between "tradition" and "modernity"—or "postmodernity," for that matter. Nor, as others before us have said, is much to be gained from typological contrasts between worlds of gesellschaft and gemeinschaft, or between economies governed by use- and exchange-value. But we are less concerned here to reiterate this point than to make a methodological observation. If such distinctions do not hold up, it follows that the modes of discovery associated with them—ethnography for "traditional" communities, history for the "modern" world, past and present—also cannot be sharply drawn. We require ethnography to know ourselves, just as we need history to know non-Western others. For ethnography serves at once to make the familiar strange and the strange familiar, all the better to understand them both. It is, as it were, the canon-fodder of a critical anthropology.

In respect of our own society, this is especially crucial. For it is arguable that many of the concepts on which we rely to describe modern life—statistical models, rational choice and game theory, even logocentric event histories, case studies, and biographical narratives—are instruments of what Bourdieu (1977:97f), in a different context, calls the "synoptic illusion." They are our own rationalizing cosmology posing as science, our culture parading as historical causality. All this, as many now recognize, calls for two things simultaneously: that we regard our own world as a problem, a proper site for ethnographic inquiry, and that, to make good this intention, we develop a genuinely historicized anthropology. But how exactly are we to do so? Contrary to some scholarly opinion, it is not so easy to alienate ourselves from our own meaningful context, to make our own existence strange. How do we *do* ethnographies of, and in, the contemporary world order? What, indeed, might be the substantive directions of such a "neomodern" historical anthropology?

II

Both history and ethnography are concerned with societies *other* than the one in which we live. Whether this *otherness* is due to remoteness in time . . . or to remoteness in space, or even to cultural heterogeneity, is of secondary importance compared to the basic similarity of perspective. . . . [I]n both cases we are dealing with systems of representations which differ for each member of the group and which, on the whole, differ from the representations of the investigator. The best ethnographic study will never make the reader a native. . . . All that the historian or ethnographer can do, and all that we can expect of them, is to enlarge a specific experience to the dimensions of a more general one.

—Claude Levi-Strauss (1963a:16–17)

These questions parse into two parts, two complementary motifs that start out separately and, like a classical pas de deux, merge slowly, step by step. The first pertains to ethnography, the second to history.

As we have noted, the current status of ethnography in the human sciences is something of a paradox. On the one hand, its authority has been, and is being, seriously challenged from both within anthropology and outside; on the other, it is being widely appropriated as a liberalizing method in fields other than our own—among them, cultural and legal studies, sociology, social history, and political science.[3] Are these disciplines suffering a critical lag? Or, more realistically, is a simultaneous sense of hope and despair *intrinsic* to ethnography? Does its relativism bequeath it an enduring sense of its own limitation, its own irony? There does seem to be plenty of evidence for Aijmer's (1988:424) recent claim that ethnography "always has been . . . linked with epistemological problems." To wit, its founding fathers, having taken to the field to subvert Western universalisms with non-Western particularities, now stand accused of having served the cause of imperialism. And generations of journeyman anthropologists since have struggled with the contradictions of a mode of inquiry that appears, by turns, uniquely revelatory and irredeemably ethnocentric.

The ambivalence is palpable also in critiques of anthropology, which accuse it both of fetishizing cultural difference (Asad 1973; Fabian 1983; Said 1989) and—because of its relentlessly bourgeois bias—of effacing difference altogether (Taussig 1987). In a recent review, for example, Sangren (1988:406) acknowledges that ethnography does "to some degree, make an object of the 'other.'" Nonetheless, he goes on to assert, it was "dialogic long before the term became popular." Similar arguments, one might add, are to be heard in other scholarly fields that rely on participant observation: Surveying the growing literature in cultural studies, for instance, Graeme Turner (1990:178) remarks that "the democratic impulse and the inevitable effect of ethnographic practice in the academy contradict each other."

But *why* this enduring ambivalence? Is ethnography, as many of its critics have implied, singularly precarious in its naive empiricism, its philosophical unreflectiveness, its interpretive hubris? Methodologically speaking, it *does* have strangely anachronistic echoes, harking back to the classical credo that "seeing is believing." In this it is reminiscent of the early biological sciences, where clinical observation, the penetrating human gaze, was frankly celebrated (Foucault 1975; Levi-Strauss 1976:35; Pratt 1985); recall, here, that biology was the model chosen, in the golden age of social anthropology, for a "natural science of society" (Radcliffe-Brown 1957). The discipline, however, never really developed an armory of objectifying instruments, standardizing strategies, and quantifying formulas.[4] It has continued to be, as Evans-Pritchard (1950; 1961) insisted long ago, a humanist art, in spite of its sometime scientific pretentions. And while it has never been theoretically homogeneous, internal differences and disputes have seldom led to thoroughgoing revisions of its *modus operandi*.[5] Indeed, the unsympathetic critic could claim that ethnography is a relic of the era of travel writing and exploration, of adventure and astonishment;[6] that it remains content to offer observations of human scale and fallibility; that it still depends, disingenuously, on the facticity of first-hand experience.

Yet it might be argued that the greatest weakness of ethnography is also its major strength, its paradox a productive tension. For it refuses to put its trust in techniques that give more scientific methods their illusory objectivity: their commitment to standardized, a priori units of analysis, for example, or their reliance on a depersonalizing gaze that separates subject from object. To be sure, the term "participant observation"—an oxymoron to believers in value-free science—connotes the inseparability of knowledge from its knower. In anthropology, the observer is self-evidently his/her "own instrument of observation" (Levi-Strauss 1976:35). This is the whole point. Even if they wanted to, ethnographers could not, *pace* the purifying idyll of ethnoscience, hope to remove every trace of the arbitrariness with which they read meaningful signs on a cultural landscape. But it would surely be wrong to conclude that their method is especially vulnerable, more so than other efforts, to know human (or even nonhuman) worlds.

In this sense, the "problem" of anthropological knowledge is only a more tangible instance of something common to all modernist epistemologies, as philosophers of science have long realized (Kuhn 1962; Lakatos and Musgrave 1968; Figlio 1976). For ethnography personifies, in its methods and its models, the inescapable dialectic of fact and value. Yet most of its practitioners persist in asserting the usefulness—indeed, the creative potential—of such "imperfect" knowledge. They tend both to recognize the impossibility of the true and the absolute and also to suspend disbelief. Notwithstanding the realist idiom of their craft, they widely accept that—like all other forms of understanding—ethnography is historically contingent and culturally configured.[7] They have even, at times, found the contradiction invigorating.

Still, living with insecurity is more tolerable to some than to others. Those presently concerned with the question of authority fault (unenlightened) ethnographers for pretending to be good, old-fashioned realists. Thus Clifford (1988:43) notes that even if our accounts "successfully dramatize the intersubjective, give-and-take of fieldwork . . . they remain *representations* of dialogue." As if the impossibility of describing the encounter in all its fullness, without any mediation, condemns us to lesser truths. Likewise, Marcus (1986:190) counterposes "realist ethnography" to a new "modernist" form that, because it "can never gain knowledge of the realities that statistics can," would "evoke the world without representing it."[8] If we cannot have *real* representation, let us have no representation at all! Yet surely this merely reinscribes naive realism as an (unattainable) ideal? Why? Why should anthropologists fret at the fact that our accounts are refractory representations, that they cannot convey an undistorted sense of the "open-ended mystery" of social life as people *experience* it? Why, instead, should ethnographers not give account of how such experiences are socially, culturally, and historically grounded or argue about the character of the worlds they evoke, with the aim of fructifying our own ways of seeing and being, of subverting our own sureties (cf. van der Veer 1990:739). Ethnography, in any case, does not speak *for* others, but *about* them. Neither imaginatively nor empirically can it ever "capture" their reality. Unlikely as it may seem, this was brought home to us in a London School of Economics toilet in 1968. It turned out to be our first foretaste of deconstruction; perhaps it was where postmodern anthropology all began. On an unhinged stall door, an unknown artist—perhaps an unhinged student—asked nobody in particular, "Is Raymond Firth real, or just a figment of the Tikopean imagination?"[9]

Ethnography, to extend the point, is not a vain attempt at literal translation, in which we take over the mantle of an-other's being, conceived of as somehow commensurate with our own. It is a historically situated mode of understanding historically situated contexts, each with its own, perhaps radically different, kinds of subjects and subjectivities, objects and objectives. Also, it has hitherto been an inescapably *Western* discourse. In it, to pick up our earlier comment, we tell of the unfamiliar—again, the paradox, the parody of doxa—to confront the limits of our own epistemology, our own visions of personhood, agency, and history. Such critiques can never be full or final, of course, for they remain embedded in forms of thought and practice not fully conscious or innocent of constraint. But they provide one way, in our culture, of decoding those signs that disguise themselves as universal and natural, of engaging in unsettling exchanges with those, including scholars, who live in different worlds.

For all this, it is impossible ever to rid ourselves entirely of the ethnocentrism that dogs our desire to know others, even though we vex ourselves with the problem in ever more refined ways. Thus many anthropologists have been wary of ontologies that give precedence to individuals over contexts. For these rest on manifestly Western assumptions: among them, that human beings can triumph over their contexts through sheer force of will, that economy, culture, and society are the aggregate product of individual action and intention. Yet, as we shall point out again below, it has proven extremely difficult to cast the bourgeois subject out of the anthropological fold. S/he has returned in many guises, from Malinowski's maximizing man to Geertz's maker of meaning. Ironically, s/he appears again in the writings of those who take ethnography to task for failing to represent the "native's point of view." Sangren (1988:416) argues vigorously that this is a legacy of American cultural anthropology or, at least, the version of it that would sever culture from society, experiencing subjects from the conditions that produce them. Under these conditions, culture becomes the stuff of intersubjective fabrication: a web to be woven, a text to be transcribed. And ethnography becomes "dialogical," not in Bakhtin's thoroughly socialized sense, but in the narrower sense of a dyadic, decontextualized exchange between anthropologist and informant.[10] We would resist the reduction of anthropological research to an exercise in "intersubjectivity," the communing of phenomenologically conceived actors through talk alone. As Hindess (1972:24) remarks, the rendering down of social science to the terms of the experiencing subject is a product of modern humanism, of a historically specific Western worldview. To treat ethnography as an encounter between *an* observer and *an* other—*Conversations with Ogotemmêli* (Griaule 1965) or *The Headman and I* (Dumont 1978)—is to make anthropology into a global, ethnocentric interview. Yet it is precisely this perspective that warrants the call for ethnography to be "dialogical"—so that we may do justice to the role of "the native informant," the singular subject, in the making of our texts.

Generations of anthropologists have said it in a wide variety of ways: In order to construe the gestures of others, their words and winks and more besides, we have to situate them within the systems of signs and relations, of power and meaning, that animate them. Our concern ultimately is with the interplay of such systems—often relatively open systems—with the persons and events they spawn; a process that need privilege neither the sovereign self nor stifling structures. Ethnography, we would argue, is an exercise in dialectics rather than dialogics, although the latter is always part of the former. In addition to talk, it entails observation of activity and interaction both formal and diffuse, of modes of control and constraint, of silence as well as assertion and defiance. Along the way, ethnographers also read diverse sorts of texts: books, bodies, buildings, sometimes even cities (Holston 1989; Comaroff and Comaroff 1991; see below). But they must always give texts contexts and assign values to the equations of power and meaning they express. Nor are contexts just *there*. They, too, have to be constructed analytically in light of our assumptions about the social world.

"The representation of larger, impersonal systems," in short, is not untenable in "the narrative space of ethnography" (Marcus 1986:190). Apart from all else, such systems are implicated, whether or not we recognize them, in the sentences and scenes we grasp with our narrow-gauge gaze. But more than this: Ethnography surely extends beyond the range of the empirical eye; its inquisitive spirit calls upon us to ground subjective, culturally configured action in society and history—and vice versa—wherever the task may take us. That spirit is present, we shall see, in the work of historians who insist that the human imagination itself is perforce a "collective, *social* . . . phenomenon" (Le Goff 1988:5; our emphasis). In this sense, one can "do" ethnography in the archives, as Darnton (1985:3) implies by the phrase "history in the ethnographic grain" (see p. 14). One can also "do" the anthropology of national or international forces and formations: of colonialism, evangelism, liberation struggles, social movements, dispersed diasporas, regional "development," and the like. Such systems seem impersonal and unethnographic only to those who would separate the "subjective" from the "objective" world, claiming the former for anthropology while leaving the latter to global theories (Marxism, world-systems, structuralism), under whose wing ethnography may find a precarious perch (e.g., Marcus 1986). In fact, systems appear "impersonal," and holistic analyses stultifying, only when we exclude from them all room for human maneuver, for ambivalence and historical inde-terminacy—when we fail to acknowledge that meaning is always, to some extent, arbitrary and diffuse, that social life everywhere rests on the imperfect ability to reduce ambiguity and concentrate power.

Of course, like all forms of inquiry, ethnography objectifies as it ascribes meaning—albeit perhaps less so than do those methodologies that explain human behavior in terms of putatively universal motives. An exacting critic from a neighboring discipline recently allowed that the work of anthropology, "which combine[s] a passion for detail with a humane aspiration, does not suffer in comparison with its ethnocentric competitors" (Fields 1985:279). In this respect, ethnography seems no more intrinsically "arrogant" than do other modes of social investigation (*pace* Turner 1990:178). Much of the difficulty has come from the fact that, for reasons deeply inscribed in the politics of knowledge, anthropologists have classically studied populations marginal to the centers of Western power—those who were unable, until recently, to answer back. In this, as we will argue, our position is little different from that of often radical social historians concerned with society's nether regions, the lives of "little people" viewed from the bottom up (Cohn 1987:39). The dangers of disclosure in such situations are real enough. Indeed, while all representations have effects, those imposed by academic brokers on communities without cultural capital are more likely to have deleterious consequences. At the very least, we have to confront the complexities of our relations to our subjects, texts, and audiences—especially because the impact of our work is never fully foreseeable. This not only demands a serious regard, once again, for contexts, our own as much as those we study. It also calls for a careful consideration of the real implications of what we do, a consideration that must go far beyond the now routine recognition that our writings are potential instruments of "othering."

But ethnography also has positive political possibilities. We ought not be too quick, for instance, to disregard the challenge that cultural relativism poses to bourgeois consciousness. Why else the special opprobrium heaped upon us by shrill absolutists, essayists of the closed mind like Alan Bloom? The fate of the Naparama may tell us that we are less influential than we often suppose. Nevertheless, our work *does* reverberate in and beyond the academy, although its legitimacy and impact vary with the way in which we choose to phrase our questions. An important moment of choice is now upon us. If we take our task to be an exercise in intersubjective translation, in speaking for others and their point of view, our hubris will cause us no end of difficulties, moral and philosophical. And if we see it to lie in the formal analysis of social systems or cultural structures, statistically or logically conceived, we evade the issue of representation and experience altogether. But if, after an older European tradition, we seek to understand the *making* of collective worlds—the dialectics, in space and time, of societies and selves, persons and places, orders and events—then we open ourselves to conventions of criticism widely shared by the nonpositivist human sciences. Then, too, we may traffic in analytic constructions, not in unverifiable subjectivities, and can acknowledge the effects of history upon our discourses. Then we may focus on interpreting social phenomena, not on the endless quest for textual means to exorcise the fact that our accounts

are not realist transparencies. Then, finally, we will be on epistemological
turf that, if only provisionally, we comprehend and control.

*   *   *

The second motif, recall, is the question of history. Or, more precisely, of
historical anthropology.

In the late 1970s and early 1980s, it became common to temper the
anthropological turn toward history-as-panacea by posing the problem:
"What history? Which anthropology?" We ourselves raised the issue,
arguing that

> any substantive relationship between disciplines is determined *not* by the
> intrinsic nature of those disciplines—if any such thing exists—but by prior
> theoretical considerations. It would seem obvious, for example, that historical
> analysis assumes different significance for structural functionalists than it
> does for either Marxists or structuralists. . . . Hence to assert that anthropol-
> ogy should be "more" historical, or history "more" anthropological, may be
> well-intentioned; but . . . the assertion remains vacuous without further
> theoretical specification. [In our view] there ought to be no "relationship"
> between history and anthropology, since there should be no division to begin
> with. A theory of society which is not also a theory of history, or *vice versa,*
> is hardly a theory at all.[11]

But there was more to the matter than this. For the space of intersection
between the two disciplines was (inevitably, it now seems) pervaded by a
particular *Geist*—a politics of perspective, so to speak. Clearly, the kind of
histories that were to find a sympathetic ear among anthropologists were
unlikely to be the Chronicles of Courts and Kings. Neither were they liable
to be event-full political narratives, however fascinating, of embassies
among empires, strife between states, or trade between chieftains; nor
latter-day quantitative accounts of past worlds that, by appeal to synchronic
sociology, sought to write "general histories" in "numbers and anonymity."[12]

Bound to be much more attractive, save in some structuralist and Marxist
circles, were richly textured accounts of things similar to what we ourselves
study—analyzed, broadly speaking, in similar ways. If the description was
suitably thick, the subject matter obviously remote, so much the better.
How could we not be appealed to by, say, Carlo Ginzburg's (1983) tale of
sixteenth-century witchcraft and agrarian cults in Europe, or his account
(1980) of the cosmos of a contemporary miller. Such studies in *l'histoire
des mentalités*[13] are not just chronicles of the quotidian, of "little people"
and their ordinary practices; nor—like their even more everyday English
equivalents—are they merely studies of "the *experience* of living men and
women" (Thompson [1978a] 1979:21; cf. Thomas 1971; Hill 1972). As

Darnton (1985:3) notes, they also "[treat] our own civilization in the same way that anthropologists study alien cultures." Hobsbawm (1990:47–48) puts it in the words, more or less, of the English novelist L. P. Hartley: For these historians "the past is another country where things are done differently . . . [in which even] the best interpreters still remain biased strangers."[14] However, it is Raphael Samuel (1989:23) who probably comes closest to us in spirit. Arguing for the kind of history that might best be taught in British schools, he says, wryly: "If one were not, like the historians of high politics, mesmerized by the glamour of power, one might suggest that horses were more interesting to study than politicians and, at least for younger children, more appealing." Perhaps for anthropologists as well. But the intention here is not to jest at the expense of politicians or historians. It is to make a profound methodological point. As Samuel shows, the move from cavalry charge to hay wain and horse-gin, from sporting prints to the text of *Black Beauty,* lays bare the cultural texture of an age. "*Cherchez la vache!*" says Evans-Pritchard of the world of the Nuer—advice offered on the same conviction: that, in the career of everyday goods, of valued things, we grasp the constitution of complex social fields. We ourselves follow this object lesson in Chapter 5, extending the concept of commodity fetishism to explore how cattle give analytical access to a changing Southern Tswana universe. In fact, in making his case against history as the biography of big men, Samuel voices the same concern as we did about an anthropology "from the native's point of view": that it tends to focus on individual intention and action at the expense of more complex social processes. Take, for example, the Battle of Trafalgar, which looms large in standard British textbooks, not least because of Nelson's heroic death. This event, claims Samuel, was far less important to the making of an epoch than, say, the Married Women's Property Act of 1882. A product of drawn-out social struggle, the act had critical consequences for marriage, family, and gender in late nineteenth century England—in other words, for the construction of modern British society *tout court*. Yet it barely rates a footnote in any major work.

Cultural historians like Le Roy Ladurie, Ginzburg, Darnton, and Samuel give us comfort in the face of less friendly interlocutors partly because they reassure us that our methods ("suspiciously like literature" to the hard social sciences [Darnton 1985:6]) are more rigorous and revealing than they appear. But most fundamentally, they see virtue in—indeed, make no apologies for—disinterring and disseminating the lives of insignificant "others." For many of them, far from an act of domination or appropriation, this is the first step in a subversive historical sociology, a history written against the hegemony of high bourgeoisies, the power of parliaments, and the might of monarchies. Their work, moreover, bears more than passing similarity to colonial historiography in the so-called subaltern mode. This is not merely because the latter concerns itself with "faceless masses," people who have left few documentary traces of Promethean careers. Subaltern historiography also challenges the very categories through which colonial pasts have been made. In so doing, it resonates with the democratizing impulse of our own craft, of which we have already spoken: the well-intentioned—some would say self-satisfied—view that ethnography celebrates the narratives, the consciousness, and the cultural riches of non-Western populations, especially those threatened with ethnocide.

In anthropology, as we have noted, the liberal urge to speak for others has had its comeuppance. Social history may seem less vulnerable to counterattack: Its subjects, often well dead and buried, can neither answer back nor be affected any longer by the politics of knowledge. This, however, is much too simple. Not only do scholars work increasingly on history-in-the-making (cf. Bundy 1987), but also anyone who writes of times past must recognize that there will be people who stand to suffer from the way in which social memory is fixed (cf. Ashforth 1991). In addition, there are those, both revisionist and radical, who champion the cause of historical populations. Thus Rosaldo (1986) contends that, for all his efforts to capture the life-world of the peasants of Montaillou from within, Le Roy Ladurie (1979) derives his narrative primarily from the standpoint of a contemporary inquisitor; Rosaldo, in fact, likens his perspective to that of a colonial anthropologist. Spivak (1988) goes yet further: She questions whether the subaltern can speak at all, even through the texts of a radicalized history. It appears that in representing the point of view of "natives," living or dead, cultural historians are on no firmer epistemological ground than are ethnographers—and no less embroiled in the politics of the present (Croce [1921] 1959:46f).

This calls to mind Jacques Derrida's critique of Foucault's history of madness and, as significantly, Ginzburg's rejoinder. Both are instructive for anthropologists—especially for those drawn by deconstruction, those troubled by the tyranny of a totalizing social science. They are also salient in light of our own analysis (Chapter 6) of the historical consciousness borne, in apartheid South Africa, by an alleged "madman." It is impossible, says Derrida (1978:34f) in dismissing Foucault's *History* (1967), to analyze dementia save in "the restrained and restraining language" of Western reason. Yet this is the very language that constituted *folie* in the first place— the very means of its repression. It follows, therefore, that there is no point in the discursive structure of Western rationalism from which an interrogation of abnormality may proceed. Derrida (1978:35–36) adds: "All our European languages, the language of everything that has participated, from near or far, in the adventure of Western reason [are implicated in the objectification of madness]. . . . *Nothing* within this language, and *no one* among those who speak it, can escape. . . . [T]he revolution against reason can only be made within it . . . [and] always has the limited scope of . . . a disturbance." For all his determination to write a history of insanity "without repeating the aggression of rationalism," then, Foucault is accused of self-delusion; the project, implies Derrida, was itself pure folly, madness. And so his act of subversion disappears before the deconstructive eye. The parallel with the politics of ethnography is obvious. Its analytic gaze, too, appears entrapped in Western reason, a party to the very relationship—between subject and object, the surveyor and the surveilled—on which colonizing power/knowledge is based.

To Ginzburg (1980:xvii), however, Derrida's critique is both facile and nihilistic. For, against all the forces of repression in the world, it allows little by way of legitimate reaction: inaction, ironic indifference, silence (cf. Said 1978).[15] Even worse, it misses the fact that "the only discourse that constitutes a radical alternative to the lies of constituted society is represented by [the] victims of social exclusion." Extraneousness, irrationality, absurdity, rupture, contradiction in the face of dominant cultures, to take the point further, are all mirrors of distortion, angles from which are exposed the logic of oppressive signs and reigning hegemonies. Despite his location within the discourses of Western reason, concludes Ginzburg, Foucault *did* succeed in using the history of madness, the politics of sanity, to unmask the coerciveness of convention and (self-)discipline.

We should not draw false comfort from this. It is one thing to acknowledge the *possibility* that rupture, absurdity, or resistance may disclose—even disable—the world from which it emanates, but quite another to ensure that it does. More immediately, though, there is relevance for us in the methodological implications of Ginzburg's argument, in the kind of history to which it is dedicated. The latter, by definition, must be grounded in the singular. It can make no pretense of representativeness, of disintering a typical seventeenth-century European villager or nineteenth-century urban merchant. For all the cultural historian can ever "see" are the dispersed fragments of an epoch—just as the ethnographer only "sees" fragments of a cultural field. However, the point of recovering these fragments—be they individuals or events—is to "connect [them] to an historically determinate environment and society" (1980:xxiv).[16] They may come to us largely by chance and may in some measure be unintelligible. But to recognize and respect that unintelligibility, which we have perforce to do, "does not mean succumbing to a foolish fascination for the exotic and incomprehensible." It is, rather, to undertake redeeming them. For "redeemed [they are] thus liberated" (1980:xxvi). Liberated, that is, in the sense of being restored to a world of meaningful interconnections.

Ginzburg's insistence on the redemptive connection between fragments and totalities brings together two critical points about cultural history in general and, in particular, its subaltern variants. The first echoes Samuel's

(1989:23) observation that " 'History from below' . . . without some larger framework . . . becomes a cul-de-sac and loses its subversive potential." Improperly contextualized, the stories of ordinary people past stand in danger of remaining just that: stories. To become something more, these partial, "hidden histories" have to be situated in the wider worlds of power and meaning that gave them life. But those worlds were also home to other dramatis personae, other texts, other signifying practices. And here is the second point: there is no basis to assume that the histories of the repressed, in themselves, hold a special key to revelation; as we show in Part Three, the discourses of the dominant also yield vital insights into the contexts and processes of which they were part. The corollary: There is no great historiographic balance that may be restored, set to rights once and for all, merely by replacing bourgeois chronicles with subaltern accounts—by "topping and tailing" cultures past (Porter 1989:3). History, Antonio Gramsci reminds us, is made in the struggle among the diverse life worlds that coexist in given times and places—between the "tendentious languages" that, for Bakhtin (1981:263; Holquist 1981:xix), play against one another and against the "totality" (posited, *real*ized) that gives them meaning. For historiography, as for ethnography, it is the relations between fragments and fields that pose the greatest analytic challenge.

How, then, do we connect parts to "totalities"? How do we redeem the fragments? How do we make intelligible the idiosyncratic acts, lives, and representations of others? How do we locate them within "a historically determinate environment"? It is here that cultural history, for all its brilliant achievements, runs out of answers for us. Not that this should be a surprise. Just as we were turning to history for guidance, at the moment when our early paradigmatic foundations were crumbling, many historians began to repay the compliment. Just as we were inclined to see history as "good"—as if time might cure everything—they seemed to see ethnography as a panacea. This should have warned us that they were in as much theoretical trouble as we were ourselves.

In fact, much historiography still proceeds as if its empirical bases were self-evident, as if "theory" were an affectation only of those of philosophical bent (Thompson 1978b; cf. Johnson 1978). Collingwood (1935:15) might have asserted, long ago, that the "points between which the historical imagination spins its web . . . must be achieved by critical thinking." But there has been relatively little effort to interrogate the constructs through which the silences and spaces between events are filled, through which disjointed stories are cast into master narratives. In practice, of course, the way in which the "historical imagination" does its work is culturally crafted; so, too, is the fabrication of events, as we are reminded by old debates over *l'histoire événementielle* (see below). As this suggests, the cultural historian is no less prone than the cultural anthropologist to read with an ethnocentric eye. In the absence of principled theory, ethnographers of the archive and the field alike tend to become hermeneuts by default, finding in interpretive anthropology a confirmation of their own phenomenological individualism. Of those who did turn to systematic approaches—especially to some form of structuralism or materialism—many have been attracted, in the wake of recent crises, by the less deterministic visions of a Gramsci or a Foucault, or to such "counternarratives" as feminism, psychoanalysis, and subalternism. They have drawn, in other words, on an increasingly global legacy of social thought, to which we anthropologists have equal access.

What, in sum, are the lessons to be taken from this excursion into history? Clearly it is cultural historians, more than any other social scientists, who validate our endeavor as ethnographers. This they do by asserting the possibility of a subversive historical anthropology, one that focuses primarily on little people and their worlds. Like cultural studies, with which—at least, in Britain—it has had a rich conversation (see Turner 1990:68f; Johnson 1979), cultural history has been especially adept at revealing that all social fields are domains of contest; that "culture" is often a matter of argument, a confrontation of signs and practices along the fault lines of power; that it is possible to recover from fragments, discord, and even from silences, the raw material with which to write imaginative sociologies of the past and the present. But eventually we must part company. Given the reluctance of historians to reflect on matters of theory, their tendency to look to empirical solutions for analytic problems, we must find our own way through the maze of conundrums that lies along the road to a principled historical anthropology.

III

So, with all this in mind, toward what kind of historical anthropology do we strive? And how, exactly, does ethnography fit into it? It follows, from the way in which we call the question, that we do not find a ready answer in the methods and models spawned by the recent rapprochement of history and anthropology—or by its intellectual precursors, which go back much further than we often realize (see, e.g., Cohn 1980, 1981; J. L. Comaroff 1984; Rosaldo 1986). Nor, as our brief excursion into *l'histoire des mentalités* indicates, is one to be found by surveying existing historiographies and choosing the most congenial candidate. Recall Thompson's (1978b:324) admonitory metaphor—a little shopworn now, but still valuable—that ideas, ways of knowing, are not like objects in a supermarket, perishables casually bought or brushed aside, cast out or consumed.

Let us begin to answer the question in the negative voice—by disposing, that is, of the kinds of historical anthropology that we seek specifically to avoid. The method in our malice, to invoke the memory of Edmund Leach (1961:2), will reveal itself as we proceed: Some ground clearing is necessary if we are to cut fresh pathways through old thickets.

Many years ago, Nadel (1942:72) drew the attention of anthropologists to the distinction, already well inscribed in social theory and philosophy, between "ideological" and "objective" history. The first recalls Malinowski's (e.g., 1948:92f) description of myth: It is the past as told by people to account—authoritatively, authentically, audibly—for the contemporary shape of their world. By contrast, "factual" chronicles, the work of dispassionate observers, are scripted "in accordance . . . with universal critera of connexion and sequence." Nadel did not go on to point out that "ideological" history rarely exists (or ever existed) in the singular. He wrote, after all, long before culture was seen to be a fluid, often contested, and only partially integrated mosaic of narratives, images, and practices (see below); before we even perceived that, in a single African society, there may be alternative (gendered, generational, even stratified) histories and world-maps.

The distinction between ideological and objective history may no longer go unquestioned in the musings of metahistorians. But it remains deeply entrenched in Western popular discourse and, implicitly, in much historical anthropology. How often are we not at pains to show that the chronicles of kings, conquerors, and colonizers—we follow Croce's ([1921] 1959:51) usage here[17]—are distortions, pure ideology in servitude to power, the corollary being that our version is more objective, more factual? The same is true of the past as perceived, from the bottom up, by the dispossessed and the disenfranchised, the mute and the muzzled. How often do we not explain away their failure to act in their own interest, or to act at all, by seeking to show that they perforce misrecognize the "real" signs and structures that sustain their subordination? In so doing, it is all too easy to cross an invisible boundary, the now familiar line that marks out the limits of authority, ethnographic and historical alike. For it is one thing to assume that no human actor can ever "know" his or her world in its totality; one thing to situate the natives' points of view—note, now, the plural—in their appropriate context. That, as we have suggested, is entirely legitimate. But it is quite another thing to arrogate to ourselves an exclusive, emancipatory, suprahistorical purchase on reality. To dredge up the lexicon of an age gone by, social knowledge is never value-free or priceless. And there are no "universal criteria of connexion and sequence"; *vide* Joan Kelly's (1984) feminist critique of orthodox practices of periodization in European history. Universal historiography, as we should all be aware by now, is itself a myth—worse, a conceit. Indeed, the most striking thing about the very idea—the Western idea of universalism, that is—is how parochial it is.

Any historical anthropology that sustains a fixed dichotomy between the ideological and the objective is bound to run into all the old problems of brute empiricism—not to mention accusations of insensitivity to its own positioning and provisionality. In short, it invites the justifiable criticisms raised most recently by postmodernism but also by many before on the long road from the early Marx to late phenomenology. If a distinction between the ideological and the objective is to appear in historical anthropology at all, we would argue, it is primarily as a cultural artifact, a distinction that itself is to be interrogated wherever it surfaces. Who does it empower and in what manner? Are there other forms of historical consciousness in the same contexts? Are they expressed or suppressed? By what means? In sum, our historical anthropology begins by eschewing the very possibility of a realist, or an essentialist, history. This is not to say that there are no essences and realities in the world. Quite the opposite. But our objective, like the objective of many others, is to show as cogently as possible *how* they are constructed: how realities become real, how essences become essential, how materialities materialize. "Symbolic realism," a figure of analytic speech used for rather different theoretical ends by Brown and Lyman (1978:5), captures well the spirit of the matter. To the degree that our analytic strategy may still count as objectivist, then, it is highly provisional and reflexive. Perhaps this is the hallmark of a neomodernist anthropology.

If our historical anthropology is anti-empiricist, anti-objectivist, anti-essentialist—except in the amended sense in which we deploy these terms—it is also anti-statistical and anti-aggregative. Let us explain what we mean with reference, once again, to our intellectual heritage. Recall the early days of the controversy in Britain over the relationship between history and anthropology. These were the days when Evans-Pritchard (1950, 1961:20), invoking Maitland (1936:249), lined us up with art and aesthetics against science; when Leach (1961), Schapera (1962), and Smith (1962) argued that, in spite of our claims to the contrary, we had been doing history all along—and neither could nor should do otherwise; when the Association of Social Anthropologists of the Commonwealth finally blessed the rapprochement with our "sister discipline" at its annual conference (Lewis 1968).[18] It is clear, with hindsight, that there were three quite different forms of historiography being discussed.[19] But nobody, other than Leach (1954), seems to have said as much.

The first form was confined to analyses of repetitive processes of the short and medium term—analyses we would barely recognize as historical at all now, although they were often cited as proof that anthropology really *was* concerned with time (as if this were the same thing; see Chapter 4).

Most notable among them were studies of domestic groups (Fortes 1949; Goody 1958) and villages (Mitchell 1956b; Turner 1957) that sought to arrive at *aggregate* descriptions of social structures by illuminating their cyclical dynamics. Do not misunderstand us: Some of these studies, especially those of the Manchester School in Central Africa, were based on perceptive, blood-and-guts narratives of social struggles. But the latter were removed from history, consigned to the uneventful register of "structural time." However much human beings railed against the contradictions of their world, or fought with one another, their actions were always seen to reinforce the system in place, never to transform it. This reduction was not purely the preserve of British functionalism: It was to reappear later, more fashionably addressed, among Marxists concerned with the reproduction of systems of domination (e.g., Meillassoux 1981).

Altogether more recognizably "historical," if utterly undiachronic, was the second use of the past. Reminiscent of Levi-Strauss's (1963a) statistical models, of historiography founded on the "anonymity of numbers" (see p. 14), its point was to verify, in rates and incidences, descriptive accounts of existing social systems. Evans-Pritchard ([1961] 1963:55) observed that "a term like 'structure' can only be meaningful when used as an historical expression to denote a set of relations known to have endured over a considerable period of time." Echoes of *Annales,* by way of Braudel (e.g., 1980). Thus Barnes (1954:171) retraced 130 years of Ngoni history in order to show that "the form of [their] social structure [had] remained the same"; and so a long, tortured story of state formation, migration, and colonial conquest is distilled into a two-dimensional, lifeless aggregate termed "[the Ngoni] political order."[20] Less grand in scope, but similar in object and spirit, was the historical study of social institutions. If we could show, for instance, that succession among the Zulu had actually passed from father to senior son a certain number of times, we had empirical justification for the claim that the "principle" of primogeniture obtains. Similarly, if Highland Burmese men had married the daughters of their mothers' brothers in a given proportion of cases, we might be persuaded to say that they "have" an asymmetrical alliance system.[21] Note the grammatically awkward tense shift from historical past to ethnographic present: It recapitulates the methodologically uneasy move from data to generalization, event to structure, history to form.

Judiciously and imaginatively used, this kind of history may be suggestive. More often than not, however, statistical appearances, particularly when read across cultural registers, are misleading. Not only do they invite us to reify institutions, thus endowing a slippery abstraction with false concreteness, but they also erect counterfeit signposts toward causal explanations. In the Southern Tswana chiefdoms of the nineteenth and early twentieth centuries, for example, senior sons typically inherited their fathers' property and position. But they did not necessarily do so because of the principle of primogeniture, as has often been said.[22] By virtue of the manner in which succession struggles were culturally constructed, men *made* themselves into senior sons in the course of these processes (J. L. Comaroff 1978); the rules of rank might have provided the rhetorical terms in which claims were argued, but they simply could not decide matters one way or the other. As this implies, it was the logic of practice, not a set of ascriptive norms, that gave form to such struggles (Bourdieu 1977:19f). Likewise, for reasons having to do with the politics of affinity here, the close and ambiguous kinship ties that often linked spouses before marriage were commonly (re)negotiated during their lives together (see Chapter 4). Consequently, numerically based generalizations about Tswana succession and marriage may do worse than tell us nothing. They may manufacture misinformation.

Indeed, given that accounts of this kind come in a highly persuasive form, they have the capacity to render soft facts into hard fictions;[23] statistical statement,[24] as we said, is the mode of enchantment that, in our culture, makes truth "empirical." But, most distressing of all, these methods deflect our attention away from the problematic quality of habitual practices, hiding their historicity by mystifying their meaningful construction and the bases of their empowerment. For normal sociology there may be enduring appeal in ignoring cultural ambiguity, in sacrificing polyphony to the quest for certainty, in reducing messy "native" categories to measurably "scientific" ones. So be it. That is not the object of our historical anthropology.

The third mode of historiography in contemporary British anthropology, to which we find ourselves much closer in spirit, also provides a useful critical lesson. Anything but statistical or inductive, it was based on the axiom that *all* social orders exist in time; that all are inherently unstable and generically dynamic; that there are no prehistoric "anthropological societies," to recall Cancian's (1976) extraordinary term; and that, as Dumont (1957:21) once put it, "history is the movement by which a society reveals itself as what it is." Perhaps most representative of this position was Leach's remarkable *Political Systems of Highland Burma* (1954), a study sometimes said to have anticipated by many years (1) the move in anthropology toward practice theory (Fuller and Parry 1989:13), (2) the call to situate local systems in the wider political and social worlds of which they are part (Ortner 1984:142), and (3) the recognition that all human communities are shaped by an interplay between internal forms and external conditions (Leach 1954: 212). It also resonated with Bakhtin's (1981:270) insistence that the holism of (linguistic) systems is posited, not given, and that it is acted upon to ensure intelligibility in the face of fragmentary realities (see following discussion).

For Leach (1954:4), "every real society is a process in time": Internal change—either transformation within an existing order or the alteration of its structure (p. 5)—is perennial, ongoing, inevitable. What is more, social reality never "forms a coherent whole." It is, by nature, fragmentary and inconsistent (p. 8). "System," therefore, is always a fiction, an "as if" model of the world, for actor and analyst alike. But, Leach added, it is a necessary analytic fiction, because it affords a means by which otherwise invisible connections between social phenomena may be traced out and explained. Many are familiar with his ethnographic case: In Highland Burma, we are told, Kachin groups were caught up in a dynamic pattern of movement between two polar types, two idealized representations of political order. One was the highly centralized, hierarchical, autocratic Shan state; the other, the decentralized, egalitarian, "democratic" *gumlao* polity. Most communities, however, fell somewhere between, in so-called *gumsa* formations. But the latter were not static: They were constantly moving in the direction of either the Shan or the *gumlao* "type." As they did so, the internal inconsistencies (i.e., contradictions) of that "type" would manifest themselves, encouraging a countermovement—itself impelled by the self-interested actions of individuals who, appealing to diverse values, abetted the process of structural change by pursuing their own ends (p. 8). The net effect over the long run, some 150 years, was a pattern of oscillating equilibrium.

Political Systems of Highland Burma certainly has its shortcomings. Leach has been taken to task for (1) relying on crass utilitarianism, a universalist cliché, to account for human motives, thereby separating culture from society and reducing it to the "outer dress" of social action; (2) resorting, nonetheless, to vulgar idealism in order to rationalize the behavior of *homo economicus* in the Kachin Hills; (3) describing *gumsa, gumlao,* and Shan as ideal "types"—without subjecting them to historical analysis—and then treating them as factual realities; (4) failing to locate Highland Burmese communities in continental and global context or within linear processes of the long run; and, finally, (5) reducing history to a repetitive pattern of (bipolar) social equilibrium.

We are not concerned here with evaluating these criticisms. Whether or not they are justified (see Fuller and Parry 1989:12–13), each stands as a *general* admonition, something that any historical anthropology would want to avoid; hence they are to be added to our negative checklist. But that, too, is only part of the story. There are also three constructive lessons, or rather challenges, to be drawn from this worthy effort to give expression to the assertion—often made, rarely made good on—that societies are "processes in time."

The first concerns the fluid, fragmentary character of social reality and the question of order. Leach would have scorned any postmodern suggestion that, because the world is experienced as ambiguous and incoherent, it must therefore lack all systematicity; that, because social life seems episodic and inconsistent, it can have no regularity; that, because we do not see its invisible forms, society is formless; that nothing lies behind its broken, multifaceted surfaces. The very idea would probably have struck him as a lamentable failure of the analytic imagination. *Political Systems of Highland Burma,* remember, set out to disinter the dynamic structure underlying a diverse (dis?)array of social arrangements and representations, values and events; to show that, if our models are supple enough, they should make sense of even the most chaotic and shifting social environment. Again, whatever the merits of Leach's account, the implication is clear. We require good grounds for claiming the *non*existence of a system or a structure—the fact that we are unable to discern one at first blush is hardly proof that it is not there. Here, then, is a preemptive counterchallenge to the deconstructive impulse of the 1990s: Absence and disconnection, incoherence and disorder, have actually to be demonstrated. They can neither be presumed nor posited by negative induction.

The second lesson of *Political Systems of Highland Burma*[25] applies to the historical anthropology of the modern world order, in particular, to the currently fashionable concern with the encounter between international and parochial systems, universal and local cultures. Good intentions notwithstanding, it is impossible to restore history to peoples allegedly without it by appealing to historical models of global processes, especially processes in Western political economy, while sustaining ahistorical models of non-European "social formations"—whether these be described in the language of Levi-Strauss, Marx, or Max Weber. For, as has been said *ad nauseam,* "peripheral" populations do not acquire history only when they are impelled along its paths by the machinations of merchants, missionaries, military men, manufacturers, or ministers of state. Bluntly put, a truly historical anthropology is only possible to the extent that it is capable of illuminating the *endogenous* historicity of all social worlds.

This may seem old hat. Coquery-Vidrovitch (1976:91) said fifteen years ago that "no one doubts any longer that precolonial societies had a history." Still, it is one thing to recognize the undeniable, another to give account of it. Models of noncapitalist orders abound, yet few demonstrate their internal capacity for transformation (cf. Sahlins 1981), stressing rather the (*a priori*) mechanics of their reproduction. Terminological niceties aside, how much have we *really* advanced on our old conception of "traditional" societies, "cold" cultures? Of local worlds trapped in repetitive cycles of structural time (Gluckman 1965:285f)—until, to cite Meillassoux's (1972:101) startling revision of genesis, they suffer "historical accidents, usually due to contacts with foreign formations"? Even recent efforts to reconceptualize "precapitalist systems" (see, e.g., Guy 1987) treat them as resolutely prehistorical. So do some notable attempts to resituate them within World History (e.g., Wolf 1982), most of which merely show that they have been enmeshed in global connections for longer than previously thought; not that they were inherently, internally dynamic—if in their own particular ways—all along.

This is not to denigrate the insights that have come from looking anew at worlds other than our own through the eyes of, say, feminist anthropology (see, e.g., Collier and Yanagisako 1987) or, for that matter, Meillassoux's Marxism, Wolf's world system, Sahlins's structuralism, and Bourdieu's embodied practice. We *have* learned much from them. But we have not ended up with any generally accepted theories or models of the historicity of non-Western societies.[26] Perhaps that, in itself, is no bad thing. And yet, without some way, however provisional, of grasping those historicities—note, again, the shift to the plural, the recognition of differences—anthropology will continue to cast "other cultures" in the timeless shadows of its own dominant narratives. It will also leave intact the disabling opposition between historiography and ethnography.

The last lesson to be taken from *Political Systems of Highland Burma,* and from the arguments that followed in its wake, has to do with "units of analysis": the terms, that is, by which social science breathes life into data, thence to arrange them into expository narratives. Leach's analysis raises the difficult question of whether historical anthropology is forever compelled to share the two fundamental tropes of Western historiography, the individual and the event. Note that the master motif of the Kachin past, as he tells it, was oscillating equilibrium, a great epochal movement realized in a cumulative series of incidents animated by (universal) human motives and (rational) modes of action. In offering his methodological individualist account of structural drift, Leach falls back on a classical, and classically ethnocentric, conception of social history. Of course, he is not alone in finding it hard to escape the liberal modernism of his own European culture. Structuralism has long obsessed over the individual and the event,[27] never quite laying down their ghosts once and for all. The situation of structural functionalism is similar: For all its ostensible concern with the nomothetic, it came increasingly to rest, as we said earlier, on an empirical scaffolding of life histories, case studies, social dramas of interpersonal conflict, and the like. Indeed, albeit often unobserved, biography—the optic that fuses individual and event into both a worldview and a narrative genre—lies at the methodological core of much ethnography and history.

But there is danger here. Biography is anything but innocent.[28] Its most articulate textual vehicles in our own society are the private diary, the journal, and the memoir, which find their way into much, often methodologically naive, historical writing; in the ethnographer's notebook it typically appears in the guise of the life history, a singular dialogic contrivance of observer and subject. Yet the diary and the life history are culturally specific, patently ideological modes of inscription. The former is strongly associated with the rise, in the eighteenth century, of bourgeois person-hood; Barker (1984), among others, traces its roots back to the Cartesian "I," an image of a *self*-conscious being freed from the webs of enchantment and possessed of the capacity to gaze out at, and measure, the world. As a medium of (self-) representation, more generally, life-histories bespeak a notion of the human career as an ordered progression of acts and events; of biography as history personified, history as biography aggregated; of the "biographical illusion," Bourdieu (1987) calls it, a modernist fantasy about society and selfhood according to which everyone is, potentially, in control of his or her destiny in a world made by the actions of autonomous "agents." It is this fantasy that leads historians to seek social causes in individual action and social action in individual causes; to find order in events by putting events in order.

Inasmuch as it records such actions and events, then, the "life story" is an instrument of bourgeois history-in-the-making, one strand in the process whereby private thoughts and deeds are woven into the collective narratives of epochs and civilizations. Nor is it a passive, impartial instrument. Gusdorf (1980:29), noting that autobiography is peculiar to the Western sensibility of selfhood, argues that it "has been of good use in the systematic conquest of the universe." Anthropologists, as we well know, are alleged accessories in all this: By translating the experience of others into our own measures of being-in-time (cf. Fabian 1983), we are said to have laid down the terms in which they may be represented—and, in both senses of the word, made into subjects.

Gusdorf may or may not be correct about the "systematic conquest of the universe." Our more immediate worry, at this point, is that for the most part social science persists in treating biography as a neutral, trans-parent window into history. In so doing, it serves to perpetuate the "biographical illusion": to regard persons and performances in the Pro-methean mode, to find the motors of the past and present in rational individualism, and to pay little heed to the social and cultural forms that silently shape and constrain human action. It is a short step from this to a vision of History and Society as the dramaturgy of intersecting lives: a theater in which, as the narrative spotlight narrows ever more sharply on actors and their scripts, text—a sad proxy for life—becomes all. And context dissolves away into so many shadows.

If historical anthropology is to avoid recapitulating the eccentricities and ethnocentricities of the West, the individual and the event have everywhere to be treated as problematic. Just how are they constituted, culturally and historically? What determines, or renders indeterminate, the actions of human beings in the world? What decides whether, in the first place, the bounded individual is even a salient unit of subjectivity? What is it in any social context that constructs utilities and rationalities, "private" motives and collective consciousness, dominant worldviews and polyvalent symbols, consensual signs and contested images? Precisely how are meaningful atoms of human action and interaction contrived? The lessons we draw from *Political Systems of Highland Burma*—and, more generally, from the early rapprochement of history and anthropology—converge in these questions. Indeed, considered in light of our dialogue with *l'histoire des mentalités*, they pose three challenges to any historical anthropology: (1) to address the equations of structure and indeterminacy, of form and incoherence, involved in tracking the movement of societies and peoples through time; (2) to disinter the endogenous historicity of local worlds, both perceptual and practical, in order to understand better their place within the world historical processes of which they are part; and (3) to rupture the basic tropes of Western historiography—biography and event— by situating being and action, comparatively, within their diverse cultural contexts.

At this point a shift in voice is appropriate. Having set the scene for our historical anthropology in a critical key, we should say something of its positive conceptual foundations. We began to lay these out in *Of Revelation and Revolution* (1991). Here, consequently, we offer the briefest synopsis; in any case, as we stressed earlier, we wish to allow the essays to speak for themselves.

Clearly, the place to begin is with the idea of culture itself. Still the anthropological keyword par excellence, if anything it is enhanced, not threatened, by recent developments in cultural studies and "cultural poetics" (Greenblatt 1990:3). For reasons detailed elsewhere (Comaroff and Comaroff 1991:13f), we take culture to be the semantic space, the field of signs and practices, in which human beings construct and represent themselves and others, and hence their societies and histories. It is not merely an abstract order of signs, or relations among signs. Nor is it just the sum of habitual practices. Neither pure langue nor pure parole, it never constitutes a closed, entirely coherent system. Quite the contrary: Culture always contains within it polyvalent, potentially contestable messages, images, and actions. It is, in short, a historically situated, historically unfolding ensemble of signifiers-in-action, signifiers at once material and symbolic, social and aesthetic. Some of these, at any moment in time, will be woven into more or less tightly integrated, relatively explicit worldviews; others may be heavily contested, the stuff of counterideologies and "subcultures"; yet others may become more or less unfixed, relatively freefloating, and indeterminate in their value and meaning.

It has been widely argued in recent years that the concept of culture, in itself, is incapable of grasping the meaningful bases of economy and society, of inhabited history and imagined worlds. "Power," we are told, has to be added into the equation, since it determines why some signs are dominant, others not; why some practices seem to be consensual, others disputed—even when they are backed by the technology of terror. The general point is well taken, albeit with a cautionary amendment: Power is itself not above, nor outside of, culture and history, but it is directly implicated in their constitution and determination. It cannot, therefore, be "added" to them in such a way as to solve the great conundrums of history and society.

This, we would argue, is where hegemony and ideology, the terrible twins of much recent social theory, become salient. Although we regret the often unspecific, devalued use of these terms, they do, if carefully deployed, offer a cogent way of speaking about the force of meaning and the meaning of force—the inseparability, that is, of power and culture. They also serve to reframe the idea of culture itself in such a way as to embrace, at once, its systemic and indeterminate features: the fact that it appears, on the one hand, as an orderly worldview and, on the other, as a heterodox, even chaotic, repertoire of polyvalent images and practices.

Power, then, is an intrinsic quality of the social and the cultural; in short, their determining capacity. Sometimes it appears as the (relative) ability of human beings to shape the lives of others by exerting control over the production, circulation, and consumption of signs and objects, over the making of both subjectivities and realities. This is power in the *agentive* mode. But it also immerses itself in the forms of everyday life, forms that direct human perceptions and practices along conventional pathways. Being "natural" and "ineffable," such forms seem to be beyond human agency, notwithstanding the fact that the interests they serve may be all too human. This kind of *nonagentive* power saturates such things as aesthetics and ethics, built form and bodily representation, medical knowledge and material production. And its effects are internalized—in their negative guise, as constraints; in their neutral guise, as conventions; in their positive guise, as values.

This distinction between modalities of power and agency, we suggest, underlies the differences, and the relationship, between ideology and hegemony—which may fruitfully be regarded as the two empowered dimensions of any culture.

Let us elaborate. We take hegemony to refer to that order of signs and material practices, drawn from a specific cultural field, that come to be taken for granted as the natural, universal, and true shape of social being—although its infusion into local worlds, always liable to challenge by the logic of prevailing cultural forms, is never automatic. It consists of things that go without saying: things that, being axiomatic, are not normally the subject of explication or argument (cf. Bourdieu 1977:94, 167). This is why its power seems to be independent of human agency, to lie in what it silences, what it puts beyond the limits of the thinkable. It follows that it is seldom contested openly. Indeed, the moment that any set of values, meanings, and material forms comes to be explicitly negotiable, its hegemony is threatened; at that moment it becomes the subject of ideology or counterideology.

As this implies, ideology describes "an articulated system of meanings, values, and beliefs of a kind that can be abstracted as [the] 'worldview'" of any social grouping (Williams 1977:109). Carried in everyday practice and self-conscious texts, in spontaneous images and popular styles, this worldview may be more or less internally systematic, more or less consistent in its outward forms. Still, as long as it exists, it provides an organizing scheme, a master narrative, for collective symbolic production. Obviously, to invoke Marx and Engels (1970), the regnant ideology of any period or place will be that of the dominant group, although the degree of its preeminence may vary a good deal; so, also, will the extent to which it is empowered by the instrumental force of the state. But other, subordinate populations also have ideologies. And, insofar as they try to assert themselves, to gain some control over the terms in which the world is ordered, they too will call actively upon them—even if only to clash their symbols.

Here, then, is the basic difference between hegemony and ideology. Hegemony consists of constructs and conventional practices that have come to permeate a political community; ideology originates in the assertions of a particular social group. Hegemony is beyond direct argument; ideology is more likely to be perceived as a matter of inimical opinion and interest and hence is more open to contestation. Hegemony, at its most effective, is mute; ideology invites argument.

Hegemony, then, is that part of a dominant ideology that has been naturalized and, having contrived a tangible world in its image, does not appear to be ideological at all. Conversely, the ideologies of the subordinate may express hitherto voiceless experience, often sparked by contradictions that a prevailing culture no longer hides. The manner in which a sectarian worldview actually comes to naturalize structures of inequality—or, conversely, the commonplace comes to be questioned—is always a historically specific issue. Typically, however, it involves the assertion of control over various modes of production, both symbolic and material—control that, as Foucault understood, must be sustained in such a way as to become invisible. For it is only through repetition that things cease to be perceived or remarked, that they become so habituated as no longer to be noticed. At the same time, however, no hegemony is ever total (Williams 1977:109); it constantly has to be made and, by the same token, may be unmade. That is why it has been described as a process rather than a thing, a process to which all ruling regimes have to pay heed. The more successful any regime, the more of its ideology will disappear into the domain of hegemonic practice; the less successful, the more its unspoken conventions will be opened to contest. This, self-evidently, is most likely to occur when the gap between the world-as-represented and the world-as-experienced becomes both palpable and insupportable.

In *Of Revelation and Revolution* we take this analytic scheme further, using it to explore consciousness and representation, historical agency and social practice, domination and resistance, global and local social orders, and the politics and culture of colonialism. Here we seek to make a more general point: that it is possible for anthropology to live easily with the concept of culture and to defend it cogently against its critics. But this requires that we treat culture as a shifting semantic field, a field of symbolic production and material practice empowered in complex ways.

In sum, far from being reducible to a closed system of signs and relations, the meaningful world is always fluid and ambiguous, a partially integrated mosaic of narratives, images, and signifying practices. Its forms—which are indivisibly semantic and material, social and symbolic—appear, paradoxically, to be at the same time (and certainly over time) coherent yet chaotic, authoritative yet arguable, highly systemic yet unpredictable, consensual yet internally contradictory. The paradox, of course, is illusory. In its hegemonic dimensions, any culture *does* present itself as relatively coherent, systemic, consensual, authoritative. After all, whatever forms are powered by the force of habit are naturalized and uncontested; they do seem eternal and universal—at least for the continuing present, however long that turns out to be. But alongside them there are always countervailing forces: dialects that diverge, styles that do not conform, alternative moralities and world-maps. Sometimes these are implicated in open power struggles, sometimes they erupt in parody, sometimes they express themselves in mundane activity of indeterminate intention and consequence. Whatever. But the conclusion is clear: With a sufficiently supple view of culture, we may begin to understand *why* social life everywhere appears dualistic, simultaneously ordered and disorderly.

In the great confrontation between modernist and postmodern perspectives on the world, each of which emphasizes one side of the dualism, we are asked to make a choice. To do so is to be misled, however. The world *is* everywhere dualistic—this being one of those realities for which we ought to have respect. Note that we say *every*where. If a neomodern anthropology is to work creatively at the frontiers of ethnography and the historical imagination, it must be founded on a conception of culture and society that takes us beyond our traditional stamping grounds—one that travels easily to a newer generation of field sites, among them the metropoles, mentalities, and mass media of Europe and America. And this, finally, brings us back to the question of method.

IV

How, then, do we *do* an ethnography of the historical imagination? How do we contextualize the fragments of human worlds, redeeming them without losing their fragile uniqueness and ambiguity? To repeat: for us the answer lies in a historical anthropology that is dedicated to exploring the processes that make and transform particular worlds—processes that reciprocally shape subjects and contexts, that allow certain things to be said and done. Over time, all social fields are swept by contrary waves of unity and diversity: by forces that diffuse power and meaning and by counterforces that concentrate and fix them. The premise of unification, of some limitation to the "chaos of variety" (Holquist in Bakhtin 1981:xix), is essential to collective life—and, hence, to the very idea of society and culture. But so is the inevitability of proliferation, polyphony, and plurality. Situating our fragments is thus a challenging task, for the systems to which we relate them are systems of a complex sort. Yet, we insist, they are systems nonetheless. We should not deny them coherence merely because they refuse to reduce readily to simple structures.

We are not alone in urging that anthropology shift its concentration away from simple structures and local systems, at least as traditionally defined. This shift, however, has practical consequences. Above all, it deprives us of our conventional, all-too-easy means of bounding analytic fields, forcing us to enter rarified realms of floating texts and macro-structures, where the connective tissues—the processes and pathways of face-to-face sodalities—seem to dissolve into thin air. In the past, our strategy for studying "complex" situations was either to turn to the sociology of networks and symbolic interaction—to a methodological individualism, that is, without a generic theory of society and culture—or to find enclaves within the alienating world of modernity. We looked for "subcultures," informal economies, and marginal minorities, for ritual and resistance to capitalism; all neatly circumscribed phenomena, for us still thick with meaning. Until very recently, we have felt ill equipped to broach, in their own ethnographic right, such things as electronic media, "high" culture, the discourses of science, or the semantics of commodities. At best, these have been regarded as forces eroding traditional orders or as "significant causes of our modern difficulties" (McCracken 1988:xi).[29] And so we have remained largely in the countryside, on ethnic islands and culturally distinct archipelagoes.

We are the first to acknowledge that it is not easy to forge units of analysis in unbounded social fields. But it would be false to assume that an ethnography of the nation-state, of empire, or of a diaspora presents problems unprecedented in earlier studies of, say, domestic production, possession rites, or lineage relations. That assumption appears true only as long as we pretend that such "local" phenomena are visible in the round and are separable for heuristic purposes from anything beyond their immediate environs; as long as we sustain the primitivist fiction that traditional orders are natural and self-perpetuating—and radically different from the unruly, unbounded, even unnatural worlds of "modernity" or "capitalism." But few, surely, would wish to condemn anthropology to such pastoral archaism; what should define us is a unique analytic stance, less our locus than our focus. Whether our topic be headhunting in the Amazon or headshrinking in America (or is it vice versa?), voodoo exorcism in the Caribbean or voodoo economics on Capitol Hill, we should approach it from the same perspective: as meaningful practice, produced in the interplay of subject and object, of the contingent and the contextual.

It is precisely here that anthropology has shown a failure of imagination, however, and here that we return to our opening theme. Many of us continue to be hampered, in conceiving open systems, by the dualisms of an enduring evolutionism. We are still prompted to deal in a priori contrasts—between stasis and change, gifts and commodities, theodicy and theory, and so on—that assume the meaning and telos of social phenomena. The Naparama and their kind remain *primitive* rebels, not Promethean heroes or universal soldiers. And this impedes us as we try to dissolve the great analytic divide between tradition and modernity, to confront global issues in more inventive, less pejorative terms. Nor, as we suggested, is the problem resolved by upgrading mechanical models of local systems, grafting them onto universalist theories of society and history; or by literary critical methods that make ethnographic fragments into exemplary texts without adequately relating them to the wider worlds that produce them.

Ethnography does not have to respect a binary world-map, let alone the axes of typological difference. As a mode of observation, it need not be tied either to face-to-face scenes or to a specific sort of social subject. True, we have classically set our sights on particular persons and palpable processes, and this has determined our point of entry into any cultural field. But we are not, for that reason, limited to the writing of microsociologies or histories. The phenomena we observe may be grounded in everyday human activity; yet such activity, even when rural or peripheral, is always involved in the making of wider structures and social movements. Nor ought we to confine ourselves to history's outstations. Even macrohistorical processes—the building of states, the making of revolutions, the extension of global capitalism—have their feet on the ground. Being rooted in the meaningful practices of people great and small, they are, in short, suitable cases for anthropological treatment. Indeed, whether or not we choose to write about them directly, they must always be present in our accounts (cf. Davis 1990:32).

The methodological implications of all this are best explored by way of a specific instance. Several of the essays that follow address the anthropology of empire, in particular the nineteenth-century encounter between British Nonconformist missionaries and peoples of the South African interior. The former were footsoldiers of colonialism, the humble agents of a global movement. The latter, who would come to be known as "the" Tswana, inhabited a world with its own history, a history of great political communities built and broken. But the African past would become subservient to the European present, made into the timeless sign of the "traditional" periphery. In order to grasp this process, we had first to characterize each party as a complex collectivity, each endowed with its own historicity. And then we had to retrace the (often barely visible) minutiae of their interactions. For it is in the gradual articulation of such alien worlds that local and universal realities come to define each other—and that markers like "ethnicity" and "culture," "regionalism" and "nationalism," take on their meaning.

Elsewhere (1991:35ff) we have discussed the general problem of recovering the histories of peoples like the Tswana from evangelical and official records, a topic now receiving long overdue attention (Amin 1984; Guha 1983). Here we are more specifically concerned with the question of how to do a historical anthropology of dominant, world-transforming processes (cf. Cohn 1987; Cooper and Stoler 1989). Clearly, colonial evangelism must be understood both as a cultural project in itself and as the metonym of a global movement; its participants certainly saw themselves as an integral part of the grand imperial design. This, then, is an appropriate site for an imaginative sociology, a context in which anthropologists might recognize their kinship with cultural historians and embark on an ethnography of the archives. In our own work, the point of entry was obvious enough: We began with the conventional chronicles of the Nonconformist missions. But, in trying to make sense of the churchmen's various writings, as well as the wealth of reported speech about them, we soon learned not to rely on any preconstituted "documentary record." Rather, we had to pursue what Greenblatt (1990:14) terms the "textual traces" of the period, traces found in newspapers and official publications as well as in novels, tracts, popular songs, even in drawings and children's games.

Instead of a clear-cut chain of events, or a discernible perspective, the colonial archives revealed a set of arguments. They were dialogic in

Bakhtin's (1981:272f) sense; that is, they partook of diverse genres, of cultural and historical heteroglossia that gave voice to complex patterns of social stratification. If the colonizers formed a single block, it was one fractured by internal difference—and by diverging images of empire locked in "socio-ideological" struggle (p. 273). The latter expressed itself in disputes about such things as abolition, evangelism, and the way to rule and save savages. But, at root, it involved a contest over both the shape and meaning of "natural facts" and the major constituents of modern knowledge: its constructs of person, agency, and work, of Africa and Europe, wildness and civilization. It was only by reconstructing this field of argument—and, going perhaps beyond Bakhtin, by redeeming its politics—that we began to understand the cultural revolution entailed in both the rise of European capitalism and the imperial gesture. Here, amidst all the contradictions of the age, were forged the precepts and projects of a new hegemony, a new bourgeois modernism with universalist horizons and global ambitions. These, of course, included the Christian overseas mission.

A historical ethnography, then, must begin by constructing its own archive. It cannot content itself with established canons of documentary evidence, because these are themselves part of the culture of global modernism—as much the subject as the means of inquiry. As anthropologists, therefore, we must work both in and outside the official record, both with and beyond the guardians of memory in the societies we study (Cohn 1987:47f). In order to reconstruct the annals of a cultural imagination, moreover, we have to operate with a working theory not merely of the social world, but also of the role of inscriptions of various kinds in the making of ideology and argument. For only then can we situate individual expressions and signifying practices within a wider field of representation. After all, locating our fragments requires a sense of the way in which they ride the crosscurrents of division and unity at any moment; of how the autonomous creative urge runs up against cultural constraint. Sahlins (1990:47) notes that, although persons and collectivities "somehow determine" each other, they cannot, by that token, be reduced to one another. But our methods should tell us something of the way in which personal acts become social facts. In the case of colonial evangelism, we had to address the matter by locating a flood of rapportage from the imperial frontier in the complex textual field wrought by the industrial revolution, the consequences of so-called print capitalism (Anderson 1983). But this is just a specific instance of the general problem of reading social processes from exemplary representations: If texts are to be more than literary topoi, scattered shards from which we presume worlds, they have to be anchored in the processes of their production, in the orbits of connection and influence that give them life and force.

The writings of the South African evangelists are especially interesting in this regard. They differed a good deal in their intent and formality: The ambiguities, agonies, and self-doubts aired in letters to kin were not exposed to morally vigilant mission overseers, for example; nor to philanthropists, who were more responsive to evocative accounts of savagery; nor to the churchgoing masses, with their strong taste for Christian heroics. Not only was similar material carefully contrived for diverse audiences, revealing the range of purposes and constraints at work in the civilizing quest, but the historical role of these writings varied likewise. Once addressed to the mission societies, correspondence was political property, to be liberally edited and recycled for campaigns in parliament and the public domain. Letters became pamphlets. And pamphlets became books, eyewitness epics of "labors and scenes" beyond the frontiers of civilization. Thus were layers of texts produced—indeed, an entire stratigraphy. By excavating the career of a particular document it is possible to follow the editor's pen as it refigured authorial statements, rationalizing them into publishable forms that framed the doctrine of humane imperialism. And so an ethnography of this archive begins to disinter the processes by which disparate, even divisive, discourses were fused into a consistent ideology, by which coherence was distilled out of the often chaotic, episodic stream of missionary experience (cf. Bakhtin 1981:272f).

We would insist, though, that a historical ethnography must always go beyond literary traces, beyond explicit narrative, exegesis, even argument. For the poetics of history lie also in mute meanings transacted through goods and practices, through icons and images dispersed in the landscape of the everyday (Comaroff and Comaroff 1987; Cohn 1987:49). Again, this is as true of world historical movements as it is of the most local processes. Just as the Reverend John Philip saw that any effort to re-form "the" Tswana supposed "[bringing about] a revolution in their habits" (see Chapter 10), so Corrigan and Sayer (1985) hold that the making of the modern British state was a cultural revolution borne in large measure by the humdrum rituals and routines that shaped the lives of subjects. Certainly, the great empires of the past established themselves as much in a welter of domestic detail and small-scale civilities as by assertive political and economic means. Such are the tools that build hegemonies, that work thoroughgoing social transformations behind the back of a declarative, heroic history.

This implicit dimension—the study of symbolic practice—is a crucial contribution of ethnography to history, since it brings a nuanced understanding of the role of meaning and motivation to social processes. At its best, anthropology has never been content to equate meaning merely with explicit consciousness. In fact, the relationship of individual experience to the collective, often unconscious logic of sociocultural categories and designs has long been our stock-in-trade. We may have come to distrust formal, overly coherent notions of culture, but we ought not to jettison the subtle semantic models that so enhance our sensitivity to the power of signs in the world.[30] For, however open ended, systems of meaning have determinations of their own. They do not just bend to the will of those who wish to know and act upon them; to the contrary, they play a significant part in shaping subjectivity. The "motivation" of social practice, in other words, always exists at two distinct, if related, levels: first, the (culturally configured) needs and desires of human beings; and, second, the pulse of collective forces that, empowered in complex ways, work through them.

This distinction informs the analysis of all historical processes, but its significance has been underlined by the humanist turn in social science, which has led to calls for a greater concern with agency. Its salience becomes particularly visible when we examine epochal movements like European colonialism, in which purposive, "heroic" action was a central motif, even a driving impulse. Yet, from our perspective, that impulse is not enough to account for the determination of the processes involved— or even to tell very much of the story. Witness, once again, the imperial mission, an initiative moved by contradictory forces whose consequences differed radically from the stated motives of those involved. Although they were eminently effective in transforming local lives, the evangelists failed precisely where they most hoped to succeed, namely, in implanting an orthodox Protestant peasantry on African soil.

Here, then, was a paradox of motivation, a paradox that ran to the heart of the colonial encounter. While the mission spoke of itself and its intentions in the language of Christian conversion, its practice proclaimed something else. Motivated, silent and unseen, by the very situation of the evangelists in the European scheme of things, this narrative told of the reconstruction of a living culture by the infusion of alien signs and commodities into every domain of Tswana life. Methodologically, it commanded us to pursue the colonizing gesture beyond audible ideologies and visible institutions into the realm of such unspoken forms as bodies, buildings, magic, and merchandise. And this, in turn, took us back to our archives—to letters, lists, illustrations, and photographs—albeit now less for what they declared than for what they disclosed as maps of the mundane. It also prompted a cultural archaeology of the sites of earlier evangelical activity: for example, the windswept ruins of Tiger Kloof, a mission school built for Southern Tswana early this century, where it was possible to disinter, from the sediments of a dead community, aspects of colonial pedagogy invisible in the written accounts.

The scattered signs retrieved in this quest all pointed to wider social transformations borne *unwittingly* by the missionaries. In many respects, these actually ran counter to their own desires and motives. For the churchmen were themselves contradictory products of a contradictory bourgeois world. Although they wished to recreate, in Africa, the British yeomanry of yore, their tools and tropes also carried the imprint of the industrial marketplace and its commodity culture. And their actions played a major role in processes of proletarianization, the likes of which they had decried back home. This is where the relationship between the two dimensions of colonial evangelism—itself a highly specific encounter of the "local" and the "global"—took on its real complexity. At one level, it involved an odyssey, a highly purposive journey aimed at converting "savages" into pious peasants and citizens of Christendom. At another, it participated in seeding a pervasive new order that would, along with other colonizing forces, make Africans into impoverished, subordinated subjects of empire. At times, these two levels reinforced one another, at times they produced nightmarish disjunctions and discontinuities. We have argued elsewhere (n.d.[b]), in fact, that it was in the space between the liberal worldview of the mission and the racist world of settler society that modern black nationalist consciousness was to take root. In the longer run, as this suggests, the implications of evangelical imperialism were to be fixed by the wider context in which it was embedded, just as they were to be mediated by the responses of the Tswana themselves (see Part 3).

And the general methodological point? There are several. The first is that our current conceptual obsession with agency, subjectivity, and consciousness can be addressed only in *ethnographic* terms, and thereby rescued from vapid theoreticism, under a pair of conditions: that (1) we treat as problematic the manner in which persons are formed and action determined and (2) we insist that individual action is never entirely reducible to social forces, nor social forces to the sum of unique acts (above, p. 25). Second, because it is multiply motivated, social history, as we have stressed, will always be both predictable yet subject to the innovative and the unforeseen. Hence our historical ethnographies must be capable of capturing the simultaneous unity and diversity of social processes, the incessant convergence and divergence of prevailing forms of power and meaning. But they must do so without falling into the trap of typifying history in general— or histories in particular—as an expression of the radical contrast between modern (or postmodern) worlds and their "traditional" antecedents. Or between commmoditized societies and natural economies.

It follows from all this, third, that our methodological concern is less with events than with meaningful practices—which, perhaps, remains one of the principle distinctions between historical anthropology and social history.[31] Like most anthropologists, we are more preoccupied with ambiguous processes than with contained acts or isolable incidents that, in themselves, can be said to make a difference. To us, social life is continuous activity—activity that, because it is always a product of complex experience and contradictory conditions, simultaneously reproduces *and* transforms the world. It will be evident, too, that we take meaning to be largely, if not entirely, implicit in practice; we do not see it to reside in abstract schemes or in categories that endure or change in all-or-none fashion. From this perspective, history involves a sedimentation of micropractices into macroprocesses, a prosaic rather than a portentous affair in which events mark rather than make the flow of existence (cf. Cohn 1987:45). This is not to deny the importance of extraordinary human agency. Some acts do have more consequence than others and, in certain contexts, actors can become metonyms of history or, more accurately, of heroic-history-in-the-making (Sahlins 1985:35f). But it is this metonymy, some would even say fetishism, that we have to explain. How is it that particular persons and events seem, in their own worlds, to embody and motivate processes whose origins we, from our standpoint, ascribe to more dispersed causes? Heroes are born not of gods, but of social forces. Their charisma camouflages complex conditions of possibility, just as it personifies ambiguously authored action.

In the "newer social history," says Davis (1990:28), events serve less as motors of change than to exemplify the mingling of the prescribed and the contingent[32] and/or to reveal the effect of cultural form upon social processes. This approach does not so much "nullify" the event—as did an earlier structuralist history (cf. Sahlins 1990:39; also above)—as resituate it in an unfolding sequence of action. It also democratizes human agency by shifting attention from the subjectivity of big men to the force of communal projects and cultural practices. This entails a move, to cite Davis (1990:28) again, from such major episodes as wars and revolutions to processes of domination, representation, and resistance. Recall our earlier discussion: in particular, Samuel's plea for the significance of the Married Women's Property Act over the Battle of Trafalgar in shaping nineteenth-century Britain. The former has been neglected because it was the product of diffuse conflict and long-term collective action; it is not reducible, except in the most banal sense, to an event. Yet, although the impact of the Act—the changing nature of property, womanhood, and marriage—calls for a processual perspective, its history remains rich with agency, some of it even "heroic."

Much the same may be said of the revolution that occurred when the forces of European imperialism sought to insinuate themselves into the non-European world, giving rise to the double context—the global stage and the local *mise en scène*—in which all "Third World" ethnographies would later be done. Colonial history does not lack for heroes or events. But neither is it reducible to a series of fortuitous encounters or fateful actions. As pilgrims to the South African "wilderness," the Nonconformist evangelists were moved by humanitarian ideals and imperial dreams at home, ideals and dreams especially compelling to those at the margins of the rising bourgeoisie. And their reception by the often bemused Africans was determined, in large part, by the predicament of these peoples in a fraught, rapidly transforming political arena.

The incorporation of "the" Tswana into the colonial world, as we have pointed out, was a drawn-out process involving two dynamic social systems, two historical orders, each with its own indeterminacies and internal contradictions. The players in this theater of the ordinary changed one another by means of humble acts within the terrain they came to share—although their behavior also moved, increasingly and in ways barely realized, to the beat of global imperatives. The pulse of these processes may be discerned, as we show in Chapter 9, in everyday struggles over such things as agricultural technique, language and speech, the use of land and water, and modes of healing, each small thing summoning up a hinterland of signs and practices. The plough, for instance, seemed an innocent enough instrument. In this context, however, it bore within it the whole culture of commodity production and turned out to have enormously complex social consequences. It is not that the historical encounter between the evangelists and the Africans was un-event-ful. There *were* many notable episodes: epic first meetings, dramatic demonstrations of "miraculous" technology, acrimonious public arguments. Clearly, these made a difference. But they did not make *the* difference. Nor, in themselves, did they occasion moments of great rupture, cataclysms that led to the reconstruction of otherwise unchanging social systems. They were, rather, significant icons of—and elements in—an unfolding, multileveled engagement between worlds.

Insofar as global systems and epochal movements always root themselves somewhere in the quotidian, then, they are accessible to historical ethnography. In Africa, as elsewhere, the colonial "state" was both a political structure *and* a condition of being; hence the former (its institutional order of governance) might be interrogated through the latter (the routines and habits oriented toward it). Similarly, the body politic and the body personal are everywhere intimately related—so much so that their connection has become almost a truism. Yet, we would suggest, the human body—or, more precisely, its analytic use and abuse—provides a nice commentary on the interpretive methodology of which we speak.

While the body has long been an important construct in Western social thought (Durkheim 1947:115–116; Mauss 1973), it has recently gained extraordinary prominence in the discourse of the human sciences. Perhaps because critical postmodernism has challenged fixed notions of power and meaning, it has assumed a unique concreteness; it is, to be sure, something on which we can always lay hands. For that reason, it has been treated as one of the only permanent points in a shifting world, especially by Foucault and his followers. The human body, in short, has been fetishized. And, like all fetishes, it is given credit for animating social life, yet it is strangely elusive—notably so in recent writing on the topic. Often no more than an alibi, a site, for equally elusive constructs like the "person," "the subject," and "social experience," it is named only to be dismissed; thus we perpetuate what Corrigan (1988:371) terms the "Great Erasure of the Body," long characteristic of Western scholarly discourse. (How different this is from the frank sensuality with which some creative writers, from D. H. Lawrence to Toni Morrison, have expressed their opposition to established conventions!) A notable instance of this absent presence occurs in Bryan Turner's *The Body and Society* (1984), which uses corporality as the ostensible focus for "explorations in social theory." In his journey through issues of selfhood, sexuality, and social order, Turner seldom confronts physicality at all (see T. Turner 1986). Displaced by the text, by a concern with representation severed from material being, the body actually loses all social relevance.

None of this is new. Admittedly, in the great dialectic of the "social" and the "natural," a classical concern of social theory, the body has long been seen as quintessential raw material for collective representation (see Chapter 3; Durkheim 1947:115f). Still, in striving to demonstrate the sui generis quality of society and culture, scholars have repeatedly treated the human physique as a tabula rasa, plastic material to be formed by arbitrary semantic categories (cf. van Gennep 1960; Douglas 1970; Bourdieu 1977). Poststructuralist and deconstructionist writers have perpetuated this form of idealism. Outside of discourse or the splintering subject or the floating sign there is, for them, no enduring object world. Rejecting all traffic with reality as brute "positivism"—as a matter of physical properties imposing themselves on passive subjects (T. Turner 1990:10)—they are unreceptive to the idea that material facts have any role at all in human experience.

Yet there is undeniable evidence that biological contingencies constrain human perception and social practice, albeit in ways mediated by cultural forms (see Sahlins 1976b; Chapter 3). And this is the point: Precisely because history *is* a synthesis of the heterogenous, we cannot ignore the role in it of such culturally mediated materialities. These, in turn, find their prime instance in the body, the physical object that also becomes a social subject (T. Turner 1990:1). It is here, where physical facts meet social values, that collective modes of being emerge as dispositions or motives. That is why movements of social reform, whatever they do at the level of collective institutions, tend also to work on the body as *fons et origo* of the world (below, Chapter 3). Hegemony, at least in the cultural sense we give it, has its natural habitat in the human frame. As a result, that frame can never be a struggle-free zone, least of all when major historical shifts are under way.

We might anticipate, then, that those who seek to forge empires, or to remake existing worlds, will try to impress themselves upon the physiques of their would-be subjects. States old and new have built their esprit de corps by shaving, clothing, vaccinating, and counting their citizens, just as rising classes, ethnic groups, religious movements, and political associations tend to wear their self-awareness on their skin. For their part, conquerors and colonizers seem typically to feel a need to reverse prior corporeal signs, often making bodies into realms of contest. The ancient English subdued recalcitrant Scottish highlanders by cutting their hair and banning their kilts (Brain 1979:150); their descendants in Africa would attempt to force Tswana converts into the dress of Christian decency.

Such tangible processes are eminently susceptible to the kind of ethnographic scrutiny that may divulge the hidden hand of history. Take our colonial evangelists once again: While they talked of spiritual verities that disparaged the flesh and condemned Africans for their "carnal" ways, their actions displayed an intense interest in corporeal politics. The black body was seldom far from their thoughts or deeds, disrupting their rhetoric when least expected. As our encounter with Foucault, Derrida, and Ginzburg would lead us to expect, these disruptions yield vital clues. A close reading of the churchmen's diaries and records proves that body work—the effort to retune the physical registers of dark persons through grooming, dress, and comportment—was a crucial mode of colonial production. This was one of the basic methods implicit in the mission, an unremarked means by which the Christians hoped to create a new moral empire. By deciphering the small print of letters, requisitions, and reports from the field, as well as the inventories of local merchants, we were able to trace the paths of diverse goods and practices converging on the African anatomy. Again, this is an instance of a universal process (Comaroff and Comaroff 1991:19f): No technique was too trivial, no mannerism too meaningless to be drawn up into the sweep of history-in-the-making.

In their campaign to domesticate the black body, moreover, the colonizers intervened in "native" cooking, hygiene, sexuality, and work. Wherever they could, they set about breaking the "communistic" interdependence of African persons and productive processes, thereby to create a world of "free" individuals; free, that is, to consume and be consumed by European commodities. We discern this process most clearly in the expanding stock of objects (pots, fabrics, soap, tools, clocks, locks, and so on) that the whites saw as essential implements of modernity and progress. These objects moved along the prosaic pathways that bore the traffic of global capitalism and its culture to Southern Africa—and carried their recipients toward material dependency. Abroad, as at home (see Chapter 10), civilizing goods ushered in new orders of relations—relations both symbolic and substantial—that bound local consumers to an expanding world order. Such were the fragments of which novel totalities were being constructed. The mundane practices to which they gave rise speak coherently to us from the ethnographic record. Together they weave compelling narratives of a world historical movement and its many local variants, each different in critical respects.

Such symbolic processes, we stress, are not limited to colonizing moments. The making of what we term modernity in Europe can be read as much in the evolution of table manners, sanitation, or the passport photograph (Elias 1978; Jephson 1907; Fussell 1980) as in the development of formal state institutions. Body work also had its parallels in the realm of architecture and domestic space: Rybczynski (1986), for example, finds a hidden history of the bourgeoisie in the rise of the modern European sense of "home." And the relentless social engineering of twentieth-century totalitarian states, whether they be in Eastern Europe or Southern Africa, is nowhere more clearly revealed than in their oppressively uniform public housing.

We ourselves draw on these insights in Chapter 10. There we explore the remarkable similarity between, on the one hand, efforts of colonizers to reshape the habits and habitations of nineteenth-century Africans and, on the other, the apparently unrelated attempt back home to "improve" the domestic lives of the urban underclass. Evangelists in Britain and Bechuanaland expressed the same conviction: that "uncouth" populations could be tamed through the orderly deployment of windows and walls, soap and sanitation, locks and lamps. How are we to interpret this coincidence? Was it a co-incidence? The answer, once more, lay in drawing fragments together and situating them within a wider historical field, thus to make sense of the embracing totality of which they were part. By tracing out the imaginative linkages among disparate texts and tropes, we were able to see that these seemingly independent instances of domestic reform were complementary sides of one process; indeed, that colonialism was as much a movement of re-formation *within* British society as it was a global gesture; that each site, the sickening England slum and the bestial African bush, became a model of and for the "other"; that this whole process was the political expression of a universalizing hegemony, a push to rebuild "savage life" on both continents to the specifications of bourgeois enlightenment.

In both contexts the process would succeed, above all else, in standardizing an aesthetics of class distinction; an architecture of othering for the metropole as well as the colony. Such discourse—and the philanthropic practice it empowered—stressed the morality of properly inhabited space: In a world driven by property and propriety, the home was heavily invested with elemental values, framing middle-class images of personhood, production, sexuality, and gender. Bodies, houses, and everyday routines bore the capillaries of a full-blooded imperialism, capillaries that ran from the palace gates to the "mud huts" on the colonial frontier. In the late nineteenth century, evangelical effort was increasingly superseded by the work of civic-minded professionals (like the engineers and doctors of the Domestic Sanitation Movement; Adams 1991) and by the rise of state schooling. Ultimately, any anthropology of the bourgeois revolution will have to explore how homemade hegemonies played into such national (and nationalist) projects. But that is a topic for another place (Comaroff and Comaroff n.d.[a]: Chaps. 4, 5).

More immediately, as we have remarked, the effort to colonize bodies and buildings did not go unchallenged. In South Africa, indigenous rulers at first resisted the Nonconformists' gentle persuasion. They seemed alive to the fact that the white men's designs on their people were anything but trivial. Later, many Tswana would rework those designs into provocative patterns, giving free reign to an independent, often subversive imagination. In London likewise, Cockney costermongers, poor street traders, ignored middle-class moralism and fashioned flamboyant life-styles of their own (Mayhew 1851,1). We should learn from them. For costers, chiefs, and churchmen alike appear to have sensed that it is things like clothing that make subjects—again, in both senses of the term. The Tswana "style wars," in which local leaders tried to fight off Western dress and architecture, were as much the site of colonial politics as were formal confrontations with government personnel or settler statesmen. In the fantastic fashions that flourished on the frontier we catch a glimpse of the consciousness of ordinary Africans, those who left little other imprint on the historical record. Here, along the line that divided the increasingly marked domains, the ideological spaces, of "tradition" and "modernity" they made new identities by retooling old values, redeploying the very signs that the colonizers imprinted on the supple surfaces of their lives.

Reading these poetic practices is by no means straightforward. Because bodies and domestic space were vital terrains of colonization, the struggles that occurred around them exhibited all the complexities of the colonial process itself—all the multiple motivations, the indeterminacies, and internal contradictions of complex historical conjunctures everywhere. Great social movements seem always to achieve both more and less than intended. For, even as would-be subject populations take issue with the manifest messages and overtures that intrude upon them, they often internalize alien cultural *forms* along the way—without either knowing or meaning to do so. That, as we show in Chapter 9, is why new hegemonies may take root amidst ideological argument, why people may be deeply affected by the media that bear the messages they reject, why such processes are never reducible to a simple calculus of accommodation or resistance. Thus even those Tswana who most strenuously refused the dress of baptism, preferring to pick and choose what they fancied from the mission, were profoundly changed by the world of commodities admitted with these innocent objects.

By the end of the nineteenth century, black identities in South Africa were being shaped less by either indigenous or mission intentions than by the gathering forces of the colonial state. Whatever were their local meanings, bodies, dress, and "life-style" were made over into signs of gross difference; into the distinctions of race, gender, and culture by which Africans were being incorporated into the lowest reaches of a rising industrial society. There is a general point here, and a concluding one. Far from being primordial, "ethnicity," "tribalism," and other forms of identity reside in tangible practices—as, of course, does "modernity." They are the social and ideological products of particular processes, of the very conjunctures that set the terms of, and relations between, "local" and "global" worlds. Such phenomena, we have argued, are not to be treated as received categories or analytic objects conjured up as universals from our own folk sociology. They are both polymorphous and perverse. Our task is to establish *how* collective identities are constructed and take on their particular cultural content; *how* they are made real, essential, embodied qualities for those who live them; *how* they become the natural atoms of social existence. Only then will the diverse forms of the modern world—indeed, the very terms of modernity itself—become the subjects of an ethnography of the historical imagination.

V

And so we conclude our voyage into method. The journey began with the Naparama—or, at least, their representation in the Western mass media. It was they who confronted us with the paradoxes and ironies that propel this essay: that, for all our obsession with the effect of anthropology on the "other," the discipline has had very limited impact on our own culture; that, for all the efforts of generations of ethnographers, the radical opposition between prehistorical "tradition" and capitalist "modernity" survives in the discourses of our age, popular and professional alike. Indeed, in directing much of our attention to peoples on the other side of the great rift, do we not still foster a lurking primitivism? And, with it, all the myths of our own disenchantment? The Naparama, in short, are a powerful metonym of our scholarly predicament, a mirror in which we see ourselves divided. They reveal our tendency, as a caustic critic once put it, to see people as everywhere the same except where they are different—and as everywhere different except where they are the same. In sum, the "mystic warriors" of Mozambique compel us to consider our wanton ambivalences, and so to reflect upon the way in which we ourselves reflect on others.

Such reflections persuade us that the conundrum of similarity and difference is only to be resolved by turning anthropology on itself, by treating modernity (and postmodernity) as a problem in historical ethnography. For the malignancy of primitivism—and its most notable symptom, exoticism—should disappear when we estrange our own culture, treating its signs and practices as we would theirs. This is not a call for rewriting all anthropology as "We the Nacirema" (Miner 1956) or for making all the world into an imaginary village. The purpose of estrangement, rather, is to remind ourselves that the West and the rest, long locked in historical embrace, cannot but be interrogated together. This, then, is our challenge. It is to explain the great conjunctures, the processes and practices through which have been fashioned the significant social phenomena of our times, both global and local.

These are issues of broad concern within the discipline at present; historical anthropology, patently, is more than a Chicago-cult. In order to address them we have appealed to a neomodernist method that takes seriously the message of critical postmodernism yet does not lose the possibility of social science; that takes to heart the lessons of cultural Marxism, seeking a conception of culture that recognizes the reality of power, yet does not reduce meaning to either utility or domination; that builds on the techniques of cultural history, pursuing the dialectic of fragment and totality without succumbing to brute empiricism; that, above all, proceeds, as it must, by grappling with the contradictions of its own legacy, seeking to transcend them—if only provisionally and for the moment.

Notes

1. *Chicago Tribune,* Sunday, 9 December 1990, Section 1, p. 1.

2. There is widespread evidence that this ideological opposition has continuing salience in our culture. Take just one example, a token of a very common type: In a review of the successful, well-intentioned film *Dances With Wolves* (1990; director, Kevin Costner), Dorris (1991:17) notes that, even today, "Indians embody the concept of 'the other'—a foreign, exotic, even cartoonish panorama against which modern (that is, white) men can measure and test themselves, and eventually . . . be dubbed as natural leaders."

3. Note, however, that the move has not been without criticism, even in apparently receptive fields; see, for example, Johnson (1983). We return to this issue later.

4. There are exceptions to this, especially in modern American anthropology. But they are restricted to such relatively marginal areas as mathematical anthropology, cultural ecology, and highly specialized forms of network analysis and economic anthropology.

5. Once more, the exceptions prove the general rule here. Although approaches like ethnoscience and mathematical and cognitive anthropology have called for new methods and theories, they have made little lasting impact on the practices of the discipline as a whole.

6. For an insightful exploration of the tropes that ethnographic writing shares with the earlier genre of travel writing, see Pratt (1986).

7. The evidence for this is everywhere at hand, from Evans-Pritchard's curt reminder that his facts were selected in light of his theories (1940:261), through Leach's (1954:5f) insistence that ethnographic accounts of social systems, like native models, are merely "as if" constructions of the world, to Geertz's (1973:29) allegorical suggestion that cultural analysis is a matter of "turtles all the way down."

8. Marcus (1986:190–191) adds that "experimental" ethnographers "perhaps do not even recognize the priority or privileged validity of such abstractly represented realities [as statistics]." Yet, in sustaining the opposition between "evocation" and "representation," he himself perpetuates a straw man: a "realist ethnography," whose "holistic commitments" defy the "open-ended mystery" of experience, and ostensibly the possibility of "alternative explanation."

9. Nonanthropologists might wish to know that Raymond Firth was a senior professor of social anthropology at the London School of Economics, then about to retire. A very distinguished scholar, he did much of his ethnographic research on the island of Tikopia in Polynesia.

10. For an especially clear example, see Marcus (1986:191).

11. See, for example, J. L. Comaroff (1982:143f), from which the quote is drawn.

12. The phrase is from Ginzburg's (1980:xx–xxi) brief but acid comment on those historians who, like François Furet, have found panaceas for large-scale problems in demographic sociology.

13. Darnton (1985:3) points out that there is no standard English translation of *l'histoire des mentalités*, until recently a predominantly French historiographical movement (see, e.g., Vovelle 1990). Darnton himself suggests that "it might simply be called cultural history." It is difficult not to agree; as Ginzburg (1980: xiv–xv, xxii–xxiv) indicates, the final object of a history of mentalities is an account of a particular ("popular") culture.

14. Hartley's original phrasing, in the first sentence of the prologue to *The Go-Between* (1956), was "The past is a foreign country: they do things differently there."

15. There is an irony lurking here. As Derrida (1978:35) notes, Foucault (1967) himself speaks much of silence in his *History*, especially when he situates madness within the trap of Western reason (not to mention the repressive language of psychiatry). Indeed, concludes Derrida, "[Foucault's] history of madness itself is . . . the archeology of a silence."

16. The comment is made in the specific context of his discussion of Febvre's treatment of Rabelais.

17. Croce ([1921] 1959:51) contrasts chronicle with history, treating them as different "spiritual attitudes. History is living chronicle, chronicle is dead history; . . . history is principally an act of thought, chronicle an act of will." It is this last phrase—the image of an act of will—that we seek to emphasize here.

18. We pass glancingly over this terrain in Chapter 4.

19. Some might say that there was also a fourth, exemplified by Cunnison (1959; cf. also Barnes 1951), which explored "what [people] made of their history" in the course of their social lives. However, such studies tended to limit themselves to the role of ethnic historical consciousness in repetitive social processes; most were produced within the "custom and conflict" approach of the Manchester School. As a result, their methodological bases were no different from those we will discuss. In this respect, too, we do not dignify as history an old practice of British structural functionalism: the appending of residual chapters on "social

change" to otherwise synchronic ethnographies. These, typically, were no more than narrative dumping grounds for everything that escaped the deadening vision of the descriptive present.

20. A few years later Smith (1960) published the more ambitious, more theoretically sophisticated *Government in Zazzau,* which covered a span of 150 years. In contrast to Barnes (1954), his object was less to disclose the logic of stasis than to arrive at the causes of change. In historiographic terms, however, Smith's procedure remained aggregative in spirit. Events and relations were distilled into a generalized account of a political system that persisted, as if in equilibrium, until ruptured (by one of the forces specified in a set of abstract "laws"; Smith 1960:Chap. 8).

21. Our irony will be clear to those familiar with the distinctly ahistorical debates during the 1950s and 1960s over prescriptive marriage systems and, more generally, over alliance theory. For a sample of the issues involved, in the words of the protagonists, see Needham (1962), Leach (1951), Homans and Schneider (1955), and Levi-Strauss (1969, especially the preface to the second edition).

22. The notion that Tswana inheritance and succession are governed by the ascriptive principle of primogeniture goes back to missionary ethnographies, although it is often attributed to the classic writings of Schapera (e.g., 1938). Social scientists have reiterated it, usually without question, ever since. The most recent to do so are Crowder, Parson, and Parsons (1990:12f), who take issue with our early work on the topic. This is not the place to rebut their argument—which is based partly on a misrepresentation of our analysis and partly on a curiously ethnocentric, culturally barren interpretation of the historical record (see also J. L. Comaroff 1990:561, n.14 for brief comment). Indeed, theirs is the kind of account that makes it clear why history needs anthropology every bit as much as anthropology needs history.

23. The same general point has been made in a number of discourses on the human sciences—most memorably, perhaps, in McCloskey's (1985) study of the rhetoric of economics.

24. It should be clear that we do not use the term "statistical" here in its narrow, purely numerical sense. We mean it to refer, generically, to any inference of prevailing pattern or probability derived from past rates of occurrence.

25. Leach does not phrase the implications of his analysis in the terms that follow. However, they flow from his comments on the nature of social change and history (see, e.g., 1954:212, 228ff).

26. This has not been for want of trying, of course. Sahlins (1985), for one, has argued cogently for a structuralist historical anthropology. But his exertions have not gone unchallenged.

27. See, most notably, Sahlins (1990). However, it is not only cultural structuralism that continues to struggle with the individual and the event. Structural Marxism has had similar problems. Recall, for example, the debates surrounding Althusser's portrayal of history as "a process without a subject" or, in anthropology, Hindess and Hirst's (1975:45f, 78) claim that Meillassoux's (1964; 1972) accounts of Guro political economy owe less to Marx than to methodological individualism.

28. This passage on biography and the diary is excerpted, in amended form, from J. L. Comaroff (1990).

29. Recent writings suggest that such conventions might be shifting at last; for some diverse examples, see Martin (1987); Lave (1988); McCracken (1988); Spitulnik (1991). This has been a result, in part, of the influence of cultural studies, a relatively new discipline that has challenged us by applying some of our own concepts and methods to Western phenomena (see, e.g., Hall, Jefferson, and Roberts 1976; Willis 1977; Hebdige 1979, 1988). But it has also been helped along by a more general erosion of the boundaries between the human sciences.

30. These models, many of them originating in linguistics, come from a variety of sources, ranging from orthodox structuralism to Jakobsonian pragmatics and Bakhtinian dialogics. Whereas the first implied a static conception of culture—a conception now heavily under attack—both the second and third inform current concerns with the practical, political, ambiguous, and transformative qualities of meaning.

31. See Comaroff and Comaroff (1991:34f). This difference is often not acknowledged by social historians, who sometimes fault historical anthropologists for not writing "real" histories; that is, detailed chronicles of events (see, e.g., Shillington 1987).

32. This is what Sahlins (1990:47), after Ricoeur, terms a "synthesis of the heterogeneous."

2

Of Totemism and Ethnicity

THERE IS A SOCRATIC PARABLE, well-known in some quarters, about a teacher who gives his students two magnifying glasses and invites them to look at the one through the other. When each has told of all he has learned, the sage delivers his lesson in the form of a question, a *coup de grace*:

> "Of what have you told me," he asks, "the thing you have seen or the thing through which you have seen it?"

The same conundrum lurks, usually unremarked, behind the study of ethnicity. Is the latter an object of analysis, something to be explained? Or is it an explanatory principle capable of illuminating significant aspects of human existence? Does it really refer to "idols of the tribe" (Isaacs 1975), or is it in fact an idol of the scribe (Mafeje 1971)? It certainly has been treated in both ways, sometimes simultaneously. As a result, there is still a notable lack of agreement on even the most fundamental of issues: What is ethnicity? Is it a monothetic or a polythetic class of phenomena, one thing or many? Has it the capacity to determine social activity, or is it a product of other forces and structures? Do its roots lie in so-called primordial consciousness or in a reaction to particular historical circumstance? And how is it related to race, class, and nationalism? In addressing these questions, we shall use a wide-angle lens rather than a magnifying glass, and shall focus it, somewhat eclectically, on various African contexts. In so doing, moreover, we seek deliberately to turn the sage's moral on its head. For we are concerned to examine, at once, *both* an analytic object and its conceptual subject: on one hand, those processes involving the rise of ethnic consciousness in Africa and elsewhere, and, on the other, the theoretical terms by means of which ethnicity may itself be comprehended.

Contrary to the usual canons of scholarly enquiry, we proceed not by situating our discussion within the relevant literature, but by stating five propositions about the nature of ethnicity. These propositions, though, are

49

not presented in axiomatic form; rather, they are developed and exemplified as cumulative, if yet tentative, steps in pursuit of an analytic position capable of accounting for the genesis, persistence, and transformation of ethnicity and ethnic consciousness. This is not to pretend that any of them, regarded in isolation, is necessarily new—although each flies in the face of some, and sometimes most, received wisdom. Whatever their individual provenance, however, their theoretical significance lies more in the systematic relations among them than in the substance of each in its own right.

I

The first proposition is intended primarily as a point of departure, a very general statement of orientation toward the conception of ethnicity: *Contrary to the tendency, in the Weberian tradition, to view it as a function of primordial ties,[1] ethnicity always has its genesis in specific historical forces, forces which are simultaneously structural and cultural.* The corollary of this proposition ought also to be underscored. If it is true that ethnicity is a product of particular historical conditions (cf. Wallerstein [1972] 1979:Chaps. 10, 11), and not an ontological feature of human organization, it follows that it cannot be treated as a truly "independent" explanatory principle, a "first cause" in and of itself (Moerman 1968:160f).[2] This is not to deny either its reality or the fact that action is regularly conducted in its name. Nor is it to ignore that such action has concrete implications for everyday relations [see below, p. 60]. It is, rather, to recognize that, in order to understand ethnicity at all, we have not merely to reveal the conditions of its genesis, but also to establish its place in the sociological chain of being. It is to these two problems that much of this essay is addressed; for it is only by resolving them that the first proposition—and the overall position to which it speaks—may finally be sustained.

It is instructive to begin with the long-standing contention that the roots of ethnicity lie in the original "fact" of human cultural difference and ascribed status group affiliations; after all, the tenacity of the "primordial" thesis is itself significant. This thesis rests, in large part, on the compound notion (i) that culturally defined communities—or, in Weberian terms, "status groups" (*stande*)—everywhere entertain an intrinsic awareness of their own identity; (ii) that the traditional loyalties vested in this identity are the source of ethnic consciousness and affiliation; and (iii) that the latter provide the basis for collective action and intergroup relations. The counter thesis, of course, suggests that expressions of ethnicity do not arise in any community save as a *reaction* to threats against its integrity and self-determination. As long as that integrity remains unchallenged, goes the argument, ethnic sensibilities either do not exist or remain dormant.[3]

Both these theses, we believe, are simultaneously correct and incomplete. On the one hand, the precapitalist world, where primordial affiliations and loyalties are tacitly presumed to have had their origins, was never so atomistic that communities did not have relations with others. And, in so far as this is true, it would be plainly absurd to pretend that their members could have lacked common identities or a concern for sociocultural differences; consider, for example, the acute awareness that the diverse peoples of the Luapula valley are known to have had for each others' "customs" (Cunnison 1959:53–61). On the other hand, this form of awareness is distinctly different from ethnic consciousness *sui generis* (Skinner 1978:193).

Let us elaborate. In as much as collective social identity always entails some form of communal self-definition, it is invariably founded on a marked opposition between "ourselves" and "other/s"; identity, that is, is a *relation* inscribed in culture. Patently, the social and material boundaries involved in any such relations—not to mention their content—are historically wrought; they change in the course of economic and political processes [see below]. Still, whatever the substance of particular relations between groupings, the irreducible fact of identity implies the cultural structuring of the social universe. All this merely echoes the anthropological truism, after Durkheim and Mauss (1963), that classification, the meaningful construction of the world, is a necessary condition of social existence. But, we stress, it is the *marking* of relations—of identities in opposition to one another—that is "primordial," not the substance of those identities.

This, it will be recalled, was the point that Bergson (1935:172–5) made about the essence of totemism, the point upon which Levi-Strauss (1963b) was to build his thesis. The genius of Bergson's insight lay in the observation that it was not the intrinsic nature of totemic objects ("their animality") that gave them their significance. It was, rather, "their duality"; the fact that relations between these objects stood for relations between social groups (1935:175). Totemism, then, is just one form—and, it is to be added, an historically specific form—of the universal process of classification. It is one in which groupings define themselves as independent or interdependent units within a common humanity; formulate collective identities in contrast to one another; and portray themselves and others, in symbolic terms, as similar yet different. Whether such relations are signified in animate or inanimate objects makes little difference. These are the media of *totemic consciousness,* a particular species of *conscience collective.*

Ethnic consciousness also entails the formulation of collective identities and their symbolic embodiment in markers of contrast between social groupings. For ethnicity, like totemism, exists above all else as a set of relations. In this respect, they are formally similar. But they differ clearly in their substance. However the former is defined—and, to be sure, it has been defined in very many ways (see, for example, R. Cohen 1978)—it appears to have two generally recognized and closely related properties. One refers to the subjective classification, by the members of a society, of the world into social entities according to cultural differences. The other involves the stereotypic assignment of these groupings—often hierarchically—to niches within the social division of labor.[4] Neither property, of course, is unique to ethnic consciousness; the first applies equally to totemism, the second to class. But it is in their fusion that the particular character of ethnicity resides [below, p. 54]. Moreover, it is not coincidental that these features, among all those associated with ethnic consciousness, are the most commonly observed: for reasons which will become evident, they reflect the manner in which the forces that yield an ethnically ordered universe impress themselves upon human experience.

II

There is a good deal more to ethnicity than this, however. Not only may its character change over time—which is one reason why it is so resistant to easy definition (Hechter 1975:311)—but the way in which it is experienced and expressed may vary among social groupings according to their positions in a prevailing structure of power relations. For dominant groupings—be they Afrikaners, self-styled chosen people of South Africa (Adams and Giliomee 1979; Coetzee 1978:249), or precolonial Alur, spreading their particular concept of chiefship over the hinterland of Uganda (Southall 1956:181)—it takes on the assertive stamp of a protectionist ideology; a legitimation of control over economy and society. Concomitantly, it involves the negation of similar entitlements to others, often on putative cultural or "civilizational" grounds, and may call into doubt their shared humanity. Thus Robert Gordon (1978:215f) notes that Kavango and Ovambo mineworkers in Namibia believe, correctly, that their white supervisors "think we are animals." And nineteenth century Tswana saw Sarwa ("bushmen"), who peopled their underclass, as *phologolo,* beasts of the wild. Although these Sarwa allegedly controlled wondrous knowledge of herbal substances, they were thought properly to live in the undomesticated bush, and were only allowed into the towns of their masters by night (Mackenzie 1871:368). Ironically, the Tswana, themselves being subjected increasingly to the domination of Boer (Afrikaner) settlers, had become known to the whites as *skepsels,* "creatures" (cf. Marais 1939, quoted in Crapanzano 1985:31; also Livingstone 1857:37). According to Crapanzano (1985:40), who did fieldwork among Afrikaners some years ago, this perception persists. Indeed, he tells an anecdote that makes the point with frightening clarity. It concerns an elderly informant who, though deeply religious, had developed a quixotic theory as to why the bible should not be taken literally:

> [If you read it literally . . .] "you wouldn't be able to explain how the Black man got here," he said. "They come from baboons. That's what evolution has taught us, and the Bible doesn't say anything about evolution. God created the White man in a day. *That,* the Bible tells us. It took evolution to create the Black man."

For the subordinate, ethnic affiliation may originate in an *attribution* of collective identity to them on the part of others. On occasion, as we shall see, the creation of such identities has little foundation in pre-existing sociological reality, in which circumstances it usually involves what has been termed "the invention of tradition" (Hobsbawm and Ranger 1983). But even where they have had a social identity contrived for them, subordinate groupings typically come to define their "ethnicity" as an emblem of common predicament and interest; through it, too, they may begin to assert a shared commitment to an order of symbols and meanings and, sometimes, a moral code (Moerman 1968). This, moreover, is often expressed in the reciprocal negation of the humanity of those who dominate them. Those same Kavango and Ovambo mineworkers, for instance, repay their degradation by referring to the Europeans as "barbarians" (R. Gordon 1978:216). Similarly, the Tswana vernacular for "whites," *makgoa,* belongs to a class of nouns (sing. prefix: *le-*; pl. prefix: *ma-*) reserved for non-human animate objects and human pests; it includes such terms as *legodu* (thief) and *letagwa* (drunkard). The word *makgoa* itself originally denoted the "white bush lice" associated with the hindquarters of large animals (J. Comaroff 1985:137). In sum, then, ethnic identity, which always assumes *both* an experiential and a practical salience for those who bear it, entails the complementary assertion of the collective self and the negation of the collective other; it may call into question shared humanity; and its substance is likely to reflect the tensions embodied in relations of inequality.

We shall explore these substantive features below. For now, it is enough to reiterate that, while ethnicity is quite different in its *content* from totemism, there is, beneath this difference, a common denominator: both are, ultimately, modes of social classification and consciousness, markers of identity and collective relations. Herein, in fact, lies the point of interrogating them together. For it calls into question the roots of the contrast and, by extension, the particularity of ethnicity: why should the primordial fact of social classification, of the consciousness of identity and distinction, take on such diverse forms? The easy answer, of course, would be an evolutionary one: that totemism is the precursor of ethnicity, the

latter being a product of the movement from "simple" to more "complex" social systems. But this explanation will not do. Just as it is demonstrable that ethnic consciousness existed in precapitalist Africa [see p. 57 below], so, as Linton's classic ethnographic vignette proves (1924; see Levi-Strauss 1963b:7–8), totemic consciousness occurs in industrial societies. The solution, we suggest, is to be sought elsewhere; namely, in the historically specific social contexts in which totemism and ethnicity, respectively, arise and persist. For the signs and practices involved in each have their source in the very construction of economy and society.

Drawing all this together, then, the second proposition may be stated thus: *ethnicity, far from being a unitary "thing," describes both a set of relations and a mode of consciousness; moreover, its meaning and practical salience varies for different social groupings according to their positions in the social order. But, as a form of consciousness, it is one among many—totemism being another—each of which is produced as particular historical structures impinge themselves on human experience and condition social action.*

This proposition also has important corollaries, among them, the final repudiation of the "primordial" thesis. For, as the comparison of totemism and ethnicity has revealed, this thesis flows from a confounding not merely of two modes of consciousness, but also of quite separate levels of analysis. We reiterate that the marking of contrasting identities—of the opposition of self and other, we and they—is "primordial" in the same sense that classification is a necessary condition of social existence. But the way in which social classification is realized in specific forms of collective identity, ethnicity no less than any other, is always a matter to be decided by the material and cultural exigencies of history.[5]

III

This leads directly to the third proposition, which addresses those forces that produce totemism and ethnicity, and their associated modes of consciousness. In its most general form, it may be put as follows: *while totemism emerges with the establishment of symmetrical relations between structurally similar social groupings—groupings which may or may not come to be integrated into one political community—ethnicity has its origins in the asymmetric incorporation of structurally dissimilar groupings into a single political economy.*

More specifically, totemic consciousness arises with the interaction of social units that retain—or appear from within to retain—control over the means of their own production and reproduction. It is, in short, a function of processes in which autonomous groupings enter into relations of equivalence or complementary interdependence and, in so doing, fashion their

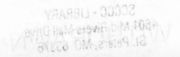

collective identities by contrast to one another. At times, such relations are enshrined in cycles of exchange of varying kinds; at others, they may entail raiding, hostility and warfare; often they embrace both. Moreover, it is possible, in fact usual, that such encounters yield short-term inequalities among the parties to them. But, if each retains its integrity and is not subordinated as a group in and of itself—which is most likely where the units bear formal structural similarity—the overall symmetry of relations is perpetuated. And, as long as it is, totemic identities and affiliations, in the general terms in which we have defined them, will be sustained—with the added qualification that the particular content of these identities will depend both on the sociocultural orders of those who bear them and on the exact nature of their engagement with others.

Totemic consciousness, and the processes that give rise to it, occurred widely in precapitalist Africa. It was realized, for instance, in relations among Sotho-Tswana chiefdoms, and between so-called acephalous societies such as the Nuer and Dinka in the Sudan (Evans-Pritchard 1956:82–4); to be sure, the ethnographic literature abounds with examples. It is true that, historically, totemic relations have also arisen in circumstances where a political community has incorporated either immigrant or conquered populations. Significantly, though, this seems to happen only when such populations are assimilated into an existing social order, not as a subordinate class, but as units of structure like those already there. In such situations, a form of totemic pluralism tends to emerge. The most striking case of this is provided by the Tswana *merafe* ("nations"), which regularly absorbed groupings from outside. These incoming groupings, whose totems differed from those of the host chiefdoms, were generally established as integral and independent wards and sections, the major politico-residential divisions within Tswana polities; their internal organization, distributions of authority and productive arrangements became an indistinguishable element of the structure in place (Schapera 1938; J. L. Comaroff 1973). Consequently, Tswana chiefdoms usually contained a large number of totemic groupings whose identities in contrast to each other were marked in ritual contexts (Schapera 1952).[6] As this implies, totemic consciousness might also surface in the wake of conquest and in complex states, depending on the manner in which social units are ordered within the polity. Where they are incorporated into symmetrical relations with other like units—as they were, say, in the "snowball state" of nineteenth century Ngoni (Barnes 1954)—the historical conditions for the production of totemic consciousness may be expected to take their due course.[7]

The emergence of ethnic groups and the awakening of ethnic consciousness are, by contrast, the product of historical processes which structure relations of inequality between discrete social entities. They are, in other words, the social and cultural correlates of a specific mode of articulation between groupings, in which one extends its dominance over another by some form of coercion, violent or otherwise;[8] situates the latter as a bounded unit in a dependent and unique position within an inclusive division of labor; and, by removing from it final control over the means of production and/or reproduction, regulates the terms upon which value may be extracted from it. By virtue of so doing, the dominant grouping constitutes both itself and the subordinate population as classes; whatever the prior sociological character of these aggregations, they are, in the process, actualized as groups *an sich*.

The creation of structured inequality of this kind, as we have already noted, demands meaningful signification; there can, after all, be no social division of labor without its representation in culture. And, in a stratified, segmentary social environment, this entails marking out the social world into identifiable classes.[9] Now these representations are not arbitrary: since they apprehend and rationalize the unequal distribution of material, political and social power by virtue of *group* membership, they must, by definition, ascribe such inequalities to the *intrinsic* nature of the groups concerned. It is thus that the "ascriptive" character of each becomes its "ethnic" identity—even though the groups themselves might only have been established, at least in their contemporary mold, in the very process of articulation which contrived that identity in the first place.

It follows that the identity imputed to a social group from the outside may be quite different from that same identity as subjectively experienced. For the construction of the collective self—and, by extension, any accounting of its entitlements (for the dominant) or predicament (for the subordinate)—depends on its *differentiation* from the collective other. "Otherness," then, becomes a contrivance in the counter image of social selfhood, not an empirical description of any particular population. Indeed, the Janus-faced nature of ethnic consciousness—the fact that it involves both the assertion of a collective self and the negation of collective other/s—is a cultural expression of the structuring of inequality; it emerges as groupings come to signify and symbolize their experience of a world of asymmetrical "we-them" relations.

The extent to which ethnic identities are rooted in previous cultural realities, moreover, is highly variable (Young 1976:34). Apart from all else, cultures tend to be transformed as the groups who bear them interact with one another (Sahlins 1981). But even if they were not, it is rarely the case, for reasons just given, that they are accurately represented in the identity assigned to others—this being true even where emergent ethnic affiliations are created out of previously bounded, homogeneous populations. Thus, just as the agencies of British colonialism had little appreciation of African social orders and acted upon distorted impressions of them—witness the common view that black South Africans had no religion (e.g. Moffat

1842:244; Burchell 1824,2:383)—so Tswana held an equally skewed image of the culture of their nineteenth-century Sarwa serfs. This is yet more likely to occur when underclasses are composed of people of diverse origins: in such circumstances, the substance of their identities, as contrived from both within and outside, is inevitably a *bricolage* fashioned in the very historical processes which underwrite their subordination.

Ethnic consciousness, as we stated earlier, existed in precapitalist Africa. It was not purely the product of colonialism or urbanization, as has sometimes been suggested, although both did (and do) contain the requisite conditions and have generally been accompanied by manifestations of ethnicity. Perhaps the most celebrated instance in the precolonial context lay in Tutsi-Hutu relations in Rwanda and Burundi (Maquet 1961), the history of which conformed closely to the above characterization. But there are many other examples (see Wallerstein [1972] 1979), the conquest and subordination of the Bairu by the Bahima in Ankole providing another immediately familiar one (Oberg 1940). Less well-known is the case of the Betsileo of Malagasy, of whom Kottak (1980:4–5) writes:

> Betsileo have not always shared . . . consciousness of themselves as a distinct ethnic unit. Prior to their conquest by the Merina, there appear to have been no Betsileo. Rather, there were several statelets and chiefdoms located in different parts of what is now the Betsileo homeland. Their conquerors . . . created the Betsileo province of the Merina state . . . and, in so doing, provided a basis for Betsileo ethnic consciousness to develop through the present.

Kottak goes on to note (1980:303, n. 1) that Bara ethnicity also originated in the nineteenth century under very similar conditions (see Huntington 1974). Ethnic consciousness, it seems, has increased throughout Malagasy as a function of political consolidation.

With colonial penetration into Africa, indigenous populations were integrated—to differing degrees and with varying rapidity—into the political economies of Europe, thereby becoming part of an increasingly global division of labor. And, as we might expect, their asymmetric incorporation into a wider order of productive and exchange relations yielded novel ethnic affiliations and groupings (Wolf 1982:380f). As Greenberg (1980:14) observes:

> The Kikuyu, for example, whose coherence is now so important to understanding Kenyatta and nationalism in Kenya, had no certain identity before the imposition of British rule and the alienation of land to the settlers; distinctive groups like the Sikhs in India, Ibo in Nigeria, and Malays in Malaysia were barely conscious of their "sameness" one hundred years ago.

But there were differences between the forms of ethnicity which had prevailed in the precolonial epoch and those bred in the wake of the expanding world system. As has been argued elsewhere (Long 1984; J. L. Comaroff 1982), the leitmotif of modern "Third World" history lies in a mutually determining interaction, a "dialectic of articulation," between global forces and the diverse social orders of Africa and elsewhere. This encounter established new, multilevelled structures of inequality both within Africa itself and between Africa and Europe. And, in so doing, it laid the basis for what might be termed "segmentary ethnicity" (cf. R. Cohen 1978:387); that is, a nesting hierarchy of ethnic identities.

At the lowest levels, local groups, which often became bounded political units by bureaucratic fiat, sought and gained dominance over others within colonial—and, later, postcolonial—states, thereby constructing internal ethnic relations. At the highest levels, the conjuncture of "Europeans" and "Africans" expressed itself in an encompassing ethnicity. This was reflected, on the one hand, in the growth of pan-Africanism and the concept of an "African culture"; on the other, it saw the crystallization of a settler-colonial social order wrought largely out of a caricature of (aristocratic) Victorian English society (Ranger 1983). And, between these polarities, there developed a variety of middle-order allegiances, attachments that crossed parochial boundaries but justified common political cause with reference to shared cultural affinities; these have been described by terms such as "supertribalism." Of the three levels, significantly, the lowest has conventionally come to be portrayed as "tribalism"; the middle, as "nationalism," sometimes with the qualifier "ethnic"; and the highest, as "race." But all had their genesis alike in the processes that gave rise to ethnic consciousness in its more complex segmentary guise. They are *interrelated* products of an historically specific confrontation between the populations of Africa and the various agencies of colonial domination.

It is not difficult to point to cases of segmentary ethnicity, since the emergence of a hierarchy of identities, all culturally marked and politically salient, has been a recurrent theme throughout modern Africa. For example, the colonial history of Zimbabwe called into being an intricate ethnological map of "tribes" whose administration under indirect rule *demanded* that their "traditional" political constitution be recognized— even, in places, where they had none. It also fostered the pre-eminence of two such entities, the Shona and Ndebele, each of which spawned the core of a (supratribal) nationalist movement. The alliance of these movements within a "patriotic front," in turn, fought the war of liberation that led to Zimbabwean independence; a war between adversaries—each with allies beyond the national borders—riven along the *racial* line of fault that divides southern Africa into inclusive (transnational) pigmentary groupings. Similar processes, if not always with the same climax, have occurred in East Africa, most notably in Uganda (Mazrui 1978) and Kenya (Parkin 1978), and in West Africa. The exact hierarchy of groupings yielded by such processes varies, of course. But the overall *structure* of nesting, opposed identities—of "tribe," "nation" and "race," each a particular refraction of ethnicity—manifests itself with remarkable frequency.

IV

The fourth proposition, which takes all this a step further, concerns the distinction between historical forces and structures, and the manner in which they are experienced in everyday life. We have argued that the forces which produce consciousness—totemic, ethnic or any other—lie in the construction and transformation of economy and society. But the terms in which they are understood by social actors have to do with the way in which the world is signified: human beings perceive and act upon their contexts not as they are formally constituted, but as they are construed in shared signs and symbols. With the emergence of class formations in which positions in the division of labor are signified by the labels of ascribed status and cultural distinction, ethnicity becomes a dominant medium through which the social order is to be interpreted and navigated.

In other words, where it becomes the basis of social classification and status relations, ethnicity, rather than the forces that generate it, takes on the ineffable appearance of determining the predicament of individuals and groups. After all, viewed from *within* any such social context, ethnic affiliation cannot but be represented as the "independent variable" that shapes careers and biographies. For, at the experiential level, it *does* seem to be ethnicity which orders social status, class membership, and so on— and not class or status that decides ethnic identities. In fact, Marx's image of the *camera obscura* ([Marx and Engels] 1970:36), whatever its other limitations (Lichtman 1975:49), is apposite here: the origins of ethnic groups and consciousness may lie in the structuring of inequality. But, once objectified as a "principle" by which the division of labor is organized, ethnicity assumes the autonomous character of a prime mover in the unequal destinies of persons and populations. To wit, just as working class black Americans do not view their blackness as a function of their class position, but their class position as a function of their blackness,[10] so underclass Hutu in Rwanda or Kgalagadi in Botswana see their status as being ascribed by virtue of their ethnic affiliation and not vice versa.

Under these conditions, then, ethnicity becomes an essential feature of the "natural" order of things, the "given" character of the world with regard to which people must conduct their lives. Nor is this confined to any particular sociological category. It applies as much to those for whom ethnic ideologies legitimize dominance as it does to those for whom ethnic labels are signs of subordination. As this suggests, such labels are not merely terms in a system of classification, although they are certainly that too. They also become a pragmatic basis for the formation of interest groups and networks, social resources for pursuing individual and communal utilities. Consequently, ethnic consciousness enters a dialectical relationship with the structures that underlie it: once ethnicity impinges upon experience as an (apparently) independent principle of social classification and organization, it provides a powerful motivation for collective activity. And this, by turn, must perforce realize an everyday world dominated by ethnic groups and relations, thereby reproducing the very social order that gave rise to ethnic consciousness in the first place. However, as we shall see, the matter is yet more complex. For social action conducted in the name of ethnicity also reveals contradictions inherent in systems of structured inequality and may transform those systems from within.

All this may sound much the same as saying that ethnicity is merely a form of false consciousness, a "phantasmic" mystification of class. But that would miss the point. For the way in which relations in any system are signified is an irreducible part of its reality. As Genovese (1971:32; see Greenberg 1980:390) puts it,

> . . . once an ideology arises it alters profoundly the material reality and in fact becomes a partially autonomous feature of that reality.

Indeed, structures of inequality and the terms of their cultural representation, whether they be subsumed in "ethnicity" or anything else, are mutually constitutive. For reasons already given, the one cannot exist without the other: both alike are elements of the dialectic of structure and practice which shapes concrete social and material relations—and, therefore, the very essence of economy and society.

The fourth proposition, in sum, argues that, *while ethnicity is the product of specific historical processes, it tends to take on the "natural" appearance of an autonomous force, a "principle" capable of determining the course of social life*. That is, by (i) configuring the particular manner in which a social system is experienced from within, it (ii) motivates social practice and rationalizes the pursuit of individual and collective utilities. This, in turn, (iii) realizes manifest relations, groups and identities; and, so, (iv) a dialectic is established between structure and practice that, in time, reproduces and/or transforms the character of the social order itself.

V

This brings us to the fifth and final proposition, which echoes a very general analytic injunction: not only are the conditions that produce an historical phenomenon to be distinguished from those that sustain it, but any such phenomenon, once created, may acquire the capacity to affect the structures that gave rise to it. So it is with ethnic identity. *Where it becomes an objectified "principle" in the collective consciousness of a society, ethnicity may be perpetuated by factors quite different from those that caused its emergence, and may have a direct and independent impact on the context in which it arose.*

We have already stressed that, in systems where "ascribed" cultural differences rationalize structures of inequality, ethnicity takes on a cogent existential reality. It is this process of reification, as we have seen, that gives it the appearance of being an autonomous factor in the ordering of the social world. As a result, ethnic identities regularly assume, for those who share them, a pervasive functionality in everyday social, economic, and political life (cf. Patterson 1977:102f). What is more, this functionality may *itself* seem to sustain the practical relevance of ethnic affiliation for both persons and groups. Behind it, however, there lies a subtle relationship between social experience and the exigencies of collective and individual practice.

Since it is cultural indices that are perceived to underlie inequalities in these systems, it follows, in the very nature of social experience, that such asymmetries would be eliminated (for groups) and upward mobility be possible (for persons) if the relevant cultural markers could be reversed or relinquished. After all, in order to have meaning, any sign must imply its complementary opposite. Thus, if the signs and principles which apparently mandate relations of inequality were no longer to apply, the inequality itself would be removed—or so it seems from the actors' perspective. In other words, such systems represent themselves as potentially navigable, their internal lines of division more or less porous, to the extent that sociocultural differences may be negotiated. This, in turn, establishes the appropriate terms in which social action is to be joined, and interests to be pursued, at the levels of both collective and individual enterprise. Let us examine each, for not only do they have contrasting dynamics, but a complex connection obtains between them.

At the level of collective action, the logic of common interest is, for the dominant, plain enough [see above, p. 52]. It lies in the authoritative protection their exclusive cultural identity and, with it, their material position. In ideological terms, such protectionism entails a stress upon the contrasts between themselves and others; although the creation of alliances with particular groupings, the internal segmentation of the underclass, and the admission of individuals into their ranks, may become strategic considerations in the defense of privilege. For the subordinate, the issue is not so clear cut. If and when any cohesive response to the common predicament is perceived as possible, two options present themselves. Either they can engage in some form of concerted direct effort—usually, but not always, political—to remove entirely the structures of inequality. Or they can seek to negate cultural differences by "proving" that these have ceased to be relevant: *vide* the attempts of South African and American blacks, earlier this century, to claim their civil rights by establishing that they had "become" sufficiently like those who oppressed them (i.e. "civilized"). It is not surprising, in light of the manner in which such systems engrave themselves upon human consciousness, that the second option tends to be the one of first resort (cf. Greenberg 1980:7–8); nor is it difficult to understand why it regularly fails, and gives way sooner or later to overt political action. In the colonial context, with the emergence of segmentary ethnicity, parochial groups (i.e. "tribes"; [see above, p. 58]) find that such exertions, while not removing higher order inequalities, bring relative success as they "rise" within the lower reaches of the (colonial) division of labor at the expense of similar groupings.

However these historical movements work themselves out in particular contexts, a fundamental contradiction inheres in them. For any activity aimed at the reversal of "ascribed" inequalities may reinforce the primacy of ethnicity as a principle of social differentiation: the very fact such activity is conducted by and for groupings marked by their cultural identities confirms the perception that these identities *do* provide the only available basis of collective self-definition and action. This is more dramatically the case where common action is seen to have been successful, but failure also tends to affirm shared affiliations, and the attribution to them of social predicament. The affirmation is clearly tautological; in analytic terms, though, it will be evident that the reproduction of ethnicity, and the reinforcement of its pragmatic salience, is as much a function of efforts directed at its erosion as it is of activities that assert its positive value. And as long as social practice continues to be pursued *as if* ethnicity did hold the key to the structures of inequality, the protectionism of the dominant and the responses of the dominated alike serve to perpetuate an ethnically ordered world.

For the same reasons that collective melioration is held by the subordinate to lie in the negation of ethnic differences, individual mobility is often perceived as a matter of relinquishing those cultural attributes which appear to ascribe social status. For individuals, the adoption of new identities is relatively easier than it is for groups; again, there is abundant documentation from Africa of the renegotiation of such identities, perhaps the most poignant case being the practice of "trying for white" by those classified as "colored" in South Africa (Watson 1970). At this level, then, the lines of ethnic division may indeed be breached if and when particular persons accumulate the social and material wherewithal to do so [see below, p. 63]. As noted before, too, there may be little resistance, on the part of the dominant, to the rise of a limited proportion of the underclass. If anything, as is indicated by the entire history of capitalism, the promise of upward mobility, as just reward for properly industrious achievement, is ordinarily seen to enjoy both practical and ideological virtue.

Once upward mobility is seen as a possibility and energies are expended to achieve it, ethnic groups must inevitably become *internally* stratified. For, in order to garner the assets with which to renegotiate their class position, individuals require first to consolidate their situations within the underclass itself. Thus Wallerstein ([1972] 1979), among others, has shown that intra-ethnic relations provide the arena in which such persons might acquire the resources for upward movement; indeed, there are few other contexts within which they might do so.[11] In addition, under colonialism, where segmentary ethnicity developed, lower order ethnic groups often assumed the character of fractions of the underclass; fractions more or less exclusively associated—much as in the segmented labor markets of the industrialized world—with relatively stratified niches within the division of labor.[12] This, in turn, opens the way for individuals to manipulate ethnic identities so as to ascend within the nether echelons of the hierarchy: it charts a series of steps that may finally lead out of the underclass itself. The regular effort to navigate this route, of course, is the very stuff of the ethnography of urban Africa. It gives rise to what is usually glossed as "situational ethnicity" (R. Cohen 1978; A. Cohen 1974), the strategic management of personal identity for social and material gain. Those who traverse the route, and ascend far enough within the class structure, become an identifiable fragment of the dominant class, an emergent local bour-geoisie. Both as individuals and as a group, however, they face an unavoid-able choice. For, on leaving the underclass, they must either seek to discard their ethnic identities—which, after all, marks the predicament from which they contrived to escape—or sustain the contradiction of being a member of a group whose primary class position is different from their own. In either case, their situation is paradoxical, since the two dimensions of their identity are at odds with each other—a contradiction most vividly embod-ied in the classical "black white men" of Africa (cf. Fanon 1968).

Drawing together the collective and individual perspectives, a significant pattern emerges. On one hand, as long as ethnic affiliations and identities provide the terms of communal action, such action—whatever its imme-diate goals, and regardless of the successes or failures of any given group-ing—reinforces the experiential salience of ethnicity as a social principle. In consequence, the seemingly ascribed character of ethnic identities is repeatedly confirmed; so, also, is the conception of ethnic groups as bounded units (cf. Barth 1969), despite the reality that membership in them is frequently the subject of social management. On the other hand, at the individual level, the achievement of upward mobility effects a transformation in the relationship of ethnicity and class. For it leads both to the internal differentiation of ethnic groups and, with the emergence of bourgeois fractions, to the loss of a one-to-one correspondence between ethnic affiliation and class membership. (Were that correspondence to be sustained, self-evidently, the paradoxes involved in both collective and individual action would either not surface, or would take a different form.) This does not obliterate the fact that, as a *statistical* frequency—and as an indigenous perception—ethnic groups continue to be predominantly associated with particular class positions. Nonetheless, class and sociocultural differences cease to be coterminous in any absolute or prescriptive sense.[13]

All this is nicely exemplified in ethnic political movements which arise among populations that were once subordinated *en toto* but, over time, have become diversified to the extent that some of their number have left the underclass. These movements are often joined, and led, by such upwardly mobile members—sometimes, we suggest, in the effort to resolve the contradiction in their own lives—and are usually framed in the rhetoric of protest and resistance; of rebellion rather than revolution, to invoke Gluckman's well-worn distinction. In some instances they have a single sociocultural grouping at their core, as did Mau Mau in Kenya; in others, like the African National Congress in South Africa and many nationalist political parties throughout the continent, they cut across local "tribal" divisions. In the latter case, too, they may reinforce a shared symbolic order where it existed only tenuously before, and weld a relatively heterogeneous social entity into a bounded status group that acts *für sich*. In so doing, ethnic political movements underscore, at once, the continuities and discontinuities in the articulation of ethnicity and class. In one respect, they express the strong (statistical) association between the two; such action *is,* patently, directed against a prevailing distribution of social, economic, and political power, and its mass support comes from those who most palpably suffer inequality. Yet they also breach the lines of class division and, as such, give the appearance of being manifestations of status group solidarities. Moreover, the dualistic character of these movements—as statements of underclass resistance, and as assertions of status group unity—may have implications that are not envisaged by those who engage in them.

Thus, under colonialism in Africa, ethnic struggles certainly had an impact on the surface contours of the social world, and they did occasionally lead to significant liberal reforms. But, insofar as they refracted class antagonisms in the cause of status group interests, they did not finally remove the *structures* of subordination. If anything, they masked those structures in an ideology of individual achievement, and, by leaving intact the correlation between ethnicity and class, served ultimately to consolidate relations of collective inequality. Nor was this restricted to Africa. As Post (1978) reveals, much the same applied to black nationalist organizations in Jamaica in the 1930s, Marcus Garvey's Universal Negro Improvement Association (UNIA) among them. These organizations tended to acquire a solidly middle class leadership (for whom political action often involved demands made in their collective *class* interest; 1978:208), and a large following among the poor, who had come to experience their suffering, "in the natural order of things" (1978:145), as the heritage of color. Post goes on to argue that such "generalized Black Nationalism" (1978:161) ultimately "refracted and atomized potential collective class consciousness" (1978:187), especially when it either receded into Ras Tafarian millenialism, or sufficed itself with the crumbs of economic palliation. In other words, by virtue of its dualistic quality, ethnicity itself became a factor in the maturation of a colonial and post-colonial capitalist order characterized by marked asymmetries. On the one hand, it continued to provide a cultural and organizational basis for a highly stratified division of labor; on the other, it rationalized the possibility of upward mobility and an ethos of achievement.

More generally, then, as ethnic groups become internally differentiated and lose their uniform correspondence to class—as they must inevitably do in the long run—they *mature* into status groups in the classical Weberian sense of the term. Now there is a double theoretical irony in this. First, in as much as ethnic affiliations are realized and solidify into status groups by virtue of such *historical* processes, they have precisely the opposite trajectory to that theorized by Weber. In the Weberian tradition, affinities based on status, being primordial, ought to come before those based on class; and they should only give way to the latter with the growth of an increasingly rationalized industrial economy (Hechter 1975:313; Greenberg 1980:6). They certainly should not emerge *with* the genesis of class structures, let alone enter a complex dialectical relationship with them. But, second, it is not only Weber who is turned on his head by the rise and persistence of ethnic groupings. In classical Marxian terms too, ethnicity should not appear with the emergence of class differences. Quite the converse: the processes that produce class societies ought to submerge "traditional" ideologies and, eventually, cause them to wither away as class consciousness is brought to the fore. However, far from disappearing, or remaining a mere epiphenomenon of "real" antinomies, ethnic identity assumes an important role in the dynamics of many historical systems— sustaining yet masking, reinforcing yet refracting, their dominant lines of cleavage. For the contradictions inherent in structures and signs of inequality not only give ethnicity the appearance of an objectified "force"; they also motivate and rationalize the very social practices which assert, with baroque circularity, that ethnicity truly is a pervasive force in the social world.

*   *   *

If the five propositions bear scrutiny, it is no wonder, *pace* both Weberian and Marxian orthodoxies, that ethnicity is as ubiquitous and tenacious as it is; and that, in spite of undergoing changes in its content, experiential character and historical relevance, it refuses to vanish—notwithstanding the once commonplace sociological tendency to predict its imminent demise. The major problem, in both theoretical and empirical terms, it seems to us, is not to account for the genesis and persistence—or even the transformation—of ethnic consciousness and affiliation. Once ethnicity is understood to exist as a set of relations, a product of specifiable historical forces and processes rather than a primordial "given," those issues become readily understandable. Much more vexing, in light of everything we have argued, is the question of when and why ethnic ideologies break down and class consciousness rises to replace it—if, indeed, this ever happens in such straightforward terms. But that is a problem which demands separate treatment. The purpose of the present exercise has been more modest. It has been to explore just some of the fundamental analytic issues surrounding the signs and practices of inequality. And, if the propositions formulated along the way remain tentative for now, they are offered in the belief, to parody Levi-Strauss, that ethnicity is good to rethink.

Notes

1. For discussion of this tendency and its Weberian origins, see, among others, Hechter (1975:313f); Greenberg (1980:13f).
2. The treatment of ethnicity as a "first cause" capable of producing autonomous effects remains the norm throughout the human sciences: see, for example, Bronfenbrenner (1979:258) in respect of psychology, Cohen (1978) of anthropology, and Wilson (1980) of sociology.
3. See, for instance, du Toit (1978:10f); Fried (1967:15, 170); Skinner (1978:192f); and Cohen and Middleton (1970). As Wallerstein ([1972] 1979:184) puts it, "Ethnic consciousness is eternally latent everywhere. But it is only realized when groups feel either threatened with a loss of previously acquired privilege or conversely feel that it is an opportune moment politically to overcome long-standing denial of privilege."
4. These properties appear with equal regularity in Weberian and Marxist discourses on ethnicity—albeit with different analytic weight. Rex (1970:48), in fact, sees them as the defining conditions for what sociologists treat under the rubric of "race relations."
5. Another variant of the "primordial" argument is the "human nature" thesis. For example, Milton Gordon (1978:73) holds that, since ethnicity cannot be shed by mobility, it "becomes incorporated into the self." Man acting in the name of his ethnic group, then, is man defending himself; and, given that "human nature" is aggressively narcissistic, ethnic consciousness and conflict is endemic. Wilson (1981:113) has countered by pointing out that this "human" predisposition is always mediated by social and cultural factors—the implication being that it may be a necessary, but can never be a sufficient condition for ethnic antagonism. We would go still further, however. It seems that Gordon has confused precisely the two levels of which we have spoken. Certainly, "I" is fused into "we" in the construction

of collective identity; that is an irreducible *social* fact, whether or not "human nature," if it exists at all, is as Gordon asserts. But why *ethnic* identity? For Gordon, the answer finally comes down to the assertion that it cannot be willingly shed. Yet the anthropological evidence is unequivocal. Ethnic identity often *can* be set aside, and may be a highly situational attribute. Of course, the relative ease with which it is sloughed off varies dramatically: for, say, Jews in Nazi Germany—who shared language, skin color, and (to a large extent) culture with their oppressors—it was well-nigh undeniable; for Central Africans on the copperbelt, although divided by language, culture, and diverse skin pigmentation, it seems always to have been negotiable. Quite clearly, ethnic mobility—like all social identity—is historically determined. But then, for many anthropologists and comparative sociologists, so too is "human nature."

6. Schapera (1952) refers to these groupings as "ethnic." By any current definition of ethnicity, however, this usage is inappropriate; clearly, it reflects the ambiguities surrounding the term in the 1950s (du Toit 1978:1f).

7. A comparable argument could be made for the rise of the Zulu state in the early nineteenth century. Here, it seems, most vanquished populations had social orders which did not differ greatly from that of their conquerors. When absorbed into the Zulu polity, they became integral units in its social and productive structure rather than a subordinate class (cf. Suret-Canale 1969; Walter 1969; Guy 1980). For a complementary discussion on ethnic identities in precapitalist Africa, see Wallerstein ([1972] 1979).

8. McGuire (1982:168), following Spicer (1971:797), offers the parallel observation that ethnic groups, the bearers of "persistent cultural systems," are born out of "opposition"; that is, out of the "efforts by those in control of the surrounding state apparatus to incorporate or assimilate" minority populations.

9. Warren's (1978) revealing study of collective identity among Guatemalan Indians— among whom subordination within a class society is vividly portrayed in ethnic terms—is built on this very premise; it shows, in considerable detail, how signs of inequality come to be elaborated into a coherent set of cultural representations.

10. It is precisely this point that lies behind much of the debate over Wilson's claim (1980) that the significance of race is declining in America. Wilson's critics have argued that skin color remains the main factor shaping the lives of blacks; its salience, therefore, cannot have decreased. At the *experiential* level, this may be true. But, whatever other arguments may be brought to bear on his case, Wilson, to his credit, does *not* deny the experiential importance of race. His thesis, rather, is that the life chances of blacks are determined primarily by other structural factors; namely, class differences. The controversy, in sum, flows from the confusion of social experience with the forces that give rise to it.

11. Greeley (1974:300) makes much the same point about ethnic relations in the United States—a point classically illustrated, as William Wilson has reminded us, by E. Franklin Frazier's *Black Bourgeosie* (1957).

12. For an especially clear example, see Mazrui's account (1978) of colonial Uganda, where the cleavage between "Nilotes" and "Bantu" was unambiguously reflected in the contemporary division of labor. Mazrui might easily have extended his analysis to take in the Indian and white settler communities, which had equally well-defined niches in that division of labor.

13. See Wilson (1984), whose penetrating analysis of race and social policy in America illuminates and gives comparative support to this aspect of our discussion.

3

Bodily Reform as Historical Practice

> Habit has its abode neither in thought nor in the objective body, but in the body as mediator of a world.
>
> —Maurice Merleau-Ponty (1970:266)

I

LIKE SEVERAL SOUTHERN TSWANA SETTLEMENTS dating back to precolonial times, Mafikeng was, in 1970, a sprawl of mudbrick homesteads clustered in circular wards about a dilapidated chiefly court. Formerly the capital of the independent Barolong boo Ratshidi (Tshidi) chiefdom, it now abutted the unfinished administrative center of a South African "ethnic homeland," or *bantustan*,[1] in whose imperious embrace the Tshidi were locked. At the time, a population of more than 20,000 lived in this old town close to the South Africa–Botswana border, a town whose involuted, concentric forms stood in stark contrast to the unfocused grids of square modern houses of both the homeland and the nearby "white" center. As darkness fell on the dusty skyline, the sound of children's voices, corn flails, and cattle would be punctuated by a more urgent and rhythmic sound: the drums that proclaimed the presence of more than fifty flourishing Zionist churches. Along the radial dirt roads, figures of distinctive dress and bearing made their way to the sources of the sound, usually the humble homesteads of "prophets" (*baparofeta*). The men in white robes and the women in tunics of an oddly Victorian cut, they would spend the night in rousing song and dance, apparently bizarre conflations of African rites and Protestant liturgy. The avowed aim of these performances was to summon the power of the Holy Spirit (*moya*), that it might imbue and reform the afflicted bodies of the faithful. But its implicit objective, as we shall see, was nothing less than to heal their troubled world itself.

69

In the pale dawn, the dancers emerged serene from their ritual retreats, returning home to work their drought-ridden fields or to labor in the white town. By no means did all Tshidi participate in these rituals, although Zionist ranks had been growing steadily since the second decade of the century. The term "Zionist," in fact, had developed specific connotations, being associated with the most "lowly" (*balala*), those "oppressed" (*patikèga*) in a generally subjugated population. Its practices were clearly marked off from what had been objectified as "tradition" (*setswana*; "things Tswana" or "Tswana ways") and from the mainstream of contemporary local life, which owed as much to the culture of colonialism as to persisting precolonial practices. To the knowing, the Zionists were people in self-imposed exile,[2] even though they inhabited the everyday Tshidi world. As one observer put it, "Whether or not you are one of them, you can tell the Zionist anywhere. His dress, the way he holds his body, and the look in his eye. What he eats, whom he may marry—it's all laid down. He's not the same person once he starts to follow the drum."

II

Bourdieu (1977:94) has noted that social groups that "seek to produce a new man through a process of 'deculturation' and 'reculturation'" set great store on the redefinition of apparently insignificant bodily habits. Why should this be? Why, for example, should the inmates of Goffman's (1961) asylums be subject to highly ritualized regimes that fix on such formerly reflex practices as posture, mode of dress, and eating? And why should these regimes resemble the fastidious physical refashioning often central to millenary movements, from cargo cults to chiliastic Christianity, Nuer prophecy to Nazism (cf. Worsley 1968; Wilson 1973; Newborn n.d.)? What accounts for the parallels between this activity and the careful "dismembering and re-membering" of bodies stressed in classic accounts of initiation rites in non-Western societies, rites that confer adult status or membership of encapsulated cults and associations (see Turner 1968:56f; La Fontaine 1972:159f; J. Comaroff 1985: Chaps. 4, 7)?

The concept of "remembering" seems apposite: As Bourdieu (1977:94) has noted, attempts to remake habit tend to treat the body as a "memory" in which are lodged, in mnemonic form, the organizing principles of an embracing context. Scrambling this code—that is, erasing the messages carried in banal physical practice—is a prerequisite for retraining the memory, either to deschool the deviant or to shape new subjects as the bearers of new worlds. Indeed, the universal salience of bodily reform in processes of social transformation is strong evidence that the human frame mediates between self and society. It is this mediating role, we suggest, that accounts for its privileged place in one widespread, yet poorly understood mode of historical practice: namely, "untheorized" collective action. By this we mean action that, while concerted, is never explicated, action whose logic seems vested more in corporeal signs than in conceptual categories.

Of course, the general problem addressed here is hardly new. Both Marx (1906) and Durkheim (with Mauss 1963) argued, if in somewhat different terms, for a perpetual dialectic between "social" and "natural" classification, a dialectic routed through human experience, where social constructs appeared axiomatic and ineffable. From this perspective, the human body is seen to provide the "raw" material, the presocial "base" upon which collective categories and values are engraved (Van Gennep 1960; Douglas 1970; Mauss 1973; Bourdieu 1977; Turner 1980). Through socialization (both formal and informal) the "person" is constructed in the image of society, tuned, in practice, to the system of meanings lying silently within the conventions of a given world. Once they have taken root in the body and have acquired a natural alibi, goes the argument, these meanings take on the appearance of transcendent truths (cf. Barthes 1973). Physically framed experience, then, seems to resonate with the forms of "objective" reality. The body is appropriated by the "structures of the world" so that it, in turn, may appropriate the world (Bourdieu 1977:89).

In their concern to show that bodies and persons are culturally constructed, however, many scholars have treated the human form as a tabula rasa (Van Gennep 1960; Mauss 1973). It becomes "a simple piece of wood each has cut and trimmed to suit him" (Van Gennep 1960:72). Or, for those of a more structuralist bent, it seems "good to think" with because it provides a homology for a dualistic social world, typically understood in terms of unidimensional oppositions (Needham 1973) and mediating anomalies (Douglas 1966; 1970). Either way, the body presents an order of contrasts to be arbitrarily colonized by society and culture.

But the ethnographic record suggests that physical facts have a more complex and determining effect on social constructions (cf. Ellen 1977; McDougall 1977). Sahlins ([1976b] 1977:166), for instance, has observed that the physiology of color discrimination challenges both the arbitrariness of the sign and the sui generis character of culture. For basic color terms in natural languages follow a universal perceptual logic; physiologically derived contrasts and combinations do seem to determine the formal structure of perceptual categories as they enter into social discourse. Yet as Sahlins ([1976b] 1977:179) stresses, these categories are themselves just one of a series of available imaginative "implements." Whether they will be selected and how they will be used in any context is clearly a function of culture rather than nature. He thus concludes that it is only through the interplay of natural facts and semantic projects that we can account for "the presence in culture of universal structures that are nevertheless not universally present."

The same is true for the universal effects of bodily form upon the social imagination. There is plenty of ethnographic evidence that certain contrasts and combinative sequences recur in diverse cultural systems, appearing to be rooted in physical constraints on human perception. This suggests a need for analytic schemes capable of acknowledging "bodily facts" and requires us to explore the processes through which they engage with specific systems of meaning. For culture is made and remade in a complex fusion of natural and social forms; it is never a matter of simple determination, either concrete or conceptual. In confronting this process here, our concern is not so much with the mechanisms through which the body, as a sensory and cognitive instrument, frames the material grounds for human perception (see, e.g., Merleau-Ponty 1962; T. Turner 1990). We are more interested in the implications of actual bodily experience for imagining and acting upon the forces of history. It is in this respect that projects of physical reform become especially revealing, for they represent efforts to rework the physical grounding of conventional realities, efforts to intervene in the dialectic of the person and the world.

The body, patently, is a complex constellation of relations and processes, some of which we experience as more or less stable, others as perpetually in flux. Relatively enduring physical structures persist for a lifetime and often become synonymous with social durability itself; such fixed forms provide paradigmatic relations of contrast (left/right, front/back, head/foot, inside/outside, center/periphery, male/female) and combination (the taxonomies that order simple contrasts into hierarchical series). Much existing discussion of the human frame as metaphor in anthropology focuses on static anatomical classifications that are treated as ideal models of, and for, unchanging social orders (Griaule 1965; Ellen 1977; Ohnuki-Tierney 1981). Although they reveal important mechanisms through which culture is essentialized, these studies *themselves* often essentialize dynamic processes, treating the body as idealized image rather than as a medium for the construction of fluid social/material realities. Less attention has been paid to the relation of physical structure to bodily process, to the containment of anatomical taxonomies in the transformative processes crucial to material life. Yet such processes map out syntagmatic principles, the combinations through which corporeal categories engage with each other and with elements of the outside world. In many non-Western contexts, such processes take the place of the static structures privileged in the Western anatomical tradition: In indigenous Chinese medicine, for one, bodily form is constantly being recreated in the flow of elements whose interplay gives rise to life itself (Farquhar 1987). Such flows, both endogenous and interactional, are distorted when reduced to neat conceptual oppositions or rigid taxonomies. Whereas reductions of this sort may be a frequent trope of ideology in the making—*vide* the place of binary oppositions in our own and other cultures (see Chapter 6)—they are inadequate as an analytic account of the life of ideology in the social world.

A growing literature on the meaning of everyday practice provides the basis for a comparative investigation of how cultures put complex bodily implements to use. In respect of the perception of shape and space, for example, Friedrich ([1970] 1977:392) has argued that certain obligatory relations, apparently rooted in physical experience, operate in all grammars: among them, the complex concept of "orifice," or curved edge; the trichotomy of long, flat, and round—or what is one, two, and three dimensions; and the abstract construct of "body" itself as a model of physical interconnection. He concludes that these qualities of shape are fundamental ideas in grammar, on a par with other basics such as "time" and "aspect."

What we have here, then, is linguistic evidence of contrasts and combinations that universally mediate human perception. The ethnographic record permits us to explore how these forms engage with particular semantic fields the world over. Take Friedrich's first obligatory category: many cultural accounts (e.g., Devisch 1984; Douglas 1966; Loudon 1977), including our own Freudian discourse, testify to the elaboration of categories associated with the perception of "orifice." The latter is not merely a universal marker of the threshold between "inside" and "outside," "self" and "other"; it is also a metonym of controlled (that is, social) process— by contrast to unbounded, asocial flux. The regulated but irreversible passage of substance through bodily orifices by means of ingestion, defecation, and sexual ejaculation serves widely both to make and mark social status.[3] Although they may be given varying emphasis in different contexts, the uncontrolled orifices of childhood and senility and the unmediated flow of menstrual blood widely signify infrasocial states of being and a less than optimal containment of the person within his/her bodily margins. On the other hand, bodily closure signals a clearly distinct, centered identity and the capacity to engage in stable exchange relations with other beings and substances in the world (see Devisch 1984; Hugh-Jones 1979:155).

Lack of closure is a widely perceived characteristic of female bodies: Women are seen, in many cultures, to be "naturally" open, most markedly during their childbearing years and at the time of menstruation. Where this is the case, it typically calls forth efforts to contain their unruly bodies. While menstruating, for instance, they are frequently prevented from interacting with others, especially those whose own status is liminal and who are hence physically vulnerable. Females are also often restricted in their access to communal space and to delicate transformative processes liable to be endangered by pollution. In places as far apart as rural England and Southern Africa, menstruation was once thought to disturb butter churning; elsewhere, it was said to endanger pot firing, or sensitive ritual (see J. Comaroff 1985; La Fontaine 1972; cf. Hugh-Jones 1979).

In other words, because they are held to be uncontained, women are often constrained in their action upon the external environment. It is as if they threaten to "spill over" into social space, breaching its order—in particular, the basic distinction between inside and outside, person and world. Yet this weakness is also a source of strength. For a body that is unstable and penetrable may be the stuff of powerful transformations, or it may serve as a willing receptacle for superhuman forces. Spirit possession, in various societies, plays with tropes of physical permeability: with mounting, copulating, and, most dramatically, with the invasion of corporeal space that is frequently, if not invariably, feminized (Matory 1986; Boddy 1989). We may note, too, that in signifying the relationship of inner and outer being, orifices function both as metonyms and metaphors. On the one hand, the flow of substances through the body actually effects a continuity of inner and outer, establishing a mutually constitutive relationship between the microcosm of the person and the macrocosm of the world. On the other, the contrast between controlled and uncontrolled orifices also serves widely as a model of social being, transactions across the thresholds of the human frame giving rise to images that tie physical to collective existence. Indeed, Devisch (1984) has argued that it is precisely through this double articulation of metaphor and metonym that the multileveled semantic mediation achieved by the body actually works.

It is not only orifices that mediate relations between the body and the world, however. The ethnographic record reveals that anatomical surfaces play a similar role. Note that the "social skin," to use Turner's (1980) term, is not necessarily coterminous with the epidermis, the "natural" husk of Western biophysical imaginings. Neither is it merely a sensory screen on which an objective environment shapes the contours of subjective being. In non-Western contexts, the bounds of personhood are seldom contained within a neat, corporeal envelope: The dressed, groomed, and elaborated exteriors of the body are regarded, in many cultures, as inseparable from the physical self. There are no nudes in Chinese painting, Hay (1989) observes, because there is no essential nature to be revealed beneath artificial drapes; the latter are integral to embodiment itself (cf. Brain 1979:64). Physical identity may be more pervasive still, extending into possessions, footprints, names, and even other bodies—like those of close kin—who share something of a person's substance. Turner (1967:392) remarked long ago that Ndembu doctors treated symptoms of illness in individual patients as signs of sickness in the corporate body; that is, in the matrilineal group to which the sufferer belonged. Such constructions do not deny the discreteness of human beings. But they do contest our own sense that organic being is unbreachable by either material or immaterial forces.

There is an interesting coda to the fact that, in many non-Western ontologies, selfhood seems to exceed Western corporeal constraints: Recent critiques from within our own tradition have suggested that, for us, subjectivity might be a good deal *less* than our physical assumptions have led us to believe. Some structuralists and postmodernists, for example, see unified selfhood as a bourgeois illusion (Althusser 1971; Derrida 1978; cf. Hebdige 1988:164ff), a myth abetted by the workings of power on the receptive surfaces of the human frame (Foucault 1980). Notwithstanding this critique, however, or the evidence that modes of selfhood have varied in human history, it is arguable that all forms of collective consciousness imply some notion of subjectivity, personhood, and agency. And, as these categories become modes of action in the world, the material body (albeit symbolically nuanced) comes into play, marking off the self from the non-self, the figure from its ground.

Physical margins are particularly implicated in processes that alter being in the world (Devisch 1984). Thus shifts in the boundaries between body and context often register changes in existential condition, subjective states being widely understood in terms of the waxing and waning of personal presence; witness such culturally modulated notions as depression, deflation, or subjection (cf. Shweder 1982). Physical compression can also serve as a powerful image of collective "oppression," as is shown by the ethnographic case that follows. These states imply a collapse of bodily boundaries, frequently accompanied by the invasion of corporeal space or by the alienation of vital substances (as in "semen" or "soul" loss; Obeyesekere 1976, Uzzell 1974). Such conditions contrast with the extension of persons into the social environment, a process that occurs through their maturation. Igbo market women, for instance, not only strive to acquire titles and reputations that extend their names in time and space; they also work to become "elephants," heavy in both physical and moral terms, whose large and copiously draped bodies shake the earth as they walk (Misty Bastian, personal communication, 1990). Yet, lest we make too glib an association between physical and social expansion, let us remind ourselves of the inverse qualities associated with obesity in our own late capitalist world. Here, where independent self-regulation is seen as essential to the production of value—at least, in bourgeois terms—emaciation becomes a sign of virtue, and "fat" typifies an absence of self-control. While our middle-class obsession with diet, exercise, and cosmetic surgery confirms that body contours define social persons everywhere, it also reinforces something else: that physical markers bequeath no more than a *means* of distinction.

The specific value attributed to these instruments, we reiterate, is always a matter of culture in particular, not nature in general.

Of course, the expansion of being in the world is also a matter of social engagement, of participation in exchanges that expand subjectivity, accumulate value, and build prestige (cf. Munn 1977; 1986). During early childhood, the management of bodily thresholds plays a crucial role in identity formation: weaning, the cutting of teeth, and the ability to ingest food or control evacuation may be signs of social viability, signaling the right to be named and to enter into relationships on one's own behalf (Weiss 1990; de Heusch 1980; Devisch 1984). The forging of collective identities and boundaries, Douglas (1966) classically suggests, also plays upon give-and-take across corporeal margins and gateways. Within extended kin groups, especially those with corporate identities, notions of consubstantiality often prevail, and individual bodily boundaries are highly porous. Food is frequently exchanged without reserve, and members (living or dead) typically have the power to invade each other in blessing or punishment (Radcliffe-Brown 1950; Fortes 1953a). Between groups of separate but equivalent status—those that intermarry, for example—bodies are also permeable, if under more regulated, ritually managed conditions; reciprocal or complementary transactions of food and physical substance occur (Marriott 1976), although they might carry the danger of mystical attack through these very avenues (Wilson 1951; Munn 1986). On the other hand, when relations are markedly unequal, such openness—and the shared subjectivity it signals—is usually absent. As Douglas (1966:147f) shows, elites in highly stratified societies often distinguish themselves, metaphorically and metonymically, in corporeal terms: They seek to reinforce their physical margins against polluting interactions with people of lower strata (cf. Stallybrass and White 1986), people made of altogether different stuff.

But the politics of physical boundaries are not merely a matter of preserving static and unambiguous categories. They are also a means of social transformation. Historians of early modern Europe have shown that changing notions of person and body were integral to the radical individuation that accompanied commodification. A range of fascinating facts concerning manners, dress, architecture, and legal categories indicate that "modernization" in the West involved the erection of unprecedented boundaries around the self (Elias 1978; Greenblatt 1980; Rybczynski 1986). By contrast to the "free" individual, who ostensibly had the capacity to negotiate his/her place in the moral and material economy, witches, madmen, and artistic grotesques were depicted, in often feminized counterimages, as beings insufficiently closed off from the world (Stallybrass and White 1986:22; cf. Thomas 1971). A similar logic pervaded the practices of Christian missions in South Africa, which sought to create bounded and inward-turning persons, physically enclosed disciples who would also be self-possessed colonial subjects (below, Chapter 9). The Africans often resisted these efforts: Many Tshidi, we shall see, strove to reverse the corporeal politics of colonialism, to construct an alternative selfhood by reestablishing permeable persons and reciprocal relations. Their efforts to counter the effects of evangelism and wage labor, and to resituate themselves in a socially responsive landscape, leaned heavily on the manipulation of body margins and thresholds.

As all this suggests, the making of social relations is often a more visceral matter than is conveyed by the categories of a Cartesian social science—in whose terms power may act upon bodies but is itself, at source, a rather abstract or cerebral force. Yet power in human society is often perceived as an innate physical capacity: a form of efficacy, virtue, or magnetism that resides, at least to some degree, as a material substance within the person. From such assumptions arise the potency of both relics and the magical concoctions that, in Africa, often purport to contain physical parts of the greatly gifted. Polynesian "mana," no less than the blood of kings, is power of the embodied sort. So, too, is the enabling "dignity" that Tswana see as emanating from the liver (both termed *sebete*).

Because it is an active force, power (like agency) must be sought in the active body, the body that lives in time and moves through space. Too frequently, anthropologies of the human form have been like the anatomies of early biology (Foucault 1975): They have been concerned with isolated and static structures, bereft of life and productive activity. Yet, as has already become clear, it is impossible to separate bodily structure from process, or bodily space from time, without distorting the complex interplay of corporeality and culture. Shape and spatial location, for instance, are inseparable from movement and metamorphosis. We have already noted that a lack of physical closure might restrict a person's mobility in the world. Likewise, systematic shifts in the positioning of the body serve to index shifts in social location. The assumption of a horizontal rather than vertical posture often accompanies a state of affliction and liminality; similarly, the raising and lowering of the body in relation to the normal planes of activity tend to imply super- or sub-social being. Authority is thus often shown by physical elevation, whereas birth and death in many societies take place on the ground (J. Comaroff 1985:97; cf. de Heusch 1980).

Furthermore, movement that differs markedly from ordinary locomotion both signals and actually achieves deviation from routine states of being. The ecstatic, drunk, or mad proclaim their state in their gait. And swinging or circling, with their attendant physiological effects on balance and perception, frequently announce conditions of dissociation or "inspiration"; that is, the eclipse of everyday existence through transporting experience. Huxley (1977:217f) has noted the widespread use of spiral motifs in rituals that seek to induce altered states of consciousness, the motif itself sometimes signifying directly the intrusion of divine power (see also Reichard 1950:161f on the spiral in Navaho ritual). Circling also welds individuals into a single "movement," achieving a heightened, ritually marked sociality (cf. Turner 1968:216f; Gell 1975, 1980; Leavitt 1985; Mitchell 1956a; Ranger 1975; Hanna 1977). Among the Tshidi, spiral movement epitomizes symbolic processes that draw individuals into an integral, tightly knit unity, dynamically fusing them into a single, rotating body (see below). It is this momentum that dissolves conventional boundaries in ecstatic rites, permitting the interpenetration of man and woman, matter and spirit.

Movement, like all bodily processes, implies the experience of differentiation, sequence, and duration—and, hence, of temporality. Here, again, widely recurring images in diverse contexts suggest the operation of a physically inscribed order upon human perceptions. Above all else, the organic processes that maintain, reproduce, and transform the body express the logical interdependence of space and time. Thus internal functions like alimentation engage the lateral contrast of "inside" and "outside" or "center" and "periphery" in dynamic sequences, for the ingestion of external substances subsumes lateral opposition into a linear irreversibility, the mouth standing in asymmetrical complementarity with the anus. Within the variety of processes held to create and recreate physical being, the digestion of food looms especially large as a model of ineluctable social incorporation and expulsion. And, predictably, its reversal signals anomaly (cf. Devisch 1984); liminal beings, such as prophets and madmen, are widely held to "eat excrement" (Loudon 1977:174). Moreover, models of sequential movement into and out of bodily space can be projected onto the social corpus as a whole. In several Southern African Bantu-speaking communities, for instance, "to be eaten" connotes consumption by a political superior or an economic patron; to be "thrown up" entails expulsion from the social community (J. Comaroff 1985:48; Guy 1979:19).

Sexual relations provide another model of transformative process, although it must be noted that the essentialist, binary constructs of gender and generation dominant in the modern West are by no means universal. In many societies, procreation serves as a paradigm for the perception of different types of temporality. As Van Gennep (1960) noticed long ago, it is widely understood by means of a tripartite scheme, centered on a liminal phase and, as such, is easily mapped upon the three-fold alimentary model described above; hence eating and sexual consumption tend to evoke each other. Van Gennep also stressed that procreative processes provide a progression of images of universal significance, most palpable perhaps in the tripartite structure of rites de passage, which build social continuities upon personal transience (Van Gennep 1960; Hugh-Jones 1979:149). But reproductive "facts" have ultimately to be recontextualized within the complex constellations of movement and stasis, space and time, that the body provides. Along with other organic processes—such as maturation, aging, and death—they have significant implications for the perception of subject and history. For these also play upon the social imagination as it thinks with the body.

The crucial issue, then, is to determine how such physical instruments are selectively elaborated in particular cultures. Western social thought, recall, has classically insisted upon the dialectic of natural and cultural form, but this in itself tells us little. For either the social has been seen as wholly determined by nature (or vice versa) or the relationship between the body and society is reduced to a functionalist tautology, in which each reinforces the other. Indeed, the organic analogy so popular in late nineteenth and early twentieth century sociology and anthropology was built on the putative resonance between "physical" and "social" systems, systems characterized as "normally" in a state of equilibrium and free from contradiction. As is shown by Turner's (1980) analysis of Kayapo cosmology, equilibrium models of this sort are not limited to our society alone. But the very transience of the worlds that functionalism sought to freeze should alert us to the fact that nature and society transform each other as they interact. The body, as we have already said, cannot escape being a vehicle of history, a metaphor and metonym of being-in-time.

More than this, the constellation of "natural" facts constituting the body is itself capable of generating multiple and potentially conflicting processes and perceptions; the human frame combines stability with transience, stasis with disease and degeneration. Of course, the "nature" of these experiences cannot simply determine how they will be read within particular semantic systems, for the latter are internally contradictory and have their own agendas. Indeed, social and cultural contradictions— emerging in everyday experience as conflicts of interest and value—often take concrete form in physical tensions. There is a widespread human tendency to signify such tensions in terms of that archetypal sign of conflict, illness (Turner 1967; Sontag 1978; J. Comaroff 1983).

We may return now to our opening fragment, and to Bourdieu's concern with bodily reform. The Zionist groups with which we are concerned share significant features with other institutions and movements that set out to produce "new" men and women—whether, like asylums, they seek to reform the deviant or, like cargo cults, aim to reconstruct the person as metonym, *pars pro toto,* of an aberrant world. In common with all such endeavors, Zionism seeks to prize apart and weave anew the social and material forms that fuse in the body. But, again like all such efforts, it has a specific historical shape, being motivated by its opposition to the neocolonial society that enfolds it: the world of *sekgoa,* "the way of the whites."[4] Thus Zionism is structurally akin to a host of other movements that have arisen in radically unequal societies (Hobsbawm 1959) or have been spawned as formerly independent communities are absorbed into colonial states (Worsley 1968). These movements tend to be defined, in Western terms, as "primitive," "subpolitical," and "ritualized." Theirs is a quest for practical transformation on the part of people who perceive themselves to be peripheral to the centers of power, outside of the purview of "heroic history" (Sahlins 1983). And they often derive their forms of protest and world-transforming practice from the accessible idioms of everyday experience, idioms that rely on local relations of production, exchange, and power—and are materialized in the human frame.

Because they so often emerge in response to social contradictions, these movements are typically rooted in images of the body at war with itself or in tension with its environment. Hence their practices are seen as forms of "healing," ways of acting upon the forces that threaten physical viability. But because the tormented body is itself an icon of the dislocated world, these curative rites act upon maladies at once personal and collective, locally embodied and expansively historical. Here, whether explicitly or not, healers treat the signs of sickness as signifiers of a conflicted society. Let us examine this in more detail in the context of Tshidi Zionism.

III

Elsewhere we have dealt extensively with the social history of South African Zionism, and with its particular manifestation among the Tshidi.[5] In the early 1970s, Tshidi Zionist churches were much like similar groups elsewhere in Southern Africa—highly segmentary, yet formally alike. They were the progeny of a process of stereotypic reproduction itself fed by their sad structural predicament: To wit, Zionism was a practical response to a set of political and economic conditions which the movement protested but could not transform. Trapped within the constraining confines of the apartheid state, it was destined to reiterate its message of estrangement and resistance. Yet these constraints did not deny the churches all creativity or historical significance. While they operated more or less autonomously at the local level, most were also branches of subcontinental organizations that cut across established boundaries and official maps (cf. Werbner 1985).

We never met a Tshidi Zionist able to offer a detailed history or theological charter of the movement as a whole. The coherence of Zionism resides in practice, resting as much in the contours of daily activity as in the symbolic elaborations of ritual. Zionists are what Zionists do, and we shall argue that the primary mnemonic for their "doing" is lodged in a reformed image of the human body—the body in itself and in its relation to its immediate context.

The semantic scheme of Tshidi Zionism retains many basic, albeit transformed, elements of its parent movement in the United States, the Christian Catholic Apostolic Church in Zion. Founded among impoverished urban workers and petty tradesmen in Chicago in 1896 (Harlan 1906), this church provided a mode of signifying practice that addressed their perceived estrangement from the world of the establishment. The movement explicitly attacked the cultural forms of Protestant orthodoxy and, by implication, the dualistic bourgeois categories they presupposed. Its practice aimed at reconstructing the fragmented person, seen to be divided by the complementary "modern" evils of a religion disengaged from worldly pragmatics and a medicine that was secular and "ungodly." Zionism sought to "heal" these breaches, working outwards from the ailing body, potentially the "temple of God." Physical reconstruction would prefigure the restoration of an "original theocracy," a radical rapprochement of man and spirit, church and state. The severed psyche and soma would be fused again by the Holy Spirit, encompassing all of the faithful into "one great family of Zion" (Harlan 1906:89). This metamorphosis would work most directly on the body and its life-world, constructing a novel order of identities and margins that prefigured a new society. The reconstructionist ambitions of the movement were awesome, but they were to be achieved through the methodical reform of the mundane: diet, gesture, greeting behavior, and the practical organization of work and devotion (Harlan 1906:15f).

We have argued elsewhere (J. Comaroff 1985) that, despite their variety, Zionist groups in South Africa all alike address the experience of alienation and displacement; they seek implicitly to reverse the impact on their world of the modern state and, in particular, to deal with the effects of migrant labor. Tshidi Zionists have typically tried to appropriate and revalue the signs of this estranging world, to counteract the disorienting consequences of proletarianization and political coercion. One of the primary ways in which they do so is by objectifying and manipulating them in the signs of sickness.

Tshidi refer to the Zionist churches interchangeably as *dikereke tsa moya* ("churches of spirit") or *dikereke tsa metse* ("churches of water"). This double usage encodes a matrix of concepts that frame Zionist semantics. First, there is the focal role of the Holy Spirit, the distinguishing feature of the whole movement, whose very name (*moya*; "breath") underlines its physical grounding. The notion of a superhuman being who remains palpably present in everyday experience contrasts strongly with the transcendent God of colonial Protestantism. Second, there is the reference to the signifying processes that lend power to the powerless and render palpable an otherwise unattainable potency: The Spirit is made tangible in water, for it is in water that it is rendered accessible to, and manipulable by, humans.

Spirit, breath, and water are alike animating, substantial yet fluid, and capable of pervading physical space and the living body. Zionist rites make considerable use of the transformative capacity of water, which, as a metonym of Spirit, can dissolve matter and usurp space. Both provide a medium within which categorical relations may be reformed and personal boundaries redrawn. Initiates are baptized (*kolobetsa*; "to make wet"), a process that dissolves prior identities resting on the social skin. Members imbibe ritually treated water, which "quenches thirst" (*itimola lenyòra*) and cools the heat engendered by a threatening world. Zionists also refer to their ritual sites as *didiba* ("wells"), an image that conflates indigenous and biblical meaning and, in this drought-ridden landscape, signifies the damming of life-giving spirit. It was to these wells that the afflicted, the "thirsty," and the "oppressed" came to "drink" (*nwa*) and be "inspired by the Spirit" (*go tsènwa ka moya*). In this manner, the alienated were reanimated, barriers transgressed, and margins redrawn. And so the substance of the body of Zion was secured.

"Thirst" and "oppression," in fact, are key signifiers of affliction for Tshidi Zionists. Both connote dissipation by means of very general images of physical depletion, images that imply an imbalance in relations between person and context. To be "thirsty" (*kgakgabala*; "parched" or "desolate," used both of bodies and the landscape) means to be desiccated by the disruption of the regular, fluid interchange between one's being and the world. "Oppression" (*patikègò*) also connotes depression, being forcibly compressed into a narrow space or becoming shriveled. It suggests a contraction of personal space through pressure on corporeal margins.

Here we see how widely shared bodily implements have been invested with particular local significance, how they have been selected and tuned to the semantics implicit in modern Zionist discourse. By specifying the orientation of the body in a particular context, these implements make concrete the objects of healing practice. As metaphors, they speak to a general state of depleted existence, their meaning deriving from the Zionist symbolic scheme as a whole. But they also serve as tangible symptoms to be worked on in the ritual context—that is, as metonyms of both acute and more thoroughgoing disruptions to be cured. Moreover, as cultural forms, these bodily signs are transformations of a precolonial Tshidi order that has been subtly revalued through the dialectics of colonization. This history, in fact, throws important light upon the processes that give form to contemporary Tshidi Zionist practice.

IV

The precolonial Tshidi polity is probably best described as having been centered on a hereditary chiefship in which were vested the mechanisms of ritual, political, and economic control. Viewed from its apex, the social order consisted of a hierarchy of social units and statuses, position within it being negotiated in the idiom of agnatic rank. Yet, as has often been noted, this "order" was also a lived-in world, comprising ego-focused networks of kin and uterine houses, themselves the basic "atoms" of social organization (Comaroff and Roberts 1981:47). The division of labor, prototypically, placed women in the agricultural domain at the periphery of highly concentrated settlements. In contrast, men engaged in the political, jural, and ritual processes—all mediated, in some form, by cattle—that created and sustained the public sphere, indeed society itself. They controlled the pastoral economy and the labor that sustained it: that of youths, impoverished clients, and subjugated "bushmen." By all accounts, adult males contributed relatively little time to the reproduction of the domestic unit. They were, rather, citizens of the royal court. The most elaborate communal rites, those of boys' initiation (*bogwèra*), transferred youths from the productive periphery (*kaha ntle*; "outside") to the center of the cosmos (*ha gare*; "the core"). In the process, they were made to experience rebirth as fully social beings and members of the body politic, of which the person of the chief was a pivotal embodiment.

The routines of everyday existence also drew Tshidi men inward to the center of the polity, reinforcing the complementary but asymmetrical relations between "core" and "periphery." This opposition, however, being based on a centrist vision of structural hierarchy, has itself to be relativized. For it coexisted with a contrasting scheme lodged within the social and cultural forms of the periphery: in the design of the homestead, in the physical activities of production and reproduction, and in the social world of women. Its root idiom was matrilateral kinship. In contrast to the rhetoric of male descent, which provided the terms for formal politics, nonranked lateral ties through females were the basis of practical cooperation in agriculture, household work, and daily life in general.

Matrilateral relations and their associated practices were anchored spatially to the house (*ntlo*) and to the female body, its metonymic referent. As the point of origin of the uterine group and, through it, of higher-order social units, the female body and the conjugal dwelling presupposed each other. The latter was circular in shape, having a single aperture for entry and exit, and was the locale of marital sexuality. Like a woman, it was perceived to lack "natural" closure; hence its thresholds were the subject of careful ritual regulation. The term for "inside the house" (*mo teng*) also meant *in utero,* and sexual access to another man's wife—as in the levirate—was referred to as *go tsena mo tlung* ("to enter the house"). The contrast between "inside" and "outside," between contained processes and unbounded flow, was used also to refer to a series of divisions of increasing scale, from the inner and outer female body to the worlds of matrilateral and agnatic relations at large.

Although complementary in their generative capacity, the gendered domains of agnation and matrilaterality were unequally incorporated into the totality of the "nation" (*morafe*). For the politics of centralization were conducted in agnatic idiom, involving the encompassment of matrilateral ties and the appropriation of female productivity for collective, male-dominated ends (J. Comaroff 1985:54ff). Of particular relevance to us here, however, is the fact that each of these domains was put at risk by the other.[6] Thus the well-being of persons and projects in the domestic sphere was constantly threatened by the effects of sorcery, itself the consequence of agnatic rivalry and political competition. Bodily images abounded here: Both aggressive politics and mystical evil were understood as attempts to "eat" (*ja*) rivals and "press" them into clientage. Sorcery itself was usually an ingested substance (*sejeso*); the very inversion of maternal nurture, it was smuggled into the otherwise benign domestic realm hidden in food and drink. Once consumed, it disrupted normal processes of alimentation and the balanced give-and-take between the body and its world. But if the domestic sphere was endangered by forces emanating from the political center, the center was subject to the reciprocal danger of being "spoiled" (*senyèga*) by the polluting effects of "heat" (*bothitho*), the by-product of unstable female fertility.

Conditions such as "thirst" and "oppression," then, seem to have implied a simultaneous physical and social disruption. They signaled interference in the orderly actions and transactions that maintained viable being in the world. But colonial conquest drastically refashioned this world. Articulation with the global political economy eclipsed local authority and set in motion mutually reinforcing processes of underdevelopment and proletarianization. The Protestant church was implicated in this process, its "civilizing mission" preparing the Tshidi for the labor market by introducing new notions of work, bodiliness, and personhood. What is more, its dualistic culture separated spirit from matter, individual from context, and religion from the state. Though they might not have fully intended it, the churchmen laid the ground for colonial overrule. In due course, the chiefship became a menial cog in the bureaucratized state machine; even local ritual functions were usurped by the Methodist mission church, whose language and organizational forms resonated with those of the "modern" society of which the Tshidi were now, for better or worse, a part. The activities of the public sphere were eroded and, as a result, agnation lost much of its social relevance. Widespread migration impoverished domestic resources, placing increased weight upon matrilateral ties—and on women, who were left to make what they could of the depleted rural economy.

These transformations had their effects on the cultural construction of the Tshidi world. For example, sorcery suspicions now bespoke new sites of conflict, revealing structural contradictions originating in colonialism itself (J. Comaroff 1980). Notions like "thirst" and "oppression" were also redefined, coming to connote, in Zionist discourse, complementary disruptions of bodily integrity and social orientation. Like other metaphors of affliction current in Tshidi usage, their connotations remained largely implicit. Although they served to situate events and experiences in both immediate and wider semantic scopes, they did not make direct *causal* connections between specific symptoms and broader sociohistorical processes. Rather, the signs of sickness were read in terms of a local dialectic of bodily space and ruptured margins, in terms of an unceasing battle between the healing Spirit and malign forces for the possession of human beings. In this sense, the metaphors of affliction would seem to have depoliticized Tshidi affliction, eclipsing its historical roots with a mystifying Zionist mythology (Barthes 1973:142ff).

Yet these medical metonyms were not emptied of all social meaning: Tswana healing practice remained, and still remains, sociosomatic: Their pathological imagery was, like all human thought, perpetually open to the rich play of symbols produced by their history. Thus the resonant notion of "thirst" seemed to suggest a range of contemporary and related afflictions to Tshidi Zionists. A physical and moral ailment it certainly was. But, in the local imagination, it was also linked to the experience of desiccation that outweighed all others in this rural reserve, where life was dominated by the battle to wrest a living from drought-ridden soil. Likewise *patikègò,* the condition of physical constriction and lost self-control; it, too, was associated with wider forms of oppression—in particular, the restricted social existence of black South Africans under a regime that thrived on the physical control of its subjects. In fact, the Zionists' millennium expressed a cogent, if implicit, rejection of the social system that contained them.

V

The American movement that spawned South African Zionism had tried to heal the divided self and restore "primitive" community in an estranged world. Tshidi Zionism sought similarly to recast the person and his/her immediate space, to give the marginalized their own dynamic fund of power. A close examination of Zionist practice suggests the impetus to create a new social order, standing between radically decentered indigenous institutions (such as the household disrupted by migrant labor) and the structures of the neocolonial state (national Protestant churches, the apparatus of the *bantustan,* and the urban economy). It incorporated elements of both local and external origin and revalued them in relation to each other, thereby creating a tertium quid—a discourse with its own distinct logic. Thus, for example, cultural forms drawn from the life of the Tswana household were fused with those of the Protestant congregation, transforming them both. In the Zionist "church," whose domestic-oriented rituals still owed something to the Nonconformist "service," a leader—part "minister," part senior matrilateral kinsman—coordinated pragmatic activities on behalf of his followers. These were predominantly women who addressed each other as siblings.

The Zionist movement achieved its synthesis, for the most part, through the reform of habitual practice, especially the reorganization of sexual relations and marriage, and the production and consumption of food. It has concentrated, in other words, on those bodily transactions that build groups and distribute persons in social space. This would appear to have been the unspoken object of enjoining endogamy—if not within particular congregations, then within Zionist ranks—and conjugal fidelity. These practices seek to encapsulate and consolidate communal ties, to reform the margins of persons and groups, and to concentrate mutually constituting exchanges within the bounds of a moral collectivity. Dietary proscriptions do likewise; Zionist rules were based on the restrictions of Leviticus, understood as a prohibition against eating "dirt" (*sejeso*; the long-standing term for ingested sorcery substances). This linked indigenous notions of malevolent invasion with biblical injunction, yet its content, the specific avoidances themselves, served to separate Zionist activity both from "tradition" and from Protestant and colonial culture. Note again how, in incorporating and resituating elements from each of these cultural sources, Zionism fashioned its unique mediations of both.

The impetus toward encapsulation and bodily reform was most evident in the preference of Zionists for eating "the work of [their] own hands" (*tiro ya diatla tsa rona*).[7] Here the physical image of a self-sufficient, "hand-to-mouth" existence captures the ideal of a community based in production for its own use, a community not polluted by transactions with the world outside. It was an unattainable ideal. Many Tshidi Zionists were returned migrants,[8] and their rituals acknowledged, perforce, the necessity of some degree of dependence on the market. Nonetheless, the effort to regulate traffic with alien goods and alienating exchanges clearly expressed the fact that commodities were seen to endanger the pristine congregation. All purchased objects were subject to ceremonial "washing" (*motlhapisò*) be-fore they could be consumed. Other things, such as dress, were also invoked in the cause of bodily reform. Thus Zionist costume ingeniously redeployed the colors, styles, and textures of colonial and neocolonial attire—most conspicuously, the uniform of the workplace. These elements were trans-formed, on the anatomies of the wearers, by fusing them in unexpected ways with features of Tshidi "tradition," thereby constructing a new synthesis—and a defiantly distinctive identity. Although they were regarded with the utmost seriousness, these creations also had a parodic quality, one that played with the material world they sought to control and transcend.

This recasting of everyday practice was paralleled in the sphere of healing rites, where attempts to remake person and community were at their most condensed and symbolically elaborate. Zionist ritual (*go dira*; "to make" or "to do" in the most general sense of the term) contrasted with Protestant worship (normally *go rapela*; "to pray" verbally, in the European manner, or "to beseech"). It was also distinguished from "work" in the sense of wage labor (*mmèrèkò*; from the Dutch/Afrikaans *werk*; see Chapter 6). Because they took place at night, and in the homes of leaders who were conduits for the descending Spirit,[9] these rites were off established maps and timetables, beyond the grasp of the modern public sphere. In carefully sealed-off nocturnal seclusion, inspired mediums went to work on bodies, both individual and collective. For these were the primary sites of social rebirth, where the power of the Spirit would dissolve ruptures among the faithful and would open up protective divisions between Zionist enclaves and the outside world.

How, exactly, did the body serve as template and tool for such meta-morphoses? At the core of the process were formal, symbolically dense rites of healing and regeneration that set about reversing signs of affliction and depletion. These had a recognizable linear structure: the tripartite sequence of all rites de passage that move from "entrance" through "action" to "exit" (cf. Hubert and Mauss 1964:19f; Van Gennep 1960). As we have already mentioned, such rituals were widely conceived in terms of physical transformation; in the Tshidi imagination they were associated with reproduction and the space of conjugal relations. Thus the afflicted were said to "enter the house"—a phrase, remember, that also implied access to the female body—and they experienced their healing in a domestic context infused with images of sexual congress and gestation. Indeed, among those schooled in Protestant puritanism, these ceremonies were dismissed as licentious. But their sensuality was the very point: Zionists countered hegemonic worldly power with a form of potency to which they had ready access, the generative force present in a pregnant body. Within the ritual enclosure (*mo teng*; see above), participants were "entered" (*go tsènwa*), "filled" (*tlala*) by the Spirit, and reconstituted by its inseminating power. Whether male or (more usually) female, their bodies were rendered passive and fructified. Where before they had been "parched," "deflated," and "pressed," they now acquired a state of "heaviness" (*boima*; also implying "pregnancy")—as if reasserting physical presence and reclaiming a space from which they had been compelled to shrink.

Zionist ritual created a sense of world-renouncing separateness, aiming to weld participants into a community reborn. This was effected in several distinct registers at once: through uniformed dress, orchestrated utterance, and articulated bodily movement. The first phase of the tripartite ceremonies framed a space in which congregants would be made to transcend their separation and suffering, being assimilated into a dynamic unity by the power of the Spirit. Within the house, they sang and swayed in unison to the increasingly urgent beat of the drum, coordinating their performances step by step to form a single body. Thus fused, they sank to the ground en masse and commenced to establish their common intent by proclaiming individual yet simultaneous utterances of personal distress. These unique outpourings reached a deafening crescendo, a swelling wave of sound that marked the culmination of the first phase.

Thus united as a body of sufferers, the congregation provided the ground on which, in the second stage, diffuse experiences of distress could crystallize in more tangible form. Symptoms manifested in a few individuals became metonyms of the affliction of the group at large. Within the circle, two or three now gave spontaneous testimony (*go bolèla*; "to tell"), interspersing short outbursts of personal misfortune with formulaic exclamations that evoked repeated communal responses. (Testifier: *Go siame, Morena?* "Is that correct, Lord?" Congregation: "Amen!") Testimony often began with the phrase "I thirst" or "I am oppressed" and continued with a breathless list of subjective symptoms, revealing the reciprocal interplay of physical sign and pernicious context ("This wasting of my inside began when I was working in Johannesburg. . . ."). Congregants listened with rapt attention, uttering responsive sighs and sounds of assent. It was as if each half-formed profession was given concreteness as it was taken up by the group. When the testimonies ceased, congregants extended their hands in support of the exhausted speakers, drawing them back into their midst. Clearly, the rhetorical form of the ritual transformed unorganized, private perceptions into a collective reality. The diffuse states of distress expressed by all the participants at the start were made into the concerted object of the healing process. Substantialized in a set of bodily signs, it had been made susceptible to specific ritual treatment. The healing phase could now proceed.

To initiate the healing, the group began to dance in a clockwise direction around their leader, moving in two concentric circles, men on the inside.[10] The drumming built up to a fever pitch and the coordination of limbs became ever tighter. As physical expression, the dance both proclaimed and promoted a high degree of social integration, minimizing the distinction between individual participants. At the center, the prophet became the vertical path for the descending force of the Spirit. Standing amidst numerous containers of water, he started to show the signs of being filled to overflowing with Spirit: He snorted, shivered, and sweated profusely. In such possession rites, as we said, the whirling of closely coordinated dancers erodes the distance between the human and the spirit worlds. Here it rendered the congregants open to intrusion, inducing the divine power to come down among them. Now it remained for their leader to transmit this force into their ailing bodies, nourishing the wasted and restoring the balance of inner and outer being. One by one they stood before him: first the testifiers, whose symptoms spoke of shared sickness, and then each congregant in turn, all drawing on the surge of power that flowed into the "well" of Zion. The prophet pressed his hand down hard on each head, "filling" (*tlatsa*) all with spirit. Thus made "whole" or "sufficient in themselves" (*itekanèla*), they "bulged" as they became replete (*totoma*). The flow of substance between persons and world was resumed, their "thirst quenched" (*itimola lenyòra*). As the ritual literally "wound down" and the circle broke up, everyone assumed a quiet composure and emerged again into the life of the town, in defiance of an afflicting world.

VI

This chapter has explored the logic of a modern historical movement among a South African people, a movement of utopian reform whose meaning was most tangibly realized through the medium of bodily signs. Bodily signification, we have argued, is an inevitable component of all social practice: Neither the most ethereal of expressions nor the most pragmatic of politics can escape being acted out through the human frame. However lofty their ideals, revolutions must also work their changes palpably on the persons they seek to re-form.

We have also suggested that the models of metamophosis provided by the body—models of production, transformation, rebirth—are of special salience to those marginal to the means of institutionalized power and ideological authority. When such populations attempt to change the world—often only to be discounted as "chiliastic," "untheorized," or "depoliticized"—they make complex, historically significant statements of defiance. The *forms* of their practice, moreover, seek to address and redress the roots of conflict-laden experience. And, although they might not be capable of finally dislodging those roots, it would be a vulgar history indeed that dismissed their efforts as a mystification of no consequence (cf. Ranger 1975:4).

The crucial role of the body here, and in all other efforts to remake history, derives from its position as a mediator between the self and the world. The human frame encodes the categories and processes that shape social systems and the subjects they presuppose, and it re-presents them as a tangible means for collective action. Cultural schemes, it is true, may permute these means and refigure the very relationship between corporeality and context; the biophysical individualism of the West, after all, is an extreme example of the stripping of the body's capacity to signify the social. Nonetheless, human experience everywhere tends stubbornly to reassert the inseparability of physical and social being.

Nor is the body just an arbitrary order of signs or a natural alibi. Physical being imposes upon our collective perceptions certain universal contrasts and processes, couched in the "realities" of material existence. Although any culture may seamlessly inscribe its self-perpetuating forms on the human anatomy, there is the ever-present risk that contradictions will find voice, as among the Tshidi, in the "natural" tensions of corporeal life: in the metaphors of affliction, depletion, and death. Such contradictions may, of course, have the effect of transforming, even decomposing, the meaningful bases of the world. But these, typically, are reconstituted again by means of media drawn directly from the body's apparently endless stock. As suggested by the practices of Tshidi Zion, such media are not mere metaphors, images of a reality that resides elsewhere. They are implements shaped by an innate, material logic, a logic that governs their entry into culture and history.

Notes

1. *Bantustans* were the ethnic "homelands" of which the vast majority of black South Africans were, until recently, compulsory citizens—and from which they migrated as "temporary sojourners" to white conurbations. These (ostensibly independent) "homelands" were the rural building blocks of the apartheid system. Although still intact in the late 1980s, they were increasingly being challenged by the reform movement.

2. Cf. Hebdige (1979), who uses the notion of "exile" with respect to categories and collectivities that, through their everyday practices, seek to set themselves off from the dominant social order.

3. In human communities, eating and sexuality typically signify the forging of social connectedness. Thus breaches in these practices often signal a sub- or semi-social state of being; witness the widespread restrictions on the feeding habits and sexual relations of persons in liminal predicaments (e.g., initiands or the bereaved; see Turner 1969:106).

4. *Sekgoa* connotes white colonial and neocolonial culture, from the Protestant church to the industrial labor market. It is not perceived as *intrinsic* to whites, however, and may refer to the activities of blacks who identify positively with European ways.

5. In this account we have perforce to deal briefly with the social and historical context of Tshidi Zionism; for a full analysis, see J. Comaroff (1985).

6. The conventions of matrilateral relations were directly opposed to those of agnation. This opposition indexed a deeper structural contradiction between the powers and interests of the chiefly center and those of the domestic periphery, between the forces of centralization and those of disaggregation (see Comaroff and Roberts 1981:46f; Chapter 4 below). For an extended acount of the "signifying economy" of this precolonial Tswana world, and for details of historical sources for its reconstruction, see J. Comaroff (1985: Chaps. 3, 4).

7. *Tiro* (work) is derived from *go dira* ("to make" or "to do") and contrasts with *mmèrèkò*, from *go bèrèka*, which implies wage labor (see Chapter 6 below).

8. Discerning rates of proletarianization for a population like the Tshidi is difficult because of the complex articulation of local production with the industrial sector. Rural poverty rendered all but a few petit bourgeois households dependent upon various forms of migrant labor: Life histories collected in 1970 in the Mafeking District suggested that 89 percent of men and 56 percent of women over the age of twenty-five had worked away from home for at least one period of nine months. Such histories showed, furthermore, that neither male nor female Zionists differed significantly from the rest of the Tshidi in this respect. (There were, however, no members of the petite bourgeoisie in their ranks.) But what distinguished the Zionists was their response to the implications of wage labor; in particular, the attempt to reverse many of its effects through their ritual and everyday practice.

9. Zionist congregations sought to establish viable, bounded social enclaves beyond the grasp of the surrounding world. It was a project that commenced, as we have noted, in domestic space. As their memberships expanded, groups tended to establish church sites alongside the homes of their leaders. Significantly, these were usually on the outskirts of the old town, in stark contrast to the centrally located Protestant churches.

10. The dance thus dramatically reproduced the sociospatial map of the precolonial community. In that community, women were peripheral to the political center, in spite of being vital mediators between the social and extrasocial worlds. Of comparative interest here is Hertz's (1973:13) classic statement: "According to a very widespread idea, at least in the Indo-European area, the community forms a closed circle at the centre of which is the altar, the Ark of the Covenant, where the gods descend and from which place divine aid radiates. Within the enclosure reign order and harmony, while outside it extends a vast night, limitless and lawless, full of impure germs and traversed by chaotic forces. On the periphery of the sacred place the worshippers make a ritual circuit round the divine centre, their right shoulders turned towards it. They have everything to hope for from one side, everything to fear from the other. The right is the inside, the finite, assured well-being, and certain peace; the left is the outside, the infinite, hostile and the perpetual menace of evil."

Part Two

Dialectical Systems, Imaginative Sociologies

4

The Long and the Short of It

Is not history, the dialectic of time spans, in its own way an explanation of society in all its reality?

—Fernand Braudel (1980:38)

I

L ONG AGO, WHEN EVANS-PRITCHARD ([1950] 1963:18f) first spoke for the unity of history and anthropology,[1] he made two critical points. Both are well worn now, but they were highly controversial at the time.[2] The first was that no social order might be analyzed adequately without reference to its internal dynamics; the second was that the communities studied by anthropologists were increasingly being "enclosed in, and [coming to] form part of, great historical societies" (1963:21). Beyond his largely descriptive account of the Sanusi (1949), however, Evans-Pritchard did not himself go far in developing the historical anthropology that he espoused in his later life. Nor did he seek to relate the inner workings of social systems to their external contexts. To be sure, he has been roundly criticized for the timeless quality of his Nuer and Zande ethnographies. But he does appear to have recognized the full complexity of the issues involved, some of which have been lost in the more recent discussion of rapprochement between the two disciplines.

The most significant of these issues, in our own view, flows from the fact that history, time, and process are *not* the same thing, despite a common tendency in the social sciences to conflate them. Indeed, it hardly need be said that history, as a discipline, has a long antiquarian tradition and that, for many historians, the unchanging epoch or the contingent event remain the stuff of their craft. Conversely, as we noted in Chapter 1, "process" is still reduced, in much of anthropology, to a sequence of actions through which social and cultural arrangements work themselves out, and are reproduced, outside of chronological time. Nobody would deny that repetitive processes and contingent events have a place in historical anthropology. But to speak of temporality purely in these terms is, at best, caricature; at worst, it perpetuates the analytic illusion that time can be set apart from social form, an illusion that conduces not to history but to an all-too-familiar functionalist sociology.[3] Nor is it possible to transform a static vision of social systems into a historically sensitive one by the cosmetic addition of methodological categories that *appear*—like "change" or "process"—to connote dynamism or diachrony (J. L. Comaroff 1984:passim).

How, then, do we set about writing a historical anthropology of rural Africa in which time is not merely "structural" or process inevitably "cyclical"; in which "noncapitalist" worlds are not made to slumber in the ether of the ethnographic present; in which the past is reduced neither to evolutionary teleology nor to a succession of random events? It is to this general problem that we address ourselves here. We do so, in classic anthropological manner, with reference to a particular context, that of a Southern Tswana people known, for the past 170 years or so, as the Barolong boo Ratshidi (Tshidi).[4] But we intend our account as a dialogue between the concrete and the concept—between a specific ethnographic narrative and the analytic terms by means of which it, and others like it, may be composed.

In order to proceed with the dialogue, however, it is necessary, following our comments above (Chapter 1), to repeat that no social world may be properly understood without reference *both* to its internal historicity and to its unfolding relationship with its wider context. But this, in turn, demands that we explore two interrelated methodological perspectives. We merely introduce them here; they will be elaborated further as we progress.

The first perspective concerns the encounter between local worlds and the universe beyond. There is no longer any need to argue against treating those worlds in hermetic isolation or to prove that their inner workings are not, and never were, insulated from external forces. Nonetheless, the *manner* in which we apprehend this encounter remains a matter of some debate. The position for which we shall argue may be summarized as follows:

1. Every society, throughout its history, is caught up in processes of articulation with the elements that compose its social environment—including, cumulatively in space and time, other local communities of broadly similar construction; regional and/or subcontinental political economies; and, finally, global forces.

2. These processes—whether they consist of exchange or economic expropriation, missionization or military domination, trade or treaty, colonial politics or cultural imperialism—are not made up of interactions between disembodied structures, modes of production, or

other abstract totalities. They involve human actors and agencies engaged in diverse, disparate, and often discordant forms of material and symbolic practice.

3. The historical encounter between two social worlds—however circumscribed the one, or expansive the other—is always *dialectical*; that is, each works to transform the other, even as they are being joined in a new order of relations. This is not to say that the process, or its social product, is determined in equal measure by both sides or that they have a commensurate impact on one another. Quite the contrary: The ratio of determination varies across situations—although local social and cultural forms invariably mediate the direction of historical movements, even when they are being radically altered by them.

4. As this implies, the lines of demarcation between the "internal" world of any society and the "external" universe beyond—between the local, the regional, and the global—are neither preordained nor fixed. They shift as processes of engagement take their course, and they alter relations of power and production. They shift, too, at the level of experience and representation, although not necessarily in direct proportion to structural changes. Indeed, what sometimes appears from within as an autonomous ("local") social order may, from a different vantage, represent a level or a fraction of an overarching one—the principles of incorporation not always being visible to those involved.

We repeat that processes of articulation between social worlds, local or global, do not begin with colonialism or capitalist penetration (as has often been suggested; see Foster-Carter 1978). In one or another form, they occur in all human societies in all periods. Clearly, too, these processes give rise to the temporal axes of the long run. For they tend everywhere to be of extended duration, often working themselves out through (indeed, even defining) epochs and ages—though their critical moments sometimes appear to occur with startling rapidity. But this makes sense only in relation to the other perspective of which we spoke: the internal workings of local worlds, their dynamics of the short run.

It is all very well to situate noncapitalist communities within more embracing movements: the rise of imperialism, of colonial and postcolonial states, of subcontinental political economies, of a global order, or whatever. Yet the danger in doing so, one recognized more often in principle than in practice, is to persist in treating them purely as "peoples without history" (Wolf 1982), peoples upon whom history acts. We shall argue that all local worlds have their own *intrinsic* historicity, an internal dialectic of structure and practice that shapes, reproduces, and transforms the character of everyday life within them—and, as we said, mediates their encounters with the universe beyond.

This historicity, we venture, has its origin in the dualistic character of all social orders. On one hand, all social orders consist of a lived-in environment: an ensemble of typically ambiguous and sometimes contested routines and rules, rituals and relations, ethics and aesthetics, values and interests, constraints and conflicts. On the other hand, behind this world of appearances lie the often unremarked forms, simultaneously material and meaningful, that configure social existence. We shall argue that these forms are *inherently* contradictory and that, as a result, they motivate practice, in the double sense of impelling and directing motion and of imparting meaning to human experience and intention. And practice, in turn, fashions "concrete" linkages among individuals, groups, and classes. It is the vehicle through which the social and semantic contours of a lived-in universe, its shifting surfaces, are made and remade—the vehicle through which enduring structures are cast and recast. In short, human agency alone has the capacity to reproduce and/or transform the substance of social life, its manifest modes of representation and relationship; human agency at once culturally constituted yet, very often, historically unpredictable.

The historicity of all social fields, political communities, and cultural milieus, then, resides in a complex equation, the elements of which are (1) the internal dynamics of local worlds, their dialectics of the short run and (2) the articulation, over the long term, between those local worlds and the structures and agencies—at once regional and global—that come to make up their total environments. This equation, moreover, will be seen to distill the essence, the long and short, of the historical anthropology for which we argue. Let us put it to work in a particular Southern African context.

II

Perhaps the most striking feature of the Tshidi world of the late nineteenth century, then rapidly being colonized, was its tendency to undergo frequent, and occasionally dramatic, transformation. At times this chiefdom appeared highly centralized, its citizenry sharply stratified into classes of royals, free persons, and serfs. Incorporated into large, internally ranked agnatic descent groups, the Tshidi lived in a populous capital town, Mafikeng, and a few satellite settlements surrounding it, and were integrated into an elaborate politico-administrative order. At the apex of this order, the chiefship—*bogosi,* the embodiment of the polity and symbolic crucible of its well-being—exercised a good deal of control over productive activities and political processes, the distribution of land and the dispensation of law, tributary labor, and, for some, ritual intercession with the ancestors. At other times, however, this same community assumed a quite different aspect. The population was wont to scatter and live in assertive isolation alongside their widely dispersed fields and cattle posts. Under such conditions, in fact, there was a palpable avoidance of aggregation beyond the level of the household, and domestic groups confined their cooperation and interaction to a few matrilaterally linked units. The chiefship seemed to lose most of its real power—its incumbent ceasing to command tribute or public support, for example—and the politico-administrative order became virtually moribund. The capital stood all but empty, its deserted labyrinth of earthen homesteads and sandy pathways a silent testimony to the ebb and flow of the social universe (see Comaroff and Comaroff 1991:Chap. 4).

In other words, Tshidi society expressed two contradictory tendencies: one toward centralization, aggregation, and hierarchy, the other, toward decentralization and the atomization of the social universe. Each had a wide spectrum of social and material correlates extending into such diverse realms as the division of labor and gender relations, household organization and the functioning of the public domain, the symbolic representation of the social order and the degree of its internal stratification (J. L. Comaroff 1987a). Over time, first one and then the other of these tendencies came to predominate and was reflected in the surface contours of everyday life. Of course, these tendencies were not always evident in extreme form, and the structure of the polity did not oscillate mechanically between them. These were contradictory *potentialities;* the visible social, political, and economic arrangements of the Tshidi world, at any moment, expressed the proportions in which they were realized as a consequence of human action.

There are two points to be made about all this. The first is that a similar contradiction—in form, if not in precise substance—was observable almost a century before. This is readily deducible from the writings of early missionaries, explorers, and other visitors to the Southern Tswana, a number of whom left behind richly detailed records of the various communities. For example, Moffat's (1842:388f) description of the Tshidi capital in circa 1824 speaks of a densely settled, centralized chiefdom under a ruler who wielded extensive power within the polity and almost absolute control over external trade (cf. Smith 1939,1:278). According to Barrow (1806:404), in fact, there were Rolong towns, at the turn of the nineteenth century, "so extensive that it required a whole day" to walk from one end to the other. The Tlhaping center, Dithakong, was portrayed in very similar terms: With 10,000–15,000 souls, it was "as large as Cape Town" (p. 390f) and was organized into a well-developed structure of wards and other internal administrative divisions (see Burchell 1824,2:511f).

This, too, was a highly centralized, hierarchical polity under a strong "king" (Stow 1905:440) who enjoyed a monopoly over the "barter" of valued objects and derived considerable wealth from tribute in labor and the spoils of the hunt (Burchell 1824,2:537f; Campbell 1822,1:249, 268; 2:194). The ruler also exerted control over public deliberations, rainmaking and initiation rites, and the allocation of land and owned large numbers of animals (see, e.g., Lichtenstein 1930,2:414; Campbell 1822,1:314f; 2:197f). And yet within three decades his chiefdom had divided into three small polities, each under the weak leadership of a man whose authority resembled more closely the prototypical village headman in colonial Central Africa than it did the *kgosi* of a large Sotho-Tswana chiefdom (Gluckman, Mitchell, and Barnes 1949).[5] Still more striking, Barrow (1806:412), among others (e.g., Smith 1939,1:240f), encountered some Southern Tswana living in autonomous political communities, each made up of a single village of no more than forty "huts." And Andrew Geddes Bain (in Steedman 1835,2:233), another traveler of the day, gives eyewitness account of small, acephalous Hurutse, Ngwaketse, and Rolong populations peppered along the eastern fringes of the Kalahari Desert, and astride the Molopo River, in the 1820s (cf. Harris 1838:66). These appear to have consisted of little more than dispersed congeries of independent households.

There is also strong indication of variations in lower-order institutional arrangements, especially in political structures and processes. This comes from what seem, at first blush, to be irreconcilable disagreements in the early records. Thus, where Burchell (1824,2:512f) took agnatic rank and relationship to be the principle on which the polity was founded, Campbell (1813:187) stressed the primacy of territoriality and administrative divisions. And where some saw a ruthless autocracy based on chiefly domination of every aspect of social and material life,[6] others were impressed by the consultative and consensual character of Tswana government and by the constraints that it imposed on officeholders.[7] Similarly, for every visitor who affirmed the emerging stereotype that, like all native Africans, the "Bechuana" placed communal over personal concerns, collective rights over private property, ascriptive norms over human achievement and initiative,[8] another spoke of their rampant individualism.[9] Yet others simply could not decide which image *truly* captured the generic African reality— and wrote accounts riddled with inconsistencies. It did not occur to these observers, just as it did not occur to some of the anthropologists and historians who came after them, that such variations and inconsistencies expressed a reasonably systematic pattern of transformation; that the "typical" chief was not a despot or a figurehead any more than Tswana society was reducible to any one stereotypic form. Both political order and social life were, by their very nature, liable to assume widely differing contours over space and time.

This is merely a small sample of a large body of evidence that confirms the mutability of early nineteenth-century Tswana communities. It is demonstrable, moreover, that their twentieth-century counterparts also underwent dramatic transformation. Thus, while a few chiefdoms remained centralized—especially in the Bechuanaland Protectorate but also in South Africa[10]—some dispersed and lost all trace of their previous form; others moved, in either or both directions, between these polarities.[11] Likewise, even though all chiefs were made into civil servants, a small number retained, or actually gained, a good deal of power and wealth. But the majority were emasculated entirely, forced into tragic personal and political oblivion by historical conditions—and often by alcohol, the liquid capital of domination and degradation. Note that these variations occurred across communities with a similar ecology and a shared cultural heritage—communities that, alike, were transformed into impoverished labor reserves at the fringes of the subcontinental political economy.

Nevertheless, and this is the second point of note, although Tswana polities have always shown a penchant for transformation over the short-run, the fluctuations of the Tshidi world during the late nineteenth and early twentieth centuries—the period with which we began—were more extreme than at any other time in their documented history. It is easy enough to find contingent factors that would seem to account for this: among them, the cumulative effects of early evangelism; the establishment, in 1885, of a formal British colonial administration; a rinderpest pandemic in 1896; the opening up of markets in grain and labor and the imposition of monetary taxation all during the same period. But we are less concerned, at this point, with contingent events than with the extended processes of which they were part—in this instance, the gradual engagement between the Tshidi and an expanding universe outside. For these processes raise the problem of the *long durée:* If the internal workings of the Tshidi world were indeed so volatile during this epoch, is there any point in seeking a pattern in its *overall* historical trajectory? Does some longer-term regularity underly the short-term vacillations?

The answer is both yes and no. In the early nineteenth century, the tendency toward centralization, hierarchy, and aggregation predominated across the chiefdoms of the region, although it did not extend to all communities. By the middle of the twentieth century, the inverse had become the case: The majority of polities had veered, in some manner and measure, toward the decentralized mode. And, during the intervening era, as we have said, movement between the two was at its greatest. But the appearance of a linear progression—which points to a correlation between increasing colonial penetration and the decentering of indigenous polities—must be regarded with care. Apart from all else, it reflects a gross statistical tendency, not a historical necessity. The fact is that many similarly structured Tswana chiefdoms, caught up in much the same circumstances, underwent very different transformations; this, if nothing else, establishes that the past and present of these peoples can be accounted for neither by reference to their internal social arrangements alone nor solely by recourse to external conditions or agencies.

Here, then, lies our problem in tangible ethnographic form. First, how do we account for the internal dynamics of the Tshidi world, its dialectics of the short run? Second, how is the long-term trajectory of Tswana economy and society—its simultaneous regularity and diversity—to be grasped and explained? Third, wherein lies the connection between the two *durées,* the long and the short? And, fourth, does this account have any general significance for historical anthropology, for the way in which we may understand other worlds, past and present? In order to address these questions, we break into the long term—arbitrarily, as we must—in the early decades of the nineteenth century, the point at which the Southern Tswana appear, with any frequency, in the documentary chronicles of Africa.

III

Although the early nineteenth-century Tshidi world could be described from a variety of angles, no single "folk model" or "actor perspective" would capture it in its entirety. It would have been perceived in quite different ways from the center or the periphery, the top or bottom; from the position of males or females, young or old, royals or serfs. For now, however, we take as our standpoint the hegemonic scheme of the period: the world as conceived and represented by those who controlled it, the men of the chief's court. For it was their worldview that served, during much of the period, to organize the lived-in environment. In due course we shall show how their ideological dominance was occasionally called into question as alternative maps and ideologies asserted themselves and how, eventually, it was dissipated for all time in the course of processes of the long run.

From within, the early nineteenth-century Tshidi world was seen as ordered yet negotiable, constant in form yet always in flux.[12] Despite the existence of an elaborate repertoire of norms and conventions (later to be formalized as *mekgwa*) and a stable administrative hierarchy (founded on a base of extended households), identity, relations, and rank were frequently objects of contention. Groups and alliances, too, seem to have been regarded as ephemeral expressions of coincident interest.[13] The dualistic, ambiguous quality of the Tshidi universe grew out of an ensemble of signs and categories, ordering principles implicit in the practices of everyday life. These signs and categories have been detailed elsewhere; here it is sufficient to note that they inscribed a contradiction at the core of the social world— a contradiction that not only motivated human action but also, in so doing, shaped manifest political and economic arrangements.

This may be illuminated with reference to two ethnographic fragments. The first is that the social world was founded on a thoroughgoing—indeed, hegemonic—distinction between agnation and matrilaterality (see, e.g., Mackenzie 1883:227). The contrast, which had wide symbolic and practical resonances, may be traced to the uterine house: to the difference between fraternal ties, the source of rank and rivalry, and the brother-sister bond, the essence of moral unity and material solidarity. Agnation was the dominant ideology in terms of which social units were defined and free men ranked. In centralized communities, it regulated the passage of property, of all positions in the administrative hierarchy, and of most forms of social value.[14] This is not to say that the rules governing status were beyond negotiation. Quite the opposite, they laid down the conventions with respect to which political rivals struggled for control over people and possessions;[15] as they strove to "build themselves up" in a hostile social field, adult males put these cultural means to work in the effort to manage political complexity and clarify ambiguous relations.

For Tshidi, then, agnation denoted ties of rivalry and inimical interest between ranked, but broadly equal, persons. These ties, we emphasize, were not contained within corporate lineages. Descent groups here were little more than genealogically defined aggregations, seniority in them being reckoned by extension from the person recognized as the most senior at any moment (cf. Kuper 1975a). But factions did arise within them, and patterns of internal stratification did express the political fortunes of their members. As all this suggests, agnation mapped out the domain of public activity, a quintessentially political context, forged by male connections, wherein some men sought to enhance their standing by "eating" others and where sorcery accusations were endemic.[16]

If agnation was associated with rank and rivalry, maleness and malevolence, public space and political processes, matrilaterality had exactly the opposite connotations. It had its origins in female-centered relations, in the privacy of the house and its confines,[17] and reached its zenith in the bonds between a mother's brother and his sister's children. Unlike agnatic ties, which were always ranked and open to management, these bonds were unranked and nonnegotiable. This was reflected both in kin terminology (see Brown 1926:55–57), and in a lifelong series of gift exchanges. Not only did maternal linkage imply supportiveness and complementarity—a man and his mother's brother never fight, went an old saying—but individual fortunes, especially in dealing with agnatic conflict, were held to depend on the connivance of matrilateral kin (Molema n.d.[a]; cf. Mackenzie 1871:410f; 1883:226f). Hence, in recalling the careers of persons dead or alive, Tshidi rarely failed to mention the part played by *bomalome* ("mother's brothers"). This was poignantly symbolized in times of trouble: The only sanctuary to which one might escape, and remain untouched, was the sequestered backyard (*segotlo*) of a maternal kinswoman.[18] Those sentenced to death in the chief's court, it was said, were set free if they were able to reach the *segotlo* of the ruler's mother. Matrilaterality, in short, was a prime source of social value, being the one mode of relationship that differentiated men from their agnates—with whom they had to compete for everything else. Finally, the opposition between agnation and matrilaterality was marked by contrast to affinity, seen here as egalitarian and cooperative, and remote agnation, a residual class of ties beyond the field of close kin.

These categories, however, must be understood in light of a second ethnographic fragment: that, throughout the nineteenth and early twentieth centuries, Tshidi men—particularly royal men—encouraged marriage with close cousins, including father's brother's daughters (J. L. Comaroff 1973:Chap. 4). It is by now an anthropological truism that unions among close patrikin yield intricate webs of ambiguous relations[19]— multiple bonds that are at once agnatic, matrilateral, and affinal. Such relations are said to blur the boundaries of descent groups and segments within them; to contrive social fields of bewildering complexity, in which people are interconnected in numerous and diverse ways; to place great emphasis on the bilateral kindred as a reservoir of active kinship bonds; to throw the onus for building effective social ties upon individuals and their domestic units. As this suggests, too, the individuation of households and the atomization of the social field counteract hierarchical divisions within the society at large.

With historical hindsight, it appears that close-kin marriage implanted a particular paradox at the heart of the Tshidi world: Multiple bonds conflated modes of relationship that, in this context, were flatly contradictory. As we have said, and as nineteenth-century ritual practice underscored (J. Comaroff 1985:Chap. 4), agnation and matrilaterality stood in stark symbolic and social contrast to one another. And yet prevailing marriage arrangements ensured that few ties could "objectively" be either one or the other. How could this be? How could such irreconcilable forms of social linkage coexist in a single relationship? The answer was that they could not. As Tshidi men often told themselves and others—in various media, including genealogies—no bond could be both hostile and supportive, politically negotiable and morally unambiguous (Matthews n.d.). Then, as now, Setswana had no term for "multiple relative" (Brown

1926:55f; Schapera 1953:43f). Here, in other words, was a disjunction between cultural categories and social realities. Its corollary was that all relations had to be reduced to something, to one thing or another, in the practical flow of everyday life.

The very construction of the Tshidi world, then, *demanded* that men (it was a gender-specific activity) manage relations and identities—a fact that conduced to the fluidity, ambiguity, and evanescence of their social lives. Moreover, because relations could not easily be fixed by ascription or genealogy, they had to be negotiated with reference to some set of received signs. We have analyzed those signs elsewhere. Here it is enough to say that when a household emerged as clearly subordinate or superordinate to another, where the bond between their heads became so unequal as to preclude rivalry, their matrilateral connection was marked, with considerations of generation and gender deciding the precise labels to be applied. By contrast, where kinsmen were more equal, the agnatic component tended to take precedence, the terms of relative seniority expressing the current state of power relations among them. Affinity, in turn, seems to have been stressed as long as a partnership of equivalent interest obtained between those involved, whereas remote agnation described attachments that had lapsed. Of course, the parties to a relationship could contest its content or its designation, there being well-recognized means by which such things might be done.

Herein lies a key to the dualistic nature of the Tshidi world. Because relations and identities were contradictory, men could not avoid acting on the social field—although, it hardly needs saying, this was not a matter of mere personal volition. Nor, *pace* Leach (see Chapter 1), was it the reflex of some "very general human motive." Rather, it flowed from the particular character of the social world, its hegemonic forms and practices. At the same time, because these relations and identities had constantly to be negotiated in terms of prevailing cultural categories—otherwise they had no social currency—they had ultimately to be defined with reference to conventional usage. Thus a man and his mother's brother did not fight; had they, they would have been seen as agnates, not matrilaterals. That this was because of a tautological connection between culture and practice is neither here nor there. The fact is that the world could, and did, appear ordered yet unfixed, highly structured yet easily altered by the protean effects of human agency.

These same conventions and categories also shaped purposive activity and the values to which it was directed. For example, the negotiation of status among men—and the efforts of rivals to cast a net of social and economic debt over one another—flowed from the fact that agnatic rank had the capacity to determine rights over property, position, and people. Likewise, because matrilateral ties were a vital resource in the pursuit of material and political success, they were carefully cultivated, even though it took time, prestations, and perhaps marriage. As this suggests, the optimal achievement of social practice was to "eat" an agnatic kinsman so thoroughly that he became a matrilateral client—thereby replacing competition over status and possessions with a tie of complementary (and distinctly unequal) interest.[20]

If relations among kin held the key to social value, marriage and affinity offered a ready context for their negotiation. Among Tshidi there was a preference for *both* matrilateral cross-cousin (MBD) and patrilateral parallel-cousin (FBD) marriage. But they had contradictory implications—just as, in Southern Tswana culture, matrilaterality and agnation were opposed to one another. Thus, had they occurred alone, as we know from the comparative literature (e.g., Fox 1967:208f; Leach 1951), MBD unions would have entailed aggregation and hierarchy; their recurrence, in fact or in retrospective construction, yielded so-called wife-giving groups in complementary relations to wife-taking ones.[21] Exchanges between equals would, in time, have become alliances between unequals as segmentary units solidified within descent groups. This tendency toward aggregation and hierarchy was actually realized, during the nineteenth and early twentieth centuries, when emergent descent group segments succeeded in transforming agnates into matrilaterals—and then repeated MBD unions with them. FBD marriages, for reasons already given, had the contrary effect: They created multiple ties, emphasized household autonomy and the competitive equality of kin, and fragmented descent groups. In contrast to both, unions between unrelated persons were egalitarian, but neutral in their impact on existing relations.

In the Tshidi world, in sum, there coexisted contradictory tendencies toward aggregation and hierarchy on one hand, and individuation and equality on the other. Patently, these tendencies had to be manifest in some measure *relative* to one another. It simply could not be otherwise. But, given the fluidity of the social field, this measure could not remain constant either. As a result, the concrete shape of Tshidi society varied widely over space and time. And its precise contours could not be determined, mechanically, from the constitution of the "social order" itself: They depended on practice, human agency whose consequences were always in part indeterminate. This is why, as we said earlier, the polity sometimes assumed the form of a hierarchical chiefdom with highly developed descent groups, whereas with others it was marked by an absence of aggregation above the household and by the fragmentation of the community. As we shall see, however, it was not merely the transient surfaces of social life that were prone to change. So, too, were its enduring forms.

But this is only a part of the picture. In introducing the inner workings of this early nineteenth-century Southern Tswana society, we have focused our gaze, albeit schematically, on its social and cultural scaffolding. What we may gloss as "political economy"—an analytic domain inseparable from the integral structure of the Tshidi world as a whole—was equally implicated in the dynamics of the short run.

*   *   *

Tshidi political economy was also founded on the contrast between agnation and matrilaterality, aggregation and individuation, hierarchy and equality. These signs and relations, after all, were the strands that made up the total social fabric (cf. Mauss 1954:1). In respect of material existence, though, the contradictions to which they gave rise were expressed in a tension between centralized chiefly control and the social ecology of domestic production. By convention, although all households were domiciled in villages, cattle were tended at distant posts, beasts hunted in the wild, and agriculture conducted at fields to which producers moved for the annual arable cycle. But the regulation of seasonal movement and its associated activities was a prerogative of the ruler. This was the crux of the tension, for its exercise was in the material *dis*interest of the population at large. Yet it was deeply inscribed in the logic of royal power, being an essential aspect of the processes through which the center dominated the domestic periphery and appropriated its surpluses.

As we would expect from the construction of the social world, relations of production emphasized the household and, within it, the uterine group.[22] Uterine houses cooperated with one another and exchanged labor and goods—usually with matrilaterals because agnates were always suspect—but they seem to have taken great care to guard their autonomy. Within the household, activities were sharply distinguished by gender and generation and were part of a more pervasive division of labor. The Tshidi political economy of the period was based on both agriculture and pastoralism, which were supplemented by hunting and gathering. Agriculture, almost entirely the work of women, yielded the bulk of everyday subsistence. On the other hand, pastoralism, which we discuss in detail in Chapter 5, provided for the ritual diet and for exchange. It was conducted by young boys, impoverished clients, and non-Tswana serfs. But these were not merely distinct and complementary spheres of production and distribution. Female cultivation (and, to a lesser extent, gathering) actually subsidized male activity in the public domain, establishing a material base on which rested the transactions of agnatic politics: Marital alliance, litigation, sacrifice, trading and raiding, and the commerce of gifts and loans needed to gather clients and supporters. To wit, the labor of women, youths, and retainers freed adult men from having to contribute much to the physical reproduction of the household, and allowed them to engage in the public domain—thereby establishing the conditions of possibility for the chiefship and the political processes surrounding it.

In addition to cultivation, women culled the fruits of the veld, just as, among males, pastoralism was augmented by hunting. Those who hunted on a regular basis, Sarwa ("bushmen") serfs, were seen as semi-human creatures; they were allowed into the town only at night to deliver skins, meat, and honey to their masters.[23] Leaving aside Sarwa, though, men and women differed in their relation to the natural world, this being expressed both in their productive activities and in the role of their respective products within the political economy. Women, corn, and bush foods stood in contrast to men, stock, and game as did an unstable mediation of the wild to a potent, stable domination of its forces. As Tswana history demonstrates, livestock could be moved to escape drought and disaster; they were regarded as the epitome of reliability and cultural control (Moffat 1842:451; below, Chapter 5). Grain, on the other hand, was vulnerable to climatic variation and harvests frequently miscarried. Cows predictably yielded milk as a finished food—a regular staple and a salvation when all else failed. The agricultural counterparts, corn porridge or beer, had to be laboriously processed by women before they could be consumed. Indeed, the entire arable cycle was metaphorically linked to procreation, being associated with both instability and the risk of abortion. As this suggests, the position of females was paradoxical. Although they created the material basis for society, they were marginal to the resources and activities most highly valued within its economy of signs and means. In fact, they were thought by male elders to threaten that economy, this being symbolized by the ambiguous quality of their own fertility. Women were held to endanger the well-being (tsididi; literally "coolness") of the community—and especially its life-giving rainfall—by their intrinsic bodily heat, itself an inevitable by-product of procreation.

The fact that livestock gave security in the face of crop failure and forced migration seemed to confirm the view that, compared to agriculture, pastoralism was an activity far more controlled. But the significance of domesticated animals stretched well beyond their worth as food. If the products of cultivation permitted men to subsist largely by the toil of others, cattle were the means for building their social identities.[24] Their herds enabled them to forge and sustain bonds within and between communities, and between the human and superhuman realms; to contract marriages and acquire reproductive rights and labor; and, by making loans (mahisa) to others, to foster relations of inequality and clientship, the currency of political dominance. Thus one of the earliest observers among the neighboring Tlhaping noted that "wealth" and "power" were synonymous and that beasts held the key to both (Burchell 1824,2:272, 347). Cattle had the capacity not only to embody value, but also to transform and revalue social bonds. In the context of exchange, sacrifice, and ritual commensalism they could construct or disentangle human identities and relations, and during rites de passage their slaughter was required to alter social status (Willoughby 1928:187, 196, 330). In short, they were the malleable symbolic media that empowered Tshidi men to shape enduring worlds out of social and spiritual connections.

Aside from their capacity to make and remake individual relations and identities, cattle served as icons of the social order at large. As such, they underpinned the authority of a specific worldview, one that validated a stratified *morafe* ("nation"). Hence they could only be owned and named by adult male citizens, whose personal stamp they bore. They also had to be kept apart from women, to whom, it is said, they had an innate antipathy (Mackenzie 1871:499; cf. Campbell 1822,2:254): As domesticated creatures, they were not fit possessions for beings who were themselves not fully socialized—females, children, and subject peoples of the wild—and who could not, therefore, enjoy the value to which they gave access. Such people were also held to lack the male quality of endurance in time, inscribed in agnatic genealogies and enshrined in ancestorhood. Yet livestock also bore testimony to the fact that, although ostensibly all equal, some men were more equal than others. Not only were the politics of rank conducted through the medium of cattle, but wealth in beasts was taken as a ready measure of social standing. The essence of the chiefship, for example, was that its holder owned the largest herd in the polity (Burchell 1824,2:347; Lichtenstein 1930:413f; see Chapter 5).

If Tshidi economy in the late precolonial era was founded on the complementary opposition of pastoralism and agriculture, wherein lay the contradiction of which we spoke earlier? And what had men's command over the labor of women to do with chiefly control of domestic production? Part of the answer to the second question has already been given. Because it subsidized the activities of males in the public arena, female cultivation was crucial to the production of a centralized polity, and hence to the office at its core. This was symbolically enacted each year: Women were made to plant fields for the ruler before going out to attend to their own. At the same time, however, agriculture here involved dispersal, the very antithesis of centralization. Thus the regulation of movement appeared as a necessary condition for sustaining a concentrated *morafe*—without which the chiefship itself would have been an empty shell. According to the conventions of Southern Tswana political culture, in fact, the power of the sovereign rested on such things as the right to appoint men to positions of authority (see, e.g., Lichtenstein 1930:414), the distribution of land (e.g., Campbell 1822,2:191), the receipt of a tributary portion of the spoils of raiding and hunting (e.g., Burchell 1824,2:545; Livingstone 1857:48), the exclusive mandate to mobilize age regiments for war and public works (e.g., Mackenzie 1871:375f), and a monopoly over external trade (e.g., Burchell 1824,2:539; Campbell 1822,2:194). All of these were held to depend on the continued aggregation of the polity. Nonetheless, as we said earlier, centralization and the royal control of arable rhythms were seen to be in the disinterest of household producers. It is here, not surprisingly, that the contradiction began to express itself.

The tension between central control and the demands of household production took a number of forms, the most concrete of which arose from the brute facts of ecology. In a semiarid region such as this, where rains were unpredictable and liable to fall unevenly over the territory, the timing of agricultural tasks was critical to the size of the yield. The Tswana, whose knowledge of their environment was profound (Livingstone 1857:22), were aware, for example, that each passing day between the first showers and the planting of their gardens diminished their eventual harvest. But it was the chief who, in a ritual pronouncement, "gave out the seed time," the "time for beginning to sow" (Willoughby 1928:226f). Anybody who departed the town before the appointed moment courted severe punishment.

The decision to set in motion the arable cycle, it seems (Molema n.d.[a]), depended on rainfall either at the capital or at the ruler's own holdings; by not allowing women to disperse earlier, he simultaneously gave demonstration of his authority and ensured that the royal lands were worked first (cf. Schapera 1943:184; 1971a:74). Given micro-ecological variations across the chiefdom, however, the delay prevented most households from exploiting optimal productive conditions. Tshidi showed their antagonism to this form of regulation by their readiness to "take to the bush" and, if they could, to establish permanent rural homes. For men who did not depend on the labor of serfs and clients, dispersal seems to have been preferable to living in poverty in the town; the latter, in any case, exposed them to the risk of being "eaten." Thus it is that early observers found some Southern Tswana living in congeries of independent households alongside their fields, with no center whatsoever (above, p. 100).

The existing sociology of production, it would seem, created a dilemma for chiefs. On one hand, the tight supervision of time and movement was vital not only to their exaction of tributary labor, but also to their material and symbolic control of the polity *tout court*. Yet the very exercise of that control threatened to provoke resistance and to encourage the popular proclivity to scatter—thereby undermining the center. As this implies, the struggle between chiefly dominance and domestic self-assertion, between centralization and decentralization, was inescapable. Rulers did not merely have to ward off attempts to dislodge them; they also had to guard against the erosion of the structures and processes on which their office rested. Indeed, this ever-present danger was acknowledged in such ritual contexts as the male initiation and first fruit ceremonies, which posited the power of centripetal forces over the dangers of dissolution (J. Comaroff 1985; cf. Bakhtin 1981:270).

We stress that the contradiction between centralization and decentralization was not reducible to a simple antagonism between chief and populace. For the town was the site of political hierarchy and the context of all social management; hence *any* activity, whether in pursuit of communal prosperity or personal status, tended to affirm hegemonic (that is, concentrated) social arrangements. Processes of disaggregation did the reverse, their localized productive activities and domestic rituals reinforcing a world of dispersed matrilateral connections. In short, the tension inhered in the very *structure* of Tshidi economy and society. Nevertheless, it was expressed most explicitly in the political arena, in which chiefly authority was the constant object of evaluation and negotiation. Although the mechanisms involved are beyond our present scope, vernacular theory had it that the rights of officeholders rose and fell in proportion to their performance, which was most audibly assessed at public assemblies;[25] to be sure, their power *did* vary a great deal within and between reigns. Significantly, where a ruler lost his legitimacy, he would eventually be unable to regulate domicile and movement. It was then that households were most likely to scatter, returning only when centralized control was reestablished. But this was not an all-or-none matter. The *degree* to which domestic units could and did disperse—or, conversely, were held at the core of the polity—reflected subtle fluctuations in chiefly dominance, in the centripetal force of power relations.

Patently, the emergence of a centralized political economy depended, in the first place, on prevailing conditions of possibility within the social world, although any move toward centralization, in turn, transformed that world. Conversely, strong resistance to a chief, arising from within the community, might lead to its social fragmentation. As long as the signs and principles underlying the Tshidi system were reproduced, so too were the contradictions to which they gave rise—and, with them, the potentiality for disaggregation and decentralization. That potentiality could not be eliminated by fiat, even by the most potent of rulers—some of whom went to great lengths to ensure the perpetuity of a centralized polity.

*   *   *

That, in essence, describes the Tshidi world, its dialectics of the short run, during the early nineteenth century. Note how, in analyzing its inner workings, we have emphasized two things above all else. The first is that sociocultural order and political economy were indivisible—as, by extension, were symbolic and material forms. Thus, for instance, the centralized political economy was validated by an authoritative cultural map of the social order, a male-centric scheme that portrayed this order as a series of concentric circles emanating from the chiefship, through the administrative hierarchy, and to the domestic periphery and the wild beyond. It was a map that stood in direct contrast to the universe as perceived from the female-centered courtyard. Nonetheless, the effort, on the part of the dominant, to impose their worldview was an essential aspect of the politics of hegemony; that is, the construction of the universe as a natural order of signs and categories, of relations of production and power.

As this suggests, second, the contemporary Tshidi world is to be analyzed at a series of interconnected levels: as a cultural order of meanings and contrasts; as a social system of relations and contradictions; and as an experiential repertoire of values and constraints, means and ends. The interplay of these dimensions gave meaning and purpose to everyday activity—which, in turn, yielded a range of productive and political configurations. In all this, it should be clear that neither individual nor collective behavior was a simple reflection, a mechanical enactment, of "social structure." Because human agency could and did produce a wide variety of manifest social arrangements, the specific outcomes of historical processes were finally indeterminate. Material contingency and social practice always intervened between structure and event.

This returns us to the one remaining question posed at the outset about the precolonial period: Why was it that centralized polities arose more often—and were more regularly sustained—during that era than in later times? In line with our earlier statement, the answer lies in the interaction between the Tshidi world and the external forces that contained it.

It goes without saying that the Tshidi did not live in isolation in the early nineteenth century. To the contrary, they raided and traded with both Tswana and non-Tswana communities to the north, south, and east. These relations, by and large, were regulated by chiefs and reinforced patterns of centralized authority. Thus rulers might accumulate a fund of power by controlling cross-regional and long-distance trade[26] and by making alliances, marital and military, with neighboring sovereigns.[27] In the late eighteenth century, such ties among Rolong leaders in the Molopo region gave rise to what some writers have termed a "confederation" (Legassick 1969a:42). Chiefs also tended to cooperate to prevent subjects from dispersing, thereby holding at bay subversive centrifugal forces; they further consolidated their position by seizing the spoils of war, especially serfs and cattle.[28] To all this was added, in the 1820s and 1830s, a monopoly of the services of the first missionaries, including their guns and technological skills.

Although chiefs were always vulnerable to the tensions in their social world, these historical factors ensured that Tshidi society was more internally stratified, circa 1830, than it was ever to be again. Colonization would collapse many of the indigenous foundations of hierarchy and reduce much of the population to dependence on the labor market. In the early nineteenth century, asymmetries of gender and age were particularly marked, being symbolically authorized by rituals that did not occur in a decentralized polity and were to be submerged after overrule (J. Comaroff 1985). During this early period, moreover, social inequalities took the form of class distinctions; that is, of major differences in access to the means of production and redistribution. For the control over serf labor and trade goods enjoyed by rulers, senior royals, and commoner head-men—and orchestrated through the chief*ship*—contributed to the subordination of the rest of the population. Indeed, as a nineteenth-century chief told a visiting missionary (Campbell 1822,1:249, 268, 316; 2:194), the trappings of government were closely tied to the regular exaction of tax and tribute. This, in turn, promoted the political processes associated with centralization: agnatic rivalry over position and power, increased rates of close-kin marriage, a stress on the creation of clientage, and so on. In sum, the realization of a centralized polity was favored, if not guaranteed, by the engagement of the local system with an external context that gave a dominant class enhanced means to control the flow of value.

IV

We turn, then, to processes of the long run.

The remaining years of the nineteenth century saw the gradual absorption of Tswana into the concentric spheres of colonial domination: the subcontinental economy, the British imperial domain, and the expanding world system. From the perspective of the Tshidi, this process had three interrelated aspects. The first grew out of the establishment of a mission amongst them and had both a material and a symbolic dimension. The Methodist vision of civilization with which they were confronted owed much to the rise of English industrial capitalism. It stressed, among other things, private property and liberal individualism, the nuclear family and its gendered division of labor, commodity production and the Protestant work ethic, literacy and self-improvement. In addition, the evangelists advocated the plough and other far-reaching technical innovations (see Chapter 9). Their immediate success—as measured in numbers of converts or in the removal of such "barbarisms" as bridewealth, polygyny, and cousin marriage—was distinctly mixed. But they were the vanguard of colonization and laid the ground for thoroughgoing transformations. Specifically, (1) the Protestant church became an alternative focus for social identity and political mobilization, especially, in the first instance, among marginal members of the community; (2) the literate leadership of the congregation, equipped with mercantile and paraprofessional skills and ambitions, became the core of a small petite bourgeoisie and of an anti-chiefly faction; (3) the introduction of the plough increasingly drew men and draught beasts into agriculture and altered the division of labor, sharpening the contradiction between household production and centralized control; and (4) the inculcation of the work ethic, and of the value of money, prepared Tshidi for entry into the commodity economy (Comaroff and Comaroff 1991).

The second facet of the colonization of the Tshidi world lay in the expansion of the regional economy and the rapid growth, from the late nineteenth century onward, of its mining and industrial sectors. The effects of this expansion on rural communities are by now familiar. It led to much of the black population being forced into the labor market, to their impoverishment, and to their confinement in reservations from which migration could be regulated: in short, to the origins of modern apartheid. The means by which this was effected are thoroughly documented.[29] Above all, they depended on the third dimension of the process of domination, the political agency of the colonial and postcolonial states.

From the 1850s onward, the Tshidi, encouraged by some of the missionaries, had sought British protection from the encroaching Boer settlers; the latter had tried increasingly to exact tribute and labor from the Southern Tswana and to extend political suzerainty over them.[30] With the active connivance of the "humanitarian imperialist" Reverend John Mackenzie (Sillery 1971), British Bechuanaland was created in 1885, further integrating the Tshidi into the regional political economy.[31] The colonial administration, and later the South African government, imposed taxes and levies on them, compelling many to seek wage work. State intervention also had an impact on internal political processes. Although "indirect rule" ostensibly left the polity intact, in practice it denuded chiefs of much of their real authority, putting an end to such activities as war and raiding—and, with them, the access of ruling cadres to their major external source of wealth and power. In addition, the royal trade monopoly was broken by colonially licensed white merchants, who bought and retailed grain and stock on terms disadvantageous to local producers (Matthews n.d.). Finally, the chiefship itself was gradually hedged about by limitations of jurisdiction. Rulers were reduced from tribute receivers to tax collectors, from politicians to civil servants, from the highest judges in their own legal order to lower functionaries in a state judiciary (J. L. Comaroff 1974).

Slowly but surely these colonizing forces were to erode the mechanisms underlying the centralization of the Tshidi world. Nevertheless, for the time being, ruling cadres still commanded greater resources than did others. They still monopolized the distribution of land and positions of authority and regulated local politico-ritual institutions; some of them also earned new forms of wealth from commerce and salaried work. And, by acting as brokers between government and population, chiefs and literate elites were often able to benefit themselves. Furthermore, everyday life continued to draw on familiar kinship categories, marriage arrangements, cattle transactions, and so on (Comaroff and Roberts 1981:Chaps. 2–7). Hence, although internal political processes were symbolically and materially undermined by the colonial state and the migrant labor system, their principal *forms* were sustained—with one essential rider: Because a centralized polity was increasingly difficult to sustain, the contradictions in the social order became more acutely manifest.

Thus it is that, by the turn of the twentieth century, the Tshidi universe was in great flux, caught up in the movement between centralization and fragmentation, hierarchy and individuation. These rapid and often dramatic swings, in sum, were a product of the encounter between external forces and the dynamics of the local system. As those forces made themselves felt, they altered Tshidi society—but in ways mediated by its internal forms. Nor is this singular: It is in the nature of processes of articulation between global and local systems that the latter affect the course of history at the same time as they are remade by it (J. L. Comaroff 1982).

It becomes clear, then, why Tshidi economy and society took on such diverse appearances at this precise period. These were the transformations of a historical system with a dynamic internal structure, itself undergoing long-term change by virtue of its engagement with the universe beyond. Such transformations were expressed in a wide range of everyday arrangements and practices. Take, for example, the domestic and public domains, family and household composition, and class and gender relations, all of which were affected by the fluctuations of the Tshidi world as a whole (J. L. Comaroff 1987a). It follows from our earlier account that, when this world was at its most centralized and hierarchical, the division between public and private sectors was highly developed. Social life was marked by intense communal activity and by a heightened concentration on agnatic politics. Because it was rank in the administrative hierarchy that gave access to value—to control over people and property, land and labor, courts and councils—political centralization, agnatic politics, and an elaborated public sector reinforced one another. By extension, too, the greater the degree of centralization, the tighter the control exercised over domestic units. Not unexpectedly, then, a well-developed public sector also tended to stress the opposition between agnation and matrilaterality, collective enterprise and household autonomy.

By contrast, under conditions of decentralization, the public domain barely existed and the symbolic and material trappings of chiefly domination withered. With much of the citizenry dispersed, they seldom took part in political activities and were rarely drawn into formal dispute;

indeed, it was their withdrawal from these activities that atomized the social field in the first place. Communal undertakings, limited to the management of such events as death and marriage, were shared among neighboring households, linked usually by matrilateral ties. During these periods, officeholding was largely a nominal affair, the indigenous state apparatus being virtually moribund; tribute could not be collected; and public meetings were infrequent and poorly attended. As this suggests, the processes by which social units were incorporated into the administrative hierarchy were effectively suspended. The major form of interaction beyond the family occurred over the exchange of labor and goods—and, for some, involvement in small Christian sects. These sects, utterly disengaged from both chiefship and mission church, were structured in a manner strikingly akin to domestic units (J. Comaroff 1974; Pauw 1960a; see Chapter 3).

A parallel contrast underlay family and domestic organization. In the decentralized mode, when household autonomy was at its most marked, domestic units usually included siblings and their families, aging parents, and other kin. But, as we can discern from genealogies, the rate of cousin marriage tended to be low, so a dense network of multiple bonds was less likely to envelop these units; the corollary was that the mechanisms that integrated them into the polity, and produced rivalries and inequalities between them, were eclipsed. As a result, they were as liable to interact with others on the basis of convenience as kinship. Within the group itself, the allocation of tasks by gender and age was less sharply drawn. Although herding was still done primarily by men and domestic work by women, agricultural and other enterprises were undertaken together, a tendency that increased with the commercialization of farming (J. L. Comaroff n.d.). Decisions concerning the use of resources were also made by adult members of both sexes, rather than by the male head alone, and heritable property was kept undivided and was commonly managed. Given patterns of migrant labor, moreover, the group and its possessions were often left under female control for long periods and, on the death of the head, were likely to remain so rather than to pass immediately to an heir. Yet in a centralized community, inter- and intra-household relations, like the division of labor at large, harked back to early nineteenth-century patterns— except that inequalities between men were translated into the currency of commodities and commercial agriculture.

Colonial overrule and the spread of capitalism certainly intensified the tensions of the Tshidi world, playing into its internal contradictions and reaching into every aspect of social and cultural being. But their more enduring effect was to embed the Tshidi at the "periphery" of a regional political economy, enclosing them in an all-embracing structure of domination. As men were drawn into commodity production and wage labor, they found it necessary to sell ever larger proportions of the domestic yield in a market that offered them decreasing returns (cf. Palmer and Parsons 1977). Matthews (n.d.) gives a graphic description of the progressive impoverishment of Tshidi families in just this predicament during the early twentieth century. Monocropping magnified their vulnerability to risk, and women lost their former influence over the distribution of household produce. The basis was laid for the thoroughgoing dependency of both sexes on the labor market. Once again, the dialectics of the short run—in this case, during the colonial epoch—became enmeshed in longer-term historical movements.

V

The story does not end there, however. For the Tshidi social order was to undergo further change as it was drawn still more tightly into a regional system dominated by the South African state. Especially after 1948, the latter exerted growing control over the fabric of everyday life, denying chiefs and headmen any effective authority and laying waste the structures that had given form to internal social processes (J. L. Comaroff 1974; 1976). Moreover, by imposing additional taxes and levies, and by allowing pressure on badly eroded land to reach unprecedented levels, the state seriously undermined both agricultural and pastoral production. With the emasculation of the local-level political economy, conventional forms of action finally lost their salience. There was no point in social management, for instance, once its cultural context and material basis had been destroyed. As this implies, the mechanisms underlying centralization were to disappear entirely. Yet the rationale for perennial dispersal—optimal domestic production in a dryland ecology—had also been superseded. With the diminishing prospect of wresting a living from infertile ground, many ceased to plough, or cultivated on a very small scale. By the 1950s, the internal dynamics of the Tshidi world had been fundamentally reconstructed. The basic principles of the precolonial society no longer obtained. What remained was a dreadfully poor community with no choice but to depend on the labor market for survival.

At the same time, the formation of such a community is never the mere sediment of historical processes centered elsewhere. The late Tshidi world was not simply a product of the implacable march of colonial capitalism. Albeit radically transformed, its inner workings retained some of their long-standing elements, if in rather different combination. The indigenous system had become indissolubly engaged with the South African state not just to be defaced by it, but also to interact with it in a reciprocal, if highly unequal, relationship. For example, Tshidi domestic groups, still identifiable as households in terms of precolonial sociocultural categories, came to stand in opposition not to the chief's court, but to other centers: the Witwatersrand, heart of the migrant labor market; Pretoria, hub of the apartheid regime; and the nearby white towns, places of proximate employment and seats of local government. It was the inclusion of these domestic units within the wider context—in a new mode of hierarchical centralization—that now determined the conditions of Tshidi existence.

From their "peripheral" perspective, contemporary Tshidi—at least those who had not thrown in their lot with the "homeland"—opposed the forces of the oppressive regime. And, even though the latter came to monopolize control over the production and exchange of value, Tshidi, like other black South Africans in the late twentieth century, struggled ceaselessly, if in varying idioms, to regain command over their everyday world. Let us examine the dynamics of this latter-day transformation in more detail.

At the time of our first fieldwork among the Tshidi in 1969, the community was still rooted in the mudbrick settlement of Mafikeng, established on the Molopo River in the nineteenth century. The royal court and "tribal" office continued to administer what remained of local authority. A half-mile from the northwest fringe of this settlement—itself now sprawled over a large area and housing more than 20,000 souls—were the headquarters of the so-called government of Bophuthatswana, the Tswana ethnic "homeland" that now subsumed the Tshidi into the political geography of apartheid. From here the majority of the population migrated to white farms and industrial centers as "foreign nationals."[32] Only a small proportion of Tshidi—a petite bourgeoisie of local traders and clerical workers and, recently, a miniscule middle class—were able to escape the cycle of wage labor and failing agricultural production (Breutz 1956:53). By 1970, no more than 45 percent of households could plough at all, and of these less than half achieved yields sufficient for their basic needs. What is more, only 26 percent owned or had rights in cattle. In such economic circumstances, rural poverty becomes both cause and effect of migration in search of work.

The structural conditions obtaining within South Africa also contributed to the internal polarization of peripheral communities. As penury and dependency increased, so did the gulf between the proletarianized majority and the few with independent access to the means of production. It was mainly the latter who were in a position to take advantage of the limited material prospects provided by the establishment of Bophuthatswana.[33] By the late 1980s, a postmodern skyline towered over the former capital, proclaiming the prominence of the new black *bantustan* elite—though for the rank and file, stark poverty militated against any real accumulation. Although wages were insufficient for most breadwinners to support their families, the collapse of African agriculture ensured that they could not survive *without* selling their labor—thereby entrapping them in the classical predicament, the tragic symbiosis, of a peasant-worker existence. Furthermore, indigenous patron-client links had all but disappeared, and the government had shut down the mission schools, former avenues to higher education and advancement. Short-term labor contracts and woefully inadequate disability payments, pensions, and countryside health services threw much of the burden of reproducing the work force on the rural households themselves. As this suggests, the modern Tshidi community— and, at the local level, it remained definitively Tshidi, not a generic Tswana community—no longer constituted a "system" in its own right. Fragmented, it now took its place amidst others at the lowest levels of the political economy of late twentieth-century South Africa.

These conditions, and especially the symbiosis of wage labor and subsistence production, implied complex cultural transformations. Particularly significant was the effect of commodity production and money on Tshidi notions of value. This was tied to the dramatic decline in the ownership of cattle, a factor of importance in light of their material and symbolic centrality in earlier times (see Chapter 5). Although beasts became reducible to cash, and were bought and sold under certain circumstances, they remained opposed to money in the perception of many Tshidi, serving still as the prime repositories of value and the preferred mode of investment among older male members of the elite. For the impoverished majority, they served as generalized symbols of a lost world of political and economic independence, the seemingly unobtainable tokens of freedom from the need to earn wages. The ideals of control and self-realization embodied by animals took on new salience in contrast to the depersonalizing experience of the industrial workplace and the eccentric, uncontrollable flow of cash. One of the few contexts in which Tshidi still transacted stock in the 1970s was marriage. But there had been a general decline in the rate of formal unions over the previous twenty-five years, most notably among those dependent on migrant labor. Conversely, there had been a rise in transient liaisons, widely referred to as *"vat en sit"* or *"donkie trou"* (Afrikaans for "snatch and squat" and "donkey marriage"), which evoke the unceremonious coupling of animals. This, it is not surprising, was accompanied by an increase both in the number of children born out of wedlock and in the proportion of female-headed domestic groups (see Chapter 6).

The rise in the number of female-headed households was closely linked to the declining significance of agnation in Tshidi social life. As noted above, with the eclipse of the chiefship and the administrative hierarchy, the ends and means of agnatic politics were made largely irrelevant—so much so that the small Christian elite, with its ideology of individual self-determination and its commitment to private enterprise, shunned the "tribal" center entirely. In the upshot, matrilaterality emerged as the primary principle of social connection. Not that this was unpredictable: The female-headed household was a transformation of the uterine house, the "atom" of structure in earlier times. This grouping, with its web of supportive ties, became the major unit of interaction and cooperation for those who remained in the countryside, its composition bearing mute testimony to the coercive processes that drew adult males not to the chiefly court, but into the national economic vortex. For labor migration was, and is, a mode of forced mobility from periphery to core. As such, it traced out a poignant historical irony. Before, in the concentrated Tshidi state, the chief had regulated space and time, supervising the movement of female producers outward to their fields while holding men at the center. Now the South African government ordered space and time, attempting to direct male workers outward to the center while holding women at the periphery. In each case, the control over movement was exercised in order to extract surplus labor. The difference, of course, is that the center of the past had become the periphery of the present, and those who dominated then were subservient now. For most Tshidi, these have become the symptoms of a world gone sadly awry, its wretchedness spelled out in hunger and poverty, sickness and mortality.

But how, finally, did they react to their predicament? With the demise of indigenous political structures and processes, and the ruthless suppression of African nationalist movements, there was no public arena in which they might engage directly with the pressures that dominated their lives. Local-level politics in the late 1960s, to be sure, were oddly divorced from broader social issues. At least in their overt form, they turned around the residual proceedings of the chiefly court, now the preserve of aging royals, who took care of the menial tasks left to "tribal administrations" by the authorities. By the 1970s, aside from formal and usually ineffective protests made by this body against the encroaching institutions of the *bantustan* government, the struggle against the apartheid regime had dispersed itself thinly and unevenly through the population. In this struggle, the Protestant church provided certain resources. In spite of its role in colonialism, Christianity had had contradictory historical implications. In addition to fostering an educated black elite, the mission had established the first context from which Africans could contest their domination. And, for a long time, it afforded Tshidi the terms with which to conceive of their place in an increasingly repressive society—although it never did forge an articulate class consciousness. From the first, the liberal struggle for civil rights in South Africa in general, and among the Southern Tswana in particular, was framed rhetorically and organizationally in the forms of European Protestantism.

For those most dispossessed in neocolonial South Africa, however, less orthodox forms of the Western Protestant tradition laid the basis for a practical expression of defiance. As we saw in Chapter 3, there was a striking profusion of churches in Mafikeng in the late 1960s. While the first Methodist building still stood near the chief's court, and continued to represent elite Christian orthodoxy, a clamorous throng of small sects had sprung up around it. These "Zionist" or "Spirit" churches were led by inspired "prophets," who were likened to ritual specialists and senior kin rather than Protestant ministers. In their effort to regain some measure of control over a runaway world, these sects tried to construct a Kingdom of Zion by building on the social forms and fertile symbols of the uterine house. Thus, for example, their members addressed each other as matrikin, and together they undertook many of the cooperative activities of the homestead. In so doing, they, like precolonial households, sought to elude the constraints of central authority—except that the latter was now situated above and beyond the local community, its power underwritten by forces of global scale.

All Tshidi, Zionists and others, strove to formulate the tension between center and periphery, the dominant and the subordinate, in explicably familiar terms. Southern Tswana, in common with other peoples of the region, often referred to themselves as feminized, "eaten"—as having to "live in sin . . . with a white master," from whose degrading embrace they tried, by various means, to escape (cf. Fry 1976:112). Here, then, was the denouement of Tshidi history in the late twentieth century: the attempt to act upon the structures of the long *durée,* the external forces of the world outside, by reducing them to the terms of the local world—the internal forms, that is, of the short run.

VI

The point of the present analysis lies at three distinct levels. At the first level, we have addressed a number of specific issues concerning the nature of the Tshidi world: What, for example, accounts for its capacity, in the past, to take on such contrasting appearances, to undergo such palpable transformations over the short run? How did it engage with external forces and agencies, over the longer term, to produce social arrangements at once diverse in content and yet, in crucial respects, similar in form? Why should its internal contradictions have expressed themselves with varying degrees of intensity during different epochs? In posing these questions, though, our intention has not merely been ethnographic. We seek, rather, to open up an enquiry—a debate, perhaps—at a second and higher analytic level. The agenda: to rethink the conception of "social system" in a manner equal to the demands of a neomodern anthropology.

As we noted at the start, it is not only the critical debates of the postfunctionalist—or, more recently, poststructuralist—era that call into doubt the worn-out paradigms of modernist African sociology. Recall that Evans-Pritchard, with whom we began, long ago posed the same challenge, citing the proven dynamism of local systems and the impact on them of the outside world. As this suggests, the image of "traditional" societies, of "cold" cultures caught up in endless cycles of social and/or semantic reproduction, is pure fiction. And poor fiction at that. But, and this was our opening proposition, the corollary ought not to be a quest for amended versions of old models and methods. It should be, instead, an effort to rethink our analytic repertoire sui generis. Here we have taken a few tentative steps in that direction—toward a conception of the social world (1) that addresses, simultaneously, its symbolic and material, social and cultural, aspects; (2) that treats its enduring forms and its everyday practices as mutually constitutive; (3) that views its internal dynamics and its external relations as inseparable elements of its total historicity; (4) that allows human action, and the social phenomena created by it, to be both determined and indeterminate, purposive and unintended, coherent and fragmentary. Here, then, lies the third and most general level of our enterprise: the pursuit of an anthropology capable of capturing the dialectical movement of history in which, as Dumont (1957:21) puts it, society reveals itself. That, finally, is the long and short of it.

Notes

1. It was Evans-Pritchard (e.g., 1961:20) who, most insistently among anthropologists, repeated Maitland's dictum (1936:249) that "anthropology must choose between being history and being nothing." It was he, too, who first inverted this dictum, arguing that, equally, "history must choose between being social anthropology or being nothing" (1961:20).

2. Fortes (1953b:42), for example, retorted that the task of anthropology ought to be restricted to "the investigation of mechanism and function in the *short-run* working of society" (our emphasis). Not coincidentally, this followed a thinly veiled attack on Evans-Pritchard: "So insidious, so apparently self-evident is the belief that the only satisfactory way of explaining social institutions is by some kind of history, that the most acute thinkers succumb to it. It has been a stumbling-block to clear thinking in the anthropological sciences for a century" (1953b:19; also 1953b:30). Nor did Fortes have the "conjectural history" of evolutionism in mind here; the objection was intended to apply to the "true historical method, applicable where there are documents and records" (1953b:29).

3. A similar point lies behind Shorter's critique (1972:141–142) of Turner's analysis of ritual processes among the Ndembu.

4. Note that, although we use an ethnic label here, we do not take it to refer to a "primordial" identity (see Chapter 2). Quite the opposite: In *Of Revelation and Revolution* we trace the development of ethnic consciousness among "the Tswana" to its historical roots in the colonial encounter. It is partly because we take that analysis as read and partly for

descriptive convenience that we use the proper noun without further qualification in this chapter.

5. For evidence on this point, see, for example, Moffat (1842) and Brown (1926:209f). On the fluctuations of chiefly power and authority, see also Solomon (1855:46f) and Campbell (1822,1:288f; 2:57, 154f).

6. The best examples, perhaps, are Lichtenstein (1930,2:414), Campbell (1822,1:314–316) and Burchell (1824,2:532, 544).

7. See, for instance, Barrow (1806:399), Moffat (1842:248f) and, for the Seleka Rolong at Thaba 'Nchu later in the century, the visiting political novelist, Anthony Trollope (1878,2:283). As noted above (n.5), Solomon and Campbell also observed the possibility of great variations in chiefly authority, between "despotic" rule at one extreme and rule by consultation at the other.

8. This view was held by most nineteenth-century missionaries to the Tswana—see, for example, Moffat (1842), Broadbent (1865), and Mackenzie (1883)—many of whom saw their task to be the inculcation of "healthy individualistic competition" (Mackenzie quoted in Dachs 1972:652). It is also true, however, that members of the Tshidi Christian elite internalized this view for themselves. The most remarkable case of this is to be found in Molema (1920:115f), whose own later writings (e.g., 1966) provided strong counterevidence for the stereotype.

9. Most notably, Burchell (1824,2:554) and Campbell (1822,1:243). It is interesting that some of the same missionaries who spoke of the absence of private property among the Tswana, and of their great stress on collective concerns (above, n. 8), also detected a strong individualistic streak in them: See Mackenzie (1871:402, 501f) and Livingstone (1857:21).

10. See, for example, the writings of Schapera (annotated in 1953), especially on the Ngwato, Ngwaketse, Kgatla, and Kwena chiefdoms.

11. See, for example, Pauw (1960b) on the Tlhaping, Ashton (1937) on the Tawana, Werbner (1971) on the Khurutse, and, for general discussion, J. L. Comaroff (1976:71–74).

12. This comes through clearly in many early sources, among them, Burchell (1824,2:552f), Moffat (1842:254), Livingstone (1857:21), and, somewhat later, Mackenzie (1871:501f, 371–452; 1883:227–262). For analytic discussion, see, for example, Comaroff and Comaroff (1991:Chap. 4).

13. We infer this from a number of sources, including Moffat (1842:248, 389), Solomon (1855:47), Mackenzie (in Dachs 1975:10), and Burchell (1824,2:546, 551f).

14. For exemplary evidence, from various times during the nineteenth century, see Burchell (1824,2:441), Moffat (1842), Campbell (1813; 1822), and Mackenzie (1871; 1883); also, from a different perspective, see Molema (1920:113f)

15. For a detailed analysis of agnatic rules and political processes in Tshidi history, see J. L. Comaroff (1973:Chaps. 4–7; 1978). Mackenzie (1871:410ff; 1883:231f) provides a comparative account of Ngwato agnatic politics in the second half of the nineteenth century.

16. On agnatic rivalry and sorcery among Southern Tswana, see Campbell (1822,1:314f), Burchell (1824,2:551), Brown (1926:134f, 152f), Mackenzie (1883:236), and Holub (1881,1:333f).

17. For analyses of the contemporary social and symbolic character of the house, see, for example, J. Comaroff (1985:Chap. 3) and Comaroff and Roberts (1981:Chap. 2).

18. A vivid comparative case—as Mackenzie's writings show (e.g., 1871:410, 419, 436)—is provided by Sekgoma, the Ngwato chief for more than thirty years (1835–1857, 1858–1866, 1873–1875; see Schapera 1938:303). Whenever he found himself in political trouble, which was often, Sekgoma took to his mother's courtyard for safety. It was there that he consorted with his allies and shaped his political schemes. Tshidi tell similar stories, both historical and apocryphal, about their own royals.

19. There is a large anthropological literature on the social implications of endogamy and patrilateral parallel-cousin marriage. Perhaps the clearest statements, however, are those in Murphy and Kasdan (1959; 1967) and Barth (1973); on the Tshidi case, see, for example, Comaroff and Comaroff (1981).

20. A dramatic example is provided by the booMakgetla, once senior members of the Tshidi line who were relegated to the status of *bomalome* (MBs) to the chiefs and became recognized as a separate descent group of "wife-givers" to them (see J. L. Comaroff 1973:Chaps. 5, 6).

21. We use the terms "wife-giving" and "wife-taking" here—despite their unfortunate general connotations—because one of the *systematic* implications of MBD marriage was a tendency toward the domination of women by men (see below).

22. We base our summary account of the contemporary Tshidi economy on a wide variety of sources, including Bain (in Lister 1949:55), Barrow (1806:394), Burchell (1824,2:346f, 358, 425, 523, 564), Campbell (1813:184, 201; 1822,1:63f, 2:207–219; n.d.:64), Lichtenstein (1973:66f, 76f; 1930,2:409f), Moffat (1842:398f), and Solomon (1855:44, 62).

23. The evidence on servitude in nineteenth-century Southern Tswana chiefdoms is copious, if not altogether consistent. For an instructive sample, see Holub (1881,1:258, 345f), Stow (1905:425f), Moffat (1842:8), and Mackenzie (1871:128f, 368; 1883:57f).

24. On the social value of cattle, see, for example, Brown (1926:92f). Campbell (1822,2:210–211) records a telling vignette about a man who, found guilty of theft, was put to death because he had no beasts with which to make restitution. His two more fortunate accomplices, stock owners both, were spared their lives.

25. For an analysis of these mechanisms, see J. L. Comaroff (1975). Primary source material on the negotiability of chiefly authority, and its expression in public discourse, is to be found in Solomon (1855:46f), Campbell (1822,1:138, 153, 288f, 314f; 2:6, 57, 154f), and Moffat (1842:248f, 289, 389).

26. The documentary record on this is very full. For just a small sample, see Smith (1939,1:278), Burchell (1824,2:537ff), Mackenzie (1883:59–61), and Campbell (1822,1:249; 2:194).

27. Again, there is too much evidence for complete annotation here. But see, for example, Campbell (n.d.:51; 1813:190). Mackenzie (1871:371ff; 1883:225f); Moffat (1842:passim); also, J. L. Comaroff (1973:Chaps. 5, 6).

28. By all accounts, the sheer magnitude of these activities was greater during this period than at any other time in history. See, for example, Smith (1939,1:408) and Burchell (1824,2:347f); all the early missionaries comment at length on this, however.

29. So thoroughly documented, in fact, that it is unnecessary to annotate sources here. For those unfamiliar with the recent social history and anthropology of colonial Southern Africa, the *Journal of Southern African Studies,* published since 1974, will provide an adequate introduction.

30. For accounts written from a wide variety of perspectives, see Molema (1966), Sillery (1952; 1971), Matthews (1945), Maylam (1980), Mackenzie (1887), and Theal (1926).

31. For the constitutional history of the period in Bechuanaland, see especially Sillery (1952; 1971; 1974).

32. For discussion of the homeland system and its application to the political organization of the Tswana, see J. L. Comaroff (1974). A detailed but purely constitutional account of Bophuthatswana itself is to be found in Vosloo, Kotzé, and Jeppe (1974). By now there is also a large critical literature on this and other homelands and on their structural role in the development of the South African political economy; for an early and especially well-known example, see Wolpe (1972).

33. Tshidi were overwhelmingly opposed to the imposition of the homeland system and registered their formal protest through the chiefship when given the opportunity. Conse-

quently, most felt ambivalent about complying with the institutions of Bophuthatswana and divided as to whether they should avail themselves of the few opportunities it offered— government loans for the few judged worthy, limited openings for secondary education, and a certain amount of local employment, largely unskilled. Much of the economic benefit resulting from the advent of the *bantustan* was reaped by white business interests in the area.

5

Goodly Beasts, Beastly Goods

Kgomo modimo wa mogae, modimo wa nkó e metse; kgomo le otlanya ditshaba, o bolaile banna ba le bantsi.

Beast, god of the home, god with the damp nose; beast that makes the chiefdoms fight, you have killed many people.

—Tswana song[1]

I

EVER SINCE THE DAWN OF MODERN SOCIAL THEORY, as we all know, efforts have been made to address the rival claims of material and conceptual forces in shaping human society. The place of cattle in Africa is especially interesting in this respect. On the one hand, their significance, even in such obviously *social* processes as marriage exchange, has been explained in entirely economistic terms (see e.g. Goldschmidt 1974; Gray 1960; cf. Schneider 1964). On the other, anthropologists have followed the Dinka insight that "the people are put together as a bull is put together"— that livestock are first and foremost metaphors of social community, signifiers of the human condition (Lienhardt 1961:23). Yet long ago, Evans-Pritchard (1940) saw that these animals embodied *both* material and symbolic value, that their prominence in indigenous consciousness and social life stemmed from their capacity to fuse the two.[2] Not only were social identities and relations represented by means of beasts (1940:18, 89). In the "bovine idiom" and "cattle clock" of the Nuer (1940:19, 101) lay a bridge between ecological conditions and collective meaning, between practical activity and its cultural construction. *The Nuer* might have succeeded, finally, in crossing that bridge "in one direction only." But Evans-Pritchard leaves little doubt that cattle here were objects *at once* economic and symbolic.

We shall attempt to build on this insight and, in looking afresh at the role of cattle in another African society, return to Marx—the Marx of

127

Capital and, especially, of the commodity. As we understand it, the latter was held to derive its significance, under capitalism, from (i) the way in which it links processes of production and exchange; (ii) the fact that it is alike a concrete object and the embodiment of an order of meanings and relations; and (iii) its capacity, through its circulation, to reproduce a total social system. Our interest here, however, is not primarily in the commodity as a *specific* historical form. Instead, we take Marx's account as a general model for analyzing relations among people and goods; as the basis, that is, for exploring the production and representation of value in all societies (Turner n.d.). Of course, Marx himself did not hold that commodit*ies* exist only in the capitalist world. They might be found anywhere. But their salience, he stressed, varied greatly across space and time; indeed, this variation was itself taken to be critical in shaping the historical character of different social systems. One obvious corollary follows: that the transformation of any society should be revealed by the changing relations of persons to objects within it.

This conception of the commodity, we believe, lays out the terms for examining the place of cattle in precolonial African societies, and for tracing the effects upon those societies of incorporation into a global order of markets and money. Taking one exemplary case, we argue that, among the Tshidi Barolong, a Tswana people, beasts were like commodities. But they were like them only in the precise sense outlined above: as the medium of transformation, in a *total* economy of signs and practices, between a material economy of things and a moral economy of persons. Further, we shall demonstrate that the changing salience of livestock here can only be fully grasped with reference to that total economy and its encounter with the forces of colonialism—a critical aspect of which was played out in the relationship between cattle and cash. At the same time, we do not wish to imply that animals meant the same thing, or played the same role, among all African pastoralists—or even among all Tswana. Quite the opposite. Recall how, in discussing the rise of capitalism, Marx set out to establish the manner in which the general principles of political economy had taken on particular historical shape, even within modern Europe. In similar vein, it may be shown that, while livestock in Africa share a number of formal properties and potentialities, these have been variously put to work in different social contexts.

II

It is sometimes said, in comparing the peoples of southern Africa, that Nguni-speakers attached "more" significance to their herds than did the Sotho-Tswana (see e.g. Sansom 1974:150). Such things are difficult to measure, of course, but the centrality of beasts in Tswana economy, culture, and society has been noted for as long as there is a documentary record. For example, John Barrow (1806:393f), among their earliest European visitors, wrote that "One great source from which they draw support is their cattle," of which they had a "very considerable" number. Nor did he intend this to refer purely to material subsistence, adding quickly "whose flesh, however, they eat but sparingly." Two of his early observations were to be repeated many times by those who followed after him (e.g. Burchell 1824,2:386; Lichtenstein 1973:66, 77–81; Moffat 1842:250): that a man's wealth was counted in livestock; and that the division of labor placed women securely in cultivation, gathering, and domestic tasks, while men devoted themselves to herding, hunting, and tanning. Burchell (1824,2:347) went on to expand upon the first observation, the association of cattle with wealth and power:

> from the possession of property [specifically cattle], the distinction of men into richer and poorer classes has followed as a natural consequence. Those who have riches, have also, it seems, power; and the word *kosi* [denotes] either *a chief* or *a rich man* [Original emphasis].

By contrast, "a *muchunka* or a *mollala* (a poor-man, or servant) had no need of cattle, as he had only to mind his duty in attending those of his superior" (1824,2:348). Another early visitor, John Campbell (1822, 2:206), a missionary with an eye for telling detail, added a further insight: that there appeared to be a direct symbolic identity between man and beast. When a woman bore twins, one of the children was put to death; when a cow had a pair of calves, one was killed or driven away. Similarly, a man was expected to place a reed on the fence around his homestead to signal either the death of a beast or the mortal illness of a member of his household.

Later missionaries were to remark again on the Tswana tendency to draw their cattle into their symbolic practices. A rich source of omens and auguries (Brown 1926:92), beasts were the medium of domestic sacrifices. They were also the focus of such rituals as male initiation, through which adolescent boys were made over into social adults (J. Comaroff 1985:Chap. 4). As Brown (1926:92) put it, the place of livestock in Tswana life was "not accounted for by the fact that they form[ed] the wealth of the people." As in many other African societies that allegedly share (or once shared) the "cattle complex,"[3] pastoralism was always distinctly secondary to cultivation in its contribution to brute subsistence. Ultimately, the significance of animals flowed from another source: that, "in a strict sense [they were] not a private, but a social possession" (Brown 1926:92). By this, Brown did not mean merely that their ownership was collective. We might gloss his use of "social possession" to imply, after Mauss (1954:1), that they were "total social phenomena"—that is, things that contained all "the threads of which the social fabric is woven."

We shall not simply be concerned here with drawing out these threads, however. As Kuper (1982:11) has pointed out, "one could pile up endless examples" of the centrality of cattle in ritual and bridewealth, of their celebration in idiom and song, and of their salience as political currency. Kuper (1982:18) himself suggests that the exchange of women for beasts is *the* central social transaction among Southern Bantu-speaking peoples.[4] It is

> related both to the more general set of exchanges between the male domain of pastoral production and the female domain of agriculture, and to the series of exchanges of goods and services (basically the gift of fertility and the return of part of the product) between superiors and inferiors.

This summarizes nicely the role of cattle, at least in times past, as (i) the mediating link between production and exchange, and (ii) a means of forging sociopolitical ties. But, in order to account for that role—and for why it was beasts, in particular, that assumed it—it is necessary to show *how* animals actually entered into the making of persons and things, relations and statuses. In short, we seek to explain how they took on the character of total social phenomena; how their unique capacity to store and transform value enabled Tshidi to sustain a viable social world; and how the fundamental changes brought about by the colonial encounter came to alter that world—with some rather unexpected consequences. Such matters, though, can only be addressed by situating relations among people and objects, historically, within the division of labor of which they were part. We enter the Tshidi *morafe,* their political community, in the first half of the nineteenth century.[5]

III

In the early nineteenth century, the Tshidi lived on the Molopo plain, along the present South Africa-Botswana border. The peoples who would soon come to know themselves as "the (Southern) Tswana," or "Bechuana," existed in a field of complex regional relations. Their inherently dynamic polities were increasingly affected by commerce with the Cape Colony, and by the shockwaves that spread across the subcontinent in the wake of the rise of the Zulu state. In the early 1800s, European visitors recorded striking variations among these polities. At one extreme was the Tshidi chiefdom, circa 1824, described by the Reverend Robert Moffat (1842:388) as a large, highly centralized city-state under a ruler who wielded great power and monopolized external trade; settlements of similar scale, some of them bigger than Cape Town, were also observed elsewhere among the Rolong and Tlhaping (e.g. by Barrow 1806:404; Burchell 1824,2:511). At the other extreme were a number of small, acephalous communities dotted over the landscape. These were made up of single, autonomous villages, some of which had, until recently, been part of sizeable chiefdoms (Barrow 1806:412; Smith 1939,1:240f). As this suggests, social fragmentation was an ever-present possibility in Southern Tswana politics, and loomed large in the Tshidi imagination; counteracting its threat, we shall see, was integrally tied to the potential of cattle to build enduring social bonds.

At the time, the Tshidi world, with its elaborate capital town, was centered upon an hereditary chiefship, in which were vested mechanisms of control at once ritual, political, and economic (cf. Okihiro 1976:Chap. 2; Schapera 1938). Radiating outward from the office was an administrative hierarchy made up of nesting residential units (households, agnatic segments, and wards), each with a position of authority at its head. Such units usually had agnatic cores and their headship devolved according to genealogical seniority, although rank was often the object of contention (see e.g. Campbell 1822,1:314–6). Despite the stress on agnation, however, the Tshidi lacked segmentary lineages. Descent groups did not coincide with administrative divisions, and their members only engaged in common action when they also belonged to the same ward. Apart from defining relative rank—and, with it, access to property and position—these groups had little collective identity. This was due, in part, to the fact that Tshidi practiced cousin marriage—including unions between close agnates, a form of endogamy which, as we have shown elsewhere (Comaroff and Comaroff 1981), prevented the emergence of large corporations. It also individuated households as units of property and production, marital alliance and social management, and created a field of overlapping social ties in which people were related in many different, often ambiguous, ways.

The features of this world to be stressed here may be subsumed into two oppositions. The first was between its center, embodied in the court and person of the chief, and its periphery of households made up of female-centered houses (see below). The chiefship was located, spatially and symbolically, at the hub of the town (*motse*), which itself stood in stark contrast to *naga,* the wild (cf. Campbell 1813:187). The settlement was visible evidence of the triumph of the social over rank nature. But it was a triumph that had to be protected by a vigilant ruler, who had to ensure that the town remained intact, its households held together within the administrative hierarchy. As a Setswana proverb put it, *motse o lwapeng,* "the town [polity] is [rooted] in the domestic courtyard" (Brown 1926:201). At the same time, the relationship between center and periphery was, potentially at least, an antagonistic one. While centralized domicile was prescribed, and was enforced where possible, families had their fields outside the settlement; and they took to them for the agricultural season once the sovereign gave the word, usually after he had them plow his gardens in the wake of the first rains (Willoughby 1928:226).[6] Tshidi showed some resentment toward this arrangement, however. They spoke of the benefits of remaining where nobody could demand their tributary labor, or delay them from cultivating their crops. And so households were wont to scatter wherever a chief lost the power to keep them at the capital (Philip 1828,2:133). In sum, while the prevailing structure of authority favored centralization, the individuation of households, encouraged by existing marriage practices, gave rise to centrifugal forces at the heart of the polity.

The second opposition involved agnation and matrilaterality, about which much has been written (e.g. Comaroff and Roberts 1981). For now, it is enough to note that agnation, the cultural idiom of political and economic status, was associated with rivalry and conflict; matrilaterality, with moral solidarity and social complementarity.[7] The former grew out of bonds among men, and tied their households into the administrative hierarchy and the public domain; the latter had its roots in relations through women, and evoked the privacy of the house[8] and its confines (Philip 1828,2:132; Solomon 1855:42). Although they might share common concerns and often cooperated, patrikin were held nonetheless to have inimical interests in property and position; it was a lamentable—but understandable—fact of life that they should constantly try to "eat" one another by means both mystical and material (Burchell 1824,2:272; Lichtenstein 1973:66f). The inherently political content of their relations was marked in kin terminology: it was impossible to refer to an agnate without ranking him relative to oneself in the positional order. By contrast, matrilaterals were always unranked, this being an expression of the fact that "a man and his *bomalome* (mother's brothers' people) never fought," never practiced sorcery, and never found themselves in competition with each other. Each, to be sure, was the other's prime social resource.

Agnatic politics, along with the ambiguous social bonds created by endogamous marriage, then, gave the Tshidi world the appearance of being highly negotiable, a fluid, dynamic universe in which practical efforts to construct identity, rank, and relations were the stuff of social action (see Mackenzie 1871:410). These processes, in turn, integrated households into the hierarchical polity—at least for as long as the centripetal forces around the chiefship could hold them there and prevent them from asserting their autonomy. It is against this background that the social division of labor is to be understood.

The Social Division of Labor

As early observers among the Southern Tswana noted, precolonial productive arrangements were based primarily on differences of gender and
generation. Women and their daughters cultivated crops, gathered the
fruits of the wild, and took care of the domestic hearth. Men, by contrast,
engaged in leather work, tool-making, and public deliberations, assisting
in the fields mainly in times of unusually heavy toil. Their major sphere of
control was the pastoral economy, and they drew on the labor of their
young sons, impoverished clients, or subjugated Sarwa ("Bushmen") to
herd their animals. They also hunted, especially in periods of scarcity. But
unlike females, adult males did not contribute much to the routine material
reproduction of the household. They busied themselves instead with the
various forms of exchange that created and recreated the social world. And,
in so doing, they transformed the yield of women's fecundity—the grain
to feed their dependants and retainers, the sons to tend their stock, the
daughters to marry off in alliances—into both political currency and more
enduring communal values.

This bald summary of the allocation of productive tasks, to which we
shall add further detail in a moment, will be readily familiar. It evokes a
very common pattern in southern and eastern Africa, at least among Bantu-
speakers (Kuper 1982:11). Yet to understand how it was elaborated into a
social division of labor we need to look briefly at the meaning ascribed by
Tshidi to human activity itself; in particular, at their conception of work
and fabrication. The vernacular term *go dira* (or *diha*) meant "to make,"
"do," or "cause to happen," and referred to a wide range of actions upon
the world, from tilling the soil to the performance of ritual. *Tiro,* the act
of fabrication (Brown 1931:308), yielded positive value in the form of
persons, things, and relations.[9] Its converse was sorcery, which negated
constructive labor, undid people, and destroyed social wealth (cf. Munn
1986 for a similar conception of sorcery in a Melanesian context).

For Tshidi, work was not an abstract quality or a thing to be exchanged.
It simply could not exist in the form of a commodity, as alienable "labor
power." Even the energies of a serf were only available to his master by
virtue of a total bond of interdependence. They could not be given over to
another person unless the relationship itself was transferred. Work, rather,
was the creative process inherent in all human existence, and was expressed
in the making of self and others in the course of everyday life (Alverson
1978:132). Yet, because people were not all the same, not all *tiro* was alike.
Or equal. The capacities and exertions of a chief or a ritual doctor, both of
whom had unusual creative powers, were more potent, more comprehensive

than those of any commoner (see J. Comaroff 1985). Above all, however, male "work" and female "work" were fundamentally different—and unequal.

The precise character of the difference flowed from the cultural construction of gender and its place in the Tshidi world. Women, associated with cultivation and reproduction in the domestic sphere, were uncertain mediators of nature. Their bodies were the source of the most prized value of all—human life—yet that very faculty imperilled the polity. For their fecundity generated heat (*bothitho*), a destructive force that threatened such things as rainmaking and initiation rites, ancestral veneration and deliberations at the chiefly court, land and cattle—all quintessentially male concerns (Schapera 1938:28; Willoughby 1909:234). Not only did their bodies require confinement, but females were denied a role in the collective world shaped through exchange; through the transaction, often, of the value created by their own productive and reproductive labor (Kinsman 1983). Debarred from contact with beasts, they were "jural minors" who had to be represented by men in the public domain.

The formal subordination of women was marked in many ways. For example, in the conjugal process, the process that reproduced the social division of labor itself (Comaroff and Roberts 1981), they were acted upon: unlike men, who married (*nyala*), they *were* married (*nyalwa*). By convention (*ka mekgwa*), moreover, they were portrayed as being unable to extend their personal influence in time and space. Their restricted powers of movement, and of inducing movement in others, was captured, according to missionary linguistics, in the very term that labelled them: the "original" meaning of the word for woman, *mosadi* (from *sala*, "stay"), Sandilands (1953:333) offers, was "the-one-who-remains-at-home." This is not to imply that wives and mothers were totally impotent in Tshidi society at the time. There is clear evidence that they wielded (sometimes considerable) influence behind the scenes in both the court and the domestic compound (see Philip 1828,2:133 for a notable Tlhaping case); in addition, royal women exercised a measure of authority over their commoner sisters through the system of age regiments (Schapera 1938:74). But, in the formal calculus of institutional power, the marginality of females was conspicuous. The point was made with great symbolic force by the place of the chief's mother—*mohumagadi*, the mother of the people—in the political architecture of the capital. Not only did her homestead stand at the edge of the chiefly court (*kgotla*) as periphery to center. It was also a house of asylum, a private, behind-the-scenes refuge for those sentenced in the public domain for crimes other than homicide (Schapera 1938:74).

In contrast, males were intrinsically stable and "cool" (*tsididi*). The latter quality was especially significant, since it was required for effective action in the public sector. Salutations at the royal meetingplace underlined this. They called for *"Pula!"* ("Let it rain!"), and implored *"A go nne tsididi!"* ("Let it be cool!"; Brown 1926:156; Solomon 1855:47). Furthermore, the term *go hodisa* ("to cool") also meant "to heal," a male skill which tempered the heat of illness and pollution (Willoughby 1928:363). As players in the public domain, men could build alliances through women, and make subordinates or clients of their rivals. In so doing, as we said earlier, they forged the social connections and status relations that shaped the hierarchical polity, a community which also embraced the invisible realm of spirit forces. Participation in these processes—and they covered a wide spectrum from flamboyantly open conflicts to secretive transactions of patronage and debt—impelled men to act potently upon the world, to engage in acts of competitive self-construction that implied "eating" or "being eaten" by others. Of course, given the fluidities of that world, such processes of social management and self-construction were unceasing. As we shall see, they also had a material expression in political economy: dominating other men and controlling the capacities of women amounted, finally, to the social production of both a workforce and a following.

The differences between male and female "work" were most apparent perhaps in everyday productive processes, the routine activities that created persons while persons created themselves. Let us explore these activities further.

Gender and Production

Agriculture, augmented by gathering, yielded the bulk of everyday subsistence, while pastoralism, along with hunting, provided largely for the ritual diet and for extra-domestic exchange. The contrast between them, as we would expect, followed the cultural logic of gender difference. Thus females, corn, and bush foods were the very opposite of males, stock, and game. While the former involved an uncertain hold over nature, ever threatening to fail, the latter were the epitome of forceful mastery of the environment. The fact that cultivation was regarded as an inherently risky business was entirely consistent with the prevailing image of women; as predictable was the notion that pastoralism was an activity far more controlled. Even though they were liable to be lost through sickness, predation, and war, beasts were held to afford security in the face of crop failure and, while meat was reserved for special occasions, milk was the most reliable component of the daily diet. In times of drought, men coordinated their hunting efforts to provide game in plenty (Burchell 1824,2:320; Livingstone 1857:28).

These associations went yet further, extending to the status of male and female products in the Tshidi scheme of values. Cattle, the essence of dependability, were largely self-reproducing, and were mobile in the face of drought and danger; they permitted the stable storage, exchange, and seemingly spontaneous growth of wealth (Burchell 1824,2:272, 347); and they supplied dung, *boloko,* the substance used to make the durable surfaces that set off domestic space from its surrounds. Their hides and bone furnished the stuff from which most lasting personal possessions were made. The hunt, too, yielded lasting material objects and trade goods— plumes, skins, and ivory—as well as consumables. On the other hand, grain was vulnerable to the climate, and, at least in the nineteenth century (Grove 1989), frequent crop failure threatened to wipe out seed altogether; it had to be arduously threshed before it was cooked, and often rotted in storage; and it had little exchange value, being worth no more than the clay pot in which it was carried (Schapera 1938:242). In addition, while cows gave forth milk as a finished product, the agricultural counterpart, corn beer, had to be prepared by women in a delicate operation that was easily spoiled, especially by their own polluting heat. In fact, the entire arable cycle was metaphorically linked to procreation and, tacitly, to the ever-present danger of miscarriage. For instance, *tlhaka* denoted "seed" or "grain" and "fetus," and *tlhakanèla dikobò* ("to plant," "fuse under the blanket") implied both sexual intercourse and the act of impregnating the land. Similarly, the term for "reap" (*go sega*) was used for cutting the umbilicus in childbirth. And where the harvest failed, it was usually attributed to the planting of an aborted fetus, an act of sorcery that "spoiled" the ground and prevented the rain from falling (Schapera 1971a:107).

But the social basis of the division of labor was most clearly marked in death. As Willoughby (1928:57) reports, a "patriarch" was buried inside the cattle byre "so that he may hear the tramp of the cattle as they [went] out to graze in the morning and return[ed] for safety at sundown"; and his corpse was shown an ox bone and a milk bowl before being placed beside some dry cow dung in its grave. His wife was interred under the threshing-floor that she might "hear the thud of the flails, threshing out each new crop"; she was shown a pestle, a winnowing fan, and domestic utensils, and was sprinkled with corn (Willoughby 1928:40). Where men became *badimo,* spirits who received regular sacrifice and continued to be central to affairs of the living, women lost their identities, being subsumed into an agnatic ancestor cult (Willoughby 1928:330). Ironically, they were sealed into their state of spiritual anonymity under a surface of the very *boloko,* the cow dung, that was made by their labor into the permanent planes of the homestead.

As all this suggests, cultivation and pastoralism were not simply opposed and complementary domains of production, just as women and men were not simply opposed and complementary social beings. It is true that females held fields in their own right, had their own granaries, and exercised some control over the use of their harvest. Yet even as producers they were anything but independent, their "works" being regularly appropriated by adult males in one or another capacity. The general point, again, was underscored in Tshidi poetics and myth. Frequent cosmogonic reference was made to the notion that the social world had its origins in the domestication, by men, of raw female fecundity, the theme being most cogently enacted in initiation rites, when males seized the capacity to generate fully social beings and communal institutions by symbolically recapitulating childbirth (J. Comaroff 1985:85f; Willoughby 1909). More practically, the fruits of female labor were appropriated in two distinct ways. First, they were harnessed to the creation—and cyclical recreation—of the polity and of the chiefship itself. And, second, they subsidized everyday male sociopolitical activity, providing a material base for inter-household transactions.

The link between female productive activity and the (re)creation of the polity hinged on the centralized controls exercised over the agricultural cycle. Specifically, the chief regulated that cycle, allowing it to begin when he "gave out the seed time" (Willoughby 1928:226f; see also Campbell 1822,2:154). This form of control empowered the ruler to extract tributary labor before people dispersed, thereby providing him with surpluses for later redistribution, a prerogative that shored up his legitimacy (Schapera 1943:184). But it also expressed a more subtle tenet of Tshidi political culture. Like work, time here was not an abstract thing, a resource that existed apart from events and actions. In the absence of activity, there literally was no time. Not surprisingly, the Setswana term *lobaka*, "[a period of] time," also translated as "space" (Comaroff and Comaroff 1991:346 n.75). In this context, then, the chiefly act of dispensing seed time, which was closely tied to his ability to bring rain, was seen actually to enable the productive season, for it set in motion the insemination of the land and the gestation of the crop. It also called into being the entire social calendar and, with it, the order which gave meaning and material form to the social world. In this respect, the two sides of centralized regulation of female labor—the regeneration of the polity and the production of a redistributable surplus—were interdependent. Together they transformed human energy into a vital political economy.

The same theme was taken a step further later on in the agricultural cycle. Once the grain had begun to ripen, the most elaborate rite of the year was performed. *Go loma thôtse*, the "tasting of the gourd," tied the maturation of the crop to the renewal of the social community (Willoughby 1928:226f). Females brought their first fruits to the court, where they were ceremonially eaten by royal males, after which a pulp of their leaves was carefully rubbed onto the body of every citizen, man and woman alike, in strict rank order (Holub 1881,1:329; Schapera 1971b:156). Between these periodic rites, of course, political fortunes rose and fell. Hence *go loma thôtse* gave annual reckoning of the state of power relations at the same time as it marked out afresh the enduring structure of the chiefdom. And so the yield of women's labor was absorbed into the body politic via its center, providing the material and symbolic substance of an hierarchical order whose living form was imprinted on the skin of all subjects.

This, in turn, throws light on the second aspect of the appropriation of female "work," namely, its subsidy of everyday male activity in the public domain. Once the polity was defined, its centralized structures annually renewed, so too was the *lobaka*, the space-time, in which agnatic politics might proceed. But for any man to participate—and, as noted before, there was little alternative but to do so—the ability to feed himself and his retainers was a basic requirement. Otherwise he had to work for others, and so lost the autonomy to act on his own account. In short, access to the yield of female labor was *the* basic provision—in both senses of that term—for entry into the political arena as a free person.[10] This was most routinely captured, in the iconography of goods, by corn beer, a beverage manufactured by wives from their surplus grain. The very essence of hospitality, it was the refreshment which a husband served to his allies and clients, enhancing his status in the process (Schapera 1943:201). In its passage from her private backyard to his public frontyard, this product of her work flowed into, and fed, the sphere of male exchange. And she lost control over its use.

But perhaps the most palpable expression of this point came after the harvest, when a woman's garden had been denuded of its corn, its broken stalks signaling the end of the arable season. At that stage, her husband's stock were led into the field, to eat what was left of her toil; the toil which ensured that, for another year, his household was provided for, thus allowing him to pursue his social career—and, as we shall see, to deploy his herd to the full in doing so. As this implies, it was the encompassment of agriculture by pastoralism that held the key to the social division of labor and, therefore, to the role of beasts themselves.

Pastoralism, Property, and Social Identity

Tshidi herds comprised cattle, goats, and somewhat fewer sheep. Both precolonial and modern observers (e.g. Schapera 1953:23) have had difficulty in assessing the size of individual and collective holdings among Tswana: beasts were widely dispersed under various forms of patronage, and any display of stock wealth was believed to invite plunder and ritual attack (Matthews n.d.; Schapera 1938:24). Moreover, postcolonial history has shown that the total animal population tends to fluctuate quite considerably over time, long-term cycles of depletion by disease and drought being followed by spontaneous recovery. But the documentary record does confirm the presence of large herds in the early nineteenth century, and gives evidence of visible inequalities in their distribution.

If the products of cultivation and gathering fueled physical subsistence, cattle were the media through which men shaped their social biographies. This flowed from the fact that, for Tshidi, they were the supreme form of property. Even late into the colonial period, they were spoken of as the only heritable wealth of real worth (Matthews n.d.; Schapera 1934:14). It is, of course, very widely the case that persons objectify themselves in things, goods either produced or circulated; that, by investing their identities in matter, they seek to project their being through space and time, enhancing their value as they are united with qualities outside of themselves (Munn 1977). However, goods differ in their culturally recognized capacity to embody value and meaning. The English word "property" is interesting in this respect. It implies both the intrinsic character of a thing ("properties") and a particular relationship to it ("possession"). And it marks a subclass of articles that may serve as vehicles of individual or collective status. Similarly, the Setswana term *khumó* ("wealth object"; from *huma*, "be [become] rich"/*humisa*, "make rich") connotes the ability to enhance wealth as well as the quality of possession. Only beasts combined both of these features. Only they, among wealth objects, could congeal, store, and increase value, holding it in stable form in a world of flux. Only they could take on, and represent, the identity of their owners.

The capacity of the beast to carry social identity, both individual and collective, was most vividly marked in two sets of conventional practices. The first involved the "cattle linkage" of siblings and bridewealth; the second arose out of inheritance.

When children were young, their fathers "cattle linked" (*go rulaganya bana*) full siblings into mixed pairs (Smith 1939,1:345). Once tied to a particular sister, the brother was obliged to look after her and to represent her, and she was to cook and care for him, especially before he married. The defining feature of the link was that the brother was the recipient of the sister's bridewealth (*bogadi*), which was to be used to support her in times of want and, if necessary, to enable his own marriage (cf. Schapera 1938:143). In practice, it was rarely put to this latter use; the conjugal process here was not a major context for the exchange of goods, *bogadi* being relatively low and rarely paid until many years had passed (J. L. Comaroff 1980). But the cultural stress on this arrangement was itself a statement of the moral and material significance of the brother-sister bond. This relationship would, in time, mature into a set of privileged matrilateral ties, ties that set men apart as individuals in relation to their agnates. In as much as his sister's bridewealth was instrumental in creating these bonds, it derived from the transfer of *her* productive and reproductive powers for a return that gave the man the *symbolic* capital with which to marry—to be endowed with food and children, and so to enter the arena of agnatic politics as a free actor. Until then, a bachelor was described as a "locust," a hapless parasite. Only through marriage could he enter into the public domain as a fully social being. Not coincidentally, the *bogadi* that placed a male between two females, a sister and a wife, and enabled his very manhood, translated literally as "womanhood" (Brown 1926:61). In sum, *go rulaganya bana* and *bogadi,* the two main forms of cattle exchange through women, established males as actors in the public domain. And it marked out the special matrilateral ties, the bonds that distinguished a man and gave him his prime social resource, an exclusive reservoir of support in the hostile world of agnatic politics (Comaroff and Roberts 1981:50f).

If *go rulaganya bana* and *bogadi* were an essential part of the making of male identity, inheritance placed men in the social field. The devolution of property here was a gradual process, cattle being passed on to children, and distributed among houses, throughout the lifetime of their father. By convention, the ideal estate had little left at death, but this residue, known as *boswa,* had great significance. Apart from all else, its passage gave public recognition to the naming of a senior heir, often a matter of contention. This son was known as *moja boswa,* the "eater" of *boswa,* the stress on "eating" as a sign of political preeminence again being noteworthy (cf. Schapera 1938:230f). So, too, was the fact that the transfer was closely linked to the renewal of the social order at large. For the domestic unit, which divided after the death of its founder, gave birth to the families that formed the core of the local agnatic segment, the grouping which tied households into the administrative hierarchy. Yet it was at this very moment that it was most likely to disband, often amidst conflict over rank. For Tshidi, *boswa* represented the integrity of the fragmenting group as it became a local segment and took up its place in the wider polity. The heir received these animals so that he might "look after" (*go disa,* "to herd") its members—a generalized metaphor for sustaining their unity. In purely economic terms, *boswa* was insufficient unto the task. But this was a *symbolic* herd which defined a bounded, if still fragile, social grouping. In "consuming" it, the heir assumed legitimate control over the people and property in the segment. If anyone was to preempt his status, they would have to "eat" him. As this suggests, inheritance turned the passage of cattle into two social facts: it provided the next generation with the core of their own estates, the material bases of their careers; and it situated individuals and households within the political field.

As this implies, beasts built social identities, individual and collective, and they gave men the basis to engage as actors in the public arena. But they did not make all males alike. Quite the contrary, in Tshidi culture the

innate qualities of cattle—like the fetishized commodity—were an alibi
for distinctions of rank, gender, and social power. The varying ability to
control them as property, to impose a personal stamp on them and put
them in circulation, was *the* major mode of distinguishing persons and
statuses (Burchell 1824,2:247f). Indeed, among Southern Bantu-speakers
in general, livestock fostered the growth and expression of great discrep-
ancies in wealth (Lichtenstein 1973:76f; Solomon 1855:42). In much the
same way as capital, they served both as standards of value and as a means
of accumulating and transforming it into other kinds of wealth in the
political economy at large (cf. Sansom 1974:153).

From Division of Labor to Political Economy

In collective representations of the polity, the chief was described as its
supreme "herdsman" (*modisa*). This metaphor ran to the heart of the
Tshidi conception of political economy. In contrast to other citizens, as
Mackenzie (1871:368) tells us, a Tswana sovereign could graze his animals
anywhere, the relevance of this being illuminated by the fact that the
vernacular term for "government" was *pusò*, which betokened both "regime" and "dominion," the area over which a ruler's authority extended
(J. L. Comaroff n.d.). This realm was not bounded by a fixed, continuous
line, but by the furthest ring of water holes to which he could lay claim for
his pasture—against other chiefs and/or by virtue of having the servants
to tend his herds over such a distance. The Tshidi sovereign might not
have been a shepherd-king, but his domain was, in the final analysis, a
range.

The chief controlled the largest herd in the community (Burchell
1824,2:272, 347). This was assured by the prerogatives of his office, among
them the right to retain a portion of fines levied at his court and, in
extreme cases, to seize the livestock of a man who consistently flouted his
authority; to keep strays (*matimèla*); to receive tribute on special occasions;
and to barter other gifts for beasts (Campbell 1822,2:194; Lichtenstein
1930,2:414; cf. Schapera 1938:64f). Significant, too, were the spoils of
raiding, the desire to increase the royal fund at the expense of neighbors
being a major motive in the mobilization of male age regiments. In fact,
the names of these regiments—*Mathibakgomo*, "those who brought back
cattle"; *Majakgomo*, "those who 'eat' cattle"; and so on—often equated
male vigor with the capture of herds (Breutz 1956:164). In principle,
Tshidi distinguished sharply between animals belonging to the chiefship
and those possessed by the office-holder; in practice, it was hard to separate
the two. But there was nothing ambiguous about the part they played in
the exercise of power. Not only did they sustain the people who actually

husbanded them, the royal servants who performed a wide range of productive and political tasks for the ruler. They could also be given away in return for support and submission. Such distributions took various forms: outright transfers to loyal followers, sometimes along with appointment to newly created headmanships; long-term loans (*mahisa*), in which the recipient might use the milk of the cows and keep a heifer, and reciprocate by giving their owner "support in public life" (cf. Schapera 1938:214); payments to specialists, such as rainmakers, who, in assuring communal well-being (*pula;* also "rain"), reinforced the legitimacy of the chief; sacrifices to the ancestors to ensure their protection; and the dispatch of gifts to other sovereigns.

As everywhere in precolonial southern Africa, then, "cattle [were] converted into fealty and political support" (Sansom 1974:163). And they had this capacity precisely because they bore the imprint, a part of the essence, of their owner. For a man to hold a beast that belonged (or had once belonged) to the ruler was to have the presence of the sovereign himself in his midst. To succour that beast was to honor the chief and, by extension, the chiefship and polity embodied in him; to hurt it was to strike against him, and to risk the sanction that might follow. Cattle, in sum, naturalized sovereign authority and gave it an enduring quality (Burchell 1824,2:272, 347). But this did not mean that rulers were all-powerful here. Quite the contrary, they had constantly to ward off the efforts of their most influential agnates to reduce their legitimacy, even to remove them (J. L. Comaroff 1973; Moffat 1842:389). Nonetheless, the chief*ship* remained above negotiation. And, as long as he occupied the office, the holder personified it. Just as the commodity bore, in both its physical existence and its circulation, the set of relations involved in its production, so the Tshidi beast carried with it the relations of authority and inequality that shaped the political economy.

Although the chief stood at the apex of the polity, it was not only for him that cattle were the currency of power. The accumulation of a large herd also gave others the opportunity to initiate ties of alliance and patronage. But this was effectively confined to those already with access to high rank and, usually, office. For most ordinary townsmen, cattle were acquired mainly through inheritance, bridewealth, and natural increase, and, except in rare circumstances, it was impossible to build up a sizeable estate in one generation. Burchell (1824,2:348), in fact, observed early on that the social order was constructed in such a way as to prevent the "poor" from rising above their station. The extension of *mahisa* loans, the major vehicle by which men might come to control others, was only open to those with substantial and, more importantly, growing herds—supported, as noted before, by food-producing wives.

For the affluent, however, *mahisa* did offer a direct medium for transforming wealth in cattle into wealth in people. But it had two quite different faces. Where these loans were made to free men of lower status, they were usually part of wider processes of social management; of "eating" others through lengthy (and often very subtle) series of transactions. In itself, each loan made a limited material difference, unless it came at a time of particular misfortune. It only added marginally to the recipient's herd, and did little for his economic fortunes. Similarly, while it gave some political advantage to the patron, who might expect generalized support in return, it was not really a basis to demand any more. Only when the client had been "consumed," and was no longer an independent person, could he actually be made to give his labor and other services. This first form of *mahisa*, in other words, was just one element in the longer-term negotiation of power relations. On the other hand, loans to *balala* (or *batlhanka;* "serfs," lit., "those laid low"), who had no access to the means of production, nurtured a more enduring relationship of servitude, that of an underclass in perennial subordination. Here the stock contributed directly to the survival of their holders, who were excluded from the politico-jural process and forced to live outside the settlement, either at hunting camps or at the cattleposts of their patrons, from where they regularly sent skins, honey, and milk to the town (Kinsman 1980:14; Lichtenstein 1973:76; Mackenzie 1871:368). This underclass comprised former captives in war, families or small communities of Sarwa and Kgalagadi, and free citizens who had been "eaten" and had lost their herds entirely. Together with young boys, these serfs made up the bulk of the pastoral workforce, swelling the surpluses that made possible the social activities of the wealthy. They were also sometimes called on, by their masters, to augment female agricultural labor. The fact that impoverished Southern Tswana were used in this way adds an interesting footnote to the cultural basis of gender and production here. In Tshidi imagery, to "be eaten," and hence "laid low," was to be feminized. Such men, in short, had become fit to do women's work. The same did not apply to Sarwa and Kgalagadi vassals, who were held to be innately "wild"; to be, literally, "*bush*men." Being incapable of leading a domestic life, they were debarred from the fundamental rights of civilized beings, namely, living in a settlement or acquiring stock (Burchell 1824,2:348).

The production and exchange of cattle, then, sustained a structure of inequality, an entire system of distinction. Built on class, gender, and rank, it was this structure that gave characteristic form to contemporary Tshidi economy and society. For citizens of the chiefdom, beasts were both the medium through which men achieved their relative standing and the social means of producing a labor force. They roused human beings to intense affect and activity, from political intrigue to praise poetry, from sorcery to warfare. Persons of rank, those who were "strong" enough to consume others, were thought actually to attract animals; that is, to draw them by being sought out as the recipients of chiefly favor and ancestral blessing, as would-be affinal allies and holders of office. As this suggests, cattle wealth was seen to reflect an inherent ability to mobilize people, to extend the self by generating support, and to radiate a personal presence. This form of wealth, in other words, had the tautological quality of all political currency: it was taken to be an expression of the very power it served to create.

For their part, Tshidi, like other Tswana, glossed the supremely creative quality of cattle by calling them "gods with wet noses" (cf. Alverson 1978:124f). They were pliable symbolic media, similar enough to human beings—yet different enough among themselves—to express a range of personal identities, common values, and states of relationship. As Lienhardt (1961:23) said of the Dinka, people were put together like livestock and could, by the same token, be rearranged through the appropriate manipulation of their bovine alters, the same principle being invoked in, among other things, Tshidi healing rites (J. Comaroff 1974; cf. Schapera 1953:59f). Along with their ability to embody particular identities, beasts were also the living products of a stratified order. Thus they could only be owned by male citizens, whose stamp they bore; they had to be kept apart from mature females, to whom they had an innate antipathy; and, being the essence of social value, they were not fit possessions for beings themselves not fully socialized (women, children, and subject peoples; Campbell 1822,2:254; Mackenzie 1871:499). As a focus of everyday activity, cattle were the epitome of social and symbolic capital; the capital, to paraphrase our opening statement, that linked a material economy of things to a moral economy of persons, and so constructed a total economy of signs and practices.

From the Past to the Present

The first sustained effort to colonize the Tshidi was made by the Methodist mission.[11] This was the thin edge of a European wedge, and it inserted itself into the fissures of their social system, opening the way for more pervasive external forces (Comaroff and Comaroff 1986; 1991). Ironically, the impact of the evangelists was less in the sphere of the sacred than in that of production and exchange. The Nonconformists introduced a world-view framed in terms of a moral economy, a free market of the spirit, in which Africans were to be cut loose from "tribal" entanglements and set on the path to individual self-construction (J. Comaroff 1985:129f). This implied a notion of person and property drawn from the industrial capitalist culture of early nineteenth-century Europe. Founded on the private family estate and the ideal of material and spiritual accumulation, it entailed a division of labor that placed agriculture in male hands and confined women to the domain of the domestic household. And, most crucially, it assumed participation in a global market economy, one that would clasp the black convert in the civilizing embrace of Christian Europe. As Livingstone (1857:34) put it:

> Sending the Gospel to the Heathen . . . [must include more than] a man going about with a bible under his arm. The promotion of commerce ought to be specially attended to, as this, more speedily than anything else, diminishes the sense of isolation which heathenism engenders . . . [I wish] to promote the preparation of the raw materials of European manufactures in Africa, for by that means we may not only put a stop to the slave-trade, but introduce the negro family into the body of corporate nations.

Above all else, it was commodity production and trade that would recreate the black person and his community: only when the 'raw material' of African agriculture became an item of exchange within the colonial system—a system at once moral and material—might the native Christian take his proper place in a new order of imperial relations. The vital medium of this transformation was to be money. Methodist ideology focused from the start on its "talents" as both a means and a measure of self-improvement (J. Comaroff 1985:133).

At the outset, Nonconformist values were clearly at odds with Tshidi social and cultural forms, and presented a bewildering array of attractions and disincentives. The evangelists sensed early on that the path to the spirit was through practical innovation, and they lost no time in introducing the plow and irrigation techniques to all who would try them (Comaroff and Comaroff 1986; 1991). Initially, it was those excluded from conventional spheres of power and prestige who identified with Christianity. But the impact of the church was soon felt further afield. The plow permitted large acreages to be brought under cultivation, and regular surpluses to be produced. Urged on by the mission's Benthamite faith in trade, Tshidi began to direct these surpluses to colonial merchants rather than to indigenous relations of exchange (cf. Bundy 1979:39; Ranger 1978:109).

The practical innovations brought by the Protestants were to have a profound effect upon the division of labor and the engendered bases of production. Plows required beasts for draught, and women were forbidden to handle them. Men, therefore, were drawn into agriculture; in any case, where grain was sold, they were quick to assert control over the wealth yielded in the process. And so, previously discrete domains of activity, of male and female "work," began to intersect and merge—one consequence being that women were relegated to the devalued tasks of tending and reaping (Holub 1881,1:339; Kinsman 1983). What is more, sexual distinctions were increasingly subsumed into relations of class. Since only those with access to sufficient oxen could use the plow effectively in this semi-arid environment, differences in cattle wealth were introduced into the domain of cultivation. Those who owned stock began to withdraw them from loans and other forms of patronage arrangements, sought to increase their arable holdings, and put ever more of their crops on the market; women, in fact, could no longer be sure of any control over the harvest, even for purposes of subsistence. As Shillington (1982:102) has pointed out of the nearby Batlhaping, this led to a cycle of dispossession as powerful pastoralists seized the most fertile land, gradually depriving other members of the community. For the first time, too, starvation became rife in many chiefdoms, and rulers found it necessary to limit the sale of produce (J. Comaroff 1985:146). Among the Tshidi, this was most visible at the centers of mission influence, where money had become a pervasive medium of exchange (Holub 1881,2:13).

The "mineral revolution" in the late nineteenth century ushered South Africa into the age of industrial capitalism. This, and the coming of the colonial state, brought radically new material conditions to bear on peoples like the Tshidi. The annexation of British Bechuanaland to the Cape Colony in 1896 led to the imposition of taxes and to systematic attempts to coerce men into the labor market, these attempts being abetted both by the practical and ideological changes initiated by the mission and by the rinderpest pandemic of the mid-1890s (Comaroff and Comaroff 1989; Shillington 1985:16f, 112). Overrule also had a direct effect on the internal political economy. By putting an end to war and raiding, it severed the ruling cadres from their major external source of power—namely, serfs and cattle (J. L. Comaroff 1987a:80). In addition, royals had their trade monopolies undercut by white merchants, who bought and sold grain and stock to the disadvantage of local producers. Under these new conditions, chiefs were reduced from recipients of tribute and fines—paid in beasts— to collectors, on behalf of the state, of taxes levied in money. The bases of a centralized Tshidi polity were gradually being eroded, although the elite still enjoyed greater wealth and self-determination than the rest.

Faced with a need for cash, men of the rank and file were increasingly compelled to sell their cattle. Tshidi had long traded animals sporadically, it is true, but they were reluctant to do so except when in dire need (cf. Schapera 1933:648). Now they had little alternative, for it was stock that yielded the highest returns; and, in any case, most had little else to sell. Those without herds were forced into the labor market very rapidly (Schapera 1947:134). Others, however, also found themselves being drawn, slowly yet inexorably, toward the same fate. For a cycle of impoverishment had been set in motion. Restricted by government decree to the contracted borders of its arid territory, the Tshidi community became increasingly polarized. Only those wealthy in beasts were able to ensure sizeable grain surpluses and withstand ecological risk. Furthermore, like other African peasants, Southern Tswana had to compete on ever less favorable terms with white producers (cf. Bundy 1977), who came to dominate the market and demand a growing black workforce. The capacity of Tshidi farmers faltered, and erosion, overcrowding, and manpower shortage took their toll on crops and herds. Growing rates of male migration drew the chiefdom into the subcontinental political economy as a reservoir of labor, and ensured that money became the prime medium of exchange. Yet wages were kept below the level at which they might support a worker and his family. The majority of the population thus gradually became a "peasantariat" (Parson 1984), trapped in an inescapable combination of wage labor and farming, neither of which sufficed to meet their subsistence needs (Murray 1981; Palmer and Parsons 1977).

As the Tshidi became more deeply imbricated in the regional political economy, relations of production and the sexual division of labor among them underwent yet further change (J. L. Comaroff 1987a:81). Most men became wage workers of some sort while women, debarred from joining their husbands in the cities, became the heads of households made up of the very young and the aged. To survive, they had either to enter the restricted local labor market or to eke out a living on ever more barren, infertile land. Agriculture fell back on female shoulders; a devalued and highly precarious activity once more, it was now synonymous with the productive uncertainty of the feminized rural reserves. Men and women had become complementary fractions of an underclass dependent upon the regulatory mechanisms of an increasingly assertive capitalist state. A new center of power controlled the space, time, and movement of all Tshidi; all, that is, save a small petty bourgeoisie which earned its comfortable income from trade, salaries, and commercial farming on large holdings accumulated in the late nineteenth century.

By the time we first did fieldwork in the Tshidi chiefdom in 1969, only 20% of families had any rights in cattle.[12] Among livestock holders, less than .01% (all of them senior royals and educated entrepreneurs) had more than 500 head; the vast majority owned no more than a handful. "Money has eaten our beasts," ordinary people would say. Those who still had cattle also husbanded what remained of the values they used to carry— those expressed in the politics of agnatic rank. But agnation, which had formerly woven domestic units into the body politic, was now eclipsed by the social and material forces that bound the community as a whole to the South African state (J. Comaroff 1985:160f; cf. Arrighi 1979; Schapera 1947; Shillington 1985). Except for the elite few, marriage had also been disengaged from the pursuit of political alliance (J. L. Comaroff 1987a).

Here, as elsewhere among the dispossessed of the earth, the overall marriage rate had declined sharply. Domestic histories collected in 1970 suggested that, over the previous 25 years, only half of all unions had involved the exchange of cattle, and *go rulaganya bana* was rarely practiced any longer (cf. Murray 1980:107f). Where bridewealth was transferred, it had come increasingly to feature cash, although, significantly, it was still spoken of in terms of a given number of beasts, a matter to which we shall return below. Caught in a web of poverty and dependance, most people had only their labor power to offer, and their depressed wages rendered them more or less impotent in a world dominated by money (see Chapter 6).

Not surprisingly, Tshidi have fashioned an elaborate symbolic discourse on the subject of money itself. The term for it, *madi*, an Anglicism, is a homonym for "blood," an irony which is put to cogent rhetorical use. Just as blood is seen as a source of life-giving motion within the body, so money seems to suggest the circulation of essential vitality in the social world (J. Comaroff 1985:174f). But, whereas bodily health is a function of the temperateness and fluidity of blood, illness and debilitation, both physical and social, bespeak its overheated, sluggish flow. Money, as we might expect, is "hot." Like a corrosive acid, it "burns" the pockets of those who try to hold on to it; like the unpredictable, dangerous fire of female fertility, it is explicitly opposed to the cool stability associated with cattle and male political control. "Money runs through your pockets and leaves you hungry. Cattle always return to make you fat," we were often told (cf. Ferguson 1985:662). While cash stands to stock as did female to male qualities in precolonial times, the former always threatening the latter, it is not a specifically feminine form of wealth. Nor is it more highly valued by women, as is the case among the Sotho (Ferguson 1985:665), although this is not to deny that they, perhaps even more than males, desire the goods that money can buy. The point, rather, is that virtually all Tshidi, now at the mercy of the capricious coin, exist in the state of subordination formerly associated with femaleness. For these people, men and women alike, the beast remains a symbol of economic and cultural self-sufficiency. It represents the freedom from the labor market of which many Tswana dream (cf. Alverson 1978:123; Peters 1983). That dream, typically, hinges upon turning cash earnings into a herd, thereby to break out of the cycle of migration and want.

The dream is seldom realized, however. Rich men, the miniscule middle class under *apartheid*, may invest in animals and still negotiate rights in people through them. But, for others, such transactions have become the stuff of an idealized, bygone age. While the market price of livestock has fluctuated greatly this century, their real cost has risen steadily "relative to the earnings from migrant labor" (Roe 1980:40), making them ever more difficult to buy. Consequently, for most Tshidi, cattle are, today, the tragic icon of a vanished world of self-determination, a mythic society in which men were men, in which women did not struggle alone in the rural wastelands, in which the control of social vitality was ultimately ensured by the goodly beast. Modern migrants offer a cynical commentary on the irony of their predicament, their world turned upside down. They describe themselves as "women," "tinned fish," and, above all, "draught oxen." Reduced to less than fully social beings, it is they who are now the animate source of value for others (Comaroff and Comaroff 1987:200).

In spite of all this, or perhaps because of it, the "bovine mystique" (Ferguson 1985) is perpetuated. In Tshidi eyes, livestock remain the ideal medium for the storage of wealth, being much more resilient to dissipation than is money. And, notwithstanding the practical difficulties of doing so, many still speak in various ways of converting cash back into cattle, of casting off their state of dependency. Given the inroads made into their environment by commerce and commodities, not to mention their brute poverty, this preoccupation is not hard to fathom. Neither is the fact that coins circulate among them as symbolically charged currency. Or that their ritual activity sometimes focuses on the manipulation of money in an attempt to bring it under control (J. Comaroff 1985:236). For the majority, as we have said, the most salient feature of cash is its sheer velocity and elusiveness. This, and its association with the dark and distant forces which dictate the rhythms of modern life, merely reiterates the contrast with beasts; with their manifest, dependable powers of increase and their resistance to the voracious demands of everyday need. Cattle, Tshidi say, are their "Barclays Bank."[13] They are not alone in speaking thus. The same sardonic imagery appears widely among Central and South African pastoralists (cf. Alverson 1978:124; Fielder 1973:351).

Certain important transactions within the community—among them, marriage and court fines, patronage loans and payments to healers—are still reckoned by everyone in terms of cattle. But, much of the time, these are "cattle without legs" (*dikgomo tse di tlhokang maoto*), the phrase used by Tshidi for tokens of (ostensibly) fixed cash value. Sansom (1976:144) has noted that, among Pedi, "signal transactions" of this kind are characteristic of bridewealth, initiation, fines, and damages; that is, of prestations and compensations involving changes of status. In signalling such transitions, nominal animal currency also distinguishes this *form* of exchange from ordinary market dealings. The monetary worth of a token beast is generally not frozen for all time. But it is always far lower than the going commercial price. The discontinuity is further underlined by the fact that nominal values are spoken of in pounds sterling, an archaic currency (Sansom 1976:145).[14] It is also significant that, while they remain well below "real" rates, such token values *do* tend to rise with inflation (cf.

Murray 1981): they are articulated with the market, yet are markedly out of step with it—as if to declare its irrelevance and, thereby, to hold at bay its intrusion into critical spheres of social life.

Tshidi "cattle without legs" carry similar signal value. They, too, mark transactions that stress the enduring quality of persons and relations. In the early 1970s, a nominal beast was worth six pounds—ludicrously below the prevailing market price, as Tshidi themselves readily pointed out. But it is precisely in this discrepancy that the significance of any symbolic currency lies. In an expanding universe, in which little seems to escape being equated with or reduced to money, "legless" livestock are a salient anachronism. By denying the universalizing rationality of commerce—its colonizing "modernity"—these "cows" inscribe the worth of local social practices in the cultural capital of *setswana* ("Tswana ways"). And, by restricting their conversion to a cash equivalent, they put such practices beyond the purview of the coin. The relations built with token animals are thereby distinguished as special and, as important, stable; in this respect, also, they are set off from the uncertainties of *sekgoa*, things "European." An extension of the opposition between the beast and the banknote, these legless animals stand as a line of defense against the erosion of what most Tshidi take to be their distinctive social wealth. They represent an effort to make cattle serve again as the guarantor of value in a world of flux, as an "enclave" that resists dissolution to the promiscuous terms of the market (cf. Ferguson 1988:494). After all, *madi ga a na mong,* money has no owner.

IV

This returns us to the issue with which we began. Marx (1967,1:82) saw money as a "special commodity," a sort of "social hieroglyph." Being a "natural object with strange properties," it serves at once as a measure of value and a standard of price for all other commodities (1967,1:94, 106). Much the same can be said of beasts among the Tshidi. They, too, may be currency and capital simultaneously; they, too, have the unusual ability to make commensurable different forms of value and to convert one form into another. It is this capacity—to equate and transform, to give worth and meaning—that quite literally animates both cattle and cash. And makes them objects of fetishism; objects, that is, which seem to have a logic all of their own, able to do things, to forge relations, and to increase of their own accord—without ever disclosing the forces that fabricate *them.* Fetishism, of course, was essential to Marx's notion of the "strange properties" of the commodity; of its role in mediating production and consumption, power and meaning. Ironically, perhaps, it is just this, the fetishism of things, that is most conspicuously absent from recent anthropological accounts of the nature of objects in the social world.

Thus, Appadurai (1986), to take one noteworthy case, defines the commodity merely as an "object in motion," and seeks the "social life of things" primarily in exchange. His approach has many virtues. For one thing, it does away with the misleading opposition between gifts and commodities (Gregory 1982). Similarly, it has no place for facile dichotomies between use and exchange value (Taussig 1980a; cf. Ferguson 1988). And it encourages us to explore the ways in which "the capitalist mode of commoditization . . . interact[s] with myriad other indigenous social forms of commoditization" (Appadurai 1986:16). On the other hand, in treating all goods like Maussian gifts, Appadurai neglects the mechanisms through which, in a single movement, (surplus) value is generated, appropriated, and naturalized; through which, by means of *some* objects, particular forms of consciousness and inequality are shaped and reproduced. Goods may indeed come to signify "regimes of value," as he says (1986:4). But both cattle and money are *particular* sorts of goods, with a peculiar aptitude for abstracting and congealing wealth, for making and breaking meaningful associations, and for permitting some human beings to live off the backs of others. And all this without ever disclosing quite how or why any of these things should, or do, happen.

While they are alike in these respects, cattle and money are dissimilar in important ways as well; this being the consequence of their situation, respectively, in very different economies of signs and meanings, very different cultures of production and exchange. Thus, beasts might have facilitated the abstraction and transaction of value among precolonial and colonial Tshidi; and, notionally at least, they still have the potential to do so. But they had nowhere near the capacity of cash in capitalist societies to free goods and services from their contexts and make them commensurable. Conversely, the coin does not have the same capacity as the cow, symbolic or substantial, to embody a biography, let alone to bear within it an entire grammar of social relations. Southern Tswana are themselves wont to note the contrast, especially when they compare the world of the workplace with life beyond its purview. Not only do they remark that "money has no owner." They also add, wryly, that "one can eat cattle but not cash."

As they have learned, however, money *can* eat cattle. In a world increasingly dominated by the commodity, little remains irreducible to a cash equivalent; little escapes the indiscriminate melting pot of the market. We have seen how, as the South African political economy engulfed the Tshidi, it undermined not only their order of values, but also their ability to make a living without resort to wage labor. Time, work, sexual and ritual "services"—all things once embodied and conveyed through animals—have been variously reified, commoditized, given a price. No wonder that the tyranny of money is most plainly and painfully visible, at least to older Tshidi, in the relentlessness with which it has eaten away at their herds and the social fabric once knitted together by them.

Perhaps this is why Southern Tswana continue to make such a great imaginative investment in livestock, marking them out as the media with which to hold the line against the ravages of the market. By struggling to prevent the goodly beast from becoming mere beastly goods, they seek to limit the Midas touch of money, to resist the implosive effects of commerce and commodities within their world. Herein lies the significance of the "bovine mystique" for black migrant laborers all over southern Africa (Ferguson 1985, 1988)—and, in particular, the salience of legless cattle among the Tshidi. Symbolic currencies of this sort are tokens of the attempt to dam the corrosive flow of cash, to force it to bear the imprint of human relations. Africa offers many examples of such currencies, and of the effort to decommoditize the coin,[15] especially in those transactions, like bride-wealth, which build enduring social ties. Indeed, in the space between old and new commodities, hybrid beasts—like the nominal "cows" of the Pedi and Tshidi—have been born; beasts that challenge the uncompromising logic of a monetary economy. The impact of cash may be everywhere to hand, and it may have converted much into its own terms. But not everything. Many Africans still cherish the ideal of reversing this process, and strive hard to do so. The Tshidi are not alone in hoping that their labors may yet yield cattle *with* legs, cattle with which to rebuild a durable world.

Notes

An earlier version of this chapter was published under the title "How Beasts Lost Their Legs: Cattle in Tswana Economy and Society," in *Herders, Warriors, and Traders: Pastoralism in Africa,* edited by John P. Galaty and Pierre Bonte (Boulder: Westview Press, 1991).

1. This song was recorded by Schapera (1934:14). We have modified his translation slightly, using the term "chiefdom" for "tribe," and have modernized the Setswana orthography.

2. Evans-Pritchard was not alone in this observation. Others before him (e.g. Casalis 1861; Hunter 1936; Schapera and Goodwin 1937) had also noted the pervasive significance of cattle in African social and cultural life.

3. As is well known, the concept was introduced by Herskovits (1926), and, states Mair (1985:743), has been misused ever since. For brief but useful comment, with reference to southern Africa, see Kuper (1982:10f).

4. Kuper's generalization is perhaps too sweeping. While bovine bridewealth was indeed crucial to cattle-keepers, some predominantly agricultural peoples exchanged other things; the Lovedu, for example, gave ceremonial hoes for wives until the end of the nineteenth century, when they switched to livestock (Krige 1981:149). Among all Southern Bantu-speakers, moreover, the role of animals in marriage prestations has undergone complex

transformation during the twentieth century. (Of course, beasts played, and continue to play, a rather different part in the social lives of such other Southern and Central African pastoralists as the Herero.)

5. Given limitations of space, we cannot hope to include an adequately detailed account of precolonial economy and society here. In summarizing their most salient features, we take for granted our earlier writings on the subject. The same applies to our sources; they are annotated and evaluated elsewhere (e.g. J. L. Comaroff 1973; J. Comaroff 1985; Comaroff and Comaroff 1991:Chap. 4).

6. Although he never worked among Rolong, Reverend Willoughby, a missionary-ethnographer, clearly intended his observations to apply to *all* Tswana, unless otherwise specified; in his writings, in fact, he was always careful to record variations in cultural practices. Willoughby was well qualified to make such comparative statements, since he knew almost as much about the Rolong and Tlhaping as he did about the Kwena, Kgatla, and Ngwato, of whom he had direct experience. Like Livingstone before him, he first made acquaintance with the "Bechuana" through his brethren in the south before going on to take up his own mission. What is more, he remained an active member of the evangelists' circle, visited them often, and read their extensive accounts of "native life." Later he became head of Tiger Kloof Native Institution, a school near Vryburg on the borders of Rolong territory.

7. Gulbrandsen (1987:239f; see also 1986) has criticized us for, among other things, making too much of the opposition between agnation and matrilaterality. He also believes that we overstress the competitive quality of agnation. It is difficult to know how to react to these criticisms, however. First, they are based on ethnographic findings among a different Tswana people (the Ngwaketse) at a different period in time (the mid-1970s), notwithstanding our efforts to contextualize our own accounts as carefully as possible. Second, they characterize our descriptions of the Tshidi sociocultural order in a somewhat oversimplified manner, so that what is being taken to task is often not exactly what we intended. Third, we have ourselves taken pains to analyze the contradictions in Tshidi views of agnation, and to account for the ambiguities surrounding their cultural categories and oppositions.

8. A house consisted of a wife and her children. In a polygamous household, the unity of the different houses was stressed: each had its own fields and share of the family estate. Most significantly, its children were differentiated from their half-siblings by their ties to their matrilateral kin. Elsewhere (e.g. J. Comaroff 1985; Comaroff and Roberts 1981), we have provided detailed analyses of the house as an "atom" of sociocultural structure.

9. We have discussed the Southern Tswana conception of *tiro* more fully elsewhere, albeit for different purposes (see Chapter 6 below). Here we merely summarize its main features.

10. It was not only the productive labor of women that subsidized a man's political enterprises, of course. His wife also bore him children—just as his mother had given him his matrikin, his most steadfast supporters—through whom to make alliances and gain control over other people.

11. This discussion draws from our current research on Nonconformist evangelism among the Southern Tswana between 1820 and 1920. In addition to ethnohistorical materials collected in the late 1960s and mid-1970s, we have made extensive use of the archives of the London Missionary Society and Wesleyan Methodist Missionary Society.

12. Tshidi who live in Barolong (or the Barolong Farms) in southern Botswana have, with few exceptions, long ceased to keep cattle in large numbers. This small community, known as the "granary of Botswana," has been given over almost entirely to cultivation, most of it for the market. Although it falls within the greater orbit of the South African political economy, Barolong has not been subjected to the oppressive controls of the *apartheid* state, and has retained much greater productive autonomy. The handful of wealthy farmers who do have sizeable herds tend now to run them on commercial ranches provided for under Botswana's national Tribal Grazing Land Policy.

13. The subsidiary of a British company, Barclays is one of the oldest banks in South Africa, and has branches in virtually every city and small town—as it once did throughout much of the empire. For black South Africans, it has long been a powerful symbol of white wealth.

14. South Africa had changed its currency from sterling to rands some years before we did our first fieldwork among the Tshidi.

15. For an especially striking example, see Hutchinson's (1988) excellent analysis of modern Nuerland.

6

The Madman and the Migrant

I

IT IS PERHAPS IRONIC that we learnt our most profound lesson about consciousness in rural South Africa from a madman. The lesson was all the more remarkable because it came in a wordless encounter, a meeting in 1973 at a mental hospital for Tswana outside Mafeking. Famous for an ingenious costume that he would never remove, the man was, literally, a prophet in polythene robes. His crazy clothes spoke the language of his obsession. His boots, standard issue for mineworkers, were topped by intricately knitted leggings, the painstaking product of many unravelled orange sacks. He wore a cloak and a bishop's mitre, fashioned from black plastic garbage bags. Across his chest was stretched a brilliantly striped sash, on which were stitched three letters: SAR. For his white attendants, these were the most obvious signs of his delusion, although they noted that he also "heard" things. The other patients, however, regarded him as an inspired healer, sent to them in their affliction. SAR was his church, and he its sole embodiment. The letters stood for South African Railways, alongside whose track the hospital lay. In fact, at the very moment we encountered him, the night train for Johannesburg rattled by with its daily cargo of migrants. Later, as we puzzled to decipher his message, we kept returning, as he did, to SAR. It was a message that spoke directly to his fellow inmates—and also to the black paramedical staff. For, in this world of peasant-proletarians, the railway forged a tangible link between rural and urban life, hitching together the dissonant worlds of the country and the city.

We had long been aware of the importance of the distinction between these worlds for the Tshidi-Barolong, the Tswana people among whom we worked. One of our earliest conversations in Mafikeng, their capital, had been with a man who, while respected, was neither rich nor high-born. This "everyman" epitomized the older generation of peasant-workers,

155

having spent his young adult life laboring in the gold mines in Johannesburg. Now he surveyed his parched corn field, and said laconically:

> Here I struggle, but I work for myself (*itirèla;* the reflexive of *dirèla,* "work [do] for"). The soil is stony and there is no rain. I struggle, but I call no-one "boss." Out there, where we labor (*bèrèka*) for the whites, they pay us money. But the mine, like the grave, has use only for your body. When it has done with you it spits you out, and you are finished! Useless!

Despite its poignancy, this commentary on the experience of alienation was in some ways unremarkable. Oppressed workers elsewhere have been apt to see the mine as a predator, the industrial workplace as a tomb (see e.g. Van Onselin 1976; Gordon 1977; Nash 1979; Taussig 1980a; cf. also D. H. Lawrence 1922; Eliade 1962). What is more, our attempt to pursue the exegesis further proved fruitless. We were simply unable to elicit statements that tied exploitation to a coherent notion of class antagonism or even racial conflict. This, it seemed, had been one of those rare moments when otherwise mute experience found voice in a fortuitous clutch of images.

But longer familiarity with the Tshidi taught us that these images were not fortuitous, and that the meaning of the old migrant's message was widely shared. The clue lay in the form of his utterance: by a subtle choice of words, the vernacular term for work (or, more precisely here, "work for myself") was nicely distinguished from that used for labor done for whites. The first, *itirèla,* implies "making oneself." It is the reflexive form of the Setswana *go dira,* "to do" or "to make." *Bèrèka* (noun, *mmèrèkò*), on the other hand, comes from the Afrikaans verb *werk,* and connotes "to do wage labor" (apparently for all Sotho-Tswana speakers; Ziervogel and Mokgokong 1985). As we shall see, these terms form a significant opposition, carrying with them a fan of associations interlaced in the Tshidi imagination: work contrasts with labor as does self-construction with self-destruction; as time logged "out there" with the creative processes of production and reproduction "at home" (*mo gae*); as the enduring value of cattle with the capricious flow of money. But these contrasts are neither frozen in a timeless cultural scheme nor played out in a narrative vision of history. Rather, they provide a versatile and poetic language, one capable of giving voice to both the musings of the migrant and the creations of the crazy prophet. In them, as in the polythene robes, lay a key to the Tshidi sense of themselves, of the making of their contemporary world.

II

It has become almost commonplace to ask why social classes seem so seldom to act for themselves (*für sich*); why class consciousness, the assertion of collective identity and interest, arises so infrequently—even under apparently favorable conditions (e.g. Wallerstein (1972) 1979:173; Marks and Rathbone 1982:26–7). The question itself raises a prior issue, however: What exactly do we take as expressions of collective consciousness? Is it possible that, for much of this century, Western social science, in both the Weberian and Marxian traditions, sought them in the wrong place? Social and political historians, especially those studying the collective consciousness of the dominated, have increasingly had to look beyond formal institutions, behind formulaic pronouncements, into the texture of the everyday (see e.g. Thompson 1963; Genovese 1972). This has also been the case in the African context. Van Onselin (1973, 1976), for instance, argues that the consciousness of Southern Rhodesian miners (1900-20) cannot be measured "by the presence or absence of associations and organizations which manifestly articulate worker interests" (1973:237). It was expressed, instead, in routine acts of resistance to the labor discipline of particular mines; in such tacit and taciturn forms of defiance as foot-dragging and absenteeism. Here, then, consciousness is not found in explicit statements of common predicament on the part of a social group, but in the implicit language of symbolic activity. Yet this only underscores the problem. In what sense does a set of inarticulate practices amount to *consciousness*? If we accept that the latter is more than just explicit social reflection—that it may hide itself in everyday activity—is it any different from the anthropological conception of culture? And, if so, does this not leave unanalyzed the relationship between conventional meaning and the processes of thought and action through which history is made?

This is the general problem which informs our analysis here, although we confine ourselves to a single social context. It is, however, a context in which issues of historical consciousness at large, and class consciousness in particular, arise in acute form: that of a black South African people drawn into the labor market and made to eke out an existence from a combination of small farming and wage work. Like others, Tshidi have been steadily impoverished by the rise of the regional political economy and have become yet another division in its reserve army of labor. In this respect, they are in no doubt that they are "oppressed" (*patikèga;* "pressed down"), though they do not have a straightforward sense of themselves as members of either a class or a community of workers. Being peasant-proletarians, they have long migrated between a rural "homeland" and the town, their journey articulating the worlds of agricultural production and wage labor, idealized past and discordant present.[1]

The Tshidi understanding of their modern situation is, quite explicitly, a consciousness of history; that is, it evokes the *making* of the social world, past and present. But this history is seldom spontaneously told in narrative style; that is, as a linear account of events.[2] Nor can it be readily distilled, from its various expressive forms, into an "objective" chronicle. It is captured, as the migrant implied—and we shall show in more detail below—in the dynamic interplay of a series of distinctions, contrasts which describe two radically different epochs that have come to coexist in time. These contrasts are sometimes acted out, sometimes spoken of, and always anchored in everyday activities.[3] Together they compose a meaningful account of a changing world and the place of the Tshidi within it.

Of course, this kind of historical reckoning is at odds with the conventional Western view of history as an account of "real" events and processes. At the heart of that view lies a distinction between reality, the actual making of history, and representation, the terms in which its story is told and acted on. Mitchell (1986), a literary critic, has recently argued that this distinction is basic to modern Western thought; it certainly underlies the familiar contrast between text and context, the concept and the concrete. But, as Mitchell goes on to suggest, representation itself is also believed to have two distinct modes: realism, where images aim to be faithful reflections of the world; and rhetoric, where those images, by their very form, evaluate the world as they portray it. The first tends to be seen as the medium of factual historical narrative, the second, of interpretive poetics. Philosophers, semioticians, and historians have disputed the soundness of this distinction as an analytic principle; few, perhaps, would defend it any longer. Yet its effects on our ways of seeing have been profound (cf. Friedrich 1979:442). Above all else, it leads directly to the assumption that poetic modes of representation are less true, more ideological, than are realistic narratives of the past. Poetic forms belong, at best, to the separate realm of aesthetics or mythology; at worst, to the dirty tricks of ideology. Either way, however, rhetoric is usually held to distort the collective imagination, breathing false life into sober social facts. In the final analysis, then, there can be no poetics of history.

But where does this leave the madman and the migrant? Neither speak in the genre of narrative realism. The madman may present the more dramatic picture; like many of his kind, he is dismissed, by those unfamiliar with his language, as a false prophet, a psychotic whose costume reflects no more than the workings of his own tortured mind. Yet even if he is defined as psychotic, he may nonetheless be the voice of history. Foucault (1967), for one, insists that the insane speak eloquently of their social world. Our madman, of course, uses visual imagery, while the migrant relies on verbal metaphor. But both use poetic expression to offer an authentic commentary on the Tshidi past and present. Friedrich (1979:441ff) has argued that the poetic is a pervasive aspect of all kinds of language; characterized by "figures and tropes, . . . intensification of form, . . . [and] association by analogy," it is the language "that most significantly interacts with the imagination (pp. 491–2)." In constructing their distinctions and contrasts, the madman and the migrant certainly use such instruments, although they do not limit themselves to words alone. Indeed, together they remind us that historical consciousness is not confined to one expressive mode. It may be created and conveyed—with great subtlety and no less "truth"—in a variety of genres.

The point is not limited to non-Western peoples, or to those at the peripheries of the modern world system. The Tshidi fondness for viewing history in terms of a set of contrasts recalls an observation made by Raymond Williams (1973). In his study of *The Country and the City* in modern English literature, he notes that the rural-urban opposition served as a very general model for interpreting a radically changing social order. Inasmuch as this opposition lent itself to the expression of differing visions of English life, it evoked a complex discourse about society, production, class, and gender—a discourse, that is, about history. Just as, among the Tshidi, the madman and the migrant spoke in contrasting ways of the same theme, so it was with different English writers. Some appeared to take the gulf between city and country as a self-evident fact of life, and proceeded to explore its social and symbolic associations. Others stressed the interdependence of the rural and urban worlds, and insisted on tracing the contradictory relations that united them in a single order. It is not only in Africa that those caught up in processes of radical change come to terms with their history by means of suggestive oppositions.

III

It is hardly surprising, in a context like South Africa, that modern Tshidi consciousness should hinge on the contrast of work and labor. For the past 135 years, after all, others have sought to induce them into the market economy and, more often than not, to transform them into laborers. In fact, one of their earliest recollections of the Boer presence in their midst goes back to 1851–2, when their chief refused the settlers military support for a punitive raid against another "recalcitrant" Tswana chiefdom (Molema 1966:41f). Southern Tswana had always showed deep suspicion of anyone who threatened their autonomy; so much so that, as early as 1820, some royals of the neighboring Tlhaping fled their capital after warning the ruler that "the missionaries will make you their servant" (Campbell 1822,1:77). And there is no question that the Tshidi believed the call for military aid to be a pretext (Molema 1966): "The Boers only wanted to make us work for them, to make us pay taxes," we were told in 1969 by a 90-year-old woman. The Tshidi were correct. Abused and attacked for their refusal, they were forced into a lengthy exile—from which they returned to find themselves being drawn ever more tightly into the colonial arena and its market for manpower and goods. Inasmuch as the past century in South Africa has "entailed the making of an African working class" (Marks and Rathbone 1982:2), its history, from the perspective of the victims, is above all else a labor history (Molema 1920:253-8)—although that is by no means all it is.

The colonial process introduced Tshidi not merely to wage work, but also to other features of commodity production—most notably, money, the supreme standard of value, and the clock, the measure of human labor time. In South Africa, as elsewhere, the experience of "time, work-discipline and industrial capitalism" (Thompson 1967) went together. But the forms of European capitalism were not implanted into a vacuum. The way in which the Tshidi set about making sense of the whole process was mediated, as it always is, by an existing set of cultural categories. Indeed, the experience of wage labor had of needs to be filtered through indigenous notions of human activity and the nature of work, just as money had to be understood in relation to local concepts of value, embodied especially in cattle (Comaroff and Comaroff 1990).

This, however, was not a confrontation between a primordial folk tradition and the modern world. Quite the contrary, Tswana "tradition" (*setswana*) was to be fashioned during the course of the nineteenth century. If not wholly invented (Hobsbawm and Ranger 1983), it was at least to be objectified: to be made into a heritage with imagined reference to the past but with its signs oriented toward the present. Moreover, *setswana* emerged in complementary opposition to *sekgoa* ("the ways of the European"), itself also a product of the encounter between Protestant imperialism and Africa. As this suggests, the discourse of contrast—of work and labor, cattle and money, and so on—had its roots deep in the colonial process itself. That process, of course, was to shape the political geography of South Africa, dividing yet binding the city and the countryside, white and black, the industrial workplace and the scheduled "native" reserve. And it was to bring the Tshidi face-to-face with the three interlocking agencies that were most active in remaking their social predicament and their historical consciousness: the mission, the market economy, and the colonial and postcolonial state.

It was the encounter with the first of these agencies, the Methodist mission, that laid the basis for the distinction between *setswana* and *sekgoa*. This encounter, in fact, paved the way for the dualistic vision of the world—and its expression in the concepts of work, time, and value— through which the political economy of apartheid was later to be understood. We have considered the role of the mission and its relationship to the other agencies of the colonial process elsewhere (Comaroff and Comaroff 1986; also J. Comaroff 1985). It is enough here to repeat a few well-established points about that process.

By the 1820s, when the Tshidi first made contact with the Methodists, their world was in the grip of forces let loose by the rise of the Zulu state. The waves of fugitives put to flight by Tshaka's regiments preyed on the settled agrarian peoples of central southern Africa (Lye 1969). In so doing, they opened the way for the missionary effort that, along with other forces, was to transform these peoples into a peasantry. The evangelists entered this theater of war with technical skills capable of making a decisive difference—guns, plows, irrigation methods and the means of long distance communication. Like other Tswana, the Tshidi actively sought them out. Almost from the start they became mediators among the displaced populations of the interior. Later that role was extended to relations between the chiefdoms and the Boers, whose trek from the Cape brought them into this same historical arena in 1837.

The role of the church in this chapter of southern African colonial history was at once ironic and contradictory. For its intervention, in the name of protecting the natives, was to prepare them for their eventual subordination—though not always in obvious ways (J. Comaroff 1985:123f). Insofar as the evangelists engaged in secular politics, they saw such activity as part of their larger "civilizing" mission. It helped in the task of enlightening the savage and bringing him into the social and cultural universe of Christian Europe. In the same vein, the Protestants quickly learned that, while the Tswana appreciated the "practical" benefits of their presence, they did not show the same enthusiasm for their "spiritual" message. This was blamed on the African's "carnal views to all spiritual things" (Broadbent 1865:178). As a result, the mission emphasized practical reconstruction, seeking to lay the basis for conversion by transforming the person through mundane activities of everyday life.[4]

Methodism was itself a product of the industrial revolution in Britain, having been directed, in particular, to the emerging working class of the northern river valleys (Troeltsch 1949; Warner 1930; cf. Weber 1958). Drawing on metaphors from the factory and the foundry, it spoke of individual salvation through arduous self-construction. And its emissaries to the slothful heathen—the "lazy Kafir," as Molema (1920:254) bluntly puts it—tried to make their stations living examples of productive enterprise. Here they demonstrated the utility of the plow and the pump, preached the virtues of sober discipline, and installed the clock and bell to mark out routines and ensure that time was well spent (Moffat 1842:339; cf. Wilson 1971:72, Oliver 1952:42). Here too, as the other side of their spiritual coin, they taught the value of the "varied treasures of commerce" (Mackenzie in Dachs 1975:72) and the supreme enabling power of money (Warner 1930:125).

Needless to say, the British evangelists shared very different concepts of personhood, production, and value from those they found among Tswana.

In the interplay of the two cultures each came to define itself in relation to the other, each reaching a new awareness of its distinctiveness at the very moment that it was being transformed by the encounter itself. From the Tshidi perspective, mission Methodism was presented to them both as a narrative—a story of the "Good News" of Christ's coming—and as a "faith" (*tumèlò*) in His "word" (*lehoko*), a coherent body of beliefs and practices offered to them as an alternative to the taken-for-granted world they inhabited. This, in turn, encouraged them to contrast the Christian message to their own mode of doing and being—and to speak of *setswana*, "Tswana ways." Even the act of naming it had the effect of making the latter appear as a systematic tradition. Of course, Christianity was itself part of an embracing colonial presence, the mission being merely its most visible face. It was this European presence that came to be described as *sekgoa*, the ways of *makgoa*, white people.

The impact of the mission was at once symbolic and material. Its faith in the moral worth of commerce ensured that evangelists would foster the production and sale of agricultural surpluses. They also nurtured a desire for "civilized" goods. Yet, while the Nonconformists cherished the ideal of a rural Christian peasantry, they actually prepared the Tswana for wage labor. For they instilled in them "wants" that could only be satisfied through entry into the colonial economy, and made them thoroughly familiar with the signs and values of the industrial work-place. In the early years of the "mineral revolution," in fact, many southern Tswana men (especially Tlhaping) spontaneously sought employment at the diamond-fields (Shillington 1982; Holub 1881,1:294). The mission had begun to convert them into colonial subjects.

But this source of "voluntary" labor was quite inadequate to the growing demand as South Africa entered an era of accelerated industrial develop-ment in the late nineteenth century. It was during this period that the Tshidi experienced firsthand the conditions of the colonial workplace. Control over the labor supply increasingly became the object of struggle among colonial capital, white farmers, the Imperial government, and the Tswana populations (sometimes championed by evangelists). It is instruc-tive, for example, that Molema (1966:180f), a Tshidi historian, describes the founding of the Union of South Africa as the result of Rhodes' sustained battle to force black labor into the market. Despite the strenuous efforts of such missionaries as Mackenzie to "save" the Tswana peasantry from destruction at the hands of "the capitalists" (Comaroff and Comaroff 1986), the Tshidi, like other native populations in the region, were pro-gressively undermined by ecological disaster and politico-economic domi-nation. The advent of the South African state formalized this process of dispossession by extending taxation, limiting access to land, and progres-sively confining blacks to the lowest and most insecure reaches of the labor market. A far cry, alas, from the liberating image of free trade and dignified labor!

IV

Let us return, then, to the signs and categories of modern Tshidi consciousness. We begin with the root contrast between work and labor.[5]

In *setswana, go dira* means "to make," "do" or "cause to happen." It includes a wide range of activities, from cultivation, cooking and creating a family to pastoralism, politics, and the performance of ritual. As in the past (Brown 1931:308), *tiro* is generally translated as "[a] work" and stresses the *act* of fabrication. It yields value in the form of persons, things and relations, although it may be undone by sorcery and other malign forces. But *tiro* is not an abstract quality or a commodity to be exchanged. It cannot exist as alienable "labor power." We were told more than once that, in the remote past (*bogologolo*), even the energies of a serf were only available to his master as part of a total bond of interdependence. They could not be given over to another person unless the relationship itself was transferred. Work, in short, is the positive aspect of human activity, and is expressed in the making of self and others in the course of everyday life.

As this implies, two interrelated features of work are foregrounded here: (i) that the self-construction of the person occurs in relation to others, and (ii) that it is a creative *process*. Not only are social beings made and remade by *tiro*, but the "product" is inseparable from the process of production itself. As Alverson (1978:132) has noted, "an individual not only produces for himself, but actually produces his entitlement to be a social person."[6] This is captured in the various inflections of *go dira*. Its simple reflexive form, *go itira*, means "to make oneself" or "to pose as," a notion with ambiguous moral implications. It suggests a form of self-enhancement that is egocentric and anti-social; hence the common usage *go itira motho* (lit. "to make oneself a distinct person") connotes "to be proud" or "haughty." Furthermore, *go itira* may be contrasted with *go itirèla*—the reflexive extension of *dirèla* ("to work for")—which translates as "to make (work, do) for oneself" in a positive sense. Alverson (1978:134) confirms that this term embodies a critical set of values for Tswana in Botswana: the building of wealth in family and social relations, in cattle and clients, in position and possessions. The creation of these forms of wealth is dubbed "great work." Value, in other words, lies in extending the self through ties of interdependence. Thus the significance of wealth objects, most notably cattle, is that they signal rights in people. By extension, power is a matter of personal autonomy, but this entails a position of control *within* a field of material and social exchange, not merely a state of individual self-sufficiency.

We have explained elsewhere[7] that the stress on the making of persons, relations, and identities was a feature of the precolonial Tshidi chiefdom. Although this polity underwent complex changes during colonial and postcolonial times, its internal organization was dominated by two principles that shaped social and material life. The first was agnation, which laid down the terms for the allocation of rank and, with it, control over people, position, and property. The second was a form of endogamy that encouraged close kin marriage, and so wove a dense fabric of overlapping relations which linked people in multiple, often contradictory ways. As a result, while free citizens were integrated into a nesting pyramid of political units—households, agnatic segments, wards, and sections—their status, the definition of social ties, and the composition of groups were always open to contention. In fact, in this system, where bonds were inherently ambiguous, individuals *had* to negotiate their social connections with one another. And so the world was always in flux, shifting with the ebb and flow of everyday social exchange—a process that placed the onus on household heads to "build themselves up" by making alliances and accumulating "greatness" and "wealth."

This process of social creativity was continuous. As elsewhere in Africa, the making of relations and statuses was typically a process rather than an event. It has long been noted, for instance, that a Tswana marriage was defined in both everyday and legal contexts with reference to the drawn out series of acts and exchanges that gradually brought it to maturity (Comaroff and Roberts 1977). A union was built up over time, the final transactions that completed it sometimes being made after the death of one or both parties (J. L. Comaroff 1980). This and other interpersonal bonds are best described as having been states of "becoming," not "being"; they existed (or, more accurately, matured) in the continuous present. As a result, Tshidi were reluctant ever to define social ties in such a manner as would close them off from the possibility of growth or transformation. Such enquiries as "Are you married?" or "Do you have children?" were often answered with a curt "Not yet!" (*ga e se*)—even by elderly women. For the Tshidi, relations and identities were potentialities to be realized and remade in the unceasing work of daily life.

The creation of social value, however, was threatened by counterveiling forces, driven by the conflicts generated within the social system itself. Thus close agnatic rivals, for example, sought to "eat" one another, to erode each other's autonomy by politico-economic and ritual means. A man who had been eaten—a metaphor, as we shall see, that suggested feminization—became not only a junior in agnatic rank, but also a client, and eventually lost all self-determination. He was, as Willoughby (1932:227) notes, "absorbed by another personality." Such a man and his family might be called upon to supply labor to his patron during the agricultural season. Like a woman, he had relatively little control over his own movement in space and time. Sorcery also played an important part in these processes of destruction, its malevolent influence undermining all positive social action. Not surprisingly, "great work" involved the protection of one's efforts, and those of one's dependants, from the ever-present danger of being undone (*dirologa;* reversive extension of *dira*). Men took great pains to fortify their homesteads and fields against attack.

The concept of *itirèla,* then, implied the work of social life. It expressed a vision of the world in which the construction of the person, the accumulation of wealth and rank, and the protection of an autonomous identity were indivisible aspects of social practice. The converse of self-construction was the eclipse of personal viability, an overshadowing caused by the invasion of malign human or spiritual forces. In extreme form, such an invasion led to the death of the self. As an early observer put it:

> When a man's relatives notice that his whole nature is changed, that the light of the mind is darkened and character has deteriorated so that it may be said that the real manhood is dead, though the body still lives; when they realize that to all intents and purposes the human is alienated from fellowship with his kith and kin, they apply to him a name (*sebibi* or *sehihi*), which signifies that though the body lives and moves it is only a grave, a place where something has died or been killed. The essential manhood is dead. It is no uncommon thing to hear a person spoken of as being dead when he stands before you visibly alive. When this takes place it always means that there has been an overshadowing of the true relationships of life . . . (Brown 1926:137–8)

As this suggests, the self lived only in its interaction with others. The object of *tiro* was to avoid social death; to continue producing oneself by producing people and things.

Of course, not all human beings were equally capable of such activity: chiefs and ritual experts, for example, had unusual creative power. Above all, though, male work differed fundamentally from that of females. Before the introduction of the plow, women were associated primarily with agriculture and reproduction. They were the source of the most basic social value, human life itself. But their very fertility generated a polluting heat (*bothithò*) that could "spoil" (*go senya*) the ritual, political, and economic projects of men (among them, rainmaking and initiation, ancestral veneration and animal husbandry). Thus they were held to need physical confinement and were denied an active role in the transactions that shaped the public world—especially cattle exchanges and politico-legal debate. By contrast, males were regarded as "cool" (*tsididi*); they had the qualities necessary for effective social production and, in particular, for the management of stock. As public actors, men represented themselves and their families through the medium of cattle, the currency against which they exchanged rights in women and dependants. With beasts they made clients of other men, and entered into alliances with both the living and the dead, extending themselves as they built and rebuilt a centralized political community.

But male and female production were not merely opposed and complementary, just as women and men were not simply opposed and complementary social beings. While wives did hold fields in their own right, had their own granaries, and exercised some control over the use of their harvest, they were not independent producers. Their "works"—the fruits of their reproductive and agricultural labor—were appropriated by men in one or another capacity. The general point was made repeatedly in Tswana poetics: thus the origin myth of the male initiation, the most comprehensive of their creative rites, told how the social world was born when the raw fertility of females was domesticated by men. The ritual itself went on to dramatize the seizure, by males, of the process of childbirth, which was then put to the purposes of social rebirth—just as, in the context of everyday life, women were harnessed to the reproduction of the polity, providing the material base that subsidized male politics and ritual.

Female "work" was controlled through communal politico-ritual processes. Crucial here was the regulation, by the chief, of the agricultural cycle and the conversion of the space-time of female activity to the rhythms of the male social calendar. Only a ruler could begin the cycle of cultivation by "giving out the seed time." Time, for Tshidi, was not an abstract entity, a resource that could be separated from the flow of human action and events. If there was no action, there was no time either to be spent or wasted; this was implicit in the processual nature of *tiro*, and in the Tswana stress on relations and identities as "states of becoming" (see above). In fact, the vernacular *lobaka*, a "period of time" (or "duration") also connotes "space." In dispensing the "time for beginning to sow," a chief, who also "owned" the land and could bring the rain, *created* the time and space within which women might produce the crop. Their work, ordered by the tempo of the growth cycle, culminated in the ritualized return of the harvest to the chiefly court at a first fruits ceremony (*go loma thôtse;* J. Comaroff 1985:66). This rite of renewal, in which households participated in their recognised order of seniority, also spelled out the hierarchical structure of the political community. The place of female labor in the recreation of the polity could not have been more vividly enacted.

The Tshidi conception of *tiro,* then, was part and parcel of a distinct world of meaning and action. It contrasts sharply with the notion of labor in the culture of nineteenth-century European colonialism.

We have noted that the Protestant missions among the southern Tswana opened the way for British colonialism; that their impact was more in the practical sphere of production and exchange than in the realm of the sacred; that they spoke of a free market of the spirit, a moral economy that required the Africans to be cut loose from their "communistic relations . . . letting in the fresh, stimulating breath of healthy competition" (Mackenzie in Dachs 1975:652). This entailed a conception of person, property, and labor cast in the fervent images of nineteenth-century industrial capitalism (Comaroff and Comaroff 1986). It celebrated the private estate, commerce, and the ideal of material and spiritual accumulation; each mortal was exhorted to lay up treasures for him or herself by dint of sheer effort. All this, of course, demanded participation in a monetized system of exchange. Quite explicitly, the black convert was to be recreated as he was drawn into the colonial economy and, through it, into "the body of corporate nations" (Livingstone 1857:34). Money was the vital medium of this transformation, alike the means and the measure of self-improvement.

The Nonconformist mission projected this ideology most tangibly in its discourse about labor. Methodist rhetoric, in particular, drew on the symbols of the industrial workplace, teaching the Tshidi that wage-labor was the divine instrument of redemption (J. Comaroff 1985:132). They spoke of labor as a commodity to be measured against other commodities, to be bought and sold in the market (cf. Marx 1967,1:167f [1867]). Counted in hours and valued in coins, it was the price of life eternal, to be husbanded wisely on individual account. Labor power was an alienable part of each human being and should be spent in pursuit of a personal salvation. The labor relation, moreover, was assumed to be an ethical one. Worker and master each had a function, performing their role as a divine calling (Warner 1930:146f). Industrious self-discipline went along with an acceptance of the given "design" of the social world. Like Wesley before them, the Protestant missionaries in South Africa encouraged docility in the workplace. Its trials and sufferings were to be bravely born, for they were the means of moral advancement.

Labor, in sum, was the key to salvation, and the missions sought to impress this on the natives of South Africa by both word and deed. Their efforts were to play into other forces of imperialism and colonialism in complex ways that we cannot pursue here. Suffice it to say that the Protestants were instrumental in instilling the signs and conventions, the values and wants, of the colonial marketplace, a fact that was exploited by the more cynical agencies of proletarianization that were to follow. With the rapid development of mining and industry in the late nineteenth century, and the rise of the South African state in the early twentieth, the southern Tswana found themselves being steadily impoverished (Shillington 1985). Coerced into the insatiable urban labor market, they were drawn ever more tightly into the industrial capitalist economy. Cattle gave way to cash as the primary currency. Yet, because income was kept below a level sufficient to support workers and their dependants, much of the population was trapped into an uneasy combination of wage-labor and subsistence farming.

Compelled to move between the urban workplace and the arid "homeland," Tshidi migrants soon produced a sardonic commentary on the lesson of free labor. This, as we might expect, was less a narrative of dispossession than a symbolic elaboration of the contrast between work and labor. For, as Alverson (1978:136) was to observe in Botswana, "wage-labor violates the very definition of 'doing'." From the earliest years of this century, Tshidi have spoken, in their everyday practices and poetic forms, of the experience of alienation. In the 1970s they talked to us of the impact of labor that depletes rather than enhances the self; labor that denies a worker control over the products in which he invests himself and so vitiates a world of meaningful relations. The testimony of Tshidi migrants dwelt particularly on the theme of dehumanization. Drawing on brute physical images born in the racist workplace, these men characterised themselves as yoked beasts with no command of the situation into which they were drawn. Having lost control over their personal time and space, they were overshadowed, eclipsed. As rural Tswana have long said, migrant workers are "outside" (*kaha ntlè*); in forced exile to the realm of the whites, they are external to the creative life of the community.

Mmèrèkò/bèrèka, the construct that captured this process in Tshidi thought, was inextricably bound up with their conception of money. As our migrant made clear, *mmèrèkò* is "work-for-money," a necessity brought upon them by the inescapable need for cash. The term *madi,* derived from English, is a homonym for "blood," a fact which, to Tshidi themselves, seemed tragically appropriate. Where working conditions were often dangerous and destructive, the equation of the wage with the worker's substance was especially direct. But the Tshidi also spoke of money in the way they did of spilled human blood, as "hot"—that is, as a negation of life. It burns those who try to hold on to it, they would assert, and "runs through your pockets, leaving you hungry." In contrast, "cattle always return to make you fat." Here the heat of money earned by *mmèrèkò* was set against the cool stability of livestock produced by *tiro.* Its destructive flow ran counter to the enriching exchanges of bovine currency. As this suggests, the beast had become the symbol of a lost world of economic self-sufficiency, representing the freedom from the labor market of which all Tswana migrants dream (cf. Alverson 1978:123; Peters 1983). But money tended to "eat" cattle, for people were often forced to convert their wealth into cash, or to concentrate all their energies into *mmèrèkò.* As workers, Tshidi men saw themselves as less than fully social beings; they were "women" or "children," "draught oxen," "donkeys" or even "tinned fish" (cf. Alverson 1978:225f). In the world of *mmèrèkò,* they were socially depleted, the vehicles of someone else's profit.

It will be patent, now, why the contrast of work and labor carried with it such a wealth of associations: why *tiro* connoted socially contextualized production that "built up" persons, generated value, and was realized in such stable media as cattle—while *mmèrèkò* occured "outside," destroyed and emasculated, and was paid in the capricious coin, which has "no real owner." Let us be clear about the status of these oppositions, however. We hold that, far from being neutral signs, they were ideological forms produced by the Tshidi engagement in a continuous history. Specifically, they emerged out of the colonial encounter, a process that incorporated the Tswana peoples into a contradictory social order, and gave rise to a discourse of cultural contrast. *Tiro* and *mmèrèkò,* it turns out, are *setswana* and *sekgoa* in the active voice, the practices that made a difference in a world of cultural distinction and social inequality. As such, we repeat, these terms have not been static—just as the relationship of black South Africans to their rulers has not gone unchanged. Indeed, it may be that the contrast itself is yielding in some contexts: for example, amongst younger wage earners oriented primarily toward the city, and those in Botswana less caught up in the radical divisions of the South African political economy (Patrick Molutsi, personal communication). But, well into the 1970s, the rhetoric of contrast provided most older Tshidi men, in the rural area at least, with an imaginative trope for organizing their experience and for wrestling with its conflicts. It is to this process, especially as personified in the madman and the migrant, that we now return.

V

In the 1970s, the contrast between work and labor, with its rich texture of associations, was called on constantly by Tshidi in their everyday lives. It was as pervasive in the implicit statements of their architecture and argot as it was in the explicit debates of their "customary" courts. Here we can offer only a few highly selective illustrations to show that the madman and the migrant drew on a shared vocabulary; that their home-made images had echoes elsewhere on the cultural landscape, and captured familiar nuances of Tshidi experience.

Perhaps the most implicit use of the rhetoric of contrast by the Tshidi was to be found in their conceptual map of the rural domain. This domain hinged on their former capital, Mafikeng, which lay just a halfmile from the white town of Mafeking. These two towns were separated by a century of colonial history,[8] and by the madman's railway line. The very name

"Mafeking," a corruption of the vernacular for "the place of rocks," made a subtle comment on that history, marking the distinction between the local white politico-economic center and the seat of the chiefship, which remained the anchor of the Tshidi sense of *setswana*. Mafeking was the most immediate citadel of *sekgoa*, and from it emanated demands for taxes, and for labor both domestic and distant. Its rectangular groundplan, broad roads, and neatly fenced bungalows contrasted sharply with the sinuous paths and circular compounds of its black counterpart. The terms on which Tshidi engaged with the wryly named "White City" were quite explicit. The only blacks allowed on its curfewed streets at night were those who carried letters of permission from their employers. In Mafikeng, the statement *"ke ya mmèrèkòng"* ("I'm going to work") implied a journey over the railway bridge beside the offices of the watchful Bantu Affairs Commissioner, who articulated all movement between the domains of work and labor.

There was a bitter historical irony in this. In the precolonial past, Tswana controlled the labor of serfs, usually Sarwa ("bushmen") and Kgalagadi. Compelled to reside in the bush (*naga*) outside the town, these subject peoples were thought of as subhuman creatures of the wild. Now the Tshidi themselves lived "outside" Mafeking, coming in to deliver their labor to masters who regulated their time and space. The pageantry of power and dehumanization could hardly have been more obvious; the center of their world had become the unmarked periphery, the wild almost, beyond the boundaries of the white town. And with every crossing of the bridge—itself a colonial metaphor of very general application, as Paul Scott has driven home[9]—the structure of their life world was physically traced out.

But, as we have stressed, the contrasts of Tshidi consciousness were not fixed or unchanging. With shifts in the line of distinction—the "border" (Williams 1973:264)—between work and labor, *setswana and sekgoa,* the imaginative weight of these categories has changed. Again the symbolism of space provides an apt instance. As a consequence of the policy of separate development and the creation of ethnic "homelands" for black South Africans, the government designated Mafeking as the first headquarters of Bophuthatswana ("the United Tswana People"). To this end, they laid the foundations, in the 1960s, of a large residential area, equidistant from Mafeking and Mafikeng. Built to accommodate the "new" citizens of the putative homeland, the township in fact recreated the familiar structure of the urban "location" for black workers. This was the architecture of wage-labor: the two-roomed, rented units stood in relentless monotony along well-lit and eminently policeable thoroughfares. No livestock could be held in its fenced yards, which were also too small for cultivation.

The Tshidi reacted immediately to this unwelcome addition to their divided landscape. They had long contested the imposition of the homeland scheme, of which this was the most recent expression (J. L. Comaroff 1974:passim; J. Comaroff 1985:38f), and they now resisted all attempts to fit them into the new residential mould. They flatly refused to move into the completed houses, which were left to the mixed population—the "sell-outs," as they dubbed them—that began to move in from elsewhere to work for the administration. The government had called its creation Montshiwa Township, named—provocatively, Tshidi assumed—after their once independent ruling dynasty. They themselves tended instead to refer to the place as the "Government Compound," evoking the restrictive enclosures of the mine. The population of the township was said to be "naked" (*ba apogile*); it had been divested of the physical and social relations of a proper *setswana* life. Thus entrapped in the habitations of *mmèrèkò*, the world of rents and wages, there was no space for self-creation, no time to generate wealth in people. Montshiwa Township might have been nearby, but, by a rhetorical leap of the imagination, it had been placed over the border. Those who lived in it might reside in the rural area, but they were unmistakeably citizens of the realm of *sekgoa*.

An altogether more explicit rhetoric of contrast was to be heard in the Tshidi courts. These courts (*makgotla;* sing. *kgotla*), and especially that of the chief, had always occupied a position of great importance in Tshidi life. Often described in the ethnographic literature as something akin to a Western law court, the *kgotla* was much more. An arena for political debate, dispute, communal ritual, and other collective processes, it was the forum in which most public discourse took place—the context in which Tshidi spoke among themselves in the language of *mekgwa le melaò ya setswana,* the conventions of *setswana*.[10] But colonial overrule transformed the *kgotla* into a cog in the adminitrative machine; it became a "customary" tribunal. As such, it could only try minor matters formally defined as *setswana,* applying *mekgwa le melaò* to arrive at its decisions. On the other hand, anything *sekgoa*—that is, anything involving relations between Tshidi and whites, or too serious for the chief—had to be handled by the colonial (and later the postcolonial) judicial system. *Sekgoa* law focused on contracts, constitutions, and individual culpability; not only did it enforce the ideas of personhood, property, and status for which the mission had prepared the Tshidi, but it seemed to underpin the entire system of wage-labor. Moreover, the chief's *kgotla*, the final court of appeal in indigenous dispute processes, now became a court of first instance, from which cases went to the Bantu Commissioner's Office. Just as Mafeking had come to encompass Mafikeng, so the kgotla was encompassed by the courts of *sekgoa*.

The procedures and aesthetic styles of these courts differed greatly. For Tshidi, who had a rich tradition of public oratory—they even nicknamed men by their known rhetorical gifts and idiosyncrasies—the *sekgoa* courts were marked by their impoverished discourse. "A magistrate only wants to know what happened," an irritated old man told us, echoing the perception of many Tshidi. " 'Quickly! Was this law or that law broken?' He is not interested in people's lives!" In the *kgotla,* time was not an issue, and "facts" were debated as part of the construction and negotiation of biographies (Comaroff and Roberts 1981); in *setswana,* by contrast to English, "fact" and "deed" are indistinguishable. A case (*tshekò*) was itself an aspect of *tiro,* a moment in the constant process of social engagement. The magistrate or the Bantu Commissioner, whose courts were invested with tangible signs of state power, belonged firmly in the domain of *mmèrèkò.* Not only were they situated in Mafeking, but, more often than not, defendants appeared before them because of an offence allegedly committed at work, because they had violated the property of whites, or because they had defaulted on the obligations of some or other *sekgoa* contract. And usually they had to pay for their crimes by "serving time" or by forfeiting their cash wages.

Not surprisingly, Tshidi complained bitterly about the South African legal system, and sometimes gave their protest a visible, if unsubtle, touch of poetic justice. In 1969, some young men named a tree behind the chief's *kgotla,* "the Bantu Commissioner's Office," and delighted in relieving themselves against it after public assemblies. More constructively, Tshidi tried, where possible, to have their disputes heard in the *kgotla,* even if the social consequences were potentially more grievous. Dealing with *sekgoa* law had itself become a part of the *setswana* dispute process; quite overtly, Tshidi used their creative powers to the full in eluding its control.

However, it was not just in respect of the structure of the legal system that Tshidi reflected on *setswana* and *sekgoa, tiro* and *mmèrèkò,* or used the categories to capture the transformations of their world. These terms also ordered the content of public discourse. An especially notable instance involved the construction of marriage. As we said earlier, a union here was held to be a "state of becoming," a relationship which matured over many years and through many social exchanges. Tshidi were quick to note that migrant labor disrupted this process, and that migrants often took partners while away. As a result, the *kgotla* was presented with innumerable cases of neglect by females and frequently had to establish the status of unions. Most commonly, it had to decide whether the woman was really "a wife" of the male defendant, or had just been a casual partner with little further claim on him. The ambiguities surrounding the marriage process had always allowed for such arguments, but the impact of wage-labor was to increase their incidence to epidemic proportions.

In order to deal with these difficulties, the Tshidi, like other Tswana, made ingenious use of loan words to extend the opposition of *setswana* and *sekgoa* to heterosexual bonding. The vernacular term for the marriage process, *nyalo* (*go nyala*, masc.; *go nyalwa*, fem.), which had formerly covered all potential conjugal ties, became restricted in its reference: it was now used only for properly constructed (that is, *setswana*) relations. Casual liaisons, especially those created in the realm of *mmèrèkò* (or between visits to that realm) were called, in Afrikaans, *donkie trou*, "donkey marriage." These liaisons, in contrast to the drawn out exchanges of *nyalo*, were established by *vat en sit* ("grab and settle"). The allusion, clearly, was to the undignified coupling of animals, an emphatically nonsocial event brought about by reducing human beings to beasts of burden. Furthermore, the use of Afrikaans, the language of domination, was not coincidental. Like the term *mmèrèkò* (or *bèrèka*) itself, it assigned blame to those who had unravelled the Tshidi social world. Over time, the *kgotla* felt it necessary to address the issues raised by these unions, and chiefs developed a policy in respect of them. They began to award some rights of support to the women concerned but, significantly, made such awards in terms of cash or consumer goods rather than cattle, the currency of *setswana* marriage. Although these settlements clearly distinguished *donkie trou* from other unions, they were explicitly intended to recognise that new forms of relationship were being produced in the wake of wage-labor, relationships that had to be situated within the Tshidi world.

But it is perhaps the madman and the migrant themselves who best illustrate how Tshidi invoked the contrast of *tiro* and *mmèrèkò* to act upon their world. As we have noted, the madman suffered "delusion" only by Western definition. To Tshidi he was a *moporofeta* (a "prophet"), a term borrowed, like the polythene robes, and put to work in the particular historical conditions of postcolonial South Africa. A visionary in popular terms, he was seen to make visible, in his idiosyncratic concoctions, something implicit in the experience of many Tshidi. There was a quality of bemused recognition in the way they responded to him, though few could explain this in words. In one sense, of course, he was a token of a type, a "Zionist"; that is, a member of a Christian cult that seeks to merge elements "traditional" and "European" (J. Comaroff 1985:Chap. 7; Fogelqvist 1986). Yet in another sense he was unique, for he had executed the Zionist collage in a highly original manner—revealing once again the unpredictability of the human imagination, even while on a short cultural rein.

The madman, then, was one of those who "insists on [making visible] the connections" (Williams 1973:264) between the elements of a contradictory world; one who bears the insignia of continuity quite literally on his chest. South African Railways had carried him to the gold mines as young migrant, and it had brought him back again when the Spirit called him to return once more and "work" (*dira*) among his own people. We never learned why he had been committed to the asylum. It may have been his fondness for standing as mute witness near the railway depot in the white town where returning laborers alighted. Like madmen and witches everywhere, he offered genteel society an image of itself that it would rather forget. For, to all who looked at him, one thing was clear: he had worked on himself with laborious care to bring together in startling anomaly things that, frequently, were kept well apart.

In contrast to the migrant, who tried to cut himself off from the signs and memories of mine-work, the prophet, despite having freed himself from wage-labor, would not give up his old miner's boots, and was said to receive spiritual inspiration from his "headquarters" in Gauteng (Johannesburg; lit. "the place of gold"). The letters "SAR," too, were a constant reminder of the connection of center and periphery. And his habit evoked both the vestments of the high church and the gaiters of the colonial military, each reproduced through the remaking of waste commodities, a characteristic activity of the peasantariat. But around his knees, neck, and wrists he also wore the strips of cowhide that Tswana have long used to bind the body in healing and protection. Indeed, he was every inch an exemplar of the interdependence of rural and urban, work and labor, *setswana* and *sekgoa*. What is more, his regalia expressed an effort to reconcile these discordant categories, recalling Foucault's (1967) claim that we label as psychotic those who confront contradictions that the rest of us suppress.

Although he expressed himself in a rather different manner, the migrant relied on the same categories, his words and actions mapping out the tension between "here" and "there," "inside" and "out," "work" and "labor." Yet his rhetoric used these distinctions to highlight discontinuities, not connections. Thus he portrayed his past as a set of contrasting moments: those of self-creation were opposed to those of alienation as life is opposed to death, *setswana* to *sekgoa*. Imagery, here, was all of a piece with biography. The migrant's response to the contradictions of his world was to try to unhitch the country from the city, to escape from the domain of *mmèrèkò*, and to return to Mafikeng ("here," "inside") to a future of *tiro*.

This attempt to reverse the signs of incorporation and domination animated much of contemporary Tshidi practice, from their pursuit of cattle wealth to their energetic healing cults. Intimate experience had convinced the migrant that the opposition of *setswana* and *sekgoa* permitted no resolution. While a younger generation of Tswana might seek, and even realize, some form of satisfaction at the workplace (cf. Guy and Thabane 1986), their elders harbored few such hopes. The latter were also unversed in, or unmoved by, a universalist discourse that spoke of democracy, liberation, or labor politics. They were keenly aware that the inroads made into their universe by wage-work had reduced them to bondage; the invocation of stark rhetorical distinctions enabled them to ponder a solution, not by synthesis or reconciliation but by separation and withdrawal. Thrust back into the realities of rural subsistence, they asserted the authority of a male-oriented "tradition" in which the fruits of *mmèrèkò* were devalued. What is more, until the late 1970s, these men seldom confronted the conflicts of neocolonialism in direct political struggle, seeking instead to remake a recognizable world beyond the predators' grasp. In so doing, they also turned their backs on a consciousness of social class—and of class relations and antagonisms—as an organizing principle of South African society. Similarly, their historical imagination, with its stress on inescapable contrasts, did not fit well with a vision of revolution; a revolution that promised to remove those very contrasts and the forces underlying them. Indeed, the revolutionary process now spreading through Southern Africa challenges this generation of Tshidi ever more insistently to reconsider its dualistic worldview.

VI

We have been concerned, in this essay, with the poetics of history. Specifically, we have tried to trace out the way in which Tshidi create a sense of themselves by imaginative play with the categories of their culture. We have shown how the opposition between *sekgoa* and *setswana* took form in the colonial process; how it came to mediate that process, with work and labor as its primary tropes. It is not of direct significance to us here whether or not oppositions are universal features of the human mind, the deep structural bases of culture; this, in any case, would tell us little about the way in which human consciousness takes its form in time and space. Our focus, rather, is upon the way in which the poetics of contrast enter into historical processes.

As we have noted, the rhetorical use of contrast is widespread, especially in situations of radical social change. It appears, with similar force, in modern English literature (Williams 1973), in the semantic categories of changing coastal Kenya (Parkin 1979), and in the values of Shetland Islanders (Cohen 1979). But perhaps there is something unusually acute about the contradictions of a racially coded colonial society, a society in which the distinction between ruler and ruled is made to seem prescriptive and unyielding. Whether or not this is true, the poetic use of contrast and opposition in the Tshidi context makes two general points about the very nature of culture and consciousness.

The first is that culture always intervenes directly in consciousness and its expression. Thus the Tshidi contrast between *tiro* and *mmèrèkò*, for instance, was not just a function of the impact of industrial capitalism; it was a product of the dynamic interplay between European cultural forms and those of the precolonial order. Many anthropologists will see the point as self-evident, but it has often been overlooked in even the most sensitive of historical analyses. Van Onselin, to return to a celebrated case (above, p. 157), treats worker consciousness as a matter of reaction and resistance to the conditions of wage labor. The behavior of miners is seen to have been shaped largely by what they were protesting against, not by the cultural categories which they carried with them into the mine. This introduces the second point, namely, that culture and consciousness are not the same thing, and cannot be reduced to one another. There is a complex set of issues tied up in this statement, for it evokes the uneasy encounter between the anthropological idea of culture and the Marxian concepts of ideology and consciousness.

Anthropological approaches to culture have long been criticized for overstressing the implicit and categorical, for treating signs and symbols as if they were neutral and above history, and for ignoring their empowering and authoritative dimensions.[11] On the other hand, Marxist theory has been taken to task for neglecting both the meaningful bases of consciousness and the expressive forms of ideology. The effort to draw together the two perspectives, and so to address the shortcomings of both, lies at the core of much theoretical debate. We have sought to make a modest point in the context of that debate. It is that consciousness is best understood as the active process—sometimes implicit, sometimes explicit—in which human actors deploy historically salient cultural categories to construct their self-awareness. Its modes, we have shown, may be subtle and diverse; and it is as crucial to explore the forms in which a people choose to speak and act as it is to examine the content of their messages.

As we have seen, a people may not express their historical consciousness as conventional history at all. Hence, if we seek a narrative of events, or an account of past relations, we may be led to conclude that they lack any such consciousness; we may even be tempted to speak of theirs as a "cold" society. But the conclusion would be false. There is every reason to expect people caught up in processes of change to use the poetics of contrast to impose meaning on their world. Tshidi, like many others, often talk of their past and present in rhetorical terms, playing on the capacity of verbal and nonverbal images to connect and separate, attract and repel, transform or reinforce. Among them, to return to Mitchell's point, history and its representation are not nicely distinguishable. History lies *in* its representation; for representation is as much the making of history as it is consciousness speaking out. Moreover, realism and rhetoric do not stand opposed.

The poetry of representation, in short, is not an aesthetic embellishment of a "truth" that lies elsewhere. Its puns and metaphors, jokes and irreverencies are the stuff of everyday thought and action—of the human consciousness through which culture and history construct each other.

Notes

1. We do not suggest that, from a structural perspective, black South Africans live in two distinct worlds (or are caught up in a "dual" economy). It is now widely recognized that the colonial process drew them into a single, overarching political economy. We shall argue that the dualistic imagery in Tshidi consciousness arises from contradictions in their experience of that process.

2. This is not to say that Tswana cannot produce narrative histories—or historians. Among the Tshidi, Molema (1966) and Matthews (1945), both mission school alumni, are notable examples. But, here as elsewhere, there is a great difference in style between formal historical scholarship and the everyday historical discourses of a people.

3. As this implies, consciousness is not merely the sum of stated attitudes found amongst a population. The point is worth stressing, as this reduction is often made in the Western social sciences—a notable instance in the recent anthropological literature being Godoy's (1985:210) critique of Taussig (1980a).

4. There is a second, more subtle level of irony here too. The spiritual message contained in the Christian narrative—the story of God and his son, Jesus Christ—was widely rejected by the Tshidi. But the practical innovations of the mission (its nonnarrative discourse) were quickly accepted. It was through them that the implicit ethos of Protestantism was impressed upon the natives. Christianity, in other words, required a nonnarrative medium—practical innovation—to serve as the vehicle of its ideological "story."

5. By translating *go dira* (*itira*) and *go bèrèka* as "to work" and "to labor," we are arbitrarily specifying the use of these English terms. However, this seems the best way of capturing the contrast. There is a theoretical precedent, of course: Marx's analyses of the special character of labor under capitalism (see e.g. Firth 1979:179f; Wolf 1982:74f; cf. Schwimmer 1979). Another point of clarification is in order here. It is difficult, in the Western context, to discuss the meaning of "work" without taking into account its opposition to "leisure"; this opposition being part of the ideological apparatus of industrial capitalism. (For a summary statement from an anthropological perspective, see Parkin 1979:317f.) The mission sought to introduce the same set of ideas to the Tshidi; a dictionary compiled by an evangelist in ca.1875 (Brown 1931) translates *boiketlo* as "leisure." This is misleading, though. *Boiketlo* (from *iketla*, "peace") connotes "ease, comfort, convenience, and taking one's time"; it is not reducible to an antonym of *tiro*. Nor, as we shall see, is it the opposite of *mmèrèkò*, which also refers to a state of being rather than a mode of activity. The converse of *mmèrèkò* is a return to the world of *tiro*.

6. Alverson (1978) found much the same in Botswana as we did in South Africa on Tswana consciousness. He also notes the contrast of *dira/itirèla* and *bèrèka* (p. 118). While there are theoretical differences in our analyses, we take this as confirmation of the ethnographic findings.

7. See e.g. Comaroff and Roberts (1981), J. L. Comaroff (1982), J. Comaroff (1985), and Chapter 4 above for analyses of Tswana social systems over both the short and the long run. We rely on those studies as background to the present account.

8. Mafeking, later famous for its Anglo-Boer War siege, was established as the headquarters of the Crown Colony of British Bechuanaland in the late nineteenth century (see J. L. Comaroff 1973). It also served as the administrative center of the Bechuanaland Protectorate until the latter became the Republic of Botswana in 1966.

9. See Paul Scott's *The Jewel in the Crown,* the first volume of *The Raj Quartet.* In the ethnographic literature, Gluckman's (1968) use of the metaphor of the bridge—to capture a dramatic moment in the contradictory relationship of colonizer and colonized—is especially well-known.

10. *Mekgwa le melaò ya setswana* is typically glossed as "Tswana law and custom," though the dictionary translations of *mekgwa* and *melaò* are usually given as "customs" and "laws," respectively (see e.g. Schapera 1938). For reasons discussed elsewhere (Comaroff and Roberts 1981:Chap.3), however, we resist such legalistic translations, and prefer to view *mekgwa le melaò* as an undifferentiated set of signs and conventions.

11. There have, of course, been several recent efforts to address and redress at least some of these criticisms (see e.g. Bourdieu 1977; Sahlins 1981, 1985).

Part Three

Colonialism
and Modernity

7

Images of Empire,
Contests of Conscience

This argument, vaguely political in nature, took place as often as the two men met. It was a topsy-turvy affair, for the Englishman was bitterly anti-English and the Indian [Dr. Veraswami] fanatically loyal . . .

"My dear doctor," said Flory, "how can you make out that we are in this country for any purpose except to steal? It is so simple . . . the British Empire is a device for giving trade monopolies to the English—or rather gangs of Jews and Scotchmen."

"My friend, it is pathetic to hear you talk so . . . [W]hile your business men develop the resources of our country, your officials are civilizing us, elevating us to their level, from pure public spirit . . . [Y]ou have brought us law and order. The unswerving British Justice and Pax Britannica."

"Pox Britannica, doctor, Pox Britannica . . ."

—George Orwell, *Burmese Days*, pp. 40–1

IN THE MID-1820S, JOHN PHILIP, Superintendent of the London Missionary Society at the Cape, stepped up his controversial campaign for the right of "coloured peoples" to sell their labor in a free market (Ross 1986:77ff). His arguments, laid out in *Researches in South Africa*, called on no less an authority than Adam Smith: the "vassalage" of the coloureds, he declared (Philip 1828,1:367), not only violated the "principles of political economy"; it also had a "depressing" moral effect on the entire population, making the "aborigines" into worthless miscreants and their masters into idle tyrants. Anticipating both Durkheim and Hegel, Philip, a technician of the soul, evoked the body corporeal to drive home his organic vision of colonialism: "The different members of a state [are] beautifully represented by the members of the human body: . . . if one member suffers, all the members suffer"; a corollary being that "the

181

ranks of the inhabitants are the vices of the system" (pp. 386, 388). Hence it was that, by freeing the coloureds, "the colonists and their families . . . [would themselves] be converted into useful farmers." With a rhetorical, historical flourish the good reverend added: "To what does England owe the subversion of the feudal system, and its high rank among the nations of the world, but to the emancipation and elevation of its peasantry?" And that through self-possessed labor, private property, and the removal of all forms of servitude.

Such arguments had long been aired in Britain, of course. Questions about the morality and the control of free labor lay at the heart of the abolitionist debate—itself part of the reconstruction, during the Age of Revolution, of bourgeois ideology in the image of industrial capitalism. Consequently, Philip's position had wide support in Whitehall, Exeter Hall, and church halls all over England. But in South Africa itself the situation was different. The colonists were simply not used to being told that they would become a useful agrarian bourgeoisie if only they allowed their laborers to cultivate in freedom. Nor did the missionary stop at delivering sermons on the theory of political economy. He also confronted the colonial government with its practical failings. Official policy might have spoken the language of free labor; but existing conditions, he alleged, encouraged administrators to perpetuate sundry forms of vassalage. Take this example, from a passage titled "Interest of the Colonial Functionaries in the Oppression of the Aborigines" (1828,1:346f):

> The landed proprietors of South Africa depend on the price of labour, and the number of hands they can command; and it is obvious, while things remain in this state, . . . magistrates [and other functionaries] are under . . . temptation to oppress the people by enslaving them, and keeping down the price of labour.

And many of them did so on a regular basis, he added—naming names. Pax Britannica, for Philip as for the fictional Flory, left much to be desired.

Not surprisingly, John Philip was sued by one of those censured in his *Researches;* the Supreme Court at the Cape awarded William Mackay substantial damages—and seriously admonished the missionary for his impolitic behavior (Ross 1986:116ff; Macmillan 1927). In England, however, the latter was seen as something of a martyr to a particular model of colonialism. His debt was paid by subscription among churchmen, philanthropists, and liberal politicians, and his crusade became a touchstone in the struggle, within the colonizing culture, to refashion the imperial project. For one thing became clear amidst all the legalities and loud acrimony. Philip had done more than call into question the deeds of a few of His Majesty's servants at a remote British outpost. Whether he intended it or not, he had opened up, to scrutiny, some of the less obvious contradictions of the colonial enterprise itself. Such was the effect of his oft-repeated claim that the tensions of empire flowed not from the idiosyncratic intentions of its agents, their "peculiar vices"; that they grew, rather, out of the "vices of the system" at large. The nature of South African colonialism had become, as it remains today, the subject of an argument of structures and practices.

Images of Colonialism

The image of colonialism as a coherent, monolithic process seems, at last, to be wearing thin. That is why we are concerned here with the tensions of empire, not merely its triumphs; with the contradictions of colonialism, not just its crushing progress. This is not to diminish the brute domination suffered by the colonized peoples of the modern world, or to deny the Orwellian logic on which imperial projects have often been founded. Nor is it to deconstruct colonialism as a global movement. It is, instead, to broaden our analytic compass; to take in its moments of incoherence and inchoateness, its internal contortions and complexities. Above all, it is to treat as problematic the *making* of both colonizers and colonized in order to understand better the forces that, over time, have drawn them into an extraordinarily intricate web of relations. This goes much further than to restate the commonplace that colonizing processes have sometimes been characterized by conflict, as well as common interest, among their perpetrators—be they administrators or industrialists, merchants or militia, the crown or the cloth. To be sure, their contradictions everywhere have run far deeper than are suggested by the tensions visible on the surface planes of empire.

In short, colonialism, as an object of historical anthropology, has reached a moment of new reckoning. Our contribution to this moment is, by design, narrowly focused. We shall explore the making, as agents of empire, of the Nonconformist missionaries to the Griqua and Tswana, the peoples of the northern frontier of early nineteenth-century South Africa. The shaping of these historical figures—which began on the changing ideological and social scape of contemporary Britain—reveals much about the contradictions of colonialism, here and elsewhere. It goes without saying that the making of any historical actor is crucial to his or her actions in the making of history; that the latter cannot be fully understood except in relation to the former. In the case of the evangelists of the London Missionary Society (LMS) and Wesleyan Methodist Missionary Society

(WMMS) in South Africa, however, there are two unusually compelling reasons for this.

First, these men, the vanguards of empire and its most active ideological agents, came from the interstices of a class structure undergoing reconstruction; many of them, as we shall see, were caught uneasily between a displaced peasantry, an expanding proletariat, and the lower reaches of the rising British bourgeoisie (Beidelman 1982:50). On the colonial stage itself, they were quite clearly a "dominated fraction of the dominant class" (Bourdieu 1984:421), the ruled among the rulers. This was exacerbated by the fact that most of them regarded themselves—and were regarded by their compatriots—as "friends and protectors of the natives" (see e.g. Wilson 1976). It was a position that often set them at odds with others in the colonial division of labor, particularly those from different fractions of the dominant class (cf. Trapido 1980:passim; Legassick 1980:46; Newton-King 1980:197f; Bundy 1979). Consequently, in viewing the colonial process through their eyes—focused as they were by the ambiguities of their own social situation—we gain an especially penetrating insight into its internal struggles and inconsistencies.

Second, the Nonconformist missionaries, bearers of the Protestant ethic in the capitalist age, saw themselves not merely as heroic figures in the creation of a new Empire of the Spirit in Africa. They also took themselves to be the conscience of British colonialism, its moral commentators; to wit, it was this self-appointed stance that was later to legitimize their occasional forays into colonial politics. In their writings are rehearsed all the arguments of images and ideology, of dreams and schemes, voiced among the colonizers as they debated the manner in which natives should be ruled, their worlds reconstructed. It is noteworthy that, for all the enormous literature on African missions, this aspect of their historical role is perhaps the least documented. And yet it gives their perspective a singular vantage—indeed, a significant advantage—in revealing the tensions of empire, the contradictions of colonialism.

We begin, then, by tracing the missions back to the society that spawned them, Britain circa 1810–40. In so doing, we concentrate, first, on the spirit of the age: on those of its social features and ideological discourses that were to affect the colonial process and the part of the churchmen in it. Thereafter, we shall examine the background of these churchmen, locating them on the changing social landscape of the time. In all this, we seek to provide a kind of imaginative sociology—that is, a sketch of the social and cultural forms that shaped their imagined world, their life-context as they regarded it. On the basis of that sociology, we shall follow the evangelists onto the colonial stage itself, looking through their gaze at its conflicts of images and practices.

The Origins of the Colonial Mission
in South Africa: Britain, 1810–40

By 1810, the industrial revolution had cut deep into the physical, social, and cultural terrain of Britain. The very term "industrial revolution" tends to direct our gaze toward its productive ecology and its technological bases; the machine, after all, was the dominant metaphor of the age. And there is no doubting the importance of its material and technical aspects, or their complex impact on the fabric of everyday life. At the same time, it is difficult to disagree with the many scholars, of both right and left, for whom the essence of the industrial revolution lay in the transformation of relations of production and, concomitantly, relations among classes. This is not to say that capitalist forms were not foreshadowed in eighteenth-century commerce and agriculture, or that social distinctions did not exist before the rise of the factory system; simply that the revolution hinged on the reconstruction of the division of labor and, with it, the social order at large.

Regarded in this light, the industrial revolution has been portrayed as the triumph of a "conquering bourgeoisie" (Hobsbawm 1962:19) over a proletariat vanquished in the process of its making (Thompson 1963). Certainly, its polarizing effect on Britain was palpable at the time, signs of class consciousness and conflict being everywhere visible, from the passing of the Combination Acts to the outbreak of Luddism (Hobsbawm 1964:5f). Moreover, it sparked an often bitter controversy over the effects of industrialization, an argument between "optimists" and "pessimists" that found its way into artistic and literary expression as well as scholarly debate (Briggs 1959:14; 1979:33). Nonetheless, for all the vital imagery that cast the common people against lordly tyrants (Shelley 1882:164), "vulgar rich" against "ill-used" worker ([Dodd] 1847), or benign captains of industry against the ungrateful, improving masses, it would be simplifying matters to describe the emerging social structure purely in terms of two classes locked in mortal embrace.

The point will turn out to be crucial for us. Interestingly, it was appreciated by a remarkable man of the period, William Dodd. Dodd had no schooling and was forced into 25 years of mill work, during which he lost an arm, but learned to write movingly of his experiences. His letters, published anonymously in 1847, are extraordinary enough; but more astonishing still is his introduction to them. In it, he gives account of social and economic divisions in England, asserting that there existed eight classes. Four (royalty; nobility; capitalists; and gentlemen of trade, the professions and the clergy) were "privileged"; they made the law and profited from the toils of others (p.11f). The latter (skilled laborers;

common laborers; honorable paupers; and the dishonorable poor) composed the nonprivileged mass, from which ascent was "attended with
difficulty." Others had spoken of class in broadly similar terms before;
notably, Charles Hall (1805). Dodd, however, made two observations of
particular salience here: that neither of the strata, the privileged nor the
poor, was solidary or united, each being caught up in its own affinities and
antagonisms; and that the "humbler . . . clergy," as the most poorly paid
members of the privileged ranks, occupied their lowest, least secure reaches.

These observations were clearly correct. Within the upper orders, relations between the increasingly powerful industrial bourgeoisie and the
landed aristocracy were often difficult, always ambiguous. And, for their
part, the "nonprivileged" were differentiated according to their positions
in the social division of labor—differences that fragmented the workforce
and were used to exercise control over it. Of course, the dominant ideology
of the period also separated laboring men from the undeserving poor.
Where the deserts of the former would one day be recognized by the great
accountant in the sky, the destiny of the latter was eternal condemnation
to a satanic hell that looked for all the world like a Mancunian mill.

An important corollary of the internal fragmentation of the classes was
that upward mobility presented itself as a possibility for those who "im-
proved" themselves. There was little to stop a common laborer from
becoming a craftsman; or the son of a skilled worker, a clerk in the lower
levels of the privileged orders. Or so the poor were told incessantly from
the pulpit and in the press. Without such gradations across the major lines
of class, this would have been implausible. A pauper could not envision
becoming a prince, and only the most star-crossed chimneysweep aspired
to be a captain of industry. Those who did make their way up the social
ladder, though, often found themselves not secure members of a more
elevated class, but the bearers of anomalous rank; neither of the rich nor
the poor, of the ruling nor the ruled. Caught in the fissures of the class
structure, they were suspended between the privileged, whose values they
shared, and the impoverished, from whence they came—and to whom, if
they failed, they would return. This is where Dodd's second observation
becomes significant. Low churchmen, more than anyone else, personified
the process: many of them, especially in northern parishes, were ex-artisans
or peasants who had climbed, unsteadily, into the middle class. And,
lacking wealth or distinction, they clung tenuously to their new social
position.

Here, then, is the thread that weaves together the general and the
particular. In the large-scale processes of the industrial revolution was
forged the specific context from which arose the army of Nonconformist
missionaries to South Africa. The fact that they came from here—from the
ideological core yet the social margins of bourgeois Britain—was not only

to affect their place in colonial society and its politics. It was also to shape the moral terms in which they were to deal both with other Europeans and with the "savage" on the frontiers of empire. For their own biographies, built on an unremitting commitment to self-improvement, were the very embodiment of the spirit of capitalism, a living testimonial to its ethical and material workings. And, inasmuch as they were to evangelize and civilize by personal example—itself part and parcel of bourgeois morality—the road along which they were to lead the heathen was to retrace their own pathways through British society. Or, rather, toward an image of that society as they wished to see it. And what they wished to see was a neat fusion of three idealized worlds: the rational capitalist age, in its most ideologically roseate form, wherein unfettered individuals were free to better themselves; an idyllic countryside in which, alongside agrarian estates, hard-working peasants, equipped with suitable tools and techniques, produced gainfully for the market; and a sovereign "Empire of God," whose temporal affairs remained securely under divine authority. Later, when we return to the roots of the South African evangelists, we shall see why these particular imagined worlds should have been so important to them. First, however, let us examine each in turn. Not only do they give us yet greater insight into the spirit of the era; they also bring us a step closer to the colonial encounter.

Imagined Worlds: (i) The Individual and Civilized Society

The triumph of the bourgeoisie in the age of revolution was most visibly expressed in the dominant worldview of early capitalism—in particular, its stress on utilitarian individualism and the virtues of the disciplined, self-made person; on private property and status as measures of success, poverty as appropriate sanction for failure; on enlightened self-interest and the free market as an instrument of the common good; on reason and method, science and technology, as the key to the progress of mankind. These values did not go uncontested, of course. For all the philosophical support they enjoyed in the liberalism of Bentham and Mill, they were freely questioned in the artistic work of the likes of Shelley and Blake; for all their backing in the political economy of Smith and Ricardo, they were subject to outspoken socialist critique and to the vocal objection of a fraction of the working class. Indeed, the entire history of the British labor movement, from the late eighteenth century onward, has been a discourse on precisely this ideology. Still, the revolution confidently forecast by Engels (1968:Chap. 9) did not arise from the squalor of Manchester. As Matthew Arnold (1903:viii) was to muse in 1865, even such popular organs as the *Saturday Review* had observed that Britain had "finally anchored itself, in the fullness of perfected knowledge, on Benthamism."

Perfected knowledge or not, the rise of capitalism, by its very nature, entailed the inculcation of a set of signs and images into the collective consciousness of Britain. Among these, perhaps the most far-reaching concerned the essence of the person.[1] Classic liberalism posited a world consisting of self-contained, right-bearing individuals who created society by the sum of their actions. "Universal History," declaimed Carlyle (1842:1), is the history of what great men accomplish. In its popular form, this philosophical individualism saw people less as products of a social context than as autonomous beings—Daltonian "atoms," says Halévy (1924:505)—with the capacity to construct themselves if they set their minds and bodies to the task. Further, the *self* was viewed as a divided entity (Foucault 1975:197). On one hand, it was the core of subjectivity: "I," the center from which a person looked and acted on the world. On the other, it was an object: "me, my-self," something of which "I" could become (self-)conscious and subject to (self-) restraint or indulgence. As Reed (1975:289) and others note, this divided self was to be a ubiquitous presence in Victorian literature, colonizing popular consciousness through such vehicles as the novel, the theater, the tract, and the diary.

The immediate corollary of this image of the self was that the social values of bourgeois ideology could be internalized as qualities of individual *person*ality. Thus the virtues of discipline, generosity, and ownership, to name a few, were embodied in self-control, self-denial, and self-possession; conversely, hedonism and indolence were, literally, self-destructive. No wonder that one archetype of the success story in contemporary heroic novels was the "self-made man," who often turned out to be a manufacturer.[2] This image of the person was cogently expressed in the doctrine of self-improvement; the notion that, through methodical behavior and the avoidance of indulgence, one might better oneself—the reward being upward mobility for men, upward nubility for women. In this respect, the outer shell of the individual was a gauge of inner essence. Neat dress and a healthy body spoke of a worthy heart and an alert mind (Haley 1978). What is more, the subjective "I" was in a position to monitor the progress of the objective self.

Self-evidently, this ideology of personhood saturated the popular discourses of the time. Take, for instance, the link between self-improvement and literacy. For all the debate in some circles as to whether the poor should be educated, reading took on a doubly positive connotation. Not only did it expand the mind; it also engaged the self in a properly profound manner. For, in addressing the written text, readers internalized it, reflected on it in the deepest recesses of their being, and entered with it into a silent conversation. And, in the process, they came to know better both the outer world and their inner selves. The rise of literacy in the nineteenth century may have been encouraged by the commoditization of the printed word

(Anderson 1983:38f). But its social impact was closely tied to the ascendance of the reflective, inner-directed self.

The partibility of the self—later to reappear as a "scientific" principle in, among other things, Freudian psychology—also manifested itself in the "natural" oppositions of mind and body, spirit and essence, consciousness and being, which came to loom so large in post-enlightenment thought (Spicker 1970). Even more crucial for the development of capitalism, it underlay the notion that individuals could separate from the rest of their being, and sell, a part of themselves: their capacity for work (Marx 1967,1:Chap. 6). We all know the implications that follow. In as much as commodity production entailed the exchange of labor power between worker and capitalist, it demanded a standardized measure of quantity (for human effort) and a universal medium of remuneration (for pay). The latter is money; the former, time. And both can be spent or used, wasted or owned.

As time and money became vehicles for dividing the self, so they came to mediate the rhythms of everyday life, detaching work-time from leisure-time, workplace from home, wage labor from unpaid domestic toil, production from consumption; imbricated in all this being the sanctification of the nuclear family with its engendered division of labor, the distinction between public and private domains, and other familiar signs and practices of a rising capitalist order. That time and money were explicitly equated in the early nineteenth century is nicely demonstrated by Thompson (1967:87), who also shows that the growing salience of the clock resonated with both secular and Protestant ideas of discipline and self-improvement. So did the notion that wealth was a just reward for effort. Wesley, after all, had spoken of its "precious talents" (Warner 1930:155); for him it was a true measure, at once spiritual and material, of human worth.

It is not necessary, after Weber and Tawney, to labor the connections—ideological, symbolic, even aesthetic[3]—between industrial capitalism and Protestantism, bourgeois culture and liberal individualism. Notwithstanding theological differences over such questions as predestination and salvation, Protestantism envisaged the human career as a cumulative moral voyage, unrelieved by the possibility of immediate atonement or absolution. The person, as a self-determining being, laid up treasures in heaven in the same way as he or she did on earth—by ascetic effort, neighborly duty, and good works. This person could not be a slave—at least, not for the Nonconformists who were to evangelize South Africa, some of whom were active abolitionists. For them, it was through free labor and commerce, self-willed moral and material improvement, that the heathen was going to pave the road to personal salvation.

At the same time, Nonconformism was quick to affirm the premises of an unequal society—at home and abroad. In preaching self-realization through work and duty, it exhorted the poor to make peace with their lot. Thus, for example, while Wesley set out to give a sense of worth to the troubled masses, and to draw them into secure social and spiritual communities, he assumed that "the labor relationship was an ethical one" (Warner 1930:146f). Employee and master had different functions by virtue of divine calling, the spiritual status of each depending on the manner in which he fulfilled his appointed role. As this implies, "a diversity of ranks" was taken to be perfectly natural and eternal (p. 125). At a stroke, the alienating experience of wage-labor became the necessary cost of salvation, and inequality was made into a sacred instrument of moral sanction. Although he advocated fair pay and prices, Wesley was as vociferous as any industrialist in decrying agitation by workers: "meddling" on the part of "those who are given to change" might threaten the providential market and, even worse, encourage sloth on the part of the poor.

The Nonconformist missions were to export these images of selfhood and society, transposing them from factory and foundry, mine and mill, pithead and pulpit onto African soil. But other members of the dominant class—settlers, merchants, and administrators among them—were also caught up in the spirit of the age. Not all of them read its signs and images in the same way, however—at least as they were to apply to the colonized. Quite the opposite: it was such things as the future of African personhood, labor, and literacy that the bearers of empire were to contest among themselves.

Imagined Worlds: (ii) The City and the Countryside

For those who lamented a paradise lost to the cause of the industrial revolution, the idealized British past was situated in a pristine countryside cast timelessly in the early eighteenth century. This idyll was inhabited by three estates: (i) the feudal establishment, in which lord and servant were bound in a web of mutual obligation; (ii) the yeomanry, independent peasants who "[produced] for the market, themselves employing wage-labour, and shared the outlook and interests of gentlemen and merchants rather than of landless labourers and subsistence husbandmen" (Hill 1969:70); and (iii) a mass of poor, honest small-holders engaged in both agriculture and domestic industry. In the public perception, the last two categories were often lumped together as one and romanticized as the "perfect Republic of Shepherds and Agriculturists" (Wordsworth 1948:54).

More than anything else perhaps, the transformation of the countryside was associated, in the British imagination, with the fall of the yeomanry—itself a process dramatized by the migration of many people to bleak northern cities. Its passing, typically ascribed to enclosure and the agrarian revolution that preceded industrialization, was taken by many to signal the unraveling of the social fabric at large.[4] In the eye of contemporary beholders, the yeomanry had embodied a "traditional" lifestyle in which domestic groups, with their customary division of labor, produced more than enough for their own needs and were free to enjoy the fruits of their toil; in which households were securely embedded in communities of kin and neighbors; in which the independence of the family was guaranteed by its private estate and its social position.[5]

This vision may have had a slim basis in history (Briggs 1959:40). Yet its appeal is attested by the fact that the nineteenth-century reformers who sparked most public interest were those who undertook to stitch back together the torn social fabric. For example, Owen's popularity among workers seems to have lain in his attempt "to reconcile . . . industry with domestic employment," and his promise of "a return to the rural existence [with its] family and community life" (Thomis 1974:148). In this respect, Hill (1969:272) has suggested that the transformation of the landscape subsumed, in a nutshell, the antagonism between the new bourgeoisie and the working class. The bitterness of the poor, he argues, flowed as much from having been dispossessed of their land as from their resentment at being forced into factories. But that bitterness was directed at more than just larceny, however grand. It was fanned by the death throes of an epoch, the most tragic symptom of which was taken to be the scarring of the earth itself, the defacing of England-as-garden.

At the same time, the industrial revolution had a contradictory impact on contemporary images of the relationship between country and city. On one hand, the chasm dividing them was seen to grow ever wider. Far from just a description of socio-spatial realities, this contrast between mill town and moor, metropolis and meadow, became a key symbolic trope in British historical consciousness. Note that it was industrial workers, many of them with no experience of rural England, who agitated most loudly for a return to the land, a mythical world of contented labor, village cricket, and county entertainments (Thompson 1963:231). In both poetry and popular conception, the country stood to the city as nature to worldliness, innocence to corruption, a harmonious past to the disjunctive present (Williams 1973).

On the other hand, as the mill and the mine made their noisy entry into the rural northern valleys, the industrial revolution blurred the ecological distinction between country and city. As Sir John Clapham (1926:36) put it:

> Rural labour and town labour, country house and town house, were divided by no clear line. In one sense there was no line at all. Very many of the industrial workpeople were countrymen, though their countryside might be fouling and blackening, their cottages creeping together and adhering into rows, courts, formless towns.

That the contrast between country and city seemed simultaneously to be growing and disappearing is not paradoxical. As the ecological and social separation between them dissolved under the impact of industrial capitalism, the resulting dislocation was acutely felt throughout Britain, leaving fragmented and discontented working populations in its wake (Briggs 1959:42). Some had to move to the city, others found that the city had moved to them. Either way, the sense of having crossed boundaries, both old and new, was unavoidable, often painful. And this, in turn, could not but highlight the contrast between the worlds separated by those boundaries.

As the perceived opposition between country and city grew in the popular imagination, then, it became a master symbol of the radical transformation of British society, picking out a counterpoint between mythic past and present reality. But the idealized countryside also stood for the possibility of paradise regained, a utopian rhapsody for the future. That is why the dreams of the likes of Owen were paid so much attention. In practice, these dreams could not be realized in a greatly changed England. However, the open vistas of the non-European world seemed to offer limitless possibilities. The missionaries to South Africa—many of whom came from the rural communities most altered in the restructuring of Britain (see below)—were to resuscitate the rural idyll as a model for Africa.

Imagined Worlds: (iii) The Empire of God

Notwithstanding the sheer vibrancy of the Protestant revival during the early nineteenth century, this was a secularizing age in which the suzerainty of organized religion was in decline (Toynbee 1969:235). At the time of the Reformation, says Hill (1969:34), ecclesiastical hegemony had been all-encompassing: not only were cloth and crown entailed in each other, but the parish church was the nub of political and social life for most Britons. What is more, the signs and practices of Christianity were taken-for-granted features of everyday existence, an unspoken condition of seeing and being. In these circumstances, temporal power appeared as a function of spiritual sovereignty—which made it hard to distinguish religion from politics, *lex Dei* from *lex naturae*. Indeed, James I, who openly identified kingly rule with divine command, equated sedition with blasphemy (Mill 1982,6:10f). No wonder that "the reformed Church of England . . . [was] inseparable from national consciousness" (Chadwick 1966:3). With the profound economic turmoil of the mid-sixteenth century, however, all of Europe witnessed a spiritual crisis and a bitter struggle for control over religious life—one consequence of which was to be the steady growth of Christian dissent and, in particular, the birth of Congregationalism, an antiestablishment movement that would spread quickly among lower-class groups (Hill 1969:111). The London Missionary Society, later to evangelize the Tswana, arose from this movement.

The breakdown of the unity and authority of Anglicanism in the 1640s, Hill (p. 190) goes on, was a critical moment: the Kingdom and God, and hence the Kingdom of God, could never again exist as one, or enjoy the same supreme hegemony. This is not to say that organized religion lost all influence in the political process, or that Protestant doctrine ceased to pervade public discourse. As nineteenth-century ecclesiastical history proves, the matter is much too complex to be captured in such general terms. The point, rather, is that spiritual sovereignty, *sui generis,* had lost its ineffability. Far from being an unquestioned order of signs and symbols through which nature and society were apprehended, Christianity had itself become an object of debate and struggle. The growing disunity of the church was an element in this. So, too, was the dissolution of doctrinal homogeneity among Nonconformists after 1800 (Briggs and Sellers 1973:6). But the most telling portent of authority undermined was the fact that the role of the church—and the relationship between the sacred and the secular— could be questioned at all. No longer did Christianity-as-culture have the capacity to dissolve the distinction between the law of God and the law of the land, the divine and the mundane; no longer was reality constructed by autonomic reference to the moral language of Christendom. Its hegemony lost, English Protestantism, too, was to be transformed by the forces that drove the age of revolution. Like most other things, it was about to be refashioned in the ethical mold of capitalism (Anderson 1983:Chap. 2).

There was, however, no reason why a Kingdom of God could not be recreated elsewhere, and nowhere seemed better than the fringes of the European world. Two things underscored this at the time. One was the abolition of the slave trade in 1807, an act taken by the mission societies as a moral mandate to right "the Wrongs of Africa."[6] The other grew out of the collapse of the "Old British Empire" (Knorr 1944:211), a reverse which made "colonial expansion so distasteful to the English that they even . . . abolished the Secretaryship of State for the Colonies" (Halévy 1924:87).[7] To Nonconformists, the chance to evangelize in an imperial vacuum was appealing: being strongly anti-establishment, and for the rigid separation of church and state, they did not welcome the presence of a colonial government (Briggs and Sellers 1973:143); it curbed their freedom to minister to an unfettered spiritual sovereignty. As time passed and conditions changed, the Kingdom of God would pave a way for the Empire of Britain, a process in which some missionaries were to play a lively part. But, at the dawn of the new century, the hiatus in colonial expansion enabled English Christians to dream of their own spiritual imperium.

This dream, nonetheless, was firmly grounded in the ethos of the age. The Kingdom of God—as the Nonconformists said repeatedly in the abolition debate—was to be built on a moral economy of Christian commerce and manufacture, methodical self-construction and reason, private property and the practical arts of civilized life. Like all utopias, it offered a future that fused the values of the present with the myths of the past. Savage society would, by careful tending, be made into an independent peasantry, much like the late British yeomanry. In talking thus, the missions relied heavily on horticultural metaphors, evoking the recreation of the spoiled English garden in Africa's "vast moral wastes" (Moffat 1842:614). The countryside would be tilled anew, civilizing the heathen as he cultivated the soil.

But the African garden was to be part of the imperial marketplace. After all, commerce, like money, was an integral—even sanctified—aspect of civilization. For many, in fact, commercial agriculture was the panacea that would establish both the material and the moral infrastructure of the Kingdom of God—an imagined world that fused the Benthamite vision of liberation through free exchange, the Protestant notion of self-construction through rational improvement, and the bourgeois ideal of accumulation through hard work. From small seeds there grew large dreams; from modest biographies, heroic visions of deeds to be done.

Modest Biographies: The Social Roots of the Nonconformist Missionaries

We have noted that most Nonconformist missionaries to South Africa were men who had risen from laboring, peasant, and artisan backgrounds to the lower end of the bourgeoisie, often via the church. Few had a university education—some had no schooling at all—and many would "have spent their lives as artisans had they not been invited to enter the ministry" (Etherington 1978:28). Indeed, the LMS *Rules for the Examination of Missionaries* (1795) stressed that candidates did *not* have to be learned; Godly men who knew "mechanic arts" were also welcome. Beidelman (1982:50) has reiterated that "the missionary movement in Britain cannot be separated from the . . . rise of the lower middle classes." Not only was it from here that most evangelists came; many of their biographies, marked by modest upward mobility and the acquisition of respectability, echoed the rise of the class itself. Nonconformism may have drawn its following from all strata (Briggs 1959:69), but its missionaries were from a narrow band of the social spectrum. Hobsbawm's (1962:270) account of the "new sects" nicely summarizes the origins of these men:

[The sects] spread most readily among those who stood between the rich and powerful on one side, the masses of the traditional society on the other: i.e., among those who were about to rise into the new middle class, those about to decline into a new proletariat, and the indiscriminate mass of small and independent men in between.

But it is not only the reconstruction of class divisions that weaves missionary biography into the social history of the age. Also salient were the other major transformations of which we have spoken: the ascendance of a new moral economy; the social, ecological, and aesthetic despoliation of the countryside; and the secularization of the age.

The most heroic British figures in South African mission history, with the possible exception of John Philip, were Robert Moffat and his son-in-law, David Livingstone.[8] Their backgrounds, if not their later lives, were typical of the first generation of Nonconformist evangelists. Moffat was the son of a ploughman who had risen to become a petty official in a Scottish salt tax office.[9] The elder Moffat's life was a model of disciplined, self-sacrificing improvement: he died leaving £2,351 and a freehold dwelling, great wealth in light of his origins. In 1795, when Robert was born, his parental home was at Ormiston, near Edinburgh. His grandparents' cottage still stands in the Ormiston public garden; the remains of his own home are now enclosed in a National Coal Board property. The one faces rural, horticultural Scotland; the other, industrial Britain. Moreover, Ormiston had been rebuilt by John Cockburn, a capitalist and reformer, who erected a distillery, introduced flax production, and revivified local agriculture. The young Robert, in short, saw the countryside and town begin to merge, and the peasantry, of which his father had been part, become an agrarian and industrial work-force. The reconstruction of northern Britain reached to his doorstep.

Moffat came from a strict Calvinist family in which improvement was equated with industry, thrift, and good works. Apparently its sense of philanthropy included a "lively evangelical interest in foreign parts" (Northcott 1961:17). For all the stress on improvement, however, Robert had almost no schooling, although reading, sewing, and knitting was a regular evening activity for both sexes. At 14, he became a gardener, and later moved to Cheshire, where he happened on a group of Independent Methodists whose views and style of worship attracted him. From this cottage prayer circle, through the good offices of a Congregationalist minister in Manchester, Moffat's path led to the LMS, ordination, and a long sojourn among the Tswana. Just as his youth was dominated by the currents of the age—hardening class lines, the transformation of the country and the peasantry, and the absorption of the poor into the bourgeois moral economy—so his later career was dedicated to the reenactment of his own life amidst those currents. The African was to be led along similar paths, learning to read and reflect, to cultivate and sell his labor, and to see the value of industry—so that he, too, might better himself. Mission biography, as we said, was mission ideology personified.

The early life of David Livingstone closely resembled that of Robert Moffat. He also grew up in the fissures of the emerging class structure; his childhood, too, was spent at the intersection of the country and the city. Blantyre, his birthplace, was 8 miles from Glasgow and boasted a major textile works; it was here that, at 10, he was employed when his family fell on hard times. His grandfather, Neil, like Moffat's father, had been a rural man—a small farmer—but lost his tenancy when the land was taken over by a commercial sheep farm. Forced to migrate to the industrial fringe of Glasgow, Neil slowly raised enough to leave mill work. However, his son, a tea salesman, could not hold on to hard-won respectability: he suffered repeated financial reverses, and the family had to move into Shuttle Row, a tenement owned by Blantyre Mill. This community, like Ormiston, was planned by the mill owner. It also abutted a park, the private garden of the works manager—thus highlighting the contrast between stark tenement and verdant countryside, laboring poor and new rich. From the Livingstone home, says Johnston (n.d.:50–1), one could see "a peep of Glasgow . . . dimly discernible through [an] irridescent mist of smoke, sunshine, and rain." Between Blantyre and Glasgow, he goes on, lay clearly visible "strips of murdered country, fields of rye alternating with fields of baking bricks."

Like the Moffats, the Livingstones devoted themselves energetically to education and self-improvement; the atmosphere and daily routine in the two households seem to have been similar. Most accounts tell how David spent two hours each evening in the company school and then went home to read—all this after a 12 hour workday. His family were also members of the established church until the 1830s, when his father, affected by Nonconformist preaching, joined the independent Hamilton Church. From there, it is said, he took home a pamphlet on medical missions in China. David had long shown an interest in medicine and found the prospect appealing. The rest is well-known: after saving the necessary funds, he went to study in Glasgow, and from there found his way, like Moffat, into the LMS.

The general pattern will be clear. Of the 17 LMS and WMMS missionaries who began work among Southern Tswana before 1860, and for whom we have sufficient information, 12 came from Scotland or the north of England, 2 from Wales, and only 3 from southern England; 13 of them being from either the industrializing river valleys, the urban peripheries or proletarianized villages. Sixteen of the 17, moreover, fit Hobsbawm's description (p. 195)—that is, of persons caught between rich and poor, either indeterminate in their class affiliation or struggling to cross the invisible boundary into the bourgeoisie. Five of them came from peasant stock, five were from artisan backgrounds, three had been petty clerks or traders, and three had risen directly from the ranks of the laboring poor. Many, like Moffat and Livingstone, were from displaced rural families. For all of them, the church conferred respectability and a measure of security in their social position, even though it did not enrich them.

All this underscores the extent to which the Nonconformists were creatures of their age and its contradictions. It also indicates why they should have been so caught up in its moral economy and ideological discourses; why, in particular, they were so drawn to the idealized worlds of expansive bourgeois individualism, of a renascent countryside, of a resurrected Empire of God. Let us follow them to Africa and see how, thus socially and culturally endowed, they took up their role as the conscience of the colonizer.

Colonialisms in Conflict:
The South African Frontier, Circa 1820–60

When the first generation of LMS and WMMS missionaries arrived in South Africa, they did not, despite their rhetoric of Africa-as-desert, en- counter an empty landscape. The Cape of Good Hope, ruled earlier by Holland and now by Britain, was already a field of tension and conflict (see e.g. de Kiewiet 1941:Chap. 2; Newton-King 1980:passim). From the perspective of the evangelists, as recorded in their accounts,[10] the terrain sported four sets of characters—aside from Africans—and three models of colonial rule. The former included (i) His Majesty's administrators and officers, most of them gentlemen of high birth and/or rank; (ii) British settlers, largely respectable middle-class burghers of Cape Town and farm- ers in the colony; (iii) Boers (lit. "farmers") of Dutch, German, and French descent who were regarded as "rude"; and (iv) themselves, agents of the various mission societies. Even more sharply distinguished were their models of colonial rule, though they would not have referred to, or labeled, them as such. The first, associated with the British administration (and, by extension, British settlers), may be dubbed *state colonialism;* the second, attributed to the Boers, was a form of *settler colonialism;* and the third, their own, was perceived as a *civilizing colonialism.* In the missionaries' view, if it may be so summarily stated, the three colonialisms were, respectively, bureaucratic, brutal, and benign (see e.g. Philip 1828,1).

We shall describe these models in a moment. But, before we do, a few qualifications are to be made. First, although each was associated with a specific set of characters, it did not follow that everyone on the colonial stage would act according to type; the Christians were quick to point out when, say, a government functionary or British settler behaved "like Boers." Second, while the three colonialisms were, in principle, quite discrete, evangelists often underplayed the differences between themselves and administrators, stressing their mutual involvement in the imperial project; for some churchmen, this was a deliberate part of the effort to persuade state officials to participate in their civilizing mission (e.g. Philip 1828; and later MacKenzie 1887). Third, the content of the different colonialisms was to be transformed, over time, by subcontinental and global forces. As this implies, the Nonconformist vision was itself to alter, and increasingly to fragment, as the years went by. However, we are concerned here with the early 1800s, when the models were clearly delineated, and the evangelical voice unified.

Three Models of Colonialism

We repeat that the three "models" are drawn from the body of mission literature—letters, reports, published works—where they are *not* laid out in formal terms. Still, it will become clear that their content and coherence are beyond question. Each captures a pervasive, consistent set of stereotypic images; images that were held up as a template—literally, a model— against which to describe and evaluate the actions of whites toward blacks.

(1) The *state* model, according to which the colonial government was seen to oversee the territory, had, as its first priority, *Pax Britannica:* the pacification of "tribes," under British law, in an ever widening radius outward from the Cape. Ideally, this was to be achieved by trade and by making alliances with native chiefs.[11] To this end, the administration sponsored the exploration of the interior, but did not concern itself with the civilization of indigenes; their "improvement," in official rhetoric, would follow naturally from trade, pacification, and contact with whites. Nor did the state impose direct rule on inland peoples, although it kept an increasingly regulatory eye on the flow of black laborers and the terms of their employment. The obligation to "protect the aborigines"—from internecine war, unscrupulous whites, and Boer enslavement—was also part of the self-appointed mandate of the administration, especially after abolition. "It is a wise policy in Government," observed Moffat (1842:210), "to *render every facility* to the advancement of knowledge and civilization among the aborigines" (our italics). But, to the evangelists, state policy was ambiguous on just this point (recall Philip; above, p. 182). It became even more so in the early 1850s when, by the Sand River Convention (1852) and Bloemfontein Convention (1854), Britain ceded control over the hinterland and its black population to Boer settlers—and to their form

of colonialism (see e.g. Thompson 1969:420–5; Davenport 1977:62–3, 124).

State colonialism, as we said, was to change over time. It would involve, in due course, the imposition of taxes, the limitation of chiefly authority, and many other (typically legalistic, punitive) forms of regulation. Above all, from the late 1860s onwards, in the wake of the mineral revolution, it would be ever more concerned with the control of "native [wage] labor." But the essence of the missionary view of the state—that it was about bureaucratic regulation not civilization, at least in their terms—would remain intact for a long time. Indeed, it was to be fed by the government: in 1878, for example, Sir Gordon Sprigg, Prime Minister of the Cape, was to go about the Colony announcing his firm resolve to make blacks into laborers—and to punish any "native rebellion" by forcing the culprits to forfeit their land. The policy of his administration, he added in an obvious dig at the evangelists, "is to teach them to work, not to read and write and sing."[12]

(2) *Settler colonialism,* the Boer model, was represented by the missionaries in starkly negative terms. To them, Boers were no more than half-savages: they led degenerate, unrefined lives, lacked a true European "spirit of improvement," and showed their "monstrous" character by treating blacks as prey to be hunted and enslaved.[13] As this suggests, settler colonialism was seen to be founded on brute coercion, domination by force—although it was justified by appeal to the biblical allegory of "the children of Ham," according to which eternal servitude was the divine calling of blacks.[14] For the evangelists, the Boer model was revealed most clearly in, and after, the Great Trek of the 1830s, when the settlers, loudly protesting abolition, left the Colony for the interior.[15] Their epic frontier movement, the mythological exodus of modern Afrikaner historical consciousness, did more than strike a blow for Boer independence from the state colonialism of Britain. It also established a new order of relations between these Europeans and the peoples of the interior. The encounter began with either war or alliance and ended, usually, with the subordination of local communities to Boer control. The latter was expressed in one or more of four ways: (a) the imposition of tax and/or demands for tribute; (b) the seizure of men, women, and children to toil as bonded servants and unpaid laborers on white farms; (c) the requirement that chiefs provide military assistance to the whites against "unfriendly natives"; and (d) the gradual appropriation of "tribal" lands. These measures, the churchmen pointed out in their various ways, added up to a deliberate, systematic process of domination. A few indigenous communities were destroyed as a result, their dispossessed members forced to become laborers and servants on the white farms that seemed to be multiplying across the South African hinterland. Others remained physically intact, but many lost their indepen-

dence, their leaders emasculated by the irresistible demand for regular tax, tribute, and labor.[16]

(3) The *civilizing colonialism* of the mission, as we would expect, was much more fully spelled out by the Christians than were the other models. Apart from all else, they believed their designs for the transformation of indigenous life to be more positively comprehensive, more finely detailed, than any other (see e.g. Moffat 1842:616f; Livingstone 1858:Lecture I). Nor were they alone in this view. It was to become an anthropological commonplace, a century later, that the mark of the early mission enterprise was its effort to reconstruct *totally* African society and culture (e.g. Bohannan 1964:22f).

Distilled to its essence, the civilizing colonialism of the Nonconformists sought to "cultivate" the African "desert" and its inhabitants by planting the seeds of bourgeois individualism and the nuclear family, of private property and commerce, of rational minds and healthily clad bodies, of the practical arts of refined living and devotion to God. All these things were of a piece; that, after all, was what was implied by *total* reconstruction. Hence, far from pursuing religious conversion alone, the evangelists set out, at once, to (a) create a theater of the everyday, demonstrating by their own exemplary actions the benefits of methodical routine, of good personal habits, and of enlightened European ways; (b) banish "superstition" in favor of rational technique and Christian belief; (c) reduce the landscape from a chaotic mass of crude, dirty huts to an ordered array of square, neatly bounded residences (with rooms and doors, windows and furniture, fields and fences), enclosure being both a condition of private property and an aesthetic expression of the sheer beauty of refinement;[17] (d) recast the division of labor by making men into hardworking farmers and bringing women "indoors" to the domestic domain, much along the lines of the English middle-class family; (e) encourage these families to produce for the market by teaching them advanced methods, the worth of time and money, and an ethos of enterprise—the explicit model being the late British yeomanry (see above); all of which (f) demanded that Africans be taught to read and reason, to become self-reflective and self-disciplined. It followed, as axiomatic, that "heathen" society would be forever destroyed. But the evangelists were less sure of their attitude toward indigenous secular authority. In light of their commitment to the separation of church and state, they promised repeatedly not to interfere in "tribal" government and politics. However, in seeking "religious freedom" for their congregants, and by "fighting superstition," they tried hard to drive a wedge between (what *they* took to be) the temporal and ritual aspects of the chiefship— which brought them into open conflict with many chiefs. Of course, the ideal solution was to convert these rulers, a stroke that would replace the benighted rule of heathenism with a new Christian sovereignty. In sum, the nub of the civilizing colonialism of the mission—and it was, quite explicitly, a colonialism, in that it sought to subordinate Africa to the dominance of the European order—lay in replacing native economy and society with an imagined world of free, propertied, and prosperous peasant families. This latter-day yeomanry would inhabit a bounded and cultivated countryside, its beauty marred neither by the nakedness of savagery nor the despoliation of an expanding industrial city. It was a world in which God-inspired authority, pervading the reasoning mind and the receptive soul of every person, would reign through ever more enlightened secular rulers.

It is in the details of this civilizing colonialism, to recall what we said at the outset, that the making of the evangelists may be seen to have shaped the way in which they sought to make history; patently, the substance of their imagined worlds, formed on the social and physical landscape of Britain, had been fused and transposed into a coherent model for Africa. Thus Moffat (1842:616–7), leaning heavily on the rhetoric of Fowell Buxton, was fond of asserting that, if only the missions were careful to rebuild African life in all its aspects, "civilization [would] advance as the natural effect, and Christianity operate as the proximate cause of the happy change." He also took pains to point out (1842:616–7) that his entire career was given over to leading the Tswana along the high road to refinement, at the apex of which lay European civil society. This objective justified all his efforts to remake the Tswana mode of production and consumption, to establish a large school and a busy printing press, to clothe the heathens and rehouse them in proper habitations, to stimulate trade and reform the social division of labor. The general point was echoed by Livingstone, who repeatedly proclaimed that he, too, was working toward the thoroughgoing "elevation of man" in Africa (1858:46) through the "inestimable blessings" of "those two pioneers of civilization—Christianity and commerce" (p. 21); it was the latter, after all, that would gain the "negro family" entry into the "body corporate of nations" (1857:34). Even when he took off for Central Africa, leaving his brethren to the more mundane tasks of the mission, he justified his exploration as a necessary step in attaining the goal of "civilization, commerce, and Christianity" (p. 18; also p. 7). And, as it was for Moffat and Livingstone, so it was with their evangelical colleagues; elsewhere (Comaroff and Comaroff 1991:Chap. 6; n.d.[a]:Chaps. 2–4) we show that the model of civilizing reform—the scheme for reconstructing the very bases of "native life"—was shared by all the Nonconformists.

As significant here is the fact that the three models, taken together, owed much to the missionaries' self-appointed role as the conscience of the colonizer. Each was a moral refraction of bourgeois ideology, a measure of the ethics of the imperial impulse. This is most obvious in the case of the settler model, which was represented as the very inverse of enlightened liberal humanism (see e.g. Philip 1828,2:318). Hence the claim that the Boers violated the principles of *free* labor and *self*-determination, the corollary being that they would happily banish Africans from the kind of personhood and society for which civilized Britain had come to stand. But bourgeois ideology and morality also permeated the churchmen's view of state colonialism—founded, as it was, on the separation of sacred from secular authority, on the recognized right of a ruling class to exercise temporal command over the people and places under its jurisdiction, and on the duty of His Majesty's functionaries to extend the imperial sphere of influence (e.g. Moffat 1842:Chap. 13). Accordingly, the appointed role of government was not merely to administer the territory and population of the Colony. It was also—to recapitulate a popular opinion at home— the creation of a space, a "body of corporate nations" under *Pax Britannica* (Livingstone 1857:34), within which British commerce, interests, and values might flourish. The spirit of the age, and its particular expression in the Nonconformist imagination, emerges unmistakably in the terms which they chose to portray the colonial process.

So, too, does the social position of the missionaries—specifically, their class background and orientations—both at home and abroad. Thus, the state model took for granted the right of a cadre of "well-born" Britons to exercise authority over the colonial population, white and black, by virtue of their membership in a ruling *class;* a *"law-making* class," as William Dodd (above p. 185; 1847:11) called them, not knowing how well the term applied to the overseas ministers of *Pax Britannica*. A number of the churchmen did not especially admire the British aristocracy, and many disapproved of the actions and ethics of His Majesty's representatives at the Cape (see e.g. Livingstone in Schapera 1960:81f; Philip 1828,2:253 passim). Yet they did not question the right of the ruling classes to govern (see e.g. Macmillan 1936:245f). At the other end of the spectrum, the settler model was thought to reflect the sheer "boorishness," the brute degeneracy of the Boers, who were compared explicitly with the "worst" of the "unimproved" masses back in Britain (e.g. Ludorf 1863:203). For their part, the evangelists saw their own position as lying between ruler and settler; as we have said repeatedly, their social situation and their ideology alike were an embodiment of middle-class respectability, an expression of the assertive bourgeois Benthamism of which Arnold was to write (see above, p. 187). The upper class gentlemen of His Majesty's administration might govern by right of their nobility and worldly author- ity. And the lowly Boers might dominate by brute force. But they, emis- saries of the Empire of God, were there to implant a reign of civility, a state of colonization more pervasive and powerful than the colonial state, more enduring than the rancher republicanism of the Boers. So it was that the triumph of the bourgeoisie at home would be made into an imperial dominion of middle-class liberal virtue.

Measured on the uncompromising scale of political and military might, the churchmen did *not* occupy a niche between ruler and settler. As they well knew, they were the least potent whites in this colonial theater: subject to the authority of the Cape government on the one hand, they lacked the social and material resources, the numbers, and the resolute strength of the Boers on the other. As we noted above, it was just this—their being a "dominated fraction"—that makes the missionaries' reading of contemporary South Africa so revealing to us. Having to justify themselves to a frequently uncooperative administration, and to defend themselves against the (always suspicious, often belligerent) settlers, they were repeatedly sensitized to the different colonizing projects that were contesting the subcontinent. Moreover, their only weapons in this political arena were their rhetorical potency and their moral sanction. Add to this their assumed role as ethicists of empire and it is no wonder that few others on the scene were as articulate in discoursing on the competing colonialisms.

But two obvious questions follow from all this. Were the evangelists' models of colonialism similarly perceived by others—in particular, by those to whom they were attributed? And how accurately did they describe the various faces of colonization? The second question is, for present purposes, the less significant, since we are concerned here with arguments of ideology and rhetorical constructions; arguments that were themselves part of the colonial process and hence, by definition, only partial accounts of it. More salient is the issue of representation itself. Did those who spoke for the Boers—then or later—concur in the settler model? What of the functionaries of the state? And what difference did it make anyway?

The Boers, who reciprocated the evangelists' contempt in full (de Gruchy 1979:12f), repudiated the negative moral charges made against them by the Nonconformists, and they were loud in ridiculing accusations of personal brutishness and spiritual degeneracy. Indeed, a sympathetic German explorer and natural historian, Lichtenstein (1928,1:59), claimed not to recognize the "barbarians, [the] half-savages" described in British accounts of the settlers and bandied about by the churchmen. Also denied were the seizure of native lands, the kidnaping of blacks for slaves, and unprovoked attacks on the various chiefdoms in pursuit of stock and prisoners. Where such attacks and seizures occurred, they were justified as due punishment for cattle theft and other infractions against European property and persons. Likewise, demands for tax, tributary labor, and military assistance were legitimized in a manner reminiscent of the constitutional spirit of *Pax Britannica:* the Boers, went the argument (see e.g. Theal 1893:517f), having established sovereign jurisdiction over the interior of South Africa by right of conquest during the Great Trek, had conferred free citizenship on peoples like the Southern Tswana. In return for protection, peace, and the right to live within the settler territories, these peoples had, like citizens everywhere, to undertake military service and to pay taxes in cash or labor. What is more, as Boer leaders liked to point out, Britain had signed the Sand River and Bloemfontein Conventions in 1852 and 1854, thereby recognizing their right to conduct "native policy" as they saw fit. As this suggests, the imputation of lawlessness or immorality was rejected out of hand—and has been ever since by a long tradition of Afrikaner historiography (see e.g. Theal 1891, 1893; Cory 1919; Muller 1969). However, the *facts* of domination—its grounding in a theology of racial inequality; its practical application in various forms of regulation and extraction; its concentration on relations of land, labor, and taxation; its enforcement by coercive, even violent means—were not questioned. Just the opposite: they were assertively defended as legal and proper. In short, the missionaries' model of the *substance* of settler colonialism, if not their reflections on its moral and legal bases, were accepted by those to whom it was meant to apply. To be sure, the ideology of domination that it described was to be sustained in broadly similar form well into the post-colonial epoch in apartheid South Africa.

In the same vein, the stereotypic image of state colonialism shared by the Nonconformists did not depart far from that essayed by the Cape authorities themselves, at least between 1820 and the 1860s. It did not capture all the complexities, of course. For example, there was a great difference between the treatment of "coloureds" and blacks within the Colony and the policy toward those who lived along or beyond the frontier. The latter, as the missionaries noted, were encouraged to retain the integrity of their polities, keeping intact the institutions of "tribal government." By contrast, the former, whose political communities had long been dismantled, had become a servant class dispersed within and around the white settlements and farms of the Cape; even after abolition, their "freedoms" were greatly restricted by both law and common practice. John Philip (1828,2:308) might have railed against this in his campaign for "civil rights"; and he well understood the sympathy with which the middle and lower echelons of "magistrates" regarded (and treated) the settlers prior to, and after, the Great Trek. But most evangelists did not fully grasp the degree to which the state had become an agency for regulating both the flow of labor and the terms on which coloureds and blacks served whites; and all this long before Sprigg's spirited defense of civilization-through-toil. Nonetheless, His Majesty's functionaries would not have disagreed with those churchmen who perceived state colonialism to be a form of limited, regulatory governance. Indeed, they, too, were often assertive in extolling the virtues of this form of imperial rule—as generations of South Africans have been told by their school history books.

Here, then, are the imaginative and ideological bases for the clash of colonialisms. At one level—the coda of domination—nineteenth-century South African history may be read as an unfolding confrontation between these three colonialisms. From the perspective of the victim, their coexistence made the encounter with Europe appear contradictory and, initially at least, difficult to fathom. It is, after all, something of an irony to the colonized that those who come to rule them spend so much time fighting among themselves over the terms of command. Indeed, African popular protest was to make a good deal of the irony, often turning it into a bitterly satirical commentary on the poetics—or, rather, the poetic injustice—of oppression. And some black South Africans were to find new forms of empowerment in the fissures among the whites. But all this was yet far into the future. In the early decades of the century, the differences among the colonialisms were to express themselves in a series of struggles over policy and the practices of power.

From Models to Struggles

It is obviously impossible, here, to offer a detailed account of these struggles. To do that would be to rewrite the colonial history of South Africa. For the present, let us give just one example, one piece of that history, and let the matter rest.

In June 1847, in a letter written before his antipathy to the Boers had reached its highest pique, David Livingstone (Schapera 1974:5) lamented that the "Dutchmen" had "a great aversion to missionaries." Their enmity, he said, was caused by the "idea that we wish to furnish the natives with fire-arms." This letter, as it turns out, anticipated a long, angry round of hostilities among settlers, evangelists, and administrators; hostilities that were to break into open violence in the terrain beyond the Cape frontier, where the western edge of Boer-claimed territory met Bechuanaland. It is not surprising that the ostensible cause of the trouble was the alleged supply of weaponry to the Tswana. *Pax Britannica* notwithstanding, many chiefs had concluded that, in the interior, a little ordnance went much further than even the most far-reaching ordinance; hence they *were* trying desperately to lay their hands on some musketry. Furthermore, guns had taken on enormous significance for both the blacks and the Boers. To the former, they were an icon of the potency of *sekgoa* ("European ways") at large, a power to be seized and harnessed; to the latter, they were an affirmation of the exclusive control over force, of the capacity to determine the lives and deaths of lesser beings—"baboons and Bechuanas" among them.[18] But the conflict ran to the very core of colonial contestation, bringing the three colonialisms into noisy collision. And it ended, after some years, in a striking denouement: the destruction—indeed, physical dismemberment—of Livingstone's house and his mission to the Kwena by settler commandos. For it was none other than Dr. Livingstone himself who was presumed, by his enemies, to be most guilty of gun-running. He denied it, of course, arguing, in the *British Banner* (1849), that it was Boer traders who, tempted by huge profits, were selling firearms to the chiefs— despite the orders of their leaders (Livingstone in Schapera 1974:14). The traffic was so large, he added, that any settler authority who thought he could stop it "might as well have bolted his castle with a boiled carrot."

Carrots and castles aside, there is evidence that Livingstone did supply some guns to the Kwena (see Schapera 1974:41). For all the Reverend Ludorf's insistence, later, that missions had been there "to furnish weapons not carnal, but spiritual,"[19] other churchmen were also drawn into the trade over the next decade or so. For example, William Ashton[20] told his LMS superiors that Moffat's son, a trader, had once brought ammunition to the Kuruman station. Some had been sold to Tswana who, at the time, were fighting a group of settlers. The rest "was stored away in his father's garden," buried, it seems, amidst the carrots. "What will become of the Station," asked the nervous pastor, "if the Boers get to know [what] is in the missionary's garden?" To add to the irony, Ashton wrote again three weeks later,[21] complaining that all this had occurred while Moffat Sr. was in Cape Town trying to persuade the government to send ammunition to two "trustworthy" chiefs. Ordnance, he commented acidly, should not enter the country "by the means of either missionaries or their sons." Despite his plea, several evangelists continued willingly to help Tswana obtain weapons. But, as even the settlers knew, their efforts were far too limited to alter the balance of forces on the frontier (Schapera 1974). Effective access to the means of violence lay elsewhere.[22]

As this suggests, and this is the point, the strife over the supply of firearms to the Tswana was as much a symbolic as a material issue. But this does not mean that it was trivial. Apart from all else, the hostilities made it clear to all concerned that the deep interior had become a combat zone, alike political and ideological, in which the various protagonists were battling to lay down the terms on which black South Africa was to be ruled. Looking at this struggle from the standpoint of the Boers, and of settler colonialism, the involvement of the evangelists betokened two things, both extremely serious. The first was that, in procuring weapons for the Tswana—thereby handing them the power over human life and death—the churchmen were acknowledging their humanity and according them a place among *homo sapiens*. It was as if the gift of a musket was a metonym for the gift of membership in mankind itself. The propriety of that gift might have been taken for granted by the civilizing mission, but it was deeply contested by the settlers: for them it was divine truth, not a mere pigment of the imagination, that humanity ended at the color bar.

According to Livingstone (Schapera 1974:19), their leaders had long made it plain to the LMS that "a Missionary should teach the natives that the boers were a superior race." It was in this context, in fact, that the simian simile had first arisen: the "Dutchmen" had told his brethren, says the good doctor, that they "might as well teach baboons as Bechuanas." To give them weaponry, then, was tantamount to taking a firearm from the hunter and handing it to his prey. The Tswana were right: guns were indeed an icon of European potency. In trying to stop the Nonconformists from supplying even one to a black, the Boers sought to turn back the revolutionary tide of the civilizing mission at large.

There seems to have been little doubt among Boers that the evangelists stood for a competing colonialism—a colonialism that promised resistance and rebellion. Thus, for instance, one community went so far as to write into its constitution that members had to "take a solemn oath to have no connection with the London Missionary Society, . . . a political association, disseminating doctrines on social questions subversive of all order in society" (Theal 1902:228). Settler leaders were well aware of the church-men's intention to reconstruct the "native" world *ab initio;* the hated Philip (1828,2:355), after all, had said over and over that "civilization supposes a revolution in the habits of the people." As Stow (1905:268) was later to suggest, the Boers firmly believed that the LMS harbored the "Utopian idea of laying the foundation, under their own special priestly guidance, of a model kingdom of 'regenerated natives'." Not Moffat nor Philip nor Livingstone, for all the clarity with which they envisaged an Eden of the Spirit, could have phrased better the charter for their civilizing colonialism.

If, for the settlers, one aspect of the conflict over guns was their struggle against civilizing colonialism, the second was their opposition to, and effort to free themselves from, state colonialism. For, as they saw matters, there was yet another side to the "interference" of the missionaries. It lay in the fact that these men continually threatened to appeal to the Cape authorities, petitioning them to restrain Boer efforts to assert their autonomy and to rule the interior. The settlers appear to have assumed that their shared Britishness would dispose Her Majesty's officials to listen to the church-men; and, on occasion, the Nonconformists *did* invoke a "British" sense of civility and justice to goad officialdom into action. Despite their claims of non-involvement in colonial politics, the LMS and WMMS were quick to enter the public arena when they wished the state to exercise authority over the Boers (Comaroff and Comaroff 1991:Chap. 7). Recall that, while his garden was being filled with shot, Moffat had been in Cape Town to obtain armed support for the Tswana against the whites. Nor was this an isolated incident. During the trouble over the guns, the mission societies and their directors had made regular contact with the government, and had sometimes succeeded in persuading it to intervene, albeit on a limited

scale, to protect black communities—thereby provoking yet further acrimony among Britons and Boers. Hence the accusation made in the annals
of Afrikaner historiography some 70 years later: that the evangelists were
responsible for "malicious calumny, native unrest, race hatred, and . . .
warfare between British and Dutch" (Cory 1919:295). Not only had they
been responsible for a dangerous form of civilizing colonialism on their
own account, but their intercession was also blamed for the perpetuation
of state colonialism in the South African interior.

The immediate reaction of the Boers to the competing colonialisms, and
to the actions of mission and government, was to assert their autonomy
and their dominion over the black communities of the interior in ever more
flagrant terms. In the late 1840s, well established in central South Africa,
they spent a good deal of effort proving to the administration that *Pax
Britannica*—and, more generally, the authority of the colonial state—was
a dead letter, ever less enforceable as the distance from Cape Town grew
larger. In making their point, and simultaneously nurturing the agrarian
roots of settler economy and society, they set about laying the bases of the
rancher republics of the Transvaal and Orange Free State. Among these
was a "native policy" founded on the four elements of their model of
domination: taxation, labor extraction, the demand for military service,
and land appropriation.

Some liberal historians have argued that these actions were meant as a
deliberate provocation to the colonial state; proof that, since it could no
longer "protect the natives," the government could do little to arrest the
settler march—the political Trek—to independence (see e.g. Agar-Hamilton 1928). Perhaps. Official Boer rhetoric had it that the settlers bore "no
hostile intention toward any native tribe—unless . . . they attacked"
(Meintjes 1973:74). But such attacks were held to occur all the time,
allegedly, as we might guess, because the evangelists and other "unscrupulous" Europeans insisted on supplying guns to the blacks. Hence
Ludorf[23] recounts how a Boer leader had personally reiterated to him that
"we shall drive all [the missionaries] away for it is them who teach the
natives to be rebellious [and] to resist the white man."

To be sure, as they tried to throw off the shackles of the state, the Boers
made increasingly aggressive efforts to thwart the civilizing mission and to
silence the political voice of the missionaries. The Nonconformists were
told that, if they either interceded with the Cape government or encouraged
the chiefs to resist the settlers any further, they would be attacked and their
stations destroyed. So belligerent did the admonitions become that, in
1849–50, rumors began to circulate in the LMS: two senior evangelists, it
was said, had actually been taken prisoner. The report that bore the "news"
to London[24] also announced gravely that "the Dutch Boers . . . [had]
peremptorily ordered Livingstone to remove from his station and never to

return to it." Over the next two years, the archival records of the LMS and WMMS are one long litany, much of it based on hearsay, of intimidation and abuse of churchmen. For their part, the Societies appealed repeatedly to the colonial authorities for protection and support.

By late 1851, the British government had had enough of trying to contain the Boers. Afrikaner historiography has it that Britain eventually came to see positive advantage in drawing closer to them and their form of colonialism (Muller 1969:149); to see, among other things, that the natives had indeed been spoiled by the civilizing mission and would no longer subject themselves easily to white authority. Whatever the reasons, and they are more complex than we can discuss here, when Britain signed the Sand River and Bloemfontein Conventions, they gave the settlers constitutional sanction for their rancher republicanism. In both the historical consciousness of black South Africa (Molema 1951:85f) and in the eyes of the evangelists (e.g. Ludorf 1854; 1863:203), this heralded the final triumph of settler colonialism over the other, more enlightened modes of colonial rule. The Reverend Roger Edwards (1853:44) captures well the ensuing despair:

> Oh! what have the Commissioners done by yielding all to the boers. Has England removed from her escutcheons one of her noblest titles—justice to the native tribes? Well may we weep over these evils, and the interruption if not the termination of mission work . . .

If ever the churchmen felt the frustrations of being a dominated fraction of the dominant class, it was now. What is more, they were not thanked by the Tswana for their exertions. As one perspicacious parson had already noted in 1851, far from winning the gratitude of the blacks, "we . . . are blamed by [them] as forerunners . . . of oppression and destruction from the hands of our fellow white men."[25] There were few rewards in being the conscience of the colonizer. But the evangelists' feeling of impotence had yet to reach its nadir. That was to come with the final chapter of the story.

In the wake of Sand River and Bloemfontein, the settlers celebrated their independence by flexing their political muscle further, extending their domination, in its now familiar form, over an ever wider circle of Tswana polities. Among those who did not take easily to Boer authority were the Kwena, the chiefdom in which David Livingstone had established his station. And so, in 1852, Transvaal commandos, citing native belligerence and missionary interference as justification, decided to attack their capital at Kolobeng. Before doing so, however, they demanded that the Tshidi-Rolong—amongst whom Reverend Ludorf lived and worked—join the expedition as footsoldiers of the republic of which they were now involuntary citizens. The Tshidi ruler refused, was attacked himself, and fled north into exile (Molema 1966).

The Boers were as good as their word. Kolobeng was sacked and the LMS outpost laid to waste, its contents—the books, medicines, and other signs and instruments of the civilizing mission—deliberately destroyed and strewn over the landscape (Schapera 1974:171). One round in the argument over the guns had come to a decisive end. Livingstone gave up his mission among the Kwena for the exploration of Central Africa. And Ludorf withdrew to Thaba 'Nchu, a distant Tswana settlement on the fringe of Basutoland where the WMMS had long had a station safe from the vicissitudes of the frontier. Like Edwards, he was sure that the Boer triumph tolled the end of the civilizing mission in Bechuanaland; his reports, significantly, were laced with images of a burned, despoiled countryside, much like accounts of rural England under the impact of industrialization. As a result, he joined in the task of making Thaba 'Nchu into a new Eden, replete with cultivated gardens and fenced properties, printing press and pulpit, and other accoutrements of yeoman life—indeed, into a "perfect republic of peasants" reminiscent of Wordsworth's romantic idyll. That project, too, was to become embroiled in a contest of colonialisms. When the discovery of diamonds in the 1860s led to yet another round of conflict throughout the interior, the irrepressible evangelist was to try to create a "United Nation" of Southern Tswana, free of both British and Boer suzerainty. He was even to write a constitution for this independent black nation-state, a constitution built on private property, peasant enterprise, and bourgeois individualism. But that is another story.

For the moment, at least, the unrelenting contest of colonialisms had reached an uneasy point of rest. Its brief denouement, interestingly, was written on the geopolitical topography of the subcontinent: the state colonialism of Great Britain was reined into the boundaries of the Cape Colony; the settler colonialism of the Boers occupied the central interior; and the civilizing colonialism of the mission was confined to stations either beyond the frontier or within insulated pockets dotted across the remote countryside. Each charted, for its protagonists, a total world; each represented the effort of one class fraction to assert its own form of hegemony over South Africa; and, as noted before, each was to be drawn back into the fray, albeit in somewhat altered form, when the pause was shattered by the mineral revolution.

Conclusion

This finally returns us, full circle, to John Philip and the fictional Flory, he of the Orwellian imagination. As Philip had foreseen long before, the battle for South Africa did not arise out of the idiosyncratic actions of individuals. It grew from a *system* of relations among members of the body politic at large. And it was, indeed, an argument of structures and images, perceptions and practices. If anything is revealed by this excursion—and it should now be clear why it was so valuably undertaken through missionary eyes—it is that the terms of domination were never straightforward, never overdetermined. They seldom are, of course. In most places, at most times, colonialism did (and does) not exist in the singular, but in a plurality of forms and forces—its particular character being shaped as much by political, social, and ideological contests among the colonizers as by the encounter with the colonized.

As we said earlier, there is a sense in which, for the latter, the niceties of competing colonialisms are beside the point. At core, subordination has an emotional and perceptual logic, a calculus of abasement, all its own. At another level, however, the struggles among fractions of a ruling class can make a difference. They certainly did in South Africa. Not only did those struggles create spaces and places in which some blacks were to discover new, if limited, modes of empowerment; others, of course, were to find novel sources of enrichment at an almost Faustian cost. But, more important over the long run, the tensions of empire—in the form of conflict among colonizers and colonialisms—were to reveal some of the contradictions of European expansionism. For they would, in due course, lay bare the hidden structures, the unspoken and undisclosed ideological scaffolding, on which its peculiar structure of domination rested. In South Africa, as in other parts of the globe, the revelation of such contradictions were to feed the rise of black protest and resistance.

If Philip was correct in seeing the inherent contradictions, the systemic "vices," in early nineteenth-century colonialism, Flory saw the cosmic pun in imperialism; that, far from *pax,* it was a *pox,* a condition that scars the body personal and social, and may eventually blind those afflicted by it. Remember who it was that failed to see the truth behind the fantasy, mistaking larceny for law, sickness for civilization: none other than Veraswami—very/swami—a highly intelligent Indian doctor. It is not difficult to misunderstand the nature of colonialism and imperialism: not for the dominant, not for the subordinate, not for the scholar-voyeur. Thus, for all the evident complexities in the colonization of Africa, there remains a tendency, in some anthropological quarters, to take an essentialist view of it; to treat it as, at bottom, a linear, inexorable process in political economy, cultural imperialism, political modernization, material expansionism, or whatever. This account confirms what a number of others have shown: that colonialism simply does not have a single, transhistorical "essence," neither political nor material, social nor cultural. Rather, its form and substance are decided in the context of its making. And its making, we repeat, is in serious part a product of struggles among dominant ideologies and their perpetrators. As it happens, the three colonialisms in South Africa each stressed one face of the imperial impulse: the state emphasized the politico-legal aspects of British rule; the settlers, the socioeconomic dimension of race relations in a new agrarian society; and the mission, the signs and practices of bourgeois European culture. But the substance of the colonizing project, over the long term, was all of these things, in proportions determined on the battlegrounds of history—the bodies and societies, the territories and cultural terrains of South Africa, white and black.

Notes

1. The early nineteenth-century image of the person was not new; like much of the ontology of the age, it was foreshadowed in earlier epochs. But it was brought into sharp focus by the industrial revolution, and loomed large in the imagined world of the missionaries of the period.

2. A good example is Mrs. Bank's hero, Jabez Clegg, the *Manchester Man*.

3. Halévy (1924:428f), for one, ascribes the "uniform ugliness" of British architecture to the combination of capitalism and Puritanism.

4. See Arbuthnot's study of contemporary agriculture (1773). Arbuthnot argued for large-scale farming, but added (p. 139): "I most truly lament the loss of our yeomanry . . . [who] kept up the independence of this nation; . . . sorry I am to see their lands now in the hands of monopolizing Lords." See Thompson (1963:219) for a less roseate view of the yeomanry.

5. One remarkable statement of the myth is to be found in Wordsworth's (1948) sketch of the Lake District. An elegy for a disappearing world, it conjured up a yeomanry who lived in a "pure Commonwealth," an "ideal society."

6. This was the title of a noted anti-slavery poem by Roscoe (1787:31).

7. Of course, the ideology of imperialism had not died. Between the demise of the old and the rise of the new colonialism, there was much debate over the pros and cons of empire—fueled by Adam Smith's hostility toward a dominion of anything but free trade (Knorr 1944).

8. We focus on Moffat and Livingstone rather than on Philip because they actually worked among the Tswana, both devoting their energies directly to the civilizing mission—albeit, in Livingstone's case, only for the earlier part of his evangelical career. Philip, by contrast, spent most of his years in South Africa living in Cape Town as Superintendent of the LMS. But the choice is largely a matter of convenience; it makes little difference to our characterization. As Ross's (1986) recent biography of Philip shows, his background in Scotland was not unsimilar to that of Moffat and Livingstone.

9. On Moffat, we draw from J. Moffat (1886), Smith (1925), and Northcott (1961); on Livingstone, from Johnston (n.d.), Jeal (1973), and others.

10. This perspective, summarily presented here, is drawn from, among other sources, Campbell (1813); Moffat (1842); Broadbent (1865); Livingstone (1857); Mackenzie (1871); and the LMS and WMMS archives.

11. Increasingly, this included paying annuities to allied chiefs. In one case, Moffat (1842:209) adds with satisfaction, the payment was intended to promote education, an unusual departure from the state model.

12. See the Diamond Fields Advertiser (11.1.1878) for a report.

13. The words are from Barrow (1801–4,1:67, 273), whose views of the Boers were widely quoted, not least in missionary writings; see e.g. Philip (1828,2:263, 273). For further evidence of the attitudes toward the settlers held by the British colonists in general, and the evangelists in particular, see Streak (1974) and Coetzee (1988:28ff).

14. For evidence that the evangelists were aware of the theological justification for the settler model see Philip (1828,2:315–6).

15. For the missionaries, it was only Boer trekkers to whom the settler model really applied—not those Boers, Livingstone explains (1857:35), who chose to stay in the Colony under English law.

16. Livingstone (1857:35) gave much "eyewitness" evidence to support the claim that these practices were both brutal and common. He added that the Boers did not hide their acts, but assertively justified them.

17. In a passage often paraphrased by missionaries, Barrow (1801–4,1:57) had written: "As none of the [lands] are enclosed there is a general appearance of nakedness in the country ... which ... if divided by fences, would become sufficiently beautiful."

18. The phrase was attributed by Livingstone (Schapera 1974:19, 19n) to "not a few" Boers and their leaders.

19. J. Ludorf, Thaba 'Nchu, 2 August 1853 [WMMS, South Africa Correspondence (Bechuana), 315].

20. W. Ashton, Kuruman, 5 July 1858 [CWM, LMS Incoming Letters, South Africa, 31-1-B].

21. W. Ashton, Kuruman, 25 July 1858 [CWM, LMS Incoming Letters, South Africa, 32-1-B].

22. The Tswana had long tried to acquire arms. Their neighbors, the Griqua, had obtained weaponry from the Colony early on and, as a result, controlled frontier trade. By mid-century, however, the Tswana had found no major source of supply (see e.g. Shillington 1985).

23. See J. Ludorf, Motito, 16 October 1852 [WMMS, South Africa Correspondence (Bechuana), 315].

24. J. Freeman, Mabotsa, 25 December 1849 [CWM, LMS Home Odds (Freeman Deputation 1849–50), 2-4-D].

25. I. Hughes, Griquatown, 12 June 1851 [CWM, LMS Incoming Letters, South Africa, 26-1-A].

8

Medicine, Colonialism, and the Black Body

A few years ago a line from Cape Town to Cairo was thought to be a romantic dream, and yet most of us now are hoping to travel that way home before many years have passed; . . . and, what to some of us is more important still, there will be less of human pain and misery and more of healthy enjoyment and progress in the poor, diseased heart of Africa.

—Rev. W. C. Willoughby (1899a:63)

M EDICINE HELD A SPECIAL PLACE in the imagination that colonized nineteenth-century Africa. In fact, the rising hegemony of biology in Europe can be read in the control of threatening populations at home and abroad—and, more generally, in the regulation of relations between the "civil" and the "unruly." But the expanding empire also fed the new science with essential "raw material" and with a natural rationale for its emerging vision of physical man. As an object of European speculation, "the African" personified suffering and degeneracy, his environment a hothouse of fever and affliction. The rhetoric of the "geographical mission" linked the advance of reason in the interior of the dark continent with the biological thrust into the dim recesses of the human person. Early evangelists in South Africa saw social and political obstacles to their "humane imperialism" as natural contagions, responsive to medical control. As their philanthropic dreams hardened into colonial realities, the black body became ever more specifically associated with degradation, pollution, and disease.

In this chapter we explore the relationship of medicine and imperialism on the South African frontier, focusing on three distinct moments widely separated in time: the shaping of an imperial vision in late eighteenth-century discourses of the afflicted continent, the advent of the mid–nineteenth-century healing mission, and the founding of the colonial state in the early twentieth century. We shall suggest that the development of British colonialism in Africa, as a cultural enterprise, was inseparable from

215

the rise of biomedicine as science. The frontiers of "civilization" were the margins of a European sense of health as social and bodily order, and the first sustained probe into the ailing heart of Africa was a "mission to the suffering." It followed that the savage was the very embodiment of dirt and disorder, his moral affliction all of a piece with his physical degeneracy and his "pestiferous" surroundings. The early soldiers of Christendom were also at the cutting edge of colonialism. When they tried to domesticate the "dark" interior, they drew heavily on the iconography and practice of healing. What is more, their accounts of life and affliction in the African "laboratory" served as grist to the mill of a growing natural science.

With the rise of the colonial state, missionary healers in South Africa were to find themselves eclipsed by the newly formed agencies of public health. By the turn of this century, their talk of civilizing Africa had given way to a practical concern with the hygiene of black populations—and to the project of taming the "native" work force. Here, as elsewhere in the colonized world, persons were disciplined and communities redistributed in the name of sanitation and the control of disease. For, as blacks became an essential element in the white industrial world, medicine was called upon to regulate their challenging physical presence. It also crystallized the political threat they posed to that world by linking racial intercourse with the origin of sickness. We shall suggest that, whereas mission healing was little more than a persuasive art, the health regimes of the colonial state rested on a much greater authority, one whose global certainties were the product of the mutually sustaining regimes of science and empire.

The point of our analysis, we stress, is not to argue that imperial expansion determined the rise of biomedical science. Neither do we claim that nineteenth-century medicine was merely an ideology of imperial control. Rather, we seek to show that each played off the other within the unfolding of a particular historical process—that they were in fact cut from the same cultural cloth. Each came to verify the other through the categories and metaphors of an underlying vision. Thus, notwithstanding its status as an emerging science, medicine drew upon social images to mediate physical realities, giving colonial power relations an alibi in the ailing human body. And colonial regimes, in turn, drew upon medical icons and practices to impose their domination upon subjects and collectivities everywhere.

Biology, Romantic Naturalism, and the African's Place in Nature

Writers on the early nineteenth-century life sciences have observed that the period was marked by a restructuring of the "chain of being," with special reference to its lower half. As Figlio (1976:20) explains, the real issue underlying debates about man's place in nature was the relationship of the human species to the rest of the living world: "There was a focusing upon the multi-faceted idea of animality, as opposed to an insistence upon a scalar, uni-dimensional hierarchy, with man at the top of the visible, and God at the top of the invisible, realm." This implied a preoccupation with continuities, with the properties common to all animate beings. Those who sought such properties had to "define the elusive notion of life; to measure and rank the degrees of its expression" (Figlio 1976:28). Rooted in the contrast between the animate and the inanimate, the enterprise fixed upon man as the embodiment of perfection, for it was he who had distinguished himself by employing reason to discover his own essence. This, in turn, led inexorably to the concept of "generic human nature" (Stocking 1987:17), a notion that separated man from beast, people from objects, and so rendered anomalous anything—like the slave trade—that confused them. Of course, "human nature" notwithstanding, the chain of being was itself to be differentiated and internally ranked, and it was to use the African to mark out the lowest limits of the human species.

In the epistemology of the era, then, the key to knowledge seemed to lie increasingly within man himself, the gendered imagery here being faithful to the language of the time. The essence of life lay in the unplumbed depths of organic being, to be grasped through the invasive thrust, the looking and naming, of the new biology (Foucault 1975). Its interior truth—merely signified in outer bodily form—gave rise to meaningful differences in the faculties and functions of living beings. This mode of seeing was becoming increasingly tangible in discourses about exploration in Africa, where the quest for knowledge of the interior likened the continent to the human body (Comaroff and Comaroff 1991:Chap. 3). But the newly charted surfaces of the African landscape had an even more direct connection with the human organism, for the geographical mission was also extending European knowledge of the global range of mankind. In investigating the savage, the West set up a mirror in which it might find a tangible, if inverted, self-image. Non-Europeans filled out the nether reaches of the scale of being, providing the contrast against which cultivated man might emerge with clarity. On this scale, moreover, the African was assigned a particularly base position. In treating him as the very embodiment of savagery, the travel literature had given descriptions of his physical form alongside clinical accounts of his "manners and customs" (Pratt 1985). African "nature" was thus grounded in the color, shape, and substance of the black physique.

With the ascendance of comparative anatomy and biology, the reduction of African society and culture to such organic bases took on more authority. For much of the eighteenth century it had been civilization—moral and politico-economic circumstances rather than physical endowment—that had separated savage man from his European counterpart(Stocking 1987:18). But the vocabulary of natural science was to formalize an existing European association of dark continents with black bodies and dim minds. Comparative anatomical scales and schemes presented the African as the human obverse of the European, the "link" between man and animal (Curtin 1964:38). Late eighteenth-century racial classifications almost invariably placed him at the bottom of the ladder to enlightenment, below such paler peoples as Asians or American Indians (see White 1799; or Cuvier 1827,1:97, who ranked the "fair or Caucasian variety" above the "yellow or Mongolian," and the latter above the "Negro or Ethiopian"). The hard facts of organic existence, of the ineffable chain of biological being, had come to determine the place of men in the world.

The life sciences, in short, drew their terms from contemporary discourses about the human condition fed by Europe's encounter with the non-European world. Elevated to a new level of self-consciousness and authority, this "value-free" knowledge found a natural validation for cultural imperialism in the inner secrets of existence. Contemporary naturalists read off the degree of animality and the perfection of life from the external forms of different organisms; these forms were taken to be a function of the relative complexity, symmetry, and refinement of the faculties within. The influential Dutch scholar Petrus Camper (see Cogan 1821), for instance, devised a scale that correlated the shape of the skull with aesthetic appearance and mental capacity. His so-called facial angle measured the projection of the jaw, a protruding profile being associated in the European mind with the long snouts, low brows, and sensory-bound state of animals. Applied to an eclectic array of evidence—including African travelers' accounts—this measurement defined and ranked national character, giving physical shape to the current philosophical concern with the relationship of race, nationality, and civilization (cf. Hume 1854). Camper's scale stretched from dog to ape to Negro, and through the European peoples to the ideal form epitomized in Greek sculpture (Cogan 1821:x; see Figlio 1976:28f). What is more, his pronouncements were publicized beyond the scientific community. The preface to an English translation of his popular lectures addressed a general audience on the practical and aesthetic implications of the science of comparative anatomy (Cogan 1821:x): "[Camper's] grand object was to shew, that national differences may be reduced to rules; of which the different directions of the facial line form a fundamental norma or canon . . . the knowledge of which will prevent the artist from blending the features of different nations in the same individual." Here nationality, culture, and physical type are condensed into a language that, in the nineteenth century, would mature into scientific racism. With his apartheid of the sketchpad, Camper imprinted the physical contours of stereotypic others on the European imagination—and, with them, a host of derogatory associations. The bestiality of his sample African profile, for instance, was quite unmistakable.

Georges Cuvier, the prestigious Swiss comparative anatomist of the early nineteenth century, took the facial angle and the biological reduction of culture to new levels of sophistication: He developed a scale that purported to evaluate the perfection not only of the intellect, but of the introspective self—the moral core of the person. By measuring the proportion of the midcranial area to that of the face, he sought to reveal the degree of dependence of an organism upon external sensations; the size of the cranium itself was taken to reflect the development of reason and self-control. On this count, the "Negro" stood between the "most ferocious apes" and the Europeans, who were themselves superseded by the men and deities of ancient Greece (Figlio 1976:28). But it was the neurological dimension of Cuvier's scheme (1827,1:49f) that addressed most explicitly the spiritual and moral capacity of man. For the nervous system was the site of internal animation, and its complexity determined the higher faculties of life—intelligence and volition (Figlio 1976:24): "Cuvier associated this compactness quite explicitly with the higher faculties, indeed, with the sense of the 'self.' Just as the nervous system coalesced into a centre from which dependent nerves arose, so too was the sense of self increasingly solidified and distinct. Thus, a grading of this . . . concentrating of the nervous system was simultaneously a grading of animal sentience and selfhood." And so the bourgeois subject, already secure in the ethic of Protestantism and rational philosophy, was given incontestable grounding in biological nature. Needless to say, the inner density and refinement associated by Cuvier with self-awareness and control were underdeveloped among non-Europeans, especially blacks, who were bound by the bestial reflexes of survival (1827,1:97; see Curtin 1964:231).

As Figlio (1976:35) notes, Cuvier's writings were elaborately summarized in the British biomedical press within months of their publication and were widely discussed by scientists, theologians, and literati. In an age when specialist knowledge was not yet set apart by technical language, such work was rapidly directed to a receptive public. Often, as in the case of one widely read translation of Cuvier's *Animal Kingdom,* some "popular and entertaining matter" was added by the editors on the "instincts and habits" of animals and primitive man (1827,1:i–ii). This included a description of the "unhappy races" of South Africa, a telling bricolage of current European curiosity substantiated by material drawn from the accounts of early travelers.

An ingredient of this bricolage was the direct observation made by Cuvier and others of the so-called Hottentot Venus, an unfortunate living exhibit of the "essential black" from the Cape Colony, who died in Paris in 1815 (1827,1:196; see Gilman 1985:212; Gould 1985:294). These descriptions show early nineteenth-century representations of Africa hardening into stereotypes as travel tales and salon exotica were given scientific credentials and directed toward a seemingly insatiable popular readership. Furthermore, such images had a perceptible effect on the eyes of subsequent European visitors to Southern Africa. The epithets used in *The Animal Kingdom* for the "Hottentots"—"degraded and disgusting," "swarthy, filthy, and greasy"—were to flow from the pens of many later writers who claimed the authority of first-hand observation.

Like others before them, Cuvier and his editors focused on the exotic, simian qualities of the reproductive organs of black women, legitimating, as medical inquiry, their barely suppressed fascination with such torrid eroticism (Gilman 1985:213). Travelers like John Barrow (1801–1804) had also written in this vein of the "genital aberrations" of "Bushman" and "Hottentot" women, and Mungo Park (1799), if in somewhat different idiom, had reduced Africa to the body of a black female yielding herself to white male discovery (Comaroff and Comaroff 1991:Chap. 3). This mytheme also appears in both the poetry of romantic naturalists and the sober prose of our missionary crusaders. But, as the Cuvier text shows, in the early nineteenth century it was science that articulated and authorized such imagery; again, the various products of current European fancy at the time sailed under the colors of biological knowledge, knowledge about "nature," health, the body, and the self.

Although the internalizing focus of biological science would eventually draw attention away from man's transactions with his social and material environment, in the early nineteenth century there was still a lively concern with maintaining an equilibrium between organism and context. There had long been controversy over the role of climate in the origin of human diversity, some early naturalists (e.g., Buffon 1791) and biologists (e.g., Blumenbach 1969 [1775; 1795]) having argued that "Negro" physical characteristics grew out of sustained life in the tropics (Curtin 1964:40). Here, scientific thought drew on European notions of environment dating back at least to the sixteenth and seventeenth centuries; in particular, to the humoral theory that "as the air is, so are the inhabitants" (cf. Hodgen 1964:283). In this legacy, the "southern climes" were associated with heat, sensuality, depletion, and decay, a connection that recurs repeatedly in the perceptions of eighteenth-century Europeans. Lichtenstein (1928,1:58), for instance, blamed the Cape Dutchman's "phlegm" on the African climate, quoting Goethe's similar observations about the indolent Neapolitans. Whites in warm climates mediated between the "antipodal constitutions" of the languid Negro and the "sanguinous Anglo-Saxon" (Cartwright 1853; Jones n.d.:48). The virulent effects of febrile disease on those Britons who attempted to establish a colony in West Africa in the late eighteenth century only reaffirmed the image of the "white man's grave," a continent inimical to civilized existence.

Although the writings and actions of the early missionaries to South Africa reveal a sense of contagion lurking in the dark continent, their vision was most directly informed by the discourses of abolitionism and romantic naturalism, which also drew upon images of corporeality and health. Rooted in the early romanticism of the mid–eighteenth century, these discourses expressed a reaction to urban bourgeois society and a celebration of preindustrial rural simplicity. Here the conventionalized savage innocent steps forth. Joseph Warton's "The Enthusiast; or, The Love of Nature" (in Park 1811:39), written in 1740, captures the mood well:

> *Happy is the first of men ere yet confin'd*
> *To smoky cities; who in sheltering groves,*
> *Warm caves, and deep-sunk valleys liv'd and lov'd,*
> *By cares unwounded; what the sun and showers,*
> *And genial earth untillag'd could produce,*
> *They gather'd grateful.*

But paradise has been blighted by those who, having tasted the fruit of knowledge, can no longer remember simple virtues. By 1750, Warton (Park 1811:52) had put the following words into the mouth of an Andean Indian:

> *I see all Europe's children curs'd*
> *With lucre's universal thirst;*
> *The rage that sweeps my sons away*
> *My baneful gold shall well repay.*

Africa's gold was its manpower and, by the closing years of the eighteenth century, the rising strain of abolitionist sympathy had blended with romantic naturalism to depict a vanquished African Eden and an exiled native son. Thus Roscoe (1787:10) writes of the blissful state from which the royal Cymbello is snatched by the slave traders:

> *Lord of his time, the healthful native rose,*
> *And seiz'd his faithful bow, and took his way*
> *Midst tangled woods, or over distant plains,*
> *To pierce the murd'rous Pard; when glowing noon*
> *Pour'd its meridian fervours, in cool shades*
> *He slept away th'uncounted hours. . . .*

The garden was overtaken by a "foul plague" from Europe—slavery—and "Nature recoiled, and tore with frantic hands her own immortal features" (1787:12). Disease and despoliation follow: Southey's (1815:39) invocation of the "Genius of Africa" recounts the violation of the enchanted landscape. Maternal Africa is despoiled, her offspring torn from her breast by slavery:

> Ah heed the mother's wretchedness
> When in the hot infectious air
> O'er her sick babe she bows opprest,
> Ah hear her when the Traders tear
> The drooping infant from her breast!

Here we encounter a theme that links the romantic poetry of the time to the accounts of famous travelers like Mungo Park, a theme that was to shape the imperial vision of Africa. It is the myth of a continent bereft of its virile manhood, exiled from Eden, and awaiting the restorative attentions of the heroic white man. The suffering abandon of Africa cultivated in such romantic poetry, especially when in the service of abolition, provided fertile ground for an ideology of colonial healing.

The Healing Mission

The rhetoric of the first generation of British evangelists in South Africa was to make effective use of the theme of Africa as savage and suffering. Robert Moffat (1842:616), father-in-law of David Livingstone and illustrious pioneer of the London Missionary Society (LMS) among the Tswana, once addressed a large and admiring philanthropic public as follows: "Africa still lies in her blood. She wants . . . all the machinery we possess, for ameliorating her wretched condition. Shall we, with a remedy that may safely be applied, neglect to heal her wounds? Shall we, on whom the lamp of life shines, refuse to disperse her darkness?" Thus did the metaphors of healing justify "humane imperialism," making of it a heroic response rather than an enterprise of political and economic self-interest.

Is it surprising, then, that those responding to this call should think of their mission in medical terms? David Livingstone (1857:5) writes: "I soon resolved to devote my life to the alleviation of human misery . . . and therefore set myself to obtain a medical education, in order to be qualified for that enterprise." Although Livingstone was the first, and for many years the only, medically trained missionary among the Tswana, his colleagues all provided some medical aid to their would-be converts (Seeley n.d.:75).[1] For the early evangelists conceived of themselves as restorers both of body and spirit, bearers not only of salvation but of a healing civilization.

Within that civilization, however, medicine remained, at least in the middle decades of the nineteenth century, a relatively unrigorous and speculative form of knowledge; note that David Livingstone almost failed to gain the license of the Faculty of Physicians and Surgeons in Glasgow in 1840 because of his advocacy of the stethoscope, an instrument whose usefulness his examiners disputed (Gelfand 1957:24). There had been pressure on the state to regulate the profession for several decades (Turner 1959:154), but access to formal training remained open to the likes of Livingstone, who started his working life as a piecer in a Scottish mill. Livingstone himself had *The Lancet* sent to him during his years in the field so that he might keep abreast of innovations; the ethos of rational discovery was as alive with respect to the "body space" of medicine as it was in the domain of geography. Yet the pharmacopoeia at his disposal consisted mainly of herbal compounds, emetics, and purgatives that he himself saw as close enough to Tswana medicaments to warrant his borrowing the latter to enhance his own stock (Gelfand 1957:63; Seeley n.d.: 79; Livingstone 1857:692f).

Livingstone's own reflections on the similarities and differences between European and Tswana healing are presented to us most succinctly in his famous dialogue with a Kwena healer (1857:25; see also Schapera 1960:239f),[2] which we quote in extenso in Chapter 9. The conversation is ostensibly evidence of the fallacious reasoning of the superstitious mind. But the text is structured to convey a more ambivalent message. Take, for example, the following extract:

[**Medical Doctor**]: . . . You can not charm the clouds by medicines. You wait till you see the clouds come, then you use your medicines, and take the credit which belongs to God only.

[**Rain Doctor**]: I use my medicines, and you employ yours; we are both doctors, and doctors are not deceivers. You give a patient medicine. Sometimes God is pleased to heal him by means of your medicine; sometimes not—he dies. When he is cured, you take the credit of what God does. . . . When a patient dies, you don't give up trust in your medicine, neither do I when rain fails. If you wish me to leave off my medicines, why continue your own?

M.D.: I give medicine to living creatures within my reach, and can see the effects, though no cure follows; you pretend to charm the clouds, which are so far above us that your medicines never reach them. . . . Could you make it rain on one spot and not on another?

R.D.: I wouldn't think of trying. I like to see the whole country green. . . .

Livingstone concludes the dialogue with a remark about the Tswana genius for argument; to be sure, it is he who has had to shift ontological ground in the exchange. The use of the term "doctor" for both participants seems to reinforce the logical equivalence of their claims. Presented in various versions in Livingstone's writings, this conversation seems to have served as a device for voicing his intellectual qualms about the mission project.

Note that it is not mere evangelical zeal that prevents him from asserting the indisputable superiority of medical science. At the time, biomedical knowledge had no clear hegemony and, in the African interior, its practitioners could not be confident that their ability to deal with serious illness exceeded that of their native counterparts (cf. Jeal 1973:17).

Indeed, if healing was salient on the colonial frontier, it was as a technique of civilization, carrying with it a pervasive philosophy about the relationship of bodies and contexts, matter and morality. Ironically, while they continued to foster the image of African affliction, nineteenth-century missionaries acknowledged that Tswana populations tended to be "remarkably" free of disease (Seeley n.d.:81; Willoughby 1899a).[3] In the eyes of the churchmen, it was their *spiritual* "suffering"—their "sentence of death"—that was at issue, and this was a function of their lack of self-determination, their filthy habits, and their brazen nakedness. The unclothed heathen body posed an especially acute threat to the fragile colonial order and became something of an obsession with the evangelists. The latter soon declared that it was impossible to open up a spiritual discourse with the Tswana, who seemed to have hopelessly "carnal views to all spiritual things" (Broadbent 1865:178) and were captivated by the white man's goods and techniques. So, instead, the whites commenced their reform of the native person from outside, working on the humble terrain of everyday practice. Here, in the name of decency, cleanliness, and health, they attempted to make the Tswana into Protestant persons, molded by the cultural forms of empire.

Contemporary mission correspondence gives insight into the disquiet that underlay the industrious effort to enclose the African body. It also shows how the churchmen tried to intervene in the uncontained physicality that seemed to pervade the life of the Tswana, from their techniques of production and reproduction to their unruly architecture and undisciplined speech. Observe, for instance, this passage from the writings of Moffat (1842:287): "As many men and women as pleased might come into our hut, leaving us not room even to turn ourselves, and making every thing they touched the colour of their greasy red attire. . . . They would keep the housewife a perfect prisoner in a suffocating atmosphere, almost intolerable; and when they departed, they left ten times more than their number behind—company still more offensive." This may have been a world not yet informed by bacteriology, but there was a persistent association of the African body with noxious organisms that threatened to invade the inviolable world of white order. As we have noted, the image of the infested, "greasy" native—indistinguishable from his pestilential surroundings— had gained currency in the texts of travelers and anatomists in the late eighteenth century. The expression probably derived from the use, especially in the hottest and driest regions of Africa, of animal fat as a moisturizing and beautifying cosmetic. But the epithet carried other derogatory associations. It suggested a body surface that was porous, dirty, and damp, one that "gave off" contagion and odor to those with whom it came into contact. Like the "grotesque body" of renaissance representation, the native person was "never closed off from either its social or ecosystemic context" (Stallybrass and White 1986:22).

Nothing could have been further from the discrete, sanitized, conserving individual of the mission ideal. On the African colonial frontier, the "lubricated wild man of the desert" contrasted with the "clean, comfortable, and well-dressed believer," as did "filthy" animal fat and skin with the "cotton and woollen manufactures of Manchester and Leeds" (Hughes 1841:523). Creating a need for "healthful" attire was also a self-conscious effort to hitch Africans to the European commodity market, itself perceived as a moral order with cultivating effects (Moffat 1842:605; Livingstone 1857:34). Skin costume was "disgusting" because it failed to separate mankind from bestial nakedness and could only foster immoderate emission and disease. Moffat (1842:503) said of the Tswana: "The child, as may be seen, is carried in a skin on the mother's back, with its chest lying close to her person. When it requires to be removed from that position, it is often wet with perspiration; and from being thus exposed to cold wind, pulmonary complaints are not infrequently brought on." This style of writing objectifies "native habit," describing it in distancing, almost subhuman terms.

Such observations reveal the cultural logic behind the civilizing mission. They also give insight into the images of Africa relayed to a large and diverse reading public in Britain. When Moffat published his *Missionary Labours and Scenes in Southern Africa* in 1842, which was dedicated to Prince Albert, he was a heroic figure whose account was eagerly awaited by adventurers, evangelists, and imperialists (1842 [1969]:x). Even more influential was Livingstone, whose writings enjoyed enormous circulation in both the scientific and popular media. It is interesting that he invoked images of disease very similar to those of his medically untrained colleagues: of illness as the product of exposure and contagion, the result of bodies improperly set off from each other and from the natural elements. Of course, these constructs underpinned European etiologic theories of the period, which were still part of the "externalizing discourse" (Young 1978) of humoral pathology. Vital bodily processes were widely held to depend upon outside stimuli—especially heat, a property dense with social and moral value.

Such constructs confirmed established beliefs about the debauched condition of Africa, and they were continually reinforced by the "evidence" collected in the natural laboratory along the colonial frontier. Thus Livingstone (in Schapera 1961:129) asserted that conditions such as inflammation of the bowels, rheumatism, and heart disease seemed to decline among the Tswana with the adoption of decent European dress. And he found particularly appealing the current theory of "noxious miasmas," in terms of which fever was caused by the inhalation of emanations from "marshy miasmata," "effluvia, poisons, and human ordure" that fermented into a substrate of contagion in moist, densely vegetated situations (Carlson 1984:38). Livingstone thought Africa especially hospitable to such dank rottenness and imagined that he had found the cause of the virulent malaria that so threatened whites on the dark continent (Gelfand 1957:297; Schapera 1960:24). These conclusions were transmitted to *The Lancet* (1861) by the Hydrographer to the Admiralty, the then intense medical interest in tropical fevers being an apt example of the marriage of imperial concern and biological speculation.

But beneath the theory lay a familiar set of associations: Disease arises from dirt, and dirt comes from the confusion of bodies and bodily secretions—especially in torrid climes—which open the pores and encourage a process of organic and moral degradation. Yet the image of decay never totally eclipsed the earlier romantic vision of the "healthful native" (see above). Thus Livingstone was also challenged by the fact that, in comparison to white men, black women seemed to display a much lower mortality from malaria (Schapera 1960:24). He speculated (with fellow evangelist John Mackenzie) that this resulted from the latter's unusually heavy menstrual discharge, which flushed the poison from their bodies, presumably to swell the tide of effluvia in which the disease was held to grow. In terms of the humoral pathology that obtained in Britain in the mid–nineteenth century, fever was associated with excess, and menstruation was regarded as a natural form of therapeutic bleeding (Jones n.d.:81). Once more, etiology found meaning in immoderate sexuality, the uncontained body of the African female being a tangible threat to European male viability. Gilman (1985:231) reminds us that the black woman served widely as an icon of sexually transmitted illness in the late nineteenth-century European imagination. At the time, in fact, some medical opinion claimed that syphilis was a form of leprosy that had long been present in Africa and had spread into Europe in the Middle Ages.

Not surprisingly, venereal disease was another of Livingstone's explicit concerns. Though he noted its presence among the Tswana, his faith in the luxuriance of black fertility led him to the conviction that syphilis was "incapable of permanence in any form in those of pure African blood" (Schapera 1961:128). His optimism was ill-founded. The disease was already following the path of migrant laborers, who left the region for the colonial towns to the south. By the turn of the century, communities of black workers were seen as cesspools of syphilis in the white man's cities, calling forth the intervention of public health authorities (Seeley n.d.:124).

But, once again, Livingstone's misperception was not random. It reinforced a well-established European mythology. In the late nineteenth-century vocabulary of sexuality, miscegenation was a particularly threatening source of pathology, a cause of decline in white populations at home and abroad (Gilman 1985:237). It was also a matter of particular sensitivity in the racially marked order of domination established along the frontier. Albeit unwittingly, mission medicine reinforced the ideological bases of this order by giving it an alibi in the defiling black body.

As this implies, missionary healing had far-reaching effects, although it was more successful in making the blacks into subjects of empire than citizens of Christendom. With the colonial state ever more visibly at their back, the churchmen had a considerable impact upon African modes of production, dress, and architecture. The Tswana, in turn, strove to gain some control over the evident potency of the Europeans—potency residing in diverse objects and practices, from guns and mirrors to irrigation and literacy. In their own world, power existed in its most condensed form in the diviner's medicine, and they were soon asking the Nonconformists for concoctions to make them read, to promote conception, or to ensure successful hunting (Livingstone 1857:146, 622; Moffat 1842:599). In seeking the white man's healing, they attempted to imbibe something of his tangible might. And while his treatment did little to displace indigenous ritual, it was so much in demand that the evangelists were sometimes driven to despair.[4] But they encouraged the enthusiasm, for they believed that the African was most impressionable on the "bed of affliction"; and they seldom missed an opportunity to give moral instruction along with their treatment (Seeley n.d.:82f). They also seem to have charged "the wealthier natives" for their potions and services, hoping thereby both to cover costs and to teach a useful lesson in monetized value.[5]

In fact, Western medicine—at least of the sort provided by the evangelists—was one of several civilizing commodities by which the church ushered the Tswana into the marketplace. Perhaps the most blatant example of how this was done is provided by the Reverend Roger Price. In 1880, Price set up a flourishing "hospital" at his station at Molepolole and, from the proceeds, eventually bought himself a farm and a handsome herd of cattle.[6] However unsystematic missionary treatment might have been, it was based on the logic of biomedicine, a logic shared by other facets of the culture that colonized nineteenth-century Africa. Accordingly, the individual was seen as the atom of production, and values such as health, wealth, and salvation were moral achievements to be secured by hard labor, effective management, and rational consumption. Illness was no longer a sign of disrupted social relations, as it had been for the Tswana: If not caused by natural accident, it was the mark of personal indigence or self-abuse.

In the South African interior of the late nineteenth century, then, the evangelists were the bearers of an expansive European worldview. Their mission was regulated neither by government nor by professional monopoly. But as they ministered to the indigenous peoples (and even to isolated white settlers),[7] they introduced a coherent mode of seeing and being, a specific conception of person, body, health, and society that anticipated the culture and economy of the colonial state.

The Emergence of Colonial Public Health

But the era of the healing ministry was coming to an end. With the discovery of diamonds near Kimberley in 1867, the expansion of white settlers into the interior took on a totally new momentum. An influx of capital fueled the burgeoning market for goods and labor, and, by 1871, Britain had annexed the diamond fields and surrounding region, including land claimed by the Tswana. In 1885, after a long period of political struggle among Boers, Britons, and blacks, the Crown Colony of British Bechuanaland was established over the territory of the southern chiefdoms; it was to be transferred to the Cape Colony a decade later. At the same time, the northern chiefdoms were incorporated into the Bechuanaland protectorate (which became Botswana in 1966). As part of the government of this protectorate, two medical officers were appointed and a military hospital was built at the administrative headquarters at Mafeking.

The introduction of biomedicine at the local level soon began to undermine missionary healing. Although the colonial medical officers provided little actual health care for Southern Tswana until well into the twentieth century (Seeley n.d.:125), their appointment was accompanied by immediate restrictions on the practice of the churchmen. By 1900, government officials were actively discouraging unqualified evangelists from giving treatment where the services of a district surgeon were available and, in 1894, the LMS issued instructions that no charge should thenceforth be levied for care offered by untrained agents.[8] In their letters from the field, the churchmen became increasingly apologetic about their healing techniques, bemoaning the burden of the work, their lack of qualifications, and the dearth of "Christian medical men."[9] But there is also the suggestion that, along with their resistance to overrule, some of the peoples of the interior resisted government medicine. The missionaries note that they were frequently consulted—by blacks and whites—in preference to the resident district surgeon.[10]

The first aim of colonial officials was to ensure the well-being both of government employees and of the expanding European communities in the interior. But the sine qua non of white wealth and welfare in this context was its thoroughgoing dependence upon black labor. Thus the control of the latter loomed large in the public health project from the start, official rhetoric expressing the contradiction built into the very constitution of South African society: that "natives" be central to its economy yet marginal to its political and moral community. The defiling tropes used to distance and subjugate the black "other" came back to haunt the whites, whose material world was deeply dependent on the proximity of native labor.

One of the earliest communications from the medical officer in Mafeking reveals the driving force of the paradox. Writing of the need, in 1890, to enforce the Contagious Diseases Act in the "native location," he says: "The public should have some protection against the spread of syphilis which is frequently effected through the servants attending children as nurses" (Great Britain 1891–1892; see Seeley n.d.:124). This statement, incidentally, reveals an important refinement in lay medical usage: Specific infections had replaced the more diffusely conceived contagion of an earlier epoch. But science still found its voice in the contradictory culture of colonization. Infection continued to emanate from the black female body, a body more immediately threatening because it had been given entrée into the enclosed white world. Note that the gateway to infection had become the innocent and vulnerable European infant, whose care, increasingly in the hands of African women, brought blacks into the most private reaches of colonial life. Tellingly, the medical officer did not acknowledge the possibility that disease might be communicated by sexual congress across the lines of color, although this was an equally present reality in settler society. But miscegenation was an inadmissible challenge to the basic premise of inequality on which this society was founded: In modern South Africa, at least until recently, interracial sex was to be known as "immorality" in everyday and legal parlance. Robbed of all other meanings, the term came to imply a crime against humanity itself.

More important still, the report of the medical officer indicates how public health was to serve in the discipline of black populations whose ambiguous physicality was a source of both wealth and danger. Evidence of the relation of state medicine and social control exists—in highly graphic, literal form—in local historical records. The only mention of health facilities for Tswana in the Mafeking District at the turn of the century, for example, was that of the "gaol hospitals" attached to local police stations (Seeley n.d.:124). But this was merely a refraction of a more embracing disposition of government: Swanson (1977:387) has argued that public authorities in South Africa at the time displayed a noticeable "sanitation syndrome"; that is, an obsession with infectious disease that shaped national policies and practices of racial segregation, especially in the growing cities. Of course, it was a disposition shared with other colonizing regimes (Lyons 1985; Headrick 1987; Cohn 1988), one influenced by nineteenth-century European sanitary reforms imposed—primarily upon urban underclasses—at home (Jephson 1907; Stedman Jones 1971; Foucault 1977).

The actions and interests of the government at the time certainly support Swanson's claim. In 1903, a commission was appointed in response to the felt need for a coherent "native policy." Its members investigated current African "life and habits" and made recommendations for the control of labor relations, taxation, and education. In addressing the problem of building a stable work force, their report showed a preoccupation with black "hygiene," especially amongst migrant populations. Where, before, local health officials had been concerned to limit the threat posed by female servants in the white household, the national administration now focused on the promotion of the health and regulation of black males in the urban workplace. The specter of disease flooding the white cities along with unregulated African labor lurked just below the surface. Nor was any of this new: As early as 1881 Sir Theophilus Shepstone, influential Secretary for Native Affairs in Natal, had called the mushrooming multiracial towns, with their populations of unemployed or casual native labor, "the pest spots of our body social and political" (Swanson 1977:391). It is not surprising that the 1903 commission kept returning to the topic of sanitation, urging that it be given priority in the education of blacks and that those responsible for transporting and housing migrant workers pay special attention to the control of their toilet arrangements (South Africa 1905:73).

In fact, as Swanson (1977:390) shows, the social and architectural character of South Africa's multiracial cities was already being transformed in response to contagion and medical emergency. The outbreak of bubonic plague in 1900 focused more diffuse notions of danger: Although fewer blacks contracted the disease than did whites or so-called coloureds, they were immediately targeted as the source of infection, to be expelled from the body public. The Medical Officer of Health in Cape Town, for one, declared that "uncontrolled Kafir hordes were at the root of the aggravation of Capetown slumdom brought to light when the plague broke out" (Swanson 1977:392). As an immediate measure, sanitary inspectors were sent to rout out such "scattered nests of filth" throughout the city, but the longer-term solution was to be nothing less than the mass removal of the black population (Swanson 1977:393). In the name of medical crisis, a radical plan of racial segregation was passed under the emergency provisions of the Public Health Act. It established an enduring system of peri-urban "native locations" that were to spread from the cities of the Cape Province to become an enduring feature of the South African landscape. Swanson shows how powerful the sense of medical menace really was: Inseparable from the fear of an unregulated black presence in the white world, it repeatedly overcame all efforts to resist the separatist social engineering of the regime.

What was the role of the mission in all this? The evangelists were forced to adapt to changing circumstances—to the fact that their field had become the rural periphery of the South African state and now served as a recruiting ground for migrant labor. In the upshot, formal education became their primary civilizing technique; it is, therefore, in the provision of schooling that we must trace their primary impact upon the everyday world of black South Africans in the early twentieth century. As we have seen, the churchmen had long participated in a moral discourse about pollution and reform, a discourse that permeated their pedagogic policy and practice. They, too, were children of their time, and their activities also seem to have been organized by an increasingly specific biomedical conception of infection and hygiene. At the turn of the century, their letters displayed a growing anxiety about effluent and the management of the dirt generated by populations around their stations. It is no coincidence that, when the Reverend William Willoughby arrived to take command of the mission at Palapye (Bechuanaland Protectorate) in 1894, he found that the "W.C." (lavatory) built by his predecessor was "the most prominent object" on the skyline.[11] It is also noticeable in missionary correspondence that specific names were now frequently being given to diseases: generic "fever" gave way to "malaria" or "typhoid," conditions that, although rare in the region, were invoked as a rationale for replacing indigenous residential arrangements with more "hygienic" alternatives (Willoughby 1899a:21).

These orientations became particularly evident in the mission school itself. In writing a proposal for the establishment of a training college among the Tswana, LMS evangelists devoted three-quarters of their report to issues of hygiene, sanitation, and the regulation of daily ablutions.[12] And, when it was actually founded in 1904, the Tiger Kloof Native Institution (initially for male students alone) was equipped with accommodations specially designed for the close supervision of toilet arrangements (Comaroff and Comaroff n.d.[a]:Chap. 4). Furthermore, dormitory chiefs ensured that pupils made their beds "in that neat and uniform manner that prevails in some hospitals," and a "General Officer of Health" did weekly inspections of student quarters (Willoughby 1912:90). Rules of dress, comportment, and table manners all reinforced rituals and routines that, even more relentlessly than the formal curriculum, worked to create persons of individual, uniform, and contained identity. Their stated goal was to instill in the inmates "moral backbone," the wherewithal to live "clean and healthy" Christian lives (Willoughby 1912:70). Although not altogether intentionally, the desire of the churchmen to produce self-controlled and wholesome subjects resonated well with the political and economic interests of the state: The LMS strove to mold just the kind of disciplined worker of whom policymakers dreamed.

It is no wonder that, over the years, student resistance in South African mission schools would often protest against regimes of bodily discipline. In the Tswana case, its earliest expression—already in the 1890s—took the form of a refusal to comply with sanitary prescriptions, particularly the use of the "privy." It was a practice the black youths deplored, ironically, as "defecation in the house."[13]

Conclusion

Medical icons are no more "real" than "aesthetic" ones. Like aesthetic icons, medical icons may (or may not) be rooted in some observed reality. Like them, they are iconographic in that they represent these realities in a manner determined by the historical position of the observers. . . . Medicine uses its categories to structure an image of the diversity of mankind. . . . The power of medicine, at least in the nineteenth century, lies in the rise of the status of science.

—Sander L. Gilman (1985:205–206)

We have tried to show something of the dialectical interplay of nineteenth-century medicine and the colonizing project in South Africa. The two were in many senses inseparable. Both were driven by a global sense of man that emerged out of the Enlightenment. Both concerned the extension of "rational" control over domains of nature that were vital and dangerous. Although ostensibly an autonomous field of knowledge and practice, medicine both informed and was informed by imperialism, in Africa and elsewhere. It gave the validity of science to the humanitarian claims of colonialism while finding confirmation for its own authority in the living laboratories enclosed by expanding imperial frontiers.

Although imperialism and biomedicine have not been engaged in precisely the same reciprocal relationship everywhere, there is much evidence of their elective affinity. Whatever else it might have been, nineteenth-century Western medicine had a powerful ontology, finding confirmation, in bodies at home and abroad, for the universalist claims of European reason. And its role in this regard did not end with formal colonialism. Notwithstanding their contribution to the human condition, biomedical knowledge and technology have played a large part in sustaining the economic and cultural dependency of the non-Western world. What is more, we are still all too ready, in the West, to seek the origins of virulent disease in the uncontained nature of "others"—in the undisciplined sexuality of Africa, for example. In that regard, it might be worthwhile to remind ourselves that, until very recently, the relics of the Hottentot Venus were still on display at the Musee de L'Homme!

Notes

1. See also W. Willoughby, Palapye, 21 July 1894 [CWM, LMS Incoming Letters, South Africa, 51-1-D].

2. Similar attempts to "reason" with rainmakers are recorded by several other evangelists from this field (Comaroff and Comaroff 1991:Chap. 6).

3. In contrast, mission correspondence gives clear evidence of the toll taken on the health of evangelists and their families. The death of infants and women in childbirth was particularly high, but dysentery, unidentified "fever," and accidents also took many lives; see, for example, S. Broadbent, Matlwasse, 31 December 1823 [WMMS, South Africa Correspondence, 300]; J. Archbell, Platberg, 20 March 1832 [WMMS, South Africa Correspondence (Albany), 303]. There is also evidence that faithful care was extended to ailing churchmen by their black servants (Moffat 1842:113; Gelfand 1957:276ff).

4. See, for example, Livingstone (in Schapera 1961:14); W. Willoughby, Palapye, 21 July 1894 [CWM, LMS Incoming Letters, South Africa, 51-1-D].

5. J. Brown, Taung, 9 July 1894 [CWM, LMS Incoming Letters, South Africa, 51-1-D].

6. Ibid.

7. Ibid.; W. Willoughby, Palapye, 21 July 1894 [CWM, LMS Incoming Letters, South Africa, 51-1-D].

8. W. Willoughby, Palapye, 21 July 1894 [CWM, LMS Incoming Letters, South Africa, 51-1-D].

9. Ibid.

10. J. Brown, Taung, 9 July 1894 [CWM, LMS Incoming Letters, South Africa, 51-1-D].

11. W. Willoughby, Palapye, 22 September 1894 [CWM, LMS Incoming Letters, South Africa, 51-2-B].

12. W. Willoughby, *Report on a Visit to Certain Native Boarding Schools in South Africa, and Proposal for the Establishment of an Institute for the Teaching of Bechuana and Other Native Youth,* Palapye, 1 February 1898 [CWM, LMS Incoming Letters, South Africa, 55-1-A].

13. Ibid.

9

The Colonization of Consciousness

MODERN SOUTHERN AFRICA is built upon a long history of symbolic struggle,[1] a bitter contest of conscience and consciousness. This is not to deny the coercive, violent bases of class antagonism and racial inequality here. Nor is it to underplay the brute material dimensions of the struggle; indeed, it is never possible simply to prize apart the cultural from the material in such processes. But, in the eyes of the Southern Tswana, the rural people with whom we shall be concerned in this essay, the past century and a half has been dominated by the effort of others to impose on them a particular way of seeing and being, to colonize their consciousness with the signs and practices, the axioms and aesthetics, of an alien culture. This alien culture is the culture of European capitalism in its various guises: capitalism as the direct extension of British commerce; capitalism, both agrarian and industrial, erected on the foundations of settler economy and society; capitalism matured in the systematic mold of the racist state. Capitalism, that is, refracted from an expanding global order into a myriad of local facets.

In the face of this assault, some black South Africans have succumbed, some have resisted, some have tried to recast the intrusive European forms in their own terms. And most have done all of these things, at one or another time, in the effort to formulate an awareness of, and gain a measure of mastery over, their changing world. It is no wonder, therefore, that any attempt to understand the Southern Tswana past and present keeps being drawn back to the colonization of their consciousness and their consciousness of colonization. Of course, the dominant theme in the modern history of these peoples has been their incorporation into a colonial, and later post-colonial, state. But it is important to stress that this is a "state" in both

235

senses of the term: an institutional order of political regulation *and* a condition of being, a structure *and* a predicament. Consequently, the effort of the colonizer to impose it upon them has been as much a matter of the politics of experience as a matter of constitutional (and coercive) authority. So, too, with Tswana reactions: they have flowed well beyond the formal channels of political discourse and onto the diffuse terrains of everyday life. Nor is this unusual. Colonizers in most places and at most times try to gain control over both the material and semantic practices through which their would-be subjects produce and reproduce the very bases of their existence; no habit being too humble, no sign too insignificant to be implicated in the battle. And colonization everywhere gives rise to struggles—albeit often tragically unequal ones—over power and meaning on the moving frontiers of empire. It is a process of "challenge and riposte" (Harlow 1986:xi, after Bourdieu 1977:12) often much too complex to be captured in mechanical equations of domination and resistance—or, for that matter, in grand models of the political economy of colonialism and the modern world system.

Among the Southern Tswana, any effort to document such processes—to analyze, that is, the colonization of consciousness and the consciousness of colonization—begins with the entry of evangelical Christianity onto the historical landscape. Not only were Nonconformist missionaries the vanguard of the British presence in this part of the South African interior; they were also the most ambitious ideological and cultural agents of Empire, bearing with them the explicit aim of reconstructing the native world in the name of God and Great Britain (Comaroff and Comaroff 1986). Of course, the chronicle of evangelical Protestantism does not tell us the whole story of the Tswana past. Nothing does, in and of itself. But it does hold one key to the symbolic and material processes involved in the colonial encounter—and to the modes of cultural transformation and ideological argument, of "challenge and riposte," to which it has given rise.

We should like, in this essay, to trace out an early chapter in the confrontation between the missions and the Tswana—and, with it, an early phase in the struggle over being and consciousness here.[2] For this phase, partial and passing though it is in the broader history of Southern Africa, has some important lessons for the anthropology of colonialism in general, and for the history of consciousness in particular. In this respect, too, we offer our account with a general methodological point in mind: whether it be in the tradition of Durkheim, Marx, or Weber, anthropologists usually study consciousness and its transformations by examining its *effects* or its *expressions*. To be sure, modern anthropology has become highly skilled at describing the social and symbolic manifestations of the *conscience collective*, inferring the phenomenon, as it were, from the recurrent shadows it seems to cast upon the wall. Rarely, however, do we examine the nature of consciousness in the making—let alone in its own full historicity. Indeed, as a fashionable synonym for "culture," "ideology," "thought," or an ill-defined blend of all three, the notion of consciousness itself is seldom scrutinized. Sometimes it is regarded as the mere reflection of a reality beyond human awareness, sometimes as the site of creativity and agency. But, almost invariably, "consciousness" is treated as a substantive "model of" or "for" the world, as so much narrative content without form. Only specific historical analyses may force us to think beyond this inchoate preconception; to explore the relationship, in the making of human meaning, of form and content, sign and practice, intention and outcome.

II

The Nonconformist evangelists of the London Missionary Society (LMS) and the Wesleyan Methodist Missionary Society (WMMS) entered in the 1820s the world of the people whom we know today as the Tswana.[3] We cannot describe that world in detail here,[4] save to make two points about it. The first is that its very existence was imperilled at the time. *Difaqane,* the upheaval caused by the rise and expansion of the Zulu state under Shaka, sent shockwaves throughout the subcontinent as displaced warrior groups preyed upon the settled agricultural communities of the interior—those of the Southern Tswana among them.[5] The latter also felt themselves to be under threat from the Griqua to the south; having lived near the frontier with the Cape Colony, these people had acquired guns and horses, and alternated between allying themselves with the (more northerly) Tswana and attacking their settlements and their herds (Legassick 1969a).

The second point of relevance for present purposes is that, far from being closed communities or possessing "cold cultures," early nineteenth-century Tswana polities were dynamic structures that underwent complex transformations over space and time (see e.g. Legassick 1969b; Comaroff and Comaroff 1990; J. Comaroff 1985; J. L. Comaroff 1973). What is more, they already had a long history of interaction; interaction, over considerable distances, through trade, raiding, and—most important here—the exchange of medical knowledge and cultural practices.[6] For example, one of the earliest missionaries to visit the interior, the Reverend John Campbell (1822,1:307), tells how a party of Ngwaketse[7] traveled for almost a year, far to the north of the Tswana world, to learn techniques and obtain preparations that might bring them rain and cause their enemies drought. Such odysseys, albeit usually on less grand a scale, seem to have been undertaken quite frequently.

Nor shall we go into the social origins of the British churchmen here; it, too, is a complex issue (see above, Chapter 7). But it is necessary to stress that their mission was conditioned by an imperial vision conjured up in the fervent images of a triumphant bourgeoisie during the Age of Revolution (Hobsbawm 1962); that their position in the crevices of the changing class structure of industrial revolution Britain shaped their project, their own personal careers of upward mobility becoming an ideological mold for the moral future of Africa. In an epoch that celebrated hero-worship (indeed, as Carlyle [1842:1] asserts, almost made it into a theory of history) theirs was an epic quest, their emerging sense of "biography" as a "moral career" providing a model of and for a heroic history[8]—their own as well as that of the heathen lands that would become colonies of God and the British monarch.

This quest took them far into the Southern African hinterland; far *beyond* the colonial frontier and the gaze of its administration, with which they had very uneasy relations from the first. In fact, as a "dominated fraction of the dominant class" and as the self-styled moral conscience of the civilized world (see Chapter 7), they were to come into frequent conflict with more powerful political and economic agents of colonialism for a long time to come (see Comaroff and Comaroff 1986). In this respect, their efforts to build a new Empire of the Spirit, and later of Great Britain, were driven by tensions inherent in a rapidly changing, secularizing Europe: they wished to recreate a romantically (and mythologically) conceived society, in which spiritual authority remained unquestioned; in which technical progress, itself much admired, did not cause the massive social upheaval it had sown among the working class in the north of England; in which the countryside was not disfigured, nor its free yeomanry dispossessed—as many of their own peasant fathers and grandfathers had been.[9] They sought, in other words, a modern industrial capitalist world without its essential contradictions.

More immediately, they set about the task of "civilizing" the native by remaking his person and his context; by reconstructing his habit and his habitus; by taking back the savage mind from Satan, who had emptied it of all traces of spirituality and reason. Most of all, however, they wished to establish a viable peasantry—remaking, in Africa, the destroyed British yeomanry of their own imagined origins—tied at once to the soil and to an ethos of universal commerce. Remember that David Livingstone, perhaps the most popular missionary in the Victorian public consciousness (Jeal 1973), was to say, in a famous passage of his best selling *Missionary Travels and Researches* (1857:34):

The promotion of commerce ought to be specially attended to . . . [I wish] to promote the preparation of the raw materials of European manufactures in Africa, for by that means we may not only put a stop to the slave-trade, but introduce the negro family into the body of corporate nations.

In order to achieve these objectives, initially, the Protestants sought to hold up a mirror to the savage; a looking-glass in which he might gaze upon himself and, in a revelatory moment of self-reflection, open his eyes and ears to the Good News, the narrative of Christianity. At the same time, in the same mirror, the heathen might also come to recognize the divided self of bourgeois individualism, the subject upon whom the edifice of modern European civilization was constructed.

Of course, this was all presented to the Tswana, and to the wider world, in the non-coercive rhetoric of rational argument and free choice. Again, take David Livingstone (1857:21):

In our relations with this people we were simply strangers exercising no authority or control whatever. Our influence depended entirely on persuasion; [on teaching] them by kind *conversation* (our italics).

As the first encounter between the Tswana and the evangelists gave way to a more sustained interaction, each tried to cast the other in his own image: the missionary, to portray the native as an unregenerate savage to be transformed; the Tswana, to draw on the power of the mission to protect a world endangered. Each, in other words, found the other indispensable in making real his own fantasy—although the Europeans were ultimately to prove better positioned to impose their construction on the reality they would come to share. For the Christians brought with them goods and knowledge—guns, wealth objects, technical skills, and the capacity to act as authoritative diplomatic agents—at a time when many chiefs were desperate for just such things in their struggle to maintain their autonomy in the face of *difaqane* and early settler advance.

Indeed, the fact that this was a period of great upheaval played into the hands of the missions, facilitating greatly their entry into the Tswana world. For, while many chiefs and royals saw the Europeans as potential rivals to their authority[10]—some, it seems, even observed that their presence would "change the whole [social] system"[11]—they became too valuable to pass up, and the various chiefdoms competed for their attentions (see e.g. Moffat 1842:389f, 414). Seizing the opportunity, and showing great resourcefulness in making themselves indispensable, the evangelists soon entered into the conversation of which Livingstone wrote. But the African rulers were as assiduous in trying to limit their influence. Here we explore three crucial registers in this long argument and the battle that ensued for control over its terms. For convenience, we refer to them as (i) the politics of water, (ii) the politics of production, and (iii) the politics of language.

The Politics of Water

As soon as they gained entry into Tswana communities, the evangelists set about establishing what we might think of as a mundane theater of industry; a site for the total reconstruction of the practical world of the natives. For example, the very first act of James Read, the earliest regular missionary among the Tlhaping, was to erect a square European house[12]—even though he seems to have lived very comfortably in his wagon. He then built a smith's forge and began, before the "astonished" eyes of much of the local citizenry, to fashion the tools of peasant production. His account of these events indicates a keen awareness of their impact: "The people were struck with wonder," he wrote. "One of them said 'these men must be from God that can do such things'."[13]

Here, then, was the matter-of-fact drama of Protestant fabrication, setting forth bit by bit the mode of rural production through which the missionaries hoped to shape the servants of Christ. Spanish Catholicism in seventeenth-century Mexico used ritual drama to impress pious submission on the natives (Trexler 1984), and colonizing Anglicanism in Rhodesia took hold of the Shona by making their landscape its own icon (Ranger 1987). But the Nonconformists in South Africa sought to reconstruct the inner being of the Tswana chiefly on the more humble ground of everyday life, of the routines of production and reproduction. Not only were they predisposed to such methods by their puritan creed and by their commitment to the bourgeois ideal of self-improvement through rational labor; their ritual parsimony also struck a chord with Setswana practice, which lacked symbolic or ceremonial elaboration. As Moffat (1842:243–4) lamented early on:

> The situation of the missionary among the Bechuanas is peculiar, differing
> . . . from any other among any nation on the face of the earth . . . He seeks
> in vain to find a temple, an altar, or a single emblem of heathen worship
> . . . Thus the missionary could make no appeals to legends, or to altars, or
> to an unknown God, or to ideas kindred to those he wished to impart.

Moffat was correct. Rather than proclaim itself to the European as overtly "religious," Tswana symbolic practice operated on another plane entirely. It saturated the ground of everyday activity, breathing life into the habitual forms of social existence. It was on this terrain that the missions had to battle for control over the salient signs of the world they wished to conquer (cf. Volosinov 1973)—a battle not for sacred sites, but for mastery of the mundane.

In their effort to engage the Tswana in just such a conversation about everyday life, the evangelists soon found themselves caught up in the politics and poetics of water. As it turns out, they were encouraged by both climes and times to conceive of themselves, in horticultural idiom, as the irrigators of the African desert. "Her vast moral wastes," wrote Moffat (1842:614), a gardener by vocation in England, "must be watered by the streams of life." Such is the force of the poetic that this analogy, so good for the missionaries to think with, was to give particular form to their deeds in the "field." But the "wastes" of the Tswana world had already called forth a torrent of indigenous symbolic techniques to conserve this most precious and capricious resource. Furthermore, control over water was a vital aspect of chiefly power: the annual rains were held to be the inseminating force bestowed on the land and the people by a virile ruler, "made" (*do dira*) either by his own hand or by a rainmaker (*moroka*) of his choosing (Schapera 1971a); without these royal rites the productive cycle could not begin. In fact, the political symbolism of rain, *pula*, was central in public life. Not only did chiefs open and close all assemblies by greeting their people "*ka pula*," with rain (Campbell 1822,2:157; Solomon 1855:47), but the term itself was associated with the achievement of collective well-being. The word for water, *metse*, was the plural form of the vernacular for *town*—which, in Tswana cosmology, was the nucleus of all human life, and stood for the triumph of social order (metonymically represented in the chiefship) over the threatening, chaotic wild beyond the settlement.

The provision of a regular water supply was vital, too, in the Protestants' scheme of things. After all, they intended to create a Christian peasantry—to recreate, as we said, the lost British yeomanry—in the "desolate vineyard" of Africa (Moffat 1842:330). They had also to grow enough for their own survival. To this end, they began to dig wells and trenches with which to irrigate their gardens, an activity that soon set them at odds with local values and interests. Reverend Hamilton writes from the Kuruman River in 1823:[14]

> Our channel from the spring ran through the land of the Great Lady [chief wife, Mahutu], who refused last year to let our water pass. We appealed in the matter to [the chief] Mathebe, who upheld the women's right to do with the land and water as they please. At present we are supplied from a fountain about two miles east of us and the water of this fountain is a bone of contention betwixt us and the women. They will have it for the town and we will have it to our gardens . . . It gives us a great deal of trouble every evening to walk four miles to turn it in that we might have it for the night.

For Southern Tswana, water and land were given not by nature, but by the chief to households whose womenfolk, as primary producers, had direct control over them. In this dryland ecology, water was too scarce a domestic resource to be put to the irrigated cultivation of mission "gardens"; no wonder the women regarded the whole idea as unreasonable. These gardens—a term seldom used, incidentally, by the churchmen to refer to native horticulture—were a great source of pride to the Europeans. Laid out almost at once within neat fences, they were icons of the civilizing mission at large. Described in dispatches home as "examples to the natives of industry,"[15] it was in their cultivated shade that the few would-be converts who died in the early years were laid to rest.[16] The Tlhaping, on the other hand, expressed their resentment by repeatedly stealing their fruits—and finally by destroying all efforts made to water them (Moffat 1842:286). Indeed, Tswana resistance dates back to the very beginnings of the colonizing process and, from the first, involved women.

While the war with the women was waged over the productive deployment of water, another struggle raged over its ontology. In the absence of elaborate ritual or explicit iconography, the rites of rainmaking presented the Europeans with Tswana "superstition" in its most tangible form. In these revered rites, performed at the direction of the chief, the missionaries read the essence of savage unreason. "Rainmakers," said Moffat (1842:305), "are our inveterate enemies, and uniformly oppose the introduction of Christianity amongst their countrymen to the utmost of their power." The evangelists became fairly obsessed with rainmaking and regarded its eradication, which they linked to the triumph of bourgeois reason, as a major measure of their success.

From their perspective, it was all a matter of empirical demonstration. Thus, when Samuel Broadbent (1865:99), a Methodist minister among the Seleka-Rolong,[17] dug a simple waterhole to irrigate his garden, he was pleased that the chief poured scorn upon him, and insisted that "water comes from the clouds." For this gave the evangelist the chance to prove the ruler wrong—and to prove "once and for all" the fallacy of rainmaking. People thronged to witness the spectacle of water issuing from beneath the earth, and Broadbent wrote joyfully that he had earned the "respect and gratitude" of the Seleka rank and file for having shown that the rain magic was a "vile imposture," a "transparent deception." He was less quick to note the resentment of the chief, although it soon became clear when the ruler and his advisors met to discuss the matter in full battle-dress, as was required when the polity was threatened (Broadbent 1865:102). The sovereign's reaction was to be expected. Since any wealthy man—that is, anyone who could muster the labor—might sink his own wells, the new source of water and well-being threatened to weaken the spiritual bases of chiefly legitimacy.

Indeed, the displacement of water from the domain of "ritual" to that of "technical management" created a legitimation crisis for the chiefship. But we concentrate, here, on the ontological rather than the temporal struggle. For there was a contradiction in the evangelical message—and an especially ironic one at that. On the one hand, the Christians introduced technical innovations and a "scientific" rationale into the production of water, seeking thereby to demystify its magicality. Yet, on the other hand, they tried to prove that the Christian God was the provenance of a superior water supply. And so they presented themselves as rainmakers of a competing power.

There was another, more subtle dimension to all this, however. Rainmakers might have known how to use the magic with which to activate the clouds and bring *pula*. But, for the Tswana, their power could only work when the community was in a state of moral balance, of "coolness" (*tsididi*). Any breach of that balance—through improper conflict among humans, or between them and the non-human realm—might pollute the cosmic order, and create the heat that dried up the rain. The rainmaker "made" the rain purely in so far as he ensured that the condition of the social world met the standards of ancestral beneficence. In this sense, he no more manufactured it than did a churchman praying to God, a point that was lost on the missionaries. As a result, most of them tried to convince indigenous practitioners, in "reasoned" argument, of the illogicality and dishonesty of their activity (Reyburn 1933). While a surprising number of them recorded their efforts, Livingstone (1857:25f; also [ed. Schapera] 1960:239f) alone described his debate with a Kwena practitioner in such a way as to suggest that there was little to choose between their positions:

> [**Medical Doctor**]: So you really believe that you can command the clouds? I think that can be done by God alone.
>
> [**Rain Doctor**]: We both believe the very same thing. It is God that makes the rain, but I pray to him by means of these medicines, and, the rain coming, of course it is then mine. It was I who made it for the Bakwains [Kwena] for many years . . . ; through my wisdom, too, their women became fat and shining. Ask them; they will tell you the same as I do.
>
> **M.D.**: But we are distinctly told in the parting words of our Saviour that we can pray to God acceptably in his name alone, and not by means of medicines.
>
> **R.D.**: Truly! but God told us differently. . . . God has given us one little thing, which you know nothing of. He has given us the knowledge of certain medicines by which we can make rain. *We* do not despise those things which you possess, though we are ignorant of them. We don't understand your book, yet we don't despise it. *You* ought not to despise our little knowledge, though you are ignorant of it. [Original italics.]
>
> **M.D.**: I don't despise what I am ignorant of; I only think you are mistaken in saying that you have medicines which can influence the rain at all.
>
> **R.D.**: That's just the way people speak when they talk on a subject of which they have no knowledge. When first we opened our eyes, we found our forefathers making rain, and we follow in their footsteps. You, who send to

Kuruman for corn, and irrigate your garden, may do without rain; *we* can not manage in that way . . .

M.D.: I quite agree with you as to the value of the rain; but you can not charm the clouds by medicines. You wait till you see the clouds come, then you use your medicines, and take the credit which belongs to God only.

R.D.: I use my medicines, and you employ yours; we are both doctors, and doctors are not deceivers. You give a patient medicine. Sometimes God is pleased to heal him by means of your medicine; sometimes not—he dies. When he is cured, you take the credit of what God does. I do the same. Sometimes God grants us rain, sometimes not. When he does, we take the credit of the charm. When a patient dies, you don't give up trust in your medicine, neither do I when rain fails. If you wish me to leave off my medicines, why continue your own?

In this carefully crafted dialogue, Livingstone presents himself as an uneasy spokesman for God and science, seeming to argue with himself over the logical impasse of the mission. The parallel use of the title "doctor," as much as the symmetry of the actual debate, implies the conviction that a contest is being waged on equal ontological ground. Thus he allows his opponent to suggest a functional correspondence between Tswana material icons and European verbal signs, and to cast reasoned doubt on the Christian distinction between the sacred and secular. In so doing, Livingstone anticipated by eighty years Evans-Pritchard's (1937) spirited defense of the rationality of African "magical" thought. But this did not deter him, or his brethren, from trying to persuade the Tswana to accept the Christian message on "rational grounds." Take the following report sent by Archbell from a Methodist station in 1832:[18]

In the sermon, the preacher observed to them that some of the Rainmakers . . . had been making rains all the last week, but had produced none. [H]e therefore recommended them to put no confidence in their ability, but themselves pray to God that he might graciously look upon our land, and send down the dew of heaven. The people prayed to God . . . and shortly after the heavens gathered blackness and the rain commenced which continued through the night. The people were greatly rejoiced at so reasonable a supply, while the Rainmakers were ashamed and confounded.

It is hardly necessary to labor another of Evans-Pritchard's (1937) observations: given that criteria of technical efficacy are culturally specified, established knowledge is not falsified by evidence external to its (tauto)logical structure. What the evangelists took to be definitive proof of the "vain pretensions" of the natives in no way undermined Tswana cosmogonic assumptions. Instead, such events merely confirmed that the whites had introduced a distinct and competing power into the local world (see e.g. Hodgson [ed. Cope] 1977:23). At the same time, everything pointed to the fact that this power was substantial. Their technological prowess and wealth, after all, must have come from somewhere, and the capacity to produce water from under the ground *was* impressive. It certainly seemed to many Tswana that it was worth pursuing the conversation with the Europeans—and trying to learn the techniques which held the key to their potency. Recall, here, the long-standing indigenous value placed on the exchange of cultural knowledge and practices.

Of course, as the participants on both sides searched for signs and symbols through which to communicate, they began also to recognize the distinctions between them. And so the speakers of each language came gradually to *objectify* their world in relation to a novel other, thereby inventing for themselves a self-conscious coherence and distinctness—even while they accommodated to the new relationship that enclosed them. As is now well-known, the self-awareness of post-enlightenment Europe had long been sharpened in contrast to the non-European. The first generation of Protestant missionaries continued this reflexive process on the moral frontier with savage superstition. For the Tswana, the encounter with a people preoccupied with techniques of self-representation and rationalization brought forth a sense of opposition between *sekgoa* (European ways) and *setswana* (Tswana ways). The latter was perceived, for the first time, as a coherent body of knowledge and practice in relation to the former, which they had learned to see as a *system* of "belief" (*tumèlò*, lit. "agreement," itself a notion of doctrine as consensus; see Moffat 1842:246f). In this moment of self-objectification, we suggest, lie the cultural origins of modern Tswana ethnicity. For, until this time, "the Bechuana"—who had no name for themselves, other than *batho*, human beings[19]—were divided into political communities distinguished by their totemic affiliations, a quite different form of collective consciousness (J. L. Comaroff 1987b; see Chapter 2).

Increasingly, then, the argument over such issues as rainmaking became a confrontation between two cultures, two social orders. For their part, the Tswana were motivated by a desire to appropriate the cultural and technical power of the whites without losing their autonomy. In the effort to harness that power to their own ends, however, they joined the conversation that was so profoundly to alter their sense of themselves and their world, the conversation of which David Livingstone had written (see above). And here is the point: in so doing, they were inducted into the *forms* of European discourse; into the ideological terms of rational argument and empirical reason. Who, indeed, *was* the better rainmaker? How was it possible to decide the issue? The Tswana were not necessarily persuaded by the claims of the evangelists. Nor did this new mode of discourse simply take over their cultural universe. Still, they could not but begin slowly to internalize the terms through which they were being challenged. To be sure, in order even to respond to the arguments of *sekgoa,* it was necessary to use those terms. This, as we shall see in due course, was a critical moment in the colonizing process. But let us turn, secondly, to the politics of production.

The Politics of Production

The central role of agriculture in the evangelical vision of reconstruction has already been anticipated. Not only did many of the early Nonconformists have close ties with the recently marginalized British peasantry and a nostalgic sense of a lost rural world. They were also heirs to an idea of colonization that linked cultivation to salvation. Missionaries, wrote Moffat (1842:616–7), ought to "put their hand to the plough," preparing the stony African ground for "a rich harvest of souls." As agriculture flourished, so too would civilization. Given the African concern with cattle-keeping, it may seem curious that this imagery makes no mention of pastoralism. But the belief in the civilizing role of cultivation was as old as English colonialism itself. In the seventeenth century, Spenser had advocated a settled agrarian existence as the solution to the problem of the "wild Irish," whose barbarous and warlike state he ascribed to their semi-nomadic, pastoral pursuits (Muldoon 1975:275). Similar notions were carried to the new world and Africa, for they corresponded with what Europeans had come to regard as the natural evolution of their own superior world. Agriculture made men peaceful, law-abiding, and governable.

Agriculture, in short, would cultivate the worker as he cultivated the land: The production of new crops and the production of a new kind of selfhood went together in the evangelical imagination. Above all else, this new mode of production would encourage the would-be convert to yield enough of a surplus to tie him through trade with Christian Europe (Bundy 1979:39)—to a Kingdom of God, that is, which looked just like the imperial marketplace. Blighted no more, the dark continent would become a "fruitful field," a rural periphery of the established centers of civilization (Broadbent 1865:204).

As we have already noted, the irrigated garden was an icon of the civilizing mission at large. Within its fenced confines, the churchmen enacted the principles of material individualism: the creation of value by means of self-possessed labor; the forceful domination of nature; the privatization of property; and the accumulation of surplus through an economy of effort. Broadbent (1865:104) gives evidence of their faith in such forms of practice:

Our gardening operations produced a strong and favourable impression on the people. I and my colleague had each enclosed a plot of ground, which we had, of course, in English fashion, broken up and cleared of the roots of weeds, and then sown . . . [W]hat became the subject of wonder and remark was the notorious fact that these and other vegetables grew much more luxuriantly, and were more productive, in our grounds than theirs. One day a number of respectable natives came to ask the reason of this difference . . .

My first answer was, "Your idleness." "How so?" they inquired. I said, "You have seen that we have dug the ground ourselves; you leave it to your women. We dig deep into the soil; they only scratch the surface . . . Our seed, therefore, is protected from the sun and nourished by the moisture in the ground." I added "Work yourselves, as you see we do, and dig the ground properly, and your seed will flourish as well as ours."

The mission garden, clearly, was also meant as a lesson in the contrast of "labor" and "idleness"—and, no less, in the relative value of male and female work. For, to the churchmen, African production was "topsy-turvy" (Crisp 1896:16). The men, whose herds were tended by youths and serfs, appeared to be lazy "lords of creation" (Moffat 1842:505), their political and ritual exertions not signifying "work" to the missionary eye. Women, on the other hand, seemed to have been coerced into doing what was properly male labor, their desultory "scratching" on the face of the earth evoking the ineffectual efforts of mere "beasts of burden" (Kinsman 1983). There was no private property, no commerce, no sign of the "healthy, individualistic competition" or the maximization of time and effort that the Christians saw as righteous industry (Mackenzie quoted in Dachs 1972:652). As Reverend Willoughby (n.d.) put it, "The African lives a simple socialistic life, subordinating his individuality to the necessities of the tribe."

Determined to teach by example and compelled to become self-sufficient, then, the evangelist and his wife became metonyms of the European division of labor. Livingstone (1857:22) talks of "the accomplishments of a missionary in Central Africa, namely, the husband to be a jack-of-all-trades without doors, and the wife a maid-of-all-work within." Here lay another key to civilizing reform: the black woman was to be confined indoors to the sphere of domestic work—and a maid she was indeed to become in the political economy of modern South Africa.

While the first reaction of the Tswana to the fertile mission garden was to steal its fruit (below, p. 275), the LMS station at Kuruman, with its drought-resistant crops, became a "comparative Goshen to the surrounding country" (Moffat, quoted in Northcott 1961:148). The heathen, however, did not immediately learn from it what the churchmen wished to teach; namely, that its fertility was the product of rationalized hard labor and "modern" methods of cultivation. In the early days at least, its bountiful

harvest was seen to flow from the innate powers of the evangelists themselves, this expressing the Tswana sense of the continuity between persons
and their capacities to act upon the world. Among the Seleka-Rolong, for
instance, leading men vied to have their wives cultivate fields directly
adjoining the obviously potent WMMS plots.[20] But the Nonconformists
persisted in offering their new techniques and, in time, the Tswana began
to differentiate these forces of production from the personal potency of the
whites—thereby also learning another lesson in European selfhood. First
came the well and the irrigation ditch, next the plough, each being as
critical to the construction of the Protestant worldview as it was to the
material basis of the civilizing mission. Both were instruments that would
transform the "fitful and disorderly" Tswana into settled communities
founded on private property (Shillington 1985:17).

In the short-run, we stress, this aspect of the "civilizing" process was
anything but straightforward. The contemporary Tswana division of labor
separated cattle husbandry from cultivation, male from female work. There
was no initial enthusiasm for hitching them together—as was implied in
yoking the beast to the plough. Since women were tabooed from managing
stock, the introduction of the new technology called for a reorganization
of existing relations of production. Eventually, though, the plough overtook the hoe in all Tswana communities (Parsons 1977:123). Its capacity
to enlarge the scale and productivity of agriculture, especially in this
ecology, did not go unnoticed by a people with a keen interest in the
accumulation of practical knowledge. Among the Tlhaping, for example,
the yields of those using mission methods increased greatly after 1834. By
1844, in fact, many Dutch farmers near the Orange River were seen
"passing out of the colony with wagons . . . to purchase wheat of the
Bechuanas [Tswana]" (Broadbent 1865:106).

The churchmen were happy to report the steadily expanding reliance on
plough agriculture (Mackenzie 1871:72). They were also glad to note some
of its corollaries—the growing use of money from the sale of surpluses to
purchase farm implements and consumer goods; the increasing signs of
private property; and the reformation of the division of labor as women
lost control over crop production. They were not so quick to record other,
less palatable implications of their efforts: among them, the fact that
drought and disease threatened the cattle economy; that, as more pasture
was brought under cultivation, a few powerful families were gaining
control of much of the land, including the best acreages around natural
water sources (Shillington 1985:62). The material bases of inequality were
being progressively—and, as it was to turn out, disastrously—reconstructed.

Here, then, is the origin of a fragmented peasantry caught up in an
uneven transition to capitalism. As it was to turn out, Southern Tswana

communities were to splinter along similar lines to those described by Lenin (1971:14f; see also Ferguson 1976) for the agrarian population of Russia. The upper peasantry was to give birth to a small rural black petty bourgeoisie; the lower peasantry, into which the vast majority were to be trapped, was to become South Africa's notorious reserve army of labor, its emergent class of peasant-proletarians; and, in the middle, was a class of producers who were to suffer all the contradictions associated with the rapid growth of commodity production within a world of non-capitalist relations (J. L. Comaroff 1977, 1982). It was a process of fragmentation that, over time, would lay the basis for emergent patterns of class distinction and consciousness.

During the period with which we are concerned, however, this process of social differentiation was still in its infancy. More immediately, the rise of "modern" farming began to yield a growing number of dispossessed families. Encouraged by the churchmen, males increasingly took control of the harvest, cutting it loose from the domestic domain in order to sell it in the market (Kinsman 1983). Gradually freeing themselves from communal obligation, and forsaking existing conventions of exchange, they were tempted by the new range of commodities provided by missionaries and merchants, and tried to dispose of as much grain as possible. But, in times of hunger, they were often compelled to buy it back again from white traders at highly inflated prices. In the process, household resources were greatly depleted—to the extent that, in order to forestall famine, some chiefs tried to limit the proportion of the crop that might be sold (Schapera 1943:203). In addition, the widespread abandonment of shallow furrows and regular fallowing, another corollary of "modern" cultivation, increased the erosion of local soils (J. Comaroff 1985:36) and yet further disabled the small producer.

Thus, while the technological innovations of the mission gave rise to a class of commercial farmers, in the longer term the plough brought the majority a harvest of hunger. It also served to mark the onset of an era in which *all* Tswana would have to turn toward the market, orienting themselves, at least to some degree, to the culture and practices of commodity production. Of course, an ever greater number would have to do so as laborers. Having come to recreate the lost British yeomanry, the Christians had begun to prepare the ground not for an independent peasantry but for an army of wage workers; or, more precisely, for a population of peasant-proletarians snared in a web of economic dependency. And all this well before coercive colonial policies sought to force the Tswana into perennial wage labor.

Some of the Protestants took pride in their achievement. Hear Reverend Wookey, who spoke,[21] in 1884, of the effects of Christian evangelism upon the Southern Tswana:

> This is a fact which is too often overlooked, both in the colony and elsewhere—that the great success which has attended the diamond digging is [due to] the abundance of labour that has been always at hand . . . And this fact that labour has been plentiful is due largely to missionary and various other civilizing influences that have been at work for so many years. As a contrast to this, there are the valuable [Bechuanaland] gold fields . . . that cannot be worked successfully . . . because native labour is dearer. Not because natives are scarce, but because missionary work and civilization have made no progress among them.

Tragically, the great success of the South African economy later, in the wake of the mineral revolution and for many years to come, *was* due to an abundance of black labor; labor prized from its social context by a combination of rural poverty and the reconstructed "needs" and "wants" instilled, albeit unwittingly in some respects, by the civilizing mission.

The evangelists could not take all the credit for this situation, of course. There were other forces at work in the dispossession and domination of the Southern Tswana. But they certainly could claim to have contributed, culturally and materially, to the entry of these peoples into a cycle of peasant (under-) production and wage labor. For they had toiled hard to introduce an appreciation of money, time, work discipline and the other essential features of industrial capitalism; in sum, the signs and practices of the commodity *form*. Again, the Tswana reacted differentially to the call of commerce, commodities, and cash crops. And they did so along the fault-lines of class distinction, whose symbolic markers had themselves been instilled by the churchmen—the small petty bourgeoisie, which came most fully to embody mission values, showing greatest enthusiasm. But gradually all alike were drawn into the purview of a world reconstructed according to the logic of the market. All alike began to internalize its terms and, hence, to reorder their own prior system of meanings accordingly. Once more, let us bear this in mind as we move on to the third register of the conversation between the Tswana and the mission, the politics of language.

The Politics of Language

For the Protestants, it was the Word, the literal message of God, that, more than anything else, bore the divine light into the dark recesses of heathen hearts and minds. Its dynamic force, they believed, could reach the inner core of being, penetrating the blindness of man in his "natural" state. A sermon given by Reverend Read captures this well:[22]

> I told the Bechuanas [Tswana] that when God's word began to work in their hearts that their tears would wash away all the red paint from their bodies.

In this vivid image of conversion, outward signs of heathenism, themselves only skin deep, are dissolved by the internalized power of the word. Note also that such Christian rhetoric tended to braid together the themes of words and water, so that each chain of metaphors came to imply the other. Words conveyed reason to the mind as tears bore tangible witness to affected emotions. Water was distilled by the force of God's moving message, be it rain from the heavens or the weeping of the human heart. Evidence of this association is everywhere to hand in the poetics of the civilizing mission: the verbal "truth" was to irrigate the desert of the native's mind as moisture was to fructify his blighted habitat. In 1849, a LMS observer wrote:[23]

> It is a sight worth travelling some distance to see—the printing and binding operation at Kuruman. The Fountains of Civilization so far up in the interior of South Africa! And scores of men, women and children having renounced heathenism, intelligently reading the Word of Life.

The savage mind was indeed being watered by the word of life, whose truth had to be independently recognized and acknowledged by each self-willed citizen of God's Kingdom.

The Nonconformist "word" was, of course, the written word; its faith, the faith of the book (Beidelman 1982:14). An enduring stress on the Platonic sanctity of the original inscription made a textualized religion out of early Christianity, and laid the basis for its unity and control. It also set medieval scribes to their painstakingly imitative task of preserving the holy writ in pristine form, ending an earlier period of expansion, evangelism, and translation (Wonderly and Nida 1963:105). But the faith of the book was to be democratized in the age of the Reformation and "print capitalism" (Anderson 1983), when the ideal of literacy put a bible in the hands of every child of God. This process was founded on an ethos of universalism, the same ideology that spawned the imperialism of the Nonconformist mission, with its assumption that all peoples had some capacity to reason, to love, and to receive the written word.

What is more, the "fever for translation" often held to have overtaken Europe in the sixteenth century (Simon 1966:123) expressed a growing conviction that language could be made the universal medium of human communication. Knowing and naming global truths was a matter of managing signs and correspondences in a world of verifiable realities (Cohn 1985). As Max Müller (1891,1:30) reminded his contemporaries, the bible itself supported the view that language was the invention of man: "we read, 'The hand of God formed every beast of the field, and every fowl of the air; and brought them unto Adam *to see what he would call them'*" (our italics). All human beings shared this capacity to name and, therefore, were potential heirs to civilization, a state that knew no cultural constraints.

This, in turn, expedited a benevolent ideological imperialism, one that made bold assumptions about the ("indexical") properties of language, and the possibility of knowledge that transcended human differences.

It is noteworthy, for instance, that, while the evangelists doubted the competence of Tswana speakers, they did not question the capacity of their language to convey the meanings that civilization might demand of it. The heathen might lack the reflective mentality with which to analyze abstract terms. And he might be so stupid as to confuse homonyms. But the churchmen never doubted that Setswana would yield to their meticulous efforts to translate literally the English message they bore. Thus Moffat (1842:302) was sure that, while "a mass of rubbish . . . paralyze[d] the mental powers of the natives," such detritus was easily removed—whereupon their vacant minds would be receptive to the biblical text and all that it conveyed. In this spirit of optimism, he began a massive translation project. As we might expect, Moffat's work had consequences far beyond his own intentions. Not only did he hold up a Setswana mirror to the English text. He created a counterpart of the scriptures, as *he* read them, in the tongue of the natives—as he had come to understand it. In short, he transposed the bible into a cultural register true to neither, a hybrid creation born of the colonial encounter itself.

Hence, to take just one example, Moffat's use of *badimo* ("ancestors") to denote "demons" (Mathaio [Matthew] 7:22; 8:28, 32)[24] did violence to both biblical and conventional Tswana usage. Nonetheless, it reflected the mission ideology of the period, and was to become standard church usage (Brown 1926:103), with long-term effects on indigenous consciousness. The Tswana did not simply accept the revision of their key constructs, for the logic of a whole cultural scheme intervened. Yet this logic itself was gradually changing under the growing impact of another order, and an obviously powerful one at that. At the very least, they developed an awareness of the relativity of meaning, and of the politics of managing cultural distinctions. Thus all Tswana, whether or not they entered the church, were soon to learn that "ancestors" were phenomena of different valence in *setswana* and *sekgoa*. Within the European dominated field of colonial culture, they were signs of the "primitive."

The subversion of native signs, then, was part of the struggle that took place within the speech field of the mission. Indeed, the colonization of language became an ever more important feature of symbolic domination at large, and Setswana soon began to bear the lasting imprint of Christian Europe. This was evident in the commandeering of everyday words like *moruti* ("teacher") for "minister of the church," and *modumedi* ("one who agrees") for "Christian believer"; such terms, in turn, becoming marked by contrast to the lexicon of *bongaka,* "traditional" ritual and healing. The Tswana also relied increasingly on loan words to demarcate semantic

domains whose origins lay in *sekgoa:* English was most often used for signs
and practices associated with the mission (e.g. *madi* for "money"; *tikete*
for "membership ticket"), and Dutch for terms linked to their experience
of the Boers (e.g. *bèrèka*, from *werk*, for "wage labor"; *toronko* from *tronk*,
"jail").

But the process also had another, less obvious dimension. It arose from
the axiom, shared by all the Protestants, that African languages were of a
piece with African mentality. They were simple,[25] much like the peripheral
"folk" dialects of Europe. Reverend Hughes, for one, claimed that his
knowledge of Welsh was helping him to learn Setswana,[26] and Samarin
(1984:436) writes of a Belgian colonial doctor who thought that the
Breton he had picked up from a servant at home made it easy for him to
communicate with Central Africans. A few of the evangelists had studied
Greek, Latin, or Hebrew,[27] and most of them had received some education
in normative grammar. In trying to master the vernacular, they drew on
its techniques to "bring the language under some organization"—reducing
it, that is, to "simple grammatical form."[28] It was taken for granted that
the unreflective native was ignorant of the structure of his own tongue.
And so this structure was to be excavated and re-presented to him by his
white mentors. Working with the categories of Indo-European languages
(nouns, verbs, cases, declensions, and the like), the churchmen proudly
offered both their overseers and their subjects "samples" of the most
"unembarrassed and simple" Setswana grammar.[29]

The European categories did not always correspond nicely to Bantu
forms, however;[30] so much so that vernacular texts were sometimes rendered as little more than meaningless strings of discrete grammatical
particles (Wonderly and Nida 1963:127). Furthermore, their ideophonic
and tonal complexities were barely understood, as was the play on form
itself in some speech genres. As a result, the early translations done by the
Nonconformists often missed entirely the poetics of Setswana, which draw
on diverse and subtle semantic distinctions. Once again, though, this did
not persuade the missionary linguists to question the epistemological
assumptions underlying their apparently innocent stress on vocabulary and
simple normative grammar. Because language was seen to consist of words
whose referents were self-evident properties of the world, those of Setswana
simply had to be synonymous with those of basic English (see Moffat
1842:xiv). Not coincidentally, the first secular publications in the vernacular, alongside hymnals and biblical texts, were wordlists in the form of
spelling books.[31] These were to be followed by newspapers that, among
other things, defined a Tswana speech community—and, with it, an ethnic
group presumed to share material and cultural interests—by appeal to
quintessentially European linguistic media.

Through the linguistic exertions of the missionaries, in short, a new orthodox Setswana was established and "offered" to the Tswana as the gift of civilization. Taught in schools and spoken in church, it was indeed intended to be a "simple, unvarnished" tongue, carefully organized and free from the confusions that the evangelists read into vernacular poetics. Most pedagogic texts were written in "thin" narrative genre: they told spare, childlike stories in which language itself was portrayed, true to the spirit of rationalist empiricism, as an instrument of naming and knowing, speaking and specifying. Of course, the poetic can never be removed from any language, and the simplest utterance has symbolic potential; while we do not know how the Tswana read their lessons in school and church, their late nineteenth-century oratory and praise poetry suggests that their creativity was sparked by biblical idiom and the cadence of English preaching (J. L. Comaroff 1973:Chap. 5).

Nonetheless, the re-presentation of Setswana as a native "dialect," whose reduction to literate form had rescued it from its state of primitive disorder, was an integral aspect of the colonization of consciousness. The Tswana ideology of language, in which words shared in the reality of their referents, was dismissed by the Europeans as "animist," part of the heathen baggage of "spells and superstitions" (see below). Even praise poetry, itself an enormously rich literary tradition, was devalued as an aesthetic genre for "civilized" people. Later, in fact, when mission-educated Tswana intellectuals were to try to build a new literary canon, they began by writing life-stories, historical narratives, lyric poems, novels, and even translations of Shakespeare.[32] They had internalized the lessons of linguistic colonialism and the bourgeois ideology that lay silently behind it, concealed in such genres as narrative history and individual biography, in such percepts as moral universalism and semantic transparency. It was this process of cultural imperialism that the iconoclastic work of radical black poets in late twentieth-century South Africa was to protest (McClintock 1987).

So it was that, by rendering vernaculars like Setswana into written languages, and by expanding their forms of communication and representation, the Nonconformist mission interpolated itself into the politics of African systems of knowledge. The dominant terms of the long conversation had been laid down. So, too, had the terms of domination. But what part did the Tswana, their ideology and their actions, play in the process of linguistic colonization? To the extent that such things can be recovered, it seems that they did not regard language as an object in itself; nor does the word that denoted it, *loleme* ("tongue"), fall into the noun class usually used for abstract concepts. Rather, language was (literally) embodied in the power of speech, a taken-for-granted capacity of persons and an integral feature of social being. To wit, *setswana,* the term the evangelists took to mean "the Tswana language," would have been more accurately translated as "Tswana culture"; its signs and conventions, symbolic forms and everyday practices, flowed from life in a particular community. Language, in this view, was merely one of its aspects.

Moreover, the power of speech was all of a piece with the capacity of persons to act positively upon the world—most cogently in the form of curses, spells, praise poetry, and oratory, the "great words" (*mahoko a magolo*) that men might use as weapons (Alverson 1978:140; J. L. Comaroff 1975). That is why women, as beings of limited social competence, were excluded from such *mahoko* ("words") as public debate, poetic recital, or ritual incantation (Kinsman 1983:49). Among wordsmiths, as this implies, utterances were given their relative weight by personal status: the rhetoric of a ruler bore his full authority; the curse of an elder, his enhanced spiritual potency. Reciprocally, it was the act of speaking itself that called up such personal force (Alverson 1978:192). No wonder Tswana Christians retained a rather distinctive attitude toward prayer, seeking, as an evangelist put it to us in 1969, "to sway God with many words." In this view, *mahoko* were not merely effective manipulations of learned formulae. They were the audible signs of powerful personal substance.

Patently, then, there were major ontological differences between the linguistic worlds of *setswana* and *sekgoa*. We cannot analyze these in any detail here, save to emphasize the performative quality of the former; the axiom that to talk and to name in this culture was to *create* experience, to *construct* a reality. For, while utterances bore the imprint of their speakers, they also established tangible links with their referents, a property that was taken by Victorian scholars as evidence of "primitive mentality." It was this property that Tambiah (1968) was later to dub the "magical power of words"; their power, as Horton (1967:157) put it of African thought, to "bring into being the events or states they stand for." Such power goes well beyond the scope of Western ideas of the capacities of speech, further even than the missionaries' belief in the potency of the word. It implies verbal connections among forces unwilled and inanimate (Turner 1967:299f): words are enmeshed in dense fans of association that might unwittingly be activated by their mere mention. Thus Tswana have long explained their reluctance to use the term *shupa* ("seven") by observing that it also means "to point out" (i.e. with the right index finger, the digit that stands for the number "seven"), a gesture which connotes "to curse" (Willoughby 1932:143).

This notion of the continuity of word and action, cause and effect, did not merely differ from European conceptions. It violated the empiricist epistemology inherent in the *sekgoa* of the nineteenth century, for which positive knowledge lay in the definitive separation of the construct from the concrete, the word from the thing or the act. It also makes clear why the evangelists saw the Tswana as unreasoning, magical thinkers—and why it was so crucial to them to reduce Setswana to (grammatical, conceptual) order. For the Christians, remaking African consciousness entailed freeing the native from this web of animist superstition, this epistemology of unreason. It was with reference to this epistemology, too, that the Tswana were to speak back to them, to give voice to their side of the conversation.

In so doing, they were to resist many of the distinctions introduced by the Christians—especially the attempt to sever man from matter, the abstract from the concrete, the word from the world. What is more, they sometimes chose to contest the culture of the mission by seizing, reconstructing, and re-presenting its most sacred rite, the liturgy of the Holy Service. One incident among many speaks out cogently from the colonial record, being both a "riposte" to the colonizer and a redeployment of his power. In 1837, there appeared, in the *Evangelical Magazine and Missionary Chronicle,* an indignant report by Reverend John Monro (1837:396–7). It was entitled "Pretences of a Bechuana Woman to Immediate Communion with the Divine Being":

> A Bechuana woman, who had been enrolled on our list of candidates, and who had made some progress in scriptural knowledge, absented herself from class . . . [and] prevailed on others to follow her example, by telling them that she had found out the way of enjoying communion with God . . . One Sabbath-day her disciples [met] . . . and at the stated hour *Sabina* commenced her vain devices, by placing a large earthen basin in a particular spot, using certain mystical words, and muttering indistinct sounds, while she poured water into the basin. Then taking out of a bag which hung by her side a number of square patches, (chiefly calico,) she put them down singly on a board one by one. She then took up one of the patches, which she held by the corners, and uttering a number of incoherent expressions, in which texts of Scripture, verses of hymns, and portions of the Lord's prayer, were jumbled together, she shook the patch with violence; then laid it down, and told her followers that this was the way to pray to God. She then took up another of the patches, and went through the same ceremony . . . until she finished her line of patches, after which she told them, that whosoever among them had acted according to her directions should *now* see the face of God in the basin of water, and further, that, according to the sincerity of their prayers, God would speak to them out of the water. They all acknowledged their insincerity; hence no one attempted to look into the basin, and thus she continues the deception.
>
> Strange that such foolery should be countenanced, yet it is so. Neither this woman nor any of her associates will converse with me on the subject. They preserve a sullen silence when in my presence, but have said to some of the members of the church, that God will convince me and all the people in this town, that *they* are right.

While this "technician of the sacred" (Eliade 1964) refused to talk to Monro in his terms, she spoke eloquently in the register of her choosing.

In ironic recognition of the potency of Christianity, she rent the sacred robe and deconstructed the Holy Service, only to recombine its elements according to her own design. Her patchwork made concrete the logic of this recombination in a brilliant bricolage of symbolic objects and verbal utterances. And so the captured force of Christian ritual was put to work, making tangible—quite literally, condensing—the numinous promise of the European God, who had perplexed the Tswana by being pervasive and paternal, yet remote and uninvolved. Moreover, in sharp reaction to Nonconformist prayer and preaching (which the natives referred to disparagingly as "talking"; Edwards 1886:91), the woman's liturgy reunited words with actions. Its intent was clear. The evangelists had not only dismissed Tswana "magic," and its play upon the indivisibility of words, deeds, and things; they had also opposed the "native dance," which made the human body into an instrument of veneration (Broadbent 1865:186–7). *Go bina* connotes both "to sing" and "to dance." It subsumes what modern Tswana refer to as "praising with the feet." *Sabina*, as her name may well have suggested, was the mistress of this maligned activity. Her bag of calico patches evoked the diviner's bag of dice, but invested it with the material might of *sekgoa*, the capacity of the whites. And her shreds of "jumbled" prayer became spells that drew their efficacy from the new source of power. The missionary had no illusions about the seriousness of the threat she posed. He realized that she had elected to defy him in a language *he* could not master.

There is also a clear message here for the anthropologist of colonialism. Although not new, it is a message worth repeating. Sabina's refusal to answer to the voice of the dominant—or in the spoken voice at all—affirms that the argument between colonizer and subject often escapes the register of reasoned verbal debate. History in the making, like ethnography, is not always reducible to a narrative or a text. Indeed, following our earlier point, when the colonized respond in the genre of rational debate—at least as defined in European terms—the hegemony of the colonizing culture may be well on the way to instilling itself in its new subjects; that is why truly counter-hegemonic reactions so frequently seek out alternative modes of expression. Consequently, if we are to recover from the documentary record the riposte of the ruled, we have to move with them as they try, often by unexpected means, to shift the unequal encounter with Europe onto an entirely different plane; to acknowledge, that is, that this encounter may involve a struggle over the terms of representation, and is as likely to invoke the poetics of the concrete as it is to rely on a discourse of words (see Chapter 6). In this struggle, too, the politics of meaning go well beyond the appropriation of the signs of one culture to those of another. Their very essence lies in the shaping of new forms of signification to bear the transfigured images on which history insists.

In South Africa, for all the early resistance to the Christian message and the colonial impulse, the process of domination was to take its course, laying down a new hegemony of social forms—even though the surface planes of the world reconstructed in the colonial encounter were to become the site of a long and bitter political struggle.

III

This, in turn, leads to our more general conclusion. The colonization of South Africa—and many other parts of the world—began with an ideological onslaught on the part of Christian missionaries, self-styled bearers of European civilization. These men set out to "convert" heathens by persuading them of the content of their theological message and, even more profoundly, by reconstructing their everyday worlds. Modern Protestant conversion, of course, is itself an ideological construct framed in the bourgeois imagery of rational belief and the reflective self; of a moral economy of individual choice that echoes, on the spiritual plane, the material economics of the free market. It made little immediate sense along the South African frontier in the early nineteenth century. On the other hand, the *conversation* between the evangelists and the Tswana did have an enormous impact on the latter; in this respect, David Livingstone (above, p. 239) was to prove correct.[33]

The everyday discourse of the mission, its theater of the mundane, was effective primarily because it enmeshed the Tswana in the *forms* of *sekgoa:* the commodity form, linguistic forms, kinship forms, rhetorical forms. The politics of water, production, and language—and we could equally have chosen to discuss architecture, clothing, or a number of other things— all tell the same story. The content of the civilizing mission, its substantive message, was debated and often rejected; increasingly, it would turn out later, along emerging class lines. But its forms were conveyed by the very structure of the conversation from the moment that the Tswana engaged in it. Thus, even to argue over the relative success of two kinds of rain medicine was unwittingly to concede a good deal to the ideology of rational empiricism; to adopt the plough was to redefine the division of labor along the lines of the bourgeois family and its engendered signs; to read a vernacular bible was to have Setswana poetics re-presented in the mode of a thin *sekgoa* narrative; and so on. In each sphere, the discourse presupposed a certain kind of subject, and a particular mode of knowing and being.

The colonization of consciousness, in other words, entailed two levels. At its most tangible, it involved an overt effort to *convert* the Tswana, an argument of images and messages intended to convince them of the ideological content of Christianity. Here the evangelists tried to disseminate, in the heart of darkness, the Good News, a persuasive narrative of biblical morality and "truth." At a deeper level, only partially distinguished from the first, they set their sights on the total *reformation* of the heathen world; i.e. on the inculcation of the hegemonic forms, the taken-for-granted signs and practices, of the colonizing culture. The Nonconformists, as we know, were sometimes quite explicit about working on both planes at once, since the really cultivated being had to be converted *and* reformed. And they seem to have been aware that the kind of personhood and consciousness they wished to instill did not arise from dogma and revelation alone; that it inhered as much in the practical and material forms of "civilization," those "outer things" at once devalued and yet tacitly encouraged by the church. Notwithstanding the intentions of these European colonizers, however, the two levels of transformation—conversion and reformation—do not necessarily occur together. Quite the opposite, the discontinuities between them often lie at the very heart of the history of consciousness and its struggles. That is why people who reject an ideological message may yet be reformed by its medium; why new hegemonies may arise amidst the most bitter of ideological battles.

This brings us, finally, to the reactions of people like the Tswana to the modern historical processes in which they find themselves caught up; that is, to their consciousness of colonization. There is much debate at present, among historians and anthropologists, about the nature of those reactions—in particular, about the nature of protest and the so-called "weapons of the weak" (Scott 1985). Does an act require explicit consciousness and articulation to be properly called resistance? Should the term apply only to the intentions behind social and political acts, or may it refer equally to their consequences? When a people can be shown to express some measure of awareness of their predicament as victims of domination—and, better yet, can state the terms of their response—the matter is clear. Where they do not, defining and characterizing their reactions becomes an altogether more murky business. We would suggest, however, that there is an analytical lesson to be taken from the evident fact that most historical situations *are* extremely murky in just this respect.

Aside from organized protest—easily recognizable as "political action" by Western lights—much of what may be seen as the riposte of the colonized, as one or another form of (tacit, indirect) resistance, turns out to be a practical means of *producing* historical consciousness. Indeed, if anything is clear from our study, it is that much of the Tswana response to the mission encounter was an effort to fashion an awareness of, and gain conceptual mastery over, a changing world. This, it seems, is a very general phenomenon. Early on in the colonizing process, wherever it occurs, the assault on local societies and cultures is the subject of neither "consciousness" nor "unconsciousness" on the part of the victim, but something in between: recognition of varying degrees of inchoateness and clarity. Out of that recognition, and the creative tensions to which it may lead, there typically arise forms of experimental practice that seek, at once, techniques of empowerment and sources of new knowledge.

Such reactions, often seen as enough of a threat to the authority of the dominant to elicit coercive measures, seek to plumb the depths of the colonizing process. They search for the logic—and, sometimes, the *deus ex machina*—that lies behind its visible face. For the recently colonized generally believe that there *is* something invisible, something profound, happening to them; that their future may well depend on gaining control over it. Thus, for instance, many "Christianized" peoples the world over are, or once were, convinced that whites have a second, secret bible or set of rites (cricket? semaphore? tea parties?) on which their power depends. The whimsical "unreason" of such movements as cargo cults stems from precisely this conviction. These movements, as is now well known, are an early effort to grasp the bases of the colonial production of value, and to redirect it to the well-being of the dominated.

With time and historical experience, the colonized show greater discrimination, greater subtlety in interpreting the European embrace and its implications. Attempts to come to terms with it grow more diverse, and are ever more closely tied to processes of class formation. Among those drawn most fully into the forms of "modernity"—the petty bourgeoisies and "new elites" scattered along the fringes of the world system—there occurs a gradual appropriation of the images, ideologies, and aesthetics of the post-enlightenment West. And these include orthodox styles of political discourse and protest. But, for the rest, modernity and its modes of resistance are by no means inevitable, or even likely consequences of the colonization of consciousness—or of the consciousness of colonization that follows. Indeed, the dynamics of cultural imperialism are such that, while the power structure of colonialism is everywhere clearly laid down, the colonizing process itself is rarely a simple dialectic of domination and resistance.

Notes

1. Ranger (1975:166–7) makes a similar point with respect to colonial Eastern Africa. As he puts it, "at the core of [the 'colonial relationship'] was the manipulation and control of symbols."

2. The historical material for this essay is drawn, in large part, from Comaroff and Comaroff (1991, n.d.[a]); in that study we provide a comprehensive account of the encounter between the missionaries and the Tswana, and place it in the context of the colonial process at large.

3. In *Of Revelation and Revolution* we show that the emergence of a bounded ethnic group labeled "the Tswana" (or, at the time, "the Bechuana") was itself a function of the colonial process—and, in particular, of missionary activity.

4. We have analyzed Tswana culture and society, past and present, in our earlier writings, which we are compelled to take as read here; see, for example, J. Comaroff (1985), J. L. Comaroff (1982, 1987a), Comaroff and Comaroff (1991), Comaroff and Roberts (1981).

5. For accounts of this historical process, told from the Tswana perspective, see, for example, Molema (1951, 1966), Lye and Murray (1980).

6. Early European visitors to the Tswana were struck by their enthusiasm for trade (see e.g. Lichtenstein 1930,2:387f). There was an active traffic between southern and northern communities—and between Tswana and their more remote neighbors—in such things as spears, iron and copper goods (ibid:409), ivory (Livingstone 1857:45), wild animal skins (Smith [ed. Kirby] 1939,1:278), ostrich feathers (Mackenzie 1871:130), and cosmetics (Campbell 1822,2:194)

7. The Ngwaketse inhabit a large chiefdom in the Southern District of modern-day Botswana; like that of most countrymen, their culture has long been attuned to combating drought.

8. Bourdieu (1987) has pointed out how the commonsense notion of biography—or "life history"—is an ideologically loaded construct with a number of unstated presuppositions; among them, that the "life" of an individual is "a coherent and finalized whole," chronologically ordered, and thereby made meaningful (see also above, Chapter 1). "This way of looking at life," he goes on to say, "implies tacit acceptance of the philosophy of history as a series of historical events (*Geschichte*) . . . an historical narrative (*Historie*)" (p. 1). Missionary biographies partook of exactly this philosophy; their conception was the product of a bourgeois ideology that saw a life-history as a progress, in which the responsible individual, always (potentially) master of his or her position in the world, navigated a moral caeer of self-improvement or self-degradation. (In fact, in the Protestant vision, a life of virtue was capable of transcending death and time, being the entrée into a "world without end.") That the biography of the evangelist, a success story of individual improvement, should become a model for the moral career of Africa is hardly surprising. After all, if personal life-histories are metonyms of narrative histories at large, the former are easily represented as idealized versions of the latter. This is a point to which we shall return below.

9. In much early nineteenth-century romanticism, the image of a free class of yeoman families—small, economically independent, rural producers—came to represent a nostalgic image of a lost Britain. See, for example, Wordsworth's remarkable guide to the Lake District (1835, repr. 1948), or John Stuart Mill (1848, repr. 1929:256), who was later to condole over the passing of those "who were vaunted as the glory of England while they existed, and have been so much mourned over ever since they disappeared"—although, as Briggs (1959:40) has pointed out, the romantic vision of the yeomanry had a very slim basis in history. Since many of the missionaries had their origins in the British peasantry, it is no wonder that this romantic ideal of the free yeomanry appeared so central in their rhetoric.

10. J. Read, Lattakoo, 15 March 1817 [CWM, LMS Incoming Letters, South Africa, 7-1-C]; see also Moffat (1842:229f), Campbell (1822,1:77).

11. J. Read, New Lattakoo, 5 September 1817 [CWM, LMS Incoming Letters, South Africa, 7-3-A].

12. J. Read, Lattakoo, 14 March 1817 [CWM, LMS South African Journals, 3]. The emphasis on the *square* house was not coincidental either. As we (1986; below, Chapter 10) and others (e.g. Levi-Strauss 1972:204) have shown, the imposition of the square on the circle was part of the cultural evangelism of the West in many parts of the world. Certainly, among Tswana, the Europeans took the indigenous stress on the arc and the circle to be indicative of a lack of rationality and discipline, and tried hard to "correct" it.

13. J. Read, Lattakoo, 14 March 1817 [CWM, LMS South African Journals, 3].

14. R. Hamilton, New Lattakoo, 17 February 1823 [CWM, LMS Incoming Letters, South Africa, 9-1-A].

15. T. Hodgson, Platberg, 31 March 1827 [WMMS, South Africa Correspondence (Cape), 302].

16. T. Hodgson, Platberg, 31 March 1827 [WMMS, South Africa Correspondence (Cape), 302]; J. Archbell, Platberg, 16 March 1828 [WMMS, South Africa Correspondence (Cape), 302]; Moffat (1842:285f).

17. The Rolong were another Southern Tswana people, who, at the time, composed four chiefdoms: the Ratlou-Rolong, the Tshidi-Rolong, the Seleka-Rolong, and the Rapulana-Rolong. The earliest WMMS missionaries to the Tswana established themselves among these groupings.

18. J. Archbell, Platberg, 20 March 1832 [WMMS, South Africa Correspondence (Albany), 303].

19. Note that the term "Bechuana" (Tswana) was first used by the Europeans (see above); as Schapera (e.g. 1953) has noted, its origins and meaning are difficult to ascertain. In the early nineteenth century, it appears, *batho* ("humans") included citizens of all polities ("Bechuana" or not), but did not apply to the members of the underclass; that is, "bushmen," Kgalagari, or other serfs who lived outside the settlement and/or the social order, and were regarded as only semi-human.

20. T. Hodgson, Matlwassie, 12 January 1824 [WMMS, South Africa Correspondence, 300].

21. A. Wookey, Kuruman, 23 May 1884 [CWM, LMS Incoming Letters, South Africa, 42-3-C].

22. J. Read, New Lattakoo, 5 September 1817 [CWM, LMS Incoming Letters, South Africa, 7-2-A].

23. J. Freeman, Kuruman, 8 December 1849 [CWM, LMS Home Odds (Freeman Deputation 1849–50), 2-4-D].

24. These references are to *Bibela ea Boitshépo* (1952), a revised and reprinted version of Moffat's original *Secwana (Chuana) Bible*. The use of *badimo* for "demons" has survived all revisions of the text.

25. For example, see J. Campbell, Klaarwater, 26 July 1813 [CWM, LMS Incoming Letters, South Africa, 5-2-D], who wrote that "Setswana seemed so easy . . . that a missionary [with] a turn of mind for learning a language I think in six months would understand it so well, that [he] could be able to begin a translation of the Scripture . . ." On the more general point that African languages were seen as unchallenging to the superior European intellect, see Samarin (1984:437).

26. I. Hughes, Lattakoo, 17 December 1824 [CWM, LMS South African Journals, 4].

27. See S. Broadbent, Matlwassie, 31 March 1824 [WMMS, South Africa Correspondence, 300]; Moffat (1842:xv).

28. J. Archbell, Platberg, 7 January 1828 [WMMS, South Africa Correspondence (Cape), 302].

29. J. Archbell, Platberg, 7 January 1828 [WMMS, South Africa Correspondence (Cape), 302].

30. By modern consensus, for instance, Setswana has fifteen noun classes, a problem with which Moffat clearly grappled, but not always with great success (see 1842:260–1).

31. J. Archbell, Platberg, 7 January 1828 [WMMS, South Africa Correspondence (Cape), 302]; Moffat (1842:xiv).

32. For a study that demonstrates this especially well, see Willan's (1984) excellent biography of Sol T. Plaatje.

33. As Jeal (1973:passim) points out, however, Livingstone himself was a less than persuasive participant in this conversation, especially over the long term. Indeed, by almost any criterion, he was not a very successful missionary.

10

Homemade Hegemony

It is not so much the reality of the home that is my subject as the idea of
the home.

—Witold Rybczynski (1986:viii)

Prologue

WITNESS A CURIOUS PARALLEL BETWEEN two turn-of-the-century pieces
of social commentary. One, by the Reverend W. C. Willoughby
(1911:70), a Nonconformist missionary, describes the peoples of Bechuanaland. In it, he laments the impossibility of a "beautiful, healthy home-
life" for "people who live in one-roomed mud-huts" and goes on to speak
of the need to teach the natives how to build proper, civilized homes. The
other, by Henry Jephson (1907:31), sometime chief sanitary engineer of
London, bemoans the condition of the urban poor in England: "Physically,
mentally and morally, the overcrowded people suffered . . . [and it] was
usually at its worst in one-roomed tenements. . . . In one room they were
born, and lived, and slept and died amidst the other inmates. . . . The
consequences to the individual living in an overcrowded . . . dwelling were
always disastrous." Could the similarity in subject and tone have been mere
coincidence? Or did these texts have some historical link? Was there any
connection between the aspirations of African missions and the exertions
of London's sanitary supervisor? Between the effort to "improve" those
"who live[d] in one-roomed mud-huts" on the imperial frontier and those
who lived "in one-roomed tenements" at its core, within walking distance
of the palace gates? Was the making of modern "home-life" in black South
Africa—which is what Willoughby sought to justify—somehow implicated
in the making of modern English society? Linking all these questions are
three historical motifs: domesticity, modernity, and colonialism. Together
they weave a compelling tale, a nineteenth-century narrative about the

265

establishment of modern bourgeois hegemony in Europe and its overseas "possessions."

Precepts, Programs, and Problems

Several studies have argued recently that "the home"—as place and precept—was a crucial focus of European efforts to colonize Africa (e.g., Hansen 1989; Gaitskell 1983; Cock 1980), in particular to instill "Western family ideology" (Hunt 1990:449). But these studies have left a number of problems unresolved. Precisely *which* Western models of domesticity, for instance, were exported to the colonies? How stable and consensual were they in their own societies? Were they merely the vehicles of European "family ideology" or did they implicate more thoroughgoing social and cultural forces? Most significantly, was this imperialist gesture a simple act of domination of the "periphery" by the "center" or were the changes wrought on the colonial fringe also entailed in the making of the world from which they came?

If we are to analyze the connection between domesticity and colonialism, then, we have first to situate the phenomenon of "domesticity" itself. This construct, Rybczynski (1986) reminds us, had its roots in the seventeenth century: It was with the demise of "the public, feudal household" that "the private family home" (p. 49) began to seed itself as a generic European social and cultural form. Social historians now observe, as a commonplace, (1) that the development of a distinct "domestic domain"—associated with women, unwaged housework, the raising of children, and the "private"—was a corollary of industrial capitalism (see, e.g., Davidoff and Hall 1987; Hall 1985; Morgan 1985; Hausen 1981; Darrow 1979); (2) that "domesticity" was integral to the cult of "modernity" at the core of bourgeois ideology; and (3) that, far from being a natural or universal social institution, it grew to maturity with the rise of the factory system, which entailed the reconstruction of relations of production, of personhood and value, of class and gender. Oakley (1974:42f) points out, however, that the "doctrine of (female) domesticity" had not spread far beyond the bourgeoisie before the 1840s; that is, well after the start of African evangelism. Only after 1841, with the call for the gradual withdrawal of women from industry (p. 43), did this doctrine begin "to permeate downwards to the working classes" (p. 50).

Of course, there remained great variation in actual patterns of family organization within and across the social strata of Europe (see, e.g., Pawley 1971:6; cf. Stedman Jones 1971). To be sure, this variation persists today. But that is sociology. The ideological struggle to naturalize the doctrine of domesticity was, from the first, part of the middle-class endeavor to secure its cultural hegemony. It was a struggle, Gallagher (1985:passim) observes, that reverberated through the literary discourses of the age. We use the term "naturalize" advisedly here. The effort to disseminate the idea of domesticity was saturated with natural imagery, as Oakley (1974:43–46) goes on to show: The Report of the Royal Commission on the Mines (1842), for example, spoke of women workers as "disgusting and unnatural"; Engels (1968 [1844]:160–161) added that factory toil deformed their bodies, making mothers liable to miscarry. In another genre, Charlotte Tonna's *The Wrongs of Woman* (1844) decried female employment for having "reversed the order of nature." If the likes of Foucault are correct, this process of naturalization was an element in the making of a total moral order, a silent edifice in which family and home served as mechanisms of discipline and social control. Vested in dispersed regimes of surveillance and in the texture of everyday habit, goes the general argument, the doctrine of domesticity facilitated new forms of production, new structures of inequality. Still, we repeat, it did not prevail immediately or without resistance—nor everywhere in just the same way.

All this underscores the danger of assuming that a full-grown, stable model of "home life" was taken from Europe to the colonies. Nor can we safely assume, *pace* Fortes (e.g., 1978:14f), that "the domestic" may be conceptually freed from its historical context; that is, that "the domestic" is universal and thus had existed in some form in precolonial Africa. In its precise English sense, "domesticity" connoted a particular order of values and dispositions. It cannot be used, without distortion, for *any* form of cohabitation, residence, and/or reproduction. In Africa and Europe alike the construction of the domestic world was a highly specific cultural and social project. And it was invariably shaped by—and, in turn, influenced— the political worlds in which it occurred (J. L. Comaroff 1987a).

But there is more to the matter than this. Carefully disinterred and read anew, the evidence suggests that colonialism itself, and especially colonial evangelism, played a vital part in the formation of modern domesticity *both* in Britain and overseas; that each became a model for, a mirror image of, the other; and that historians have underplayed the encounter with non-Europeans in the development of Western modernity in general, and of "home" in particular. The imperial fringe, as Achebe (1978) points out, was an imaginative frontier on which Europe retooled its self-awareness, its metaphysical reflections on its own "nature"—while incorporating Africa into the political economy of the metropole. Scenes of distant battles with savagery, we shall see, became the cautionary currency of an urgent moral offensive in the urban "jungles" of Victorian Britain (Hebdige 1988:20f), where the poor were seen to be as uncivilized as the most beastly blacks in the bush.[1] Here lay the basis of a *dialectic* of domesticity, a simultaneous, mutually sustaining process of social reconstruction at home and abroad.

Unnatural Africa

In the late eighteenth century, Britain was caught up in a vigorous debate about humanity, reason, and civilization. It was a debate in which Africa occupied a singular symbolic place (Curtin 1964). In the varied discourses of modernity, themselves fueled by the upheavals of the Age of Capitalism, the "dark continent" loomed as a negative trope, an inversion of all that had evolved toward enlightenment (Brantlinger 1985). Europe came to stand in relation to Africa as does the refined to the raw, light to dark, the saved to the damned, the knower to his object. In due course, this relationship took on a historical imperative: The blank spaces of the continent were to be mapped, the wild cultivated, the suffering saved. The black man was to be encompassed by the white.

The Nonconformist mission to South Africa was a product of this historical moment. Spawned by the great British revival of the period, the London and Wesleyan Methodist Missionary Societies (LMS and WMMS) sent agents into the interior in the early nineteenth century and built permanent stations among the Southern Tswana in the 1820s. After the long sea voyage to the Cape, the churchmen trekked deep into the uncharted hinterland (cf. Beidelman 1982:63), their tales of epic journeys coming to hold a special place in contemporary popular literature. For these writings added moral authority to the titillating images of otherness that framed the Victorian imagination—and ethical virtue to cultural imperialism.

The evangelical gaze perceived Africa as a "desert." This was a result less of its climate than of the fact that it was preconceived as a moral wasteland. Its inhabitants, peoples of the wild, shared its qualities: Unable to master their environment, they lacked all culture and history (cf. Ranger 1987). The popular accounts of early missionaries and travelers fostered this view: Sarwa ("Bushmen") "prowled about" the veld,[2] sleeping in beds "like the nest of an ostrich" (Barrow 1801–1804,1:275). And "Bechuanas" were incapable of proper cultivation, merely "scratching the surface" of the earth (Broadbent 1865:105; Pratt 1985:124). They covered themselves in "filthy animal fat and skins" instead of wearing clothes (Hughes 1841:523), indulged in "monotonous thumping to barbarous airs" instead of singing or dancing (Edwards 1886:91), and "moped" in mud huts instead of living in houses (Moffat 1842:507). In telling of "dreadful heathenism," the evangelists reserved special opprobrium for native domestic life—or, rather, its absence. Broadbent (1865:204) wrote that they *had no marriage,* nor any proper domestic order, nor acknowledged any moral obligation to the duties arising out of that relation. Females were exchanged for others, bartered for cattle, given away as presents, and often discarded by the mere caprice of men.

The misery arising out of this state of society cannot be easily described. . . . [Nor can the] absence of the proper domestic affections, and unnatural treatment of the children. . . . [A]lthough much yet remains to be done . . . the Divine institution [of marriage] has been introduced . . . and domestic and social order and happiness are extending.

One might well ask, "Whose misery? Whose happiness?" But such questions went unanswered. By this time, the image of "diseased, suffering Africa" was taken for granted in Europe (see Chapter 8). Indeed, Broadbent and his brethren were wont to suggest that the "dark continent" was more than just sick: Its condition was downright unnatural. Satan, they were sure, had succeeded here in setting up his riotous realm, wiping clean the savage mind and corrupting the laws of nature.

During the 1820s the Tswana world was changing from both within and outside; the latter, in part, was a result of the rise of the Zulu state and of long-distance trade with the colony. For present purposes, however, its internal dynamics may be summarily described in terms of a few general principles.[3] Viewed from the center, each chiefdom comprised a hierarchy of social and administrative units (households, family groups, wards, and sections). All of these units were founded ultimately on the model of the polygamous family—itself made up of uterine houses[4]—and were ranked according to often-contested agnatic rules of seniority. And all were bound to the chiefship by a complex set of connections at once substantial and symbolic. At the same time, the Tswana expressed a preference for marrying close kin, which limited the emergence of large descent corporations and bred a field of ambiguous, individuated social ties. Great onus was placed on families to forge social and material relations on their own account and to keep as free as possible from bonds of dependency. As a result, the forces of political centralization and hierarchy were countered by tendencies toward the dispersal and autonomy of households—just as the royal ideal of a unified polity was countered by a commoner map of a social field made up of dispersed homesteads linked through women. As this suggests, there existed, anywhere and at any time, a variety of social forms on the landscape. Broadly speaking, the more centralized and hierarchical a chiefdom, the less independent were households, the more gender roles were marked, and the greater was male control; conversely, the less the degree of centralization, the more autonomous were households, the less marked was the sexual division of labor, and the more attenuated was male authority (J. L. Comaroff 1987a).

Such variations notwithstanding, agriculture centered on the household: Uterine houses were the primary units of cultivation, just as they were the primary units in the social and imaginative production of the political community. Women did most of the work—which, again, struck the evangelists as profoundly unnatural—and often cooperated with their own kin in the process. Given an uncertain ecology, farming had to be supplemented with gathering, both activities drawing mothers and their children away from the densely populated town for long periods. Rather than the bounded British "home," then, it was a matricentric group, with a radiating network of ties through females, that was the focus of material subsistence, reproduction, and nurture among contemporary Tswana.

The male world, by contrast, centered on the chiefly court. Here men participated in political and legal processes; here, too, they performed the communal rites on which depended the triumph of the state over the social and natural forces that threatened it. As this suggests, their major role in the division of labor was nothing less than the making of the body social itself. It was a role that made little sense to the missionaries, however. In their eyes, Tswana men appeared distressingly indolent, lacking in all ambition. The Europeans simply failed to see that the Africans engaged in social management with great energy and acuity, the major currency with which they did so being cattle. These beasts served as units of wealth, signs of status, and media of relationship.

Pastoralism, in fact, was male activity par excellence: It denoted forceful control over the wild. Agriculture, on the other hand, like female procreation, was fragile and perpetually endangered. It is no wonder that the Christian idea of a civilized division of labor was greeted with astonishment or that, in about 1820, some local women offered to plant fields for the benighted white men. Among the Tswana, the objective of adult males was to own beasts and to transact the value embodied in them (Comaroff and Comaroff 1990), although day-to-day herding was done by their dependents, their "bushman" serfs, or their sons. By means of these beasts, they produced and reproduced the bonds that wove together the social fabric: Through bridewealth they made marital ties, exchanging rights in women's labor and offspring; through the loan of stock they forged loyalties and relations of clientship; and through sacrifice they communed with ancestors. In addition to accumulating allies and dependents, such exchanges transformed the yield of female effort—grain to feed retainers, sons to tend herds, daughters to marry off—into social resources and wealth.

It will be clear why the evangelists, themselves drawn from the lower fringes of the rising British middle class, saw African life as moral and social chaos (cf. Vilakazi 1962:121). In violation of the bourgeois ideal of domesticity, Tswana houses were enmeshed in dense kinship networks and social units; marriages were bonds between groups; polygyny seemed no more than undignified promiscuity. Furthermore, the labyrinthine architecture of "native" homes and towns was palpable proof of the lack of clear boundaries in this strange society—boundaries between persons, their property, and their productive practices. Before all else, then, the missionaries would have to liberate would-be converts from the enchanted webs of their world, to domesticate the breeding grounds of savagery. In their restored Kingdom of God, marriage was to be a sacred union between consenting, loving, and faithful individuals; the nuclear household was to be the basis of the family estate; male and female were to be associated, complementarily, with the "public" and the "private," production and reproduction. After all, domestic order was meant to be a microcosm of the church and the world. Wesleyans had long preached that, as the "husband is head of the wife," so "Christ is head of the Church" (Whitefield 1772:185), and nineteenth-century social paternalism taught that "society could be regenerated by duplicating the family's benevolent hierarchy" (Gallagher 1985:117). Moreover, *proper* domestic arrangements were held to be vested in specific forms of *property*. Flora Tristan, a remarkable early French feminist, noted in her *London Journal* (1980 [1840]:192) that this image of family life was "far removed from reality." A "pretence" even among the wealthy, it had little purchase on the British working population. But such things did not stand in the way of its enthusiastic export to Africa.

Capturing Hearths and Minds:
The Domestication of Satan's Kingdom

The evangelical ideal of domesticity was not easily put into practice in Africa.[5] As the Reverend John Philip (1828,2:355) wrote, "The elevation of a people from a state of barbarism to a high pitch of civilization supposes a revolution in [their] habits." Among the Tswana—who, complained Moffat (1842:243), had no idols to shatter, no altars to seize, no fetishes to smash—this revolution had to be won on the diffuse terrain of everyday life. If colonial evangelism was going "to turn the [heathen] world upside down" (Moffat 1842:235f), it would have to do so by reforming the minutiae of practical existence. And so the churchmen set about staging a matter-of-fact theater of Protestant industry in which they set forth the mode of rural production through which they hoped to remake Tswana society. Thus, soon after he arrived among the Tlhaping, James Read erected a house, making sure that he was widely observed: "Had great numbers of people flocking to see [the spectacle]," he reported, "which was as a wonder to all."[6] When he finished, he set up a forge and began to fashion ploughshares, the biblically valued tools of peasant agriculture with which Tswana families might one day make a "proper" livelihood.[7]

It is no coincidence that this early performance featured the building of a house. According to Nonconformist ideology, all self-conscious improvement was rooted in the elementary forms of life: the habits of hearth and home. These, said the churchmen repeatedly, were the key to the epic task of bringing Africa into the modern world—and, not incidentally, into the British Empire. No usage was too unimportant, no activity too insignificant to escape the stern gaze of the civilizing mission. Charity, for the English middle classes, might begin at home. For colonial evangelists, however, it began by giving heathens the very idea of home.

The missionary effort to create domesticity from degeneracy took many forms. And it had many consequences, some of them unforeseen. Here we consider two related aspects of the enterprise: the attempt to remake the realm of production and the effort to recast the tangible shape of the "home" itself. Our focus is not arbitrary: The rise of domesticity as an ideological construct in Europe—however much contested (Gallagher 1985:113–146)—involved the convergence of two conceptual planes, one socioeconomic and the other architectural. "The domestic" (1) connoted a social group (the family) whose interrelated roles, duly sanctified and naturalized, composed the division of labor at the core of "civilized" economy and society and (2) presupposed a physical space (the "private" house) that was, in principle, clearly marked and bounded.

It made perfect sense, then, that in building their kingdom on a firm domestic foundation the evangelists would work to institute the practices and forms that were its icons and instruments. As John Philip (1825:223) put it, "The private and domestic situation of mankind is the chief circumstance which forms [its] character." It followed, he added elsewhere (1828,2:72–73), that the sacred task of the civilizing mission was to "[get Africans] to build houses, inclose gardens, cultivate corn land, accumulate property, and . . . [increase] their artificial wants." As this suggests, the Nonconformists had a clear appreciation of the vital role of production in forging persons and relations; from their theological standpoint, self, society, and salvation were a laborious human construction. However, being at the vanguard of colonialism, they had little with which to realize their vision save the tools of persuasion.

As a result, the churchmen made virtue of necessity as they made necessity into virtue. They built from the bottom up, on humble, homely ground. But this ground was already host to the architectural forms of Tswana production and procreation. For the Africans, too, the "house" (*ntlo*) was an elemental structure—a sign in concrete (or, rather, clay) of the relations within it and the ties that radiated outward from it. Although very different from its British counterpart, it also condensed the values inscribed in a particular cultural context. Thus, as both a social and a physical entity, the "house" was destined to be a major site of challenge and contest, of the complex encounter between Africa and Europe. The dialectic of domesticity was to play itself out in various ways within Tswana communities. Some would emulate white ways, others would appropriate them piecemeal, and a few would refuse them outright. The patterns were complex: Mission converts were not beyond reproducing "traditional" forms, whereas self-conscious "traditionalists" often conjured with those forms in creative ways. Nonetheless, although unanticipated, these patterns were far from random: The manner in which the Tswana engaged with European signs and practices turned out to be closely connected to emerging lines of social difference in this part of South Africa.

Moral Economics, Material Signs

To the missionary eye, at home in the bounded and enclosed English countryside, the Tswana landscape appeared uncontained and unfixed. Biblical Hebrews might have been nomadic pastoralists, but modern civilization was built on a solid foundation of immovable wealth. "Shifting" peoples were "shifty," inherently incapable of sustaining a lawful society based on individual rights and stable families (Muldoon 1975). The relative mobility of the Tswana, their complex territorial arrangements, and the transhumance of women during the agricultural cycle thwarted the evangelists from the beginning and offended their sense of order. As Dr. Philip told his colleagues in 1830, "When men have no settled homes . . . it is easy for them to desert the means of instruction on any provocation" (Macmillan 1929:76). The civilizing mission thus encouraged its subjects to take possession of the land by investing themselves in it, anchoring themselves through their labor and the weight of domestic possessions.

For the churchmen, cultivation was almost synonymous with salvation. The belief in the civilizing role of horticulture was as old as English colonialism itself: In the seventeenth century, Edmund Spenser had advocated a settled agrarian existence for the "wild Irish"; their "barbarous and warlike" state, he said, resulted from their seminomadic pastoralism (Muldoon 1975:275). Similar notions were carried to the peoples of Africa, whose devotion to cattle-keeping was taken as proof of their primitiveness. Moreover, some Europeans, having lived too long on the "wasted continent," were alleged to have degenerated to an equally primitive state— because they no longer cultivated. Hear Livingstone (Schapera 1974:76): "The extreme dryness of the climate in all the inland districts renders the cultivation of European grain impossible, except by means of irrigation. On this account the Boers have become exactly like the blacks,—more a pastoral than an agricultural race; and their encroachments differ essentially from the advance of civilized communities into the domain of savages elsewhere." Agriculture, the seedbed of civilization, would cultivate the worker as he cultivated the land—and then sold his produce to the market. Tswana farmers were to be encouraged to grow sufficient surpluses to link them through trade with Christian Europe (cf. Bundy 1979:39); this, believed the evangelists, would put them on the universal path to progress, albeit many paces behind white Britons. The model here was the much romanticized English yeomanry, sturdy independent peasants who had been devastated during the Age of Revolution (Comaroff and Comaroff 1991:Chap. 2).

Significantly, when the mission tried to place ploughs in the hands of Tswana males, and to consign females to "indoor" housework and the raising of children, it was the women who first resisted. Their anxieties were well-founded: Largely through the actions of the Christians, they were to lose control over agrarian production and its harvest. This change in the division of labor was meant to replicate the ideal of gentility that had enclosed bourgeois European women in idle domestic seclusion—while their poorer sisters remained in the "male" labor market as devalued beings. The Africa of which the churchmen dreamed might have evoked a vanishing yeomanry at home, a rural peasant idyll. But Nonconformist ideology grew out of the industrial revolution. It presupposed a social order that divided sharply between production and reproduction, public and private, maximization and moral nurture, male and female.

The evangelists' determination to "buy" the land that they settled and cultivated also flowed from their origins in capitalist culture. The Tswana made it quite clear that, in the circumstances, this was a meaningless gesture. But the Europeans wished to ensure that their venture was legitimately founded on the laws of private property.[8] Once they had acquired the land, they set about enclosing and planting it: The irrigated garden was held up as an example to the Africans and came to stand as an icon of the civilizing mission at large. Within its fenced confines were enacted the principles of "proper" production, rooted in material individualism: the creation of value by means of self-possessed *male* labor, the forceful domination of nature, and the accumulation of surplus through a rational expenditure of effort.

Recall our account in Chapter 9 (p. 247): Determined to instruct by example, the evangelist and his wife made themselves into metonyms of the European division of labor. Livingstone (1857:22) spoke of "the accomplishments of a missionary in Central Africa, namely, the husband to be a jack-of-all-trades without doors, and the wife a maid-of-all-work within." Here lay the key both to civilizing reform and to the problem of the displaced, uncontained black female: Many Tswana women were to be confined to home and family, and many were indeed to be maids in modern

South Africa. The missions stressed that female nature was designed for the backstage work of nurture, caring for the bodies and souls of those whose destiny lay in the cut and thrust of the public world. For his part, the Tswana male was exhorted to pursue his rightful occupation in his field over which, as "yeoman" and "breadwinner," he was called upon to assert his mastery.

The first reaction of the Tswana to the mission garden was not to take from it the lesson that the Christians wished to convey, but to steal its fruit. In the early days at least, its bounty was seen to flow from the innate powers of the evangelists themselves. Among the Rolong, for instance, men vied to have their wives cultivate fields next to the obviously fertile WMMS plots.[9] But the Christians persisted in offering new agricultural techniques and, in time, the Tswana began to differentiate these forces of production from the personal potency of their owners. First came the private well and irrigation ditch, next the plough; each was as vital to the construction of the Protestant moral order as it was to the material basis of the civilizing mission. Both were used to draw the "fitful and disorderly heathen" into settled communities founded on individual property and a new, domestically ordered division of labor (Shillington 1985:17).

Central to this process of transformation was the perceived need to recast indigenous concepts of time. The evangelists began at once to break into the cycle of seasons and communal rites and tried to disrupt the so-called cattle clock, the reckoning of diurnal rhythms with reference to pastoral practices. (For example, the Tswana term for "evening" was *maitseboa*, "when they [the cattle] returned home.") To the Christians, any notion of temporality tied to mundane routines was unable to accommodate transcendent visions of history and salvation. It was also unsusceptible to mission control. For the Europeans, time was primarily an abstract thing in itself. An objective medium capable of reducing all mankind to a common measure of fate, it had the power to order or subsume events, was a commodity to be spent in the cause of self-improvement, and served as a standard of value that allowed labor to be sold in the market. Africans, said the churchmen, were intrinsically indolent, tardy, and irrational in its use, as were the premodern producers and the neophyte proletarians of Europe (Thompson 1967; Weber 1958:63; cf. Alatas 1977). The civilizing mission hoped to make them march to the grand imperial clock and synchronize their domestic schedules to the fixed agendas of public domain: the workplace, the school, and the church. In his first letters from the field, Broadbent (1865:86f) expressed concern that, for heathens, "every day was alike." In less than a year he would note with pride that Sundays had become "as quiet and still as in England."

All this presupposed a world of commodities and wage labor; bourgeois family ideology, after all, was both an effect and a cause of the consolidation of capitalism in Europe. It did not take long for the missions to introduce market forces to the Tswana or to teach them the meaning of "real" work. Not only were the LMS and WMMS the earliest employers in the region, making much use of black toil in the building of their stations, but they were also conduits of the first sustained commerce (London Missionary Society 1830:86; Tilby 1914:192). By 1830, their reports noted that many "natives" were "becoming industrious" and that more sought work than could be hired (Livingstone 1857:46). For all their talk of creating a God-fearing peasantry, the churchmen were laying the basis for the alienation of Tswana men from the local economy by, among other things, making them receptive to wage work. In due course, the family "home" here took on features familiar in proletarian Europe, serving largely as a female-serviced dormitory for males who labored elsewhere. It also became a workplace for those women tempted or pressed to commoditize their new domestic skills. As soon as English dress became a requirement for converts, for instance, seamstresses began to sew for pay (Moffat 1967:17).

In the short run, the civilizing mission and its material innovations were bound to run into difficulties. Given their division of labor, with its rigid separation of pastoralism from cultivation, Tswana were unlikely to show enthusiasm for hitching the beast to the plough, which was demanded by the new technology. Indeed, because women were debarred from managing stock, this technology called for a thorough reorganization of relations of production. In the event, most men turned serious attention to mission agriculture only after the local economy had been disrupted and the viability of hunting and foraging had begun to decline, a result of both *difaqane,* the upheavals following the rise of the Zulu state, and the expansion of the colonial presence (Tilby 1914:193; Broadbent 1865:105; also Shillington 1985:17). Of course, only those with sufficient cattle could even consider using ploughs, and only they could profit from transporting surpluses and trade goods to distant markets. Among the Southern Tswana, it was thus junior royals who became the first members of the Christian peasant elite.

In the longer term, the plough overtook the hoe in all Tswana communities (Parsons 1977:123): Its capacity to increase the productivity of agriculture, especially in this ecology, was not liable to go unnoticed by a people with a keen interest in the accumulation of practical knowledge. In addition, the evangelists soon induced traders to settle on their stations and to supply British commodities, particularly, farming equipment, wagons, and clothing (Northcott 1961:148). The impact on cultivation, among those willing and able to use the new technology, was striking. So greatly did their arable outputs rise that, by 1844, Dutch farmers were "passing out of the colony . . . to purchase [Tswana] wheat" (Broadbent 1865:106). But there was another side to this: As drought and disease threatened the cattle economy, and as ever more pasturage was brought under cultivation, the emerging elite gained control of a disproportionate amount of land, including the best acreages around water sources (Shillington 1985:62). The material bases of inequality were being dramatically—and, as it was to turn out, irrevocably—recast in the image of commodity production.

Mission agriculture did more than force a distinction between a class of commercial farmers and a growing mass of dispossessed families. In reconstructing relations of production, it also altered the role of females, and their kin, in the social division of labor. As the evangelists had hoped, "the work of the gardens cease[d] to belong to the women" (Mackenzie 1871:70), who were reduced to doing the menial tasks of tending and reaping. Men seized control over the harvest, cut it loose from family consumption, and sold it (Kinsman 1983). Freed from communal obligation and tempted by new commodities, most marketed as much grain as possible. In so doing, they greatly depleted household resources—to the extent that, fearing famine, some chiefs tried to limit sales (Schapera 1943:203). Commercially oriented farmers grew reluctant to share with dependents or to invest in domestic brewing and hospitality; their status was now vested in other sorts of transactions and in private property. The families of the wealthy became ever more bounded, ever more nuclear. Simultaneously, accounts of destitution, especially among older women and children, became more common.

The Benthamite goal of advancement through profitable production and trade, then, was achieved by reducing a growing number of Tswana to economic dependency (Kinsman 1983:39f). Overtaken by an increasingly dominant class of farmers, who continued to enhance their royal privilege by applying agrarian techniques learned from the mission (Mackenzie 1871:70),[10] many were never able to own ploughs, could not irrigate, and gradually lost access to adequate land. Others were caught in between: While they struggled to acquire the wherewithal for viable agriculture, they found it difficult to produce even small surpluses. Still, they tried hard to maintain, and sometimes expand, their enterprises—just as those most rapidly impoverished battled to remain self-sufficient. But, by the late 1870s, the destruction of natural resources was driving more and more of them into the labor market, even those not persuaded by the myth of progress. The process was yet further accelerated by the predations of white settlers on their land and stock (Shillington 1985:99f).

Among the Tshidi-Rolong, another Southern Tswana people, it was the industrious Christian community at Mafikeng that made most use of irrigation and the plough; its "upper-class citizens," we are told, prospered from the cultivation of European cereals (Holub 1881,1:279). White visitors found the town a "pleasing" sight, with recognizable "enclosures" and "farmsteads." Although constantly harassed by Boers, by 1877 it supported considerable plough agriculture and its wealthier citizens, some of them royals, were thoroughly familiar with money and Western commodities (Holub 1881,2:13). Their houses, built in colonial style, did not merely reflect the growing importance of "Christian family life" (see below). They also signaled a standard of living far above that of the general population: Despite its overall "progress," the community was undergoing rapid internal differentiation. This process was to be exacerbated by bitter regional conflict and, in the 1890s, by rinderpest and drought, which seriously eroded local agriculture. Although the economy did not collapse altogether, the turn of the twentieth century saw most families dependent on the labor market for survival. Only the wealthiest survived with fortunes intact. This small elite stood in stark contrast to the impoverished majority and to the shrinking proportion of those trapped somewhere in between.

The impact of colonial evangelism on the Southern Tswana division of labor, in sum, varied along the emerging axes of social class. Only the affluent could effect domestic arrangements that, according to the ideology of the mission, were "civilized." As migrant labor fractured the households of the rank and file, relict wives and daughters reassumed responsibility for what survived of local agriculture. Those who remained at home had much to gain from cooperative practices; as we shall see, their life-styles continued to express the salience of extended families, and of agnatic and matrilateral relations. But new principles of domestic collaboration arose as well: for example, those of small, tightly knit Zionist churches, whose female-headed households clustered around the headquarters of male charismatic leaders (J. Comaroff 1985:199). As this implies, though Nonconformist family ideology was to influence those outside the small elite, it was also to be widely contested. Even in the 1960s, residents of old Mafikeng, with its circular homes and wards, spoke disparagingly of people who rented square, fenced houses in the nearby "government" township and worked in the wage economy. Their satirical jibes—that these people were "naked" like "plucked birds," lacking "the shelter of a homestead wall"—offered a lively critique of the discrete, self-reliant domestic unit of bourgeois orthodoxy.

The terms of this subversive rhetoric suggest a close association, in Tswana consciousness, between the forms of housing and the force of habit, between architecture and the socioeconomic arrangements of domestic life. Whatever their precolonial legacy, the Africans were powerfully affected by the churchmen's assumption that bounded dwellings begat bourgeois domesticity—and all that it entailed. In order to explore the role of built form in the colonial encounter, let us return to the early moments of the civilizing mission.

The Architecture of Modernity

From the start, the design of Tswana towns and villages was an obstacle to the evangelists' goal of establishing a stable, European-like peasantry. Indigenous settlements, some of them as large as Cape Town (Barrow 1806:404), seemed a "bewildering maze" (Moffat 1842:274) of circuitous pathways and courtyards. "Bechuanas," noted Philip (1828,2:126), "are very partial to the figure of the circle. Their houses are all of a circular form; [towns are] composed of a series of concentric lines." Like modern imperialists elsewhere (cf. Levi-Strauss 1972:204), the churchmen sought from the first to impose the square on the "primitive" arc. They were determined to rationalize the undifferentiated chaos of "native" society by laying upon it the rectangular grid of civilization (Comaroff and Comaroff 1986:13). Livingstone (1857:26) observed: "Bakwains [Kwena] have a curious inability to make or put things square: like all Bechuanas, their dwellings are made round. In the case of three large houses, erected by myself at different times, every brick had to be put square by my own right hand."

The right hand of civilization would try unceasingly to reorder the Tswana sense of space and line; to wit, evangelists came to judge the march of progress by the rectilinear extension of fence and furrow, hedge and homestead, across African soil. James Cameron records the first impact of the town of Thaba 'Nchu on the missionary gaze (Broadbent 1865:189): "Here he sees a vast assemblage of houses teeming with inhabitants. This [is] widely different from a European town. No splendid fanes, or spires, no public buildings to serve the ends of either justice or benevolence, greet the heavens; a heap of Bechuana huts jostled together without any apparent order, and their indispensable appendages, cattle-folds, make up the scene."

This scape, a jumble of human and animal life, lacked the contrasts on which rested true refinement: the heights of spirituality and justice, the separation of private and public, the marks of individuated property. Neat four-sided cottages were urgently needed to close off nuclear families and their possessions in indoor privacy; only there would they be safe from the indecent flux of heathen life (cf. Krige and Krige 1943:318 on the Lovedu). To the Christians, Tswana living arrangements were not only unaesthetic. They were unhealthy. Mackenzie (1883:222–223) wrote that "viewed from the adjoining mountain, the town . . . is really beautiful. But however charming in the distance, it is not at all pleasant to thread those narrow, winding, and gourd-shaded lanes. . . . I found the atmosphere of the town to be quite oppressive, and constantly wondered that cases of fever were not even more numerous." In the rhetoric of nineteenth-century reformers, social disorder was associated with disease, the latter being not merely an issue of dirt but also of the improper distribution of bodies in space (Foucault 1975). The absence of well bounded and visibly distinct persons, families, and habitations—or the presence of "winding paths" rather than rational roads—was often dubbed "unhygienic" and even, despite all the evidence to the contrary, "unhealthy" (J. Comaroff n.d.).

In this regard, the missionaries saw building and clothing as two sides of a single coin. They set about reforming Tswana dress along with their dwellings, seeking at once to contain the "greasy" black body in "clean, decent" habits and habitations (Moffat 1842:287). Cleanliness was taken to be a sociomoral condition: Africa was unbounded rather than merely unwashed (cf. Burke 1990). Together, European architecture and attire would enclose it and embrace its peoples in an enlightened order of production and reproduction. Each presumed the other: The modestly clothed Christian belonged in a proper house whose walls and fences segregated the person from his/her environment and segregated the nuclear family from its surrounding social context (cf. Stallybrass and White 1986). The interdependence of persons and things so volubly expressed in Tswana dress and building had to be severed because only after they were freed from entropic entanglements might human beings flourish. Only then could they build civilized relations through the circulation of modern media: commodities, money, and printed words.

Recall that Read's first act, on arrival among the Tlhaping, was to build a home, a "wonder for all to see" (see p. 240); he then offered to erect an identical one for the chief's wife. Said Livingstone (1857:46): If an evangelist "wanted to be respected by the natives," he had to have a house of "decent dimensions, costing an immense amount of manual labour." Undoubtedly, large structures made an impression on the Tswana. But the notion of decency expressed here, measured in the calculus of congealed work time, was the churchman's alone. The mission garden might have introduced Tlhaping to Nonconformist ideas of productive toil. However, it was in the "home" that they would learn to dispose of its yield through responsible habits of consumption and reproduction. The Britons were quite open in their efforts to impose their values on local domestic arrangements. And they never doubted that buildings embodied particular moral principles of conjugality and kinship—or that they spoke cogently of essential inequalities of gender, status, and power.

From the outset, the mission, with its church, house, and garden, was the irreducible atom of Christian society. When the evangelists arrived, remembers Edwards (1886:101), they had to "rough it," living in wagons and then in rudimentary residences. Yet the architecture of even the most simple station already laid out the basic design of a world conceived in the image of modern Europe. This design was built on a fundamental principle of space and time: that order and refinement inheres in functional separation and specificity. Thus the domestic should be set off from the public, the religious from the secular; similarly, sleeping and "sitting" and cooking and dining each required a discrete place and set of "things." Even the missionary's wagon—with its private interior, its communal exterior, and its black staff of guides and laborers—anticipated this principle. On it rested the bourgeois notion of advancement through growing complexity of form, both within and outside the home. Hence the distressing implications of families living primitively "all in one room" (above, p. 265).

Would-be converts were told repeatedly that minimal Christian living standards had to be signaled in their dwellings and dress; the internal transformations that were assumed to be taking place inside them and their families had to be played out on socially legible surfaces, for all to read. But there was more at issue than just the expression of change. Anticipating Bourdieu (1977) by more than a century, the evangelists believed that "houses" literally constructed their inhabitants—that their functionally specific spaces laid out the geometry of cleanliness and godliness. By contrast, "huts" and "hovels," undifferentiated within and made of all but raw materials, were brutish and transient—like filthy nests in the bush (cf. Ranger 1987). Most Tswana, it turned out, were not enamored of European architecture. Their round houses, like their cloaks, would remain undivided in form and function for a long time to come.

The evangelists persisted nonetheless and tried actively to assist the Tswana with the practical adoption of "modern" built forms. Before traders arrived with commercial materials, the churchmen advocated reshaping local substances—clay, ox hide, and powdered anthills—into square houses on enclosed lots. They stressed the value of doors that locked, ensuring the security of possessions, and windows that let in light (Tilby 1914:192; Broadbent 1865:61). The latter were especially important. Glass, as we have written (Comaroff and Comaroff 1991:Chap. 5), was the aperture of civilization for post-enlightenment Europeans. The missions sought to use its illuminating influence, thereby penetrating the dark interiors of Africa and encouraging the "domesticating" pursuits of reading and sewing. Behind secure walls, the inward-looking Protestant person would be cultivated in private, albeit under the all-seeing eye of God.

Tswana women had formerly been responsible for most building; men, for sewing and shoemaking. But those who fell within the orbit of the evangelists were pressed to reverse this "unnatural" arrangement. While mission wives set about teaching local females to stitch and cook, males learned the basic crafts of "civilized" house building, notably carpentry and ironworking.[11] All this implied a new relationship to goods and commodities, of course: Once merchants set up shop in the late 1830s, they catered to a range of wants fostered in families with an altered perception of domestic space and time—and an awakened sense of private property. Moffat (1842:507) wrote approvingly of the early converts:

> Formerly a chest, a chair, a candle, or a table, were things unknown, and supposed to be only the superfluous accompaniments of beings of another order. . . . [W]hen they had milked their cows, they retired to their houses and yards, to sit moping over a few embers; . . . at night, spreading the dry hide of some animal on the floor. . . . They soon found to read in the evening or by night required a more steady light. . . . Candle moulds and rags for wicks were now in requisition, and tallow carefully preserved . . . an indication of the superior light which had entered their abodes.

European goods had carved out a space in which the habits of the bourgeois home might take root. New furnishings, like new architecture, would lift the Tswana out of their dirty, unreflective existence. Or so said the missionaries, who had sensed that commodities have the power to socialize. Indeed, the logic of the market, and the infinitely growing wants that drive it, played an integral role in colonial evangelism. A steadily expanding range of clothes and household objects was made available to Tswana in the late nineteenth century, both by rural merchants and by urban retailers catering to the black migrant trade (Schapera 1947:228f). Although they later became wary of the dangers of "vanity," at first the churchmen blatantly encouraged competitive consumption (Mary Moffat 1967:19). Certain key items—including candles, iron bedsteads, and soap—carried great weight as signs and instruments of Christian domesticity (Schapera 1936:247; Burke 1990). Other goods such as apparel, hand mirrors, umbrellas, and toiletries were also seen as "tools" for remaking body and self in the Protestant image (cf. Hannerz 1983).

The bourgeois home was only one element, albeit the most fundamental, in the order of institutions that made up civilized society. As we have already intimated, early mission stations, the coordinates on a European map slowly unfurling across the interior, were built to be microcosms of that society. At midcentury an observer described Kuruman, the first LMS outpost, as a "village," with superior stone houses "thatched in the Devonshire style," a wagon house, a smith, and a carpenter's shop, a school and a printing office, and a merchant establishment and fenced gardens, "all lined up on either side of a dead straight street" (Burrow 1971:33f). Slowly the mission was gaining in complexity, its scale dwarfing the surrounding settlements with the shapes and routines of a colonial frontier town.

Such towns proclaimed the emerging division of labor in their spatial arrangements. Places of worship were set off from those of secular pursuits, sites of work from those of leisure, the public from the private. But, as we have already noted, all would be integrated into "rational" bourgeois routines and a universal calendar. Time was literally built into the LMS and WMMS churches from the start: Their chiming clocks and school bells punctuated the daily round, coordinating the household with communal rhythms (cf. Wilson 1971:73; Oliver 1952:52). Thus the secular schedules of the British schoolroom complemented the religious order of Sunday services, weekly classes, quarterly communions, and annual feasts. Together they imposed a temporal grid upon domestic life (J. Comaroff 1985:141).

For all the exertions of the evangelists, the transformation of the Tswana world was not a straightforward affair. Nor was it pliantly accepted. To wit, the battle over built form became implicated in a highly complex historical process. By the 1850s, colonial penetration had ensured that many Southern Tswana were living within the shadow of the mission, which had interpolated itself between black and white on the frontier. Given that the power of the Protestants was seen to inhere in *sekgoa* ("European ways"), it is not surprising that some local men learned the craft of European construction or that a growing number of "traditional" dwellings began to include windows, doors, and fences; that is, features that altered received relations between inner and outer, private and communal space. In Kuruman, wealthy Christians had put up "good houses of stone, stone-walled gardens and cornfields" (Read 1850:446), which connoted stability and domestic containment and bespoke the strength of their owners. On the other hand, Anthony Trollope (1878,2:279f), who visited the capital of the Seleka at Thaba 'Nchu in the late 1870s, reported that, although "dressed like whitemen," royals lived in homesteads comprising round mud huts, smeared courtyards, and circular brush fences. For the most part, however, the designs of *sekgoa* were appropriated selectively, as if to deploy their potency to local ends. Even in 1970, one-roomed mudbrick "huts," intricate earthen homesteads, and semicircular wards still dominated most Tswana towns. They overshadowed the weather-beaten colonial houses that dotted the landscape, themselves an epitaph to the mission dream of a prosperous black peasantry.

Indeed, vernacular architecture remained the most durable abode of *setswana* ("Tswana ways"). Given the political ecology of local chiefdoms, missions had no option but to situate themselves in large towns and villages; as a result, their followers lived at home, not in communities set apart. By contrast, stations among the more scattered Nguni were built on open terrain between hamlets. Here "conversion" entailed a tangible movement: Christians left their extended family compounds. Hence a wedge was driven between converts and conservatives (Etherington 1978:117). In the Tswana case, for the majority who did not live alongside the mission, the path to church and school traced out a journey between two worlds: between *setswana,* itself linked ever more to a marked "domestic" domain (*mo gae,* translated as "at home"), and *sekgoa,* increasingly the culture of the public (white) realm. Colonial evangelism certainly reached deep into domestic life, affecting mutable forms such as dress (Comaroff and Comaroff n.d.[a]:Chap. 3). But the churchmen were correct in their perception that Tswana architecture perpetuated an enduring order of values and routines that flourished in spaces beyond their influence.

Thus, although features of Western architecture and domestic styles were assimilated during the nineteenth century, the process was very uneven—if not, as we shall see, historically random. Perhaps the best evidence, at least for the late nineteenth century, comes from a photographic essay by the Reverend W. C. Willoughby (1899a). Intended to popularize the work of the LMS, its pictures do not focus intentionally on buildings. But they provide revealing images of "Native Life on the Transvaal Border." These photographs show that, by 1899, a tripartite scheme of architectural forms had emerged, each associated with a distinct type of domestic group. At one extreme were "traditional" dwellings, which lacked windows, doors, or other Western features and were always part of larger compounds; in the households of wealthy Christian families, such structures, where they were still found, were used as "outhouses" for storage or sleeping accommodation for young children. In this century they have become the architectural counterpart of "heathen dress," embodiments of a devalued, infantile "custom." At the other extreme were the residences of the rich, which were barely distinguishable from those of the burghers of white towns in the interior; they centered on a nuclear family with its few dependents and servants. And between the two were the synthetic structures of the majority, whose homesteads, with their mazes of courtyards and hearths, proclaimed the continuing relevance in daily life of agnatic and matrilateral ties. Still single roomed, these mudbrick houses were now square and had flat roofs, windows, and other European fixtures bought with the wages of migrant labor.

In short, most habitations, like family arrangements, gave expression to the simultaneous incorporation yet marginalization of the Tswana. They spoke of the status of their owners as peasant proletarians, of the creation, on the colonial fringe, of a new bricolage out of older forms of production and reproduction, "public" and "home" life. The architecture dominant in Bophuthatswana today still bears some imprint of Nonconformist ideas of property and privacy, domestic space and time. Yet, as with other things, these have been fashioned by the rank and file into new ensembles of aesthetic and material practice, ensembles that are neither bourgeois nor traditional yet mark out a distinct Tswana rural identity.

Reflections: Domesticating
the Tribes of London and Liverpool

We promised earlier to show that the campaign of the African mission to instill a particular idea of home was only one side of a dialectic of domesticity. The other was the effort by bourgeois reformers to mobilize Africa in the cause of remaking the British underclasses—to hold up the "dark continent" as a negative image with which to devalue its own peasants and proletarians. This presumed a likeness, even a structural equivalence, between the benighted back home and the unenlightened abroad. The presumption was often put into words, both at the colonial workplace and in the metropole. Missionaries and travelers in early nineteenth-century South Africa were quick to associate indigenous communities with peripheral peoples in Britain (Livingstone 1857:2, 22; Philip 1828,2:70, 210, 316f). John Philip, for one, said (p. 70) that in "intelligence and morals," Griqua "bear a comparison with . . . the peasantry of England." Clearly both groups remained far from the pinnacle of progress. Both, thought Philip, could do with the active ministrations of the civilizing mission. He went on (pp. 316–317): "We are all born savages, whether we are brought into the world in the populous city or in the lonely desert. It is the discipline of education, and the circumstances under which we are placed, which create the difference between the rude barbarian and the polished citizen—the listless savage and the man of commercial enterprise. . . . [In South Africa] we see, *as in a mirror,* the features of our own progenitors" [our italics].

As this implies, it was within the exploding nineteenth-century city that the bourgeoisie met with its most immediate experience of primitive unreason. The poor of London and Liverpool, went the common lament, were indeed closer to rude barbarians than to refined burghers. Their fetid, fitful presence threatened to contaminate the citadels of the middle class, to pollute all that was sane and sanitary (Jephson 1907). Hebdige (1988:20) notes that the scourge of polite society were youthful "nomads" and "street urchins" who were often compared to African savages. We are reminded, in particular, of Mayhew's (1851) classic description of costermongers, poor street traders. Younger costers, it is said, wore beaver-skin hats and moleskin collars—just as, according to contemporary accounts, Tswana wore greasy animal hides.[12] Both alike shunned civilized clothing of "cotton and woollen manufacture." Furthermore, "eyewitness" reports (e.g., Garwood 1853; Hollingshead 1861) suggest that the lack of a settled home life among these destitute youths made them seem like the "wandering tribes" of "unknown continents" (Hebdige 1988:21); their plight justified "the growing moral impetus towards the education, reform and civilisation of the working-class masses." Echoes of colonial evangelism in Africa could not be more audible. It is interesting that James Greenwood's popular travels, described in *The Wilds of London* (1874), were, in large part, guided by a missionary, from whose house in the dark innards of the uncharted city radiated the light of Christianity. The churchman's effort to "improve" the slum people—especially, their domestic lives—surfaces as a dispersed subtext in the narrative. And Greenwood was not unusual. The figure of the civilizing missionary appears in many tales of urban Britain, voyeuristic adventures and philanthropic manifestos alike. We shall return to him.

Significantly, writers like Mayhew (1851) and Greenwood (1874) portrayed themselves as "social explorers";[13] the former, in fact, introduced himself (p. iii) as a "traveller in the undiscovered country of the poor." In so doing, they evoked an obvious parallel with the geographical mission abroad, the exploratory project in which Europeans visited remote parts of the world, "discovered" them, and brought them within the compass of intellectual and material control. This recalls Stedman Jones's (1971:14) comment about the poverty-stricken districts of London: "a *terra incognita* periodically mapped out by intrepid missionaries and explorers who catered to an insatiable middle-class demand for travellers' tales." Note that the goal of *The Association for Promoting the Discovery of the Interior Parts of Africa,* formed in the late eighteenth century, had been to "penetrate the *terra incognita* of the globe" (*The Monthly Review,* 1790[2]:60–68). Note also that the products of its expeditions, most famously Mungo Park's *Travels* (1799), fed the same middle-class appetite for stories of adventure, exoticism, and the "pornography" of others' suffering. These were precursors of, and paved the way for, the mass-circulation abolitionist and evangelical writings[14] through which the progress of Africans, guided by heroic white Christians, became part of the popular literary fare of bourgeois Britain.

The connections between accounts of Africa and those of the poor in England varied in their explicitness and elaboration. Often the mere use of metaphors in otherwise unconnected descriptions conjured up potent parallels: Talk of urban "jungles"—in which the poor lived, like "wandering tribes," in "nests" and "human warrens"—brought the dark continent disconcertingly close to home (see, e.g., Hollingshead 1861:8, 165). Sometimes, however, the parallelism was less a matter of lexicon than genre. A striking instance is to be found in another text by Greenwood, published before *The Wilds of London.* In his *Seven Curses of London* (1869:20), he describes a "strange observance" in the vicinity of the Cow Cross Mission. The evangelist there had seen many "instances of this strange custom; but even he, who is as learned in the habits and customs of all manner of outcasts of civilization as any man living, was unable to explain its origin."

The "strange observance" was the prominent display by many a couple of their marriage certificate on the living-room wall, under a clock if they had one. Given the low rate of matrimony among the poor, the centrality of the conjugal family in bourgeois morality, and the role of the clock in marking work time, the symbolic logic of the practice hardly seems mysterious. To be sure, the purposeful joining of these tokens of respectability gives graphic evidence of the impact of philanthropic efforts to reform domestic values, to place legitimate marriage under the regime of responsible self-regulation. But even more salient here is the fact that this passage might easily have come from Moffat (1842) or Livingstone (1857), Broadbent (1865) or Edwards (1886), or many other missionary or explorers' accounts. It bears the unmistakable hallmarks of what Pratt (1985:120) has called the "remarkably stable subgenre" of "othering." Its distancing, objectifying style, its synthesis of the tropes of ethnography (habits, customs) and evangelism (civilization), of science (learning, explanation) and moralism (outcasts), conveyed a cogent message: The poor of Britain were "strange"—as much "other" as any African aborigine. No wonder that Mayhew (1851:iii) could preface his widely read text with the remark that less was known of these unfortunates "than of the most distant tribes of the earth." And he and his contemporaries were not in any doubt that they were as urgently in need of improvement. The charter for the civilizing mission at home (indeed, for internal cultural colonialism) speaks out clearly: The bourgeois burden in Britain, it followed, was no less pressing than the white man's burden abroad. The point was argued by a number of literary figures of the period—and persuasively supported by Charles Dickens, though his objectives were somewhat unusual.[15] Dickens asserted many times (e.g., 1908a; 1908b; cf. 1853) that the call for overseas evangelism, and for grand imperial schemes, distracted attention from England's own dire social and political problems.

The drawing of imaginative parallels between the "dangerous classes" (Stedman Jones 1971:11) at home and savages abroad, then, lay first and foremost at the level of unmarked imagery, of more or less direct intertextual and lexical references that wove a tapestry across the genre of travel and missionary literature, fusing moral homily with homeric adventure, evangelical zeal with exotic didacticism. A notable example, with particular reference to the theme of domesticity itself, is Thomas Archer's *The Pauper, the Thief, and the Convict* (1865). Its subtitle, "Sketches of Some of Their Homes, Haunts, and Habits," brings together, in avid alliteration, a hint of the naturalist's notebook, the traveler's tale, and the erotic eye. Archer begins by insisting that "there is little of the picturesque in poverty" (p. 1); in this, he recalls the evangelist to Africa who begs us, before laying out his romance, not to be romantic. And then, like the same evangelist (Comaroff and Comaroff 1991:Chap. 5), he takes us with him on a pilgrim's progress—except that his terra incognita is Bethnal Green. He refers to the inhabitants' houses as "dens" and assures us that, while "the main thoroughfares [are] ruinous and dirty," they give no idea of how awful are the "teeming and filthy rooms," how awful are the "ragged, dirty children, and gaunt women, from whose faces almost all traces of womanliness have faded" (p. 10). But we have not yet reached the depths of Archer's Africa-in-London. "Let the traveller penetrate further," he urges (p. 11), "he will enter upon a maze of streets, each of which is a social crime, and each of which contains tributary hovels many degrees worse than itself. They are not always easy to find, since, if they ever had any names, the names have been obliterated. . . . At the end of this blind court there will be found either a number of black and crumbling hovels, forming three sides of a miserable square, like a foetid tank, with a bottom of mud and slime."

And so on. In London, as in Africa, the wilderness is unnamed, unmarked, and uncharted. Archer assures us (p. 10) that this is "as foul a neighborhood as can be discovered in the civilized world." The verb, in ironic juxtaposition to its object, discloses the essential spirit of the voyage. So does the parenthetic comment that follows immediately: "(Savage life has nothing to compare to it.)" In order to reinforce the point, some writings in the same mode actually made "savages" the vehicle of observation. Thus Bosanquet (1868:1–3) tells of a "young Caffre" from South Africa who had visited London and told of his experiences when he returned home: "Many are rich and many are poor," he said, "in such a great place there is all that is beautiful and all that is bad" (p. 2).

The parallel was frequently drawn with an expressly political purpose. Rymer, for instance, wrote that the object of his *White Slave* (1844), one of several similar narratives published at the time, was "to convince the public that there were white slaves in London a great deal worse off than the black slaves in Africa" (quoted by Gallagher 1985:131). But the moral spirit, the ideological project, in the writings of this tradition[16] is most articulately—and, perhaps, intriguingly—laid out in Hollingshead's *Ragged London in 1861* (1861:v–vi): "With all our electro-plated sentiment about home and the domestic virtues, we ought to wince a good deal at the houses of the poor." The qualifier here is itself revealing: Electroplating, the coating of domestic tableware with silver by electrolysis, was a brilliant symbol of the newly acquired, skin-deep sensibilities of the bourgeoisie. Those sensibilities were offended by misery. True, the poor might themselves have been to blame—"less drunken indulgence in matrimony and child-breeding would at once better their condition"—but the point, said Hollingshead, was to do something about it. This is where the analogy with Africa took on practical salience: What was needed was an army of missionaries who would reform the needy from the core of their very beings. "In no part of the world—not even in the remotest dens of the savage wilderness—is there such a field for labour as in our London courts and alleys" (p. 221). Shades, once more, of Dickens.

The circle is closed. The wilderness of London and Africa, teeming habitats of the benighted, were little different from one another. They were equally "other," equally *undomesticated*. The primitive and the pauper were one in spirit, one in spiritlessness. And so the sacred task of the colonizing mission was to reconstruct the home lives of both—all in the cause of universal civilization. Philip (1828,2:316–317; see above, p. 285) was correct: The "dark continent" *was* a metaphorical mirror held up between savagery and civility, past and present, bourgeois ideology and its opposites at home and abroad.

In this respect, the encounter with savagery was deployed in the dialectic of domesticity in two distinct, if interrelated, ways—in two discourses— one negative, one positive—that followed upon each other conceptually and, broadly speaking, chronologically. The first has permeated everything we have said so far: namely, the invocation of Africa as an iconic inversion, a negative image, of the ideal of bourgeois refinement. Thus followed the flood of popular descriptions, distinctly didactic in tone, of the "indescribable" uncleanliness of Africans: Their "filth" and "promiscuity" became a measure against which to evaluate conditions and classes back home and to frame appropriate social and evangelical policy. For instance, in a LMS youth magazine aimed primarily at the instruction of common readers in Britain, Willoughby (1899b:84–85) offered, in a tone more polite than most, "The houses are generally not very clean. There is no ceiling, and the inside of the roof is usually dirty and festooned with cobwebs. Small scorpions often live in the thatch, and occasionally a snake. And after a year or two, creatures that the editor will not allow me to name become so numerous that even the thick-skinned natives have to clear out and build a new house."

If writings in this genre reinforced the image of Africans as leading fitful lives on intimate terms with animal nature, it remained only to show how similarly disreputable were the English poor. Jephson (1907:56) quotes an authoritative report written in London at midcentury: "It is no uncommon thing, in a room twelve feet square or less, to find three or four families *styed* together . . . filling the same space night and day—men, women, and children, in the promiscuous intercourse of cattle. . . . [I]n all offices of nature they are gregarious and public; . . . every instinct of personal or sexual decency is stifled; . . . every nakedness of life is uncovered there."

If this account had humans, promiscuous as cattle, living in styes, another had them yet further down on the scale of nature. Thomas Beames, in his extraordinary *Rookeries of London* (1852:2), likens "pauper colonies" to the nests of rooks, the "lowest" of birds. That the term "colony" is used to describe poor city districts is itself telling, but even more memorable is his description of these "colonies." In perhaps the most pejorative text of the age, he offers that (pp. 2–4) "[paupers] belong to the . . . section of the social body . . . descended to the lowest scale which is compatible with human life. Other birds are broken up into separate families—occupy separate nests; rooks seem to know no such distinction. So it is with the class whose dwellings we describe. [These colonies house] the pariahs, so to speak, of the body social, a distinct social caste." The poor here became a distinct race, the untouchables of bourgeois society. How similar this rings to the missionary sense that Tswana lacked properly bounded families, that they were caught up in unhealthy "communistic relations," and that they showed no signs of true individuality. In both cases, the discourse of pious philanthropy served to demonize the dispossessed.

The practical conclusions were clear. Both social policy and the civilizing mission had urgently to transform the domestic life of the poor (1) to create the conditions for—and an attitude of—"cleanliness," thereby achieving a world in which all matter, beings, and bodies were in their proper place; (2) to reform sexuality by encouraging legal, Christian marriage and the creation of nuclear households, thus putting an end to "drunken indulgence" in "child-breeding"; (3) to spread the ideal of private property, beginning with the family home; and (4) to reconstruct gender relations and the social division of labor. These, of course, were also the objectives of Nonconformist evangelism in Africa; it followed that the failure of the English underclass to live up to them subverted Britain's right to its own refined self-image, its claim to stand at the pinnacle of modernity and civilization. It was thus the common duty of the liberal middle classes to improve the habits and habitats of the less fortunate. But the process had its dark underside: To the extent that the enterprise failed, the poor were made responsible, like their African counterparts, for their own predicament—and for a host of other social ills besides.

Africa, then, was like a camera obscura of British civilization, a virtual portrait of all that bourgeois refinement was not. Inasmuch as anything in England could be likened to life on the dark continent, it failed the test of enlightenment and stood condemned in terms of the lexicon of domestication itself: *nomadic* costermongers; *wandering* paupers; the *teeming, filthy* poor *styed promiscuously* in their *haunts* and *hovels, dens* and *nests*. No better than savages, any of them.

Nor was the inference left unstated. On the very first page of his magnum opus, Mayhew (1851:1) quotes the ethnographic explorations of Andrew Smith in South Africa as a model for his own account. In every society, he says, wanderers are distinct from settlers, vagabonds from citizens, nomads from civilized people; in every society, elements of each "race" are to be found. According to this Africa-derived scheme, London laborers have a "savage and wandering mode of life" (p. 2)—much like "bushmen" living beside more settled ("Hottentot") peoples. Similarly, Perkin (1969:149–150) cites a widely read contemporary text by Gaskell (1836:89), from whom, he claims, Engels took "most of his notions of the development of the family":

> A [poor] household . . . in which all the decencies and moral observances of domestic life are constantly violated, reduces its inmates to a condition little elevated above that of the savage. Recklessness, improvidence, and unnecessary poverty, starvation, drunkenness, parental cruelty and carelessness, filial disobedience, neglect of conjugal rights, absence of maternal love, destruction of brotherly and sisterly affection, are too often its constituents, and the result of such a combination are moral degradation, ruin of domestic enjoyments, and social misery.

Recall, finally, the term "misery." We encountered it before (see p. 269), when Broadbent (1865:204) claimed that Tswana "had no marriage, nor any proper domestic order." It was the word used most often by the churchmen to describe African life—and particularly "home" life—before the advent of colonial evangelism. Also a favorite with abolitionists, it had, on the scale of negative tropes, deep resonance. For, in making the other a passive sufferer, it evoked the conceit of heroic salvation and, simultaneously, established an alibi for intervention. How could anyone cultivated and morally responsible ignore the plight of the ailing—or not actively support the civilizing mission everywhere? And so the metaphors of misery reverberated through the literature of outcast London, coupling the pauper and the primitive in a common destiny.

The other way in which the "dark continent" was deployed in the dialectic of domesticity, especially toward the end of the century, expressed itself in the positive voice: Africa also became a model for the possibility of constructive transformation. The rhetorical basis of this model, and its presentation in the popular media, lay in a simple, blatantly racist claim. Under the impact of the civilizing mission, some savages could be shown to have bettered themselves, to have established decent homes, and to have enjoyed just moral and material rewards. If these blacks, with their inherent limitations, could have climbed the ladder of refinement, so might the most destitute of Englishmen.

We have already come across several texts framed in the positive voice. Read's (1850:446) description of Kuruman in the 1850s (above, p. 283) was an unusually early one of its kind. In it we are told that wealthy Christians had erected "good houses of stone"—conspicuously different from "rude" mud huts—and had laid the basis for modern family living;

all around, in fact, were to be seen signs of "improvement" in building. But most revealing of all, as we suggested earlier, is Willoughby's *Native Life on the Transvaal Border* (1899a). Here we see, in a photographic series, the entire gamut of Tswana dwellings, from the most "primitive" to the most "advanced," from simple "traditional" structures to colonial-style Victorian residences. The evolutionary message is clear, as is its moral: The development of domestic life, expressed in architectural form, was an index of Christian self-improvement, successful embourgeoisement, and civilized self-realization. That is why the evangelists took such triumphal delight in telling of Africans who had demonstrated their personal cultivation in bricks and mortar. These "sable brethren" stood out not merely as a shining light, but also as a humiliating example to white people back home who still lived in the rookeries and recesses of the urban wasteland.[17] Again, the positive polemics had a stinging subtext: The willingness of blacks abroad to embrace progress doubly condemned those English indigents who seemed to spurn civility on their own doorstep.

Conclusion

We should like to end by making a few observations of general significance, some about colonialism, others about domesticity. None of them is entirely new, but all are worth reiterating.

Colonialism, it goes without saying, was an epochal movement, a world historical process. And, until recently, its dominant narratives were written as global economic epics, expansive political sagas, dramas of international conflict and center-periphery relations. Its active agents were Europeans; its objects, the "natives" of "other" lands. Colonial agency, as this suggests, was presumed to go in only one direction. Our analysis makes two points in this respect. First, as we all ought now to know, the *experience* of colonization on the part of peoples like the Tswana occurred in a quite different, much more quotidian key. The European embrace presented itself less in the form of portentious stately action than in apparently utilitarian practice, in the knowledge and techniques introduced by the frontiersmen of empire—missionaries, merchants, settlers, and smallholders. Of these, for obvious reasons, evangelists were often the most heavily implicated, at least in the first instance. They set about the task deliberately and comprehensively, as part of their calling and not as a by-product of their interests. Nor was the colonial process a highly methodical, linear affair. It proceeded amidst arguments among colonizers, some of them bitter and violent (see Chapter 7), and against resistance on the part of the colonized, albeit intermittent and often unpredictable (J. Comaroff 1985). Still, to the degree that it was effective, the colonization of the Tswana entailed the reconstruction of the ordinary. Of things at once material, meaningful, mundane. This is not to say, as we have noted many times, that global economics or regional politics did not have a significant impact on the predicament of black South Africans. It clearly did. But it was from the bottom up, through a careful reworking of the everyday environment, that the forms of European modernity were first fostered on the African landscape.

Second, we have sought to show that colonialism was not a one-sided affair. Nor was it two-sided only to the extent that the colonized may be shown to have had some influence on the way in which colonizers acted upon them. It was a more complex business all around. For, in seeking to cultivate the "savage"—with, as we said, variable success—British imperialists were actively engaged in transforming their own society as well, most explicitly in domesticating that part of the metropole that had previously eluded bourgeois control. Recall that these nether reaches of urban society were directly likened to colonies, to undomesticated primitive lands. Cultural colonialism, in short, was also a reflexive process whereby "others" abroad, the objects of the civilizing mission, were put to the purposes of reconstructing the "other" back home. The two sites, the two impulses, went hand in hand. Not incidentally, both contributed to the triumph of the bourgeoisie in the European "age of revolution" (Hobsbawm 1962). If anything is to be learned from this, it is that colonialism was as much about making the center as it was about making the periphery. The colony was not a mere extension of the modern world. It was part of what made that world modern in the first place. And the dialectic of domesticity was a vital element in the process.

This returns us to the question of domesticity itself. Given that the seeds of cultural imperialism *were* most effectively sown along the contours of everyday life, it is no surprise that the process emphasized the physical and social architecture of the household. As this implies, conversely, the inculcation of modern domesticity was much more than a matter of spreading the "Western ideology of family" (above, p. 266). It always is. As most missionaries understood, the construction of the "private" domain was fundamental to the propagation of their social order; within it were contained the elemental relations of gender and generation upon which social reproduction depended. As modernity took shape in Europe, moreover, the nuclear family became the point of articulation between civil society and the ostensibly free individual, the ideological atom upon which the bourgeois world depended.

In seeking to recast African domesticity in the same mold, then, colonial evangelists hoped to bring about a new society, a new civility. Ironically, as creatures of their time, they took for granted what was to take social scientists many decades to learn: that existing forms of domesticity and the dominant social order in which they are embedded depend, for their construction and reproduction, on one another. Hegemony is indeed homemade.

Notes

1. See Gallagher (1985:122–123) for examples.
2. J. Campbell, Klaarwater, 26 July 1813 [CWM, LMS Incoming Letters, South Africa, 5-2-D].
3. We have published a number of accounts of these systems in the nineteenth century; see, for example, J. Comaroff (1985), J. L. Comaroff (1982; 1987a), Comaroff and Comaroff (1991). Because pressures of space do not allow us to detail our sources here, we rely on those writings—which are very fully annotated—as collateral evidence.
4. A "house," in standard anthropological usage, consists of a married woman and her own children (as the latter are indigenously defined).
5. Some passages of this section are drawn, in amended form, from our *Of Revelation and Revolution*, Volume 2 (n.d.[a]); see also Comaroff and Comaroff (1989).
6. J. Read, Lattakoo, 14 March 1817 [CWM, LMS South African Journals, 3]. Note that the Tlhaping were the southernmost Tswana people.
7. This is not an isolated case; mission archives are filled with similar accounts. See, for just one further example, R. Hamilton, Lattakoo, 15 May 1817 [CWM, LMS Incoming Letters, South Africa, 7-1-C].
8. J. Archbell, Platberg, 2 September 1833 [WMMS, South Africa Correspondence (Albany), 303]; Livingstone (1857:21).
9. T. Hodgson, Matlwassie, 12 January 1824 [WMMS, South Africa Correspondence, 300].
10. See also A. Wookey, Kuruman, 23 May 1884 [CWM, LMS Incoming Letters, South Africa, 42-3-C]. J. Mackenzie, Kuruman, 17 February 1882 [CWM, LMS South Africa Reports, 2-1] details how farmers unable to irrigate were being displaced by the "wealthy" who could.
11. J. Hughes, Lattakoo, 17 December 1824 [CWM, LMS South African Journals, 4].
12. See, for example, Lichtenstein (1973 [1807]:67); Campbell (1822,2:219); Hughes (1841:523); Mackenzie (1883); Moffat (1842:502f).
13. Hebdige (1988:21) makes a similar point but does not annotate it.
14. The circulation of some missionary texts was very substantial indeed; for example, Brantlinger (1985:176) notes that Livingstone's *Missionary Travels* (1857) sold 70,000 copies in just a few months.
15. Dickens's object was *not* to draw an unflattering parallel between the English poor and savage Africans. Nor was it to stress the otherness of the former. He sought, rather, to call attention to the dreadful conditions under which they were forced to live.
16. A point is in order here. As Stedman Jones (1971:Part 3) correctly observes, late nineteenth-century writings on the predicament of the casual poor in London underwent several transformations—largely as a product of rapidly changing social and economic conditions. For present purposes, however, these transformations are not directly significant. The bourgeois ideology of domesticity did not change much over the period; nor did the efforts of middle-class reformers and missionaries to reconstruct the home life of the poor.
17. The evocation of Africa as a constructive model appeared in other popular genres as well, most notably in nursery literature. Church educators seem to have regarded children as a major target for stories of savage improvement; this flowed from the European image of the

"dark continent" as childlike, its infantilized inhabitants in need of "raising" by paternalistic whites. For a striking example of the genre, see Georgina Gollock's *Aunt Africa* (1909), published by the Church Missionary Society. Lack of space prevents us from exploring the infantilization of Africa, or its relegation to the bourgeois nursery, in late eighteenth- and nineteenth-century English literature. For further discussion, see Comaroff and Comaroff (1991:Chap. 3).

Bibliography

Achebe, Chinua. 1978. An Image of Africa. *Research in African Literatures* 9:1–15.

Adam, Heribert, and Giliomee, Hermann. 1979. *Ethnic Power Mobilized: Can South Africa Change?* New Haven: Yale University Press.

Adams, Annmarie. 1991. *Corpus Sanum in Domo Sano: The Architecture of the Domestic Sanitation Movement, 1870–1914*. Montreal: Canadian Centre for Architecture.

Agar-Hamilton, John A.I. 1928. *The Native Policy of the Voortrekkers: An Essay in the History of the Interior of South Africa—1836–58*. Cape Town: Maskew Miller.

Aijmer, Göran. 1988. Comment on "Rhetoric and the Authority of Ethnography: 'Post-modernism' and the Social Reproduction of Texts," P. S. Sangren. *Current Anthropology* 29:424–425.

Alatas, Hussein Syed. 1977. *The Myth of the Lazy Native: A Study of the Image of the Malays, Filipinos and Javanese from the Sixteenth to the Twentieth Century and Its Function in the Ideology of Colonial Capitalism*. London: F. Cass.

Althusser, Louis. 1971. *Lenin and Philosophy, and Other Essays*. [Translated by B. Brewster.] New York: Monthly Review Press.

Alverson, Hoyt. 1978. *Mind in the Heart of Darkness: Value and Self-Identity Among the Tswana of Southern Africa*. New Haven and London: Yale University Press.

Amin, Shahid. 1984. Gandhi as Mohatma: Gorakhpur District, Eastern U.P., 1921–2. In *Subaltern Studies: Writing on South Asian History and Society*, Volume 3, (ed.) R. Guha. New Delhi: Oxford University Press.

Anderson, Benedict. 1983. *Imagined Communities: Reflections on the Origin and Spread of Nationalism*. London: Verso.

Appadurai, Arjun (ed.). 1986. *The Social Life of Things: Commodities in Cultural Perspective*. Cambridge: Cambridge University Press.

Arbuthnot, John ["a Farmer"]. 1773. *An Inquiry into the Connection Between the Present Price of Provisions, and the Size of Farms*. London: T. Cadell.

Archer, Thomas. 1865. *The Pauper, the Thief, and the Convict; Sketches of Some of Their Homes, Haunts, and Habits*. London: Groombridge.

Ardener, Edwin W. 1971. The New Anthropology and Its Critics. *Man* (n.s.) 6:449–467.

Arnold, Matthew. 1903. *Essays in Criticism*. [First Series.] London: Macmillan. [First edition, 1865.]

Arrighi, Giovanni. 1979. Peripheralization of Southern Africa, I: Changes in Production Processes. *Review* 3:161–191.

Asad, Talal. 1973. Two European Images of Non-European Rule. In *Anthropology and the Colonial Encounter,* (ed.) T. Asad. London: Athlone Press.

———. 1986. The Concept of Cultural Translation in British Social Anthropology. In *Writing Culture: The Poetics and Politics of Ethnography,* (eds.) J. Clifford and G. Marcus. Berkeley: University of California Press.

Ashforth, Adam. 1991. The Xhosa Cattle Killing and the Politics of Memory. Paper read at conference, Identity, Rationality, and the Postcolonial Subject: African Perspectives on Contemporary Social Theory, Columbia University, February.

Ashton, E. H. 1937. Notes on the Political and Judicial Organization of the Tawana. *Bantu Studies* 11:67–83.

Bakhtin, Mikhail Mikhailovich. 1981. *The Dialogic Imagination: Four Essays by M. M. Bakhtin,* (ed.) M. Holquist. [Translated by C. Emerson and M. Holquist.] Austin: University of Texas Press.

Banaji, Jairus. 1970. The Crisis of British Anthropology. *New Left Review* 64:71–85.

Banks, (Mrs.) G. Linnaeus. 1876. *The Manchester Man.* Altrincham: John Sherrat & Son.

Barker, Francis. 1984. *The Tremulous Private Body: Essays on Subjection.* London: Methuen.

Barnes, John A. 1951. History in a Changing Society. *Rhodes-Livingstone Institute Journal* 11:1–9.

———. 1954. *Politics in a Changing Society: A Political History of the Fort Jameson Ngoni.* London: Oxford University Press.

Barrow, John. 1801–1804. *An Account of Travels into the Interior of Southern Africa in the Years 1797 and 1798,* 2 volumes. London: Cadell & Davies.

———. 1806. *A Voyage to Cochinchina.* London: Cadell & Davies.

Barth, Frederik. 1973. Descent and Marriage Reconsidered. In *The Character of Kinship,* (ed.) J. Goody. Cambridge: Cambridge University Press.

Barth, Frederik (ed.). 1969. *Ethnic Groups and Boundaries: The Social Organization of Cultural Difference.* Boston: Little, Brown.

Barthes, Roland. 1973. *Mythologies.* [Translated by A. Lavers.] New York: Paladin.

Beames, Thomas. 1852. *The Rookeries of London: Past, Present, Prospective.* London: Thomas Bosworth.

Beidelman, Thomas O. 1982. *Colonial Evangelism: A Socio-historical Study of an East African Mission at the Grassroots.* Bloomington: Indiana University Press.

Bell, Rudolph M. 1985. *Holy Anorexia.* Chicago: University of Chicago Press.

Bergson, Henri Louis. 1935. *The Two Sources of Morality and Religion.* [Translated by A. Audra and C. Brereton.] New York: Henry Holt & Co.

Blumenbach, Johann Friedrich. 1969. *On the Natural Variety of Mankind.* [Translated by T. Bendyshe from the 1775 and 1795 editions.] New York: Bergman Publishers.

Boddy, Janice Patricia. 1989. *Wombs and Alien Spirits: Women, Men, and the Zar Cult in Northern Sudan.* Madison: University of Wisconsin Press.

Bohannan, Paul. 1964. *Africa and Africans.* New York: Natural History Press.

Bosanquet, Charles B.P. 1868. *London: Some Accounts of Its Growth, Charitable Agencies, and Wants.* London: Hatchard.

Bourdieu, Pierre. 1977. *Outline of a Theory of Practice.* [Translated by R. Nice.] Cambridge: Cambridge University Press.

_____. 1984. *Distinction: A Social Critique of the Judgement of Taste.* [Translated by R. Nice.] Cambridge: Harvard University Press.

_____. 1987. *The Biographical Illusion.* Working Papers and Proceedings of the Center for Psychosocial Studies, no. 14. Chicago: Center for Psychosocial Studies.

Bradbury, Malcolm. 1991. The Scholar Who Misread History: A Review of *Signs of the Times: Deconstruction and the Fall of Paul de Man,* David Lehman (New York: Poseidon, 1991). *New York Times Book Review,* Section 7, 140 (24 February):9.

Brain, Robert. 1979. *The Decorated Body.* London: Hutchinson.

Brantlinger, Patrick. 1985. Victorians and Africans: The Genealogy of the Myth of the Dark Continent. *Critical Inquiry* 12:166–203.

Braudel, Fernand. 1980. *On History.* [Translated by S. Matthews.] Chicago: University of Chicago Press.

Breutz, Paul Lenert. 1956. *The Tribes of Mafeking District.* Pretoria: Department of Native Affairs.

Briggs, Asa. 1959. *The Age of Improvement, 1783–1867.* London: Longman.

_____. 1979. *Iron Bridge to Crystal Palace: Impact and Images of the Industrial Revolution.* London: Thames & Hudson.

Briggs, John, and Sellers, Ian (eds.). 1973. *Victorian Nonconformity.* London: Edward Arnold.

Broadbent, Samuel. 1865. *A Narrative of the First Introduction of Christianity Amongst the Barolong Tribe of Bechuanas, South Africa.* London: Wesleyan Mission House.

Bronfenbrenner, Urie. 1979. *The Ecology of Human Development: Experiments by Nature and Design.* Cambridge: Harvard University Press.

Brown, J. Tom. 1921. Circumcision Rites of the Becwana Tribes. *Journal of the Royal Anthropological Institute* 51:419–427.

_____. 1926. *Among the Bantu Nomads: A Record of Forty Years Spent Among the Bechuana.* London: Seeley Service.

_____. 1931. *Secwana Dictionary.* Tiger Kloof: London Missionary Society.

Brown, Richard Harvey, and Lyman, Stanford M. 1978. Introduction. In *Structure, Consciousness, and History,* (eds.) R. Brown and S. Lyman. Cambridge: Cambridge University Press.

Buffon, George Louis Leclerc. 1791. *Natural History, General and Particular.* [Translated by W. Smellie.] London: A. Strahan

Bundy, Colin. 1977. The Transkei Peasantry, c. 1890–1914: Passing Through a Period of Stress. In *The Roots of Rural Poverty in Central and Southern Africa,* (eds.) R. Palmer and N. Parsons. Berkeley: University of California Press.

_____. 1979. *The Rise and Fall of the South African Peasantry.* Berkeley: University of California Press.

_____. 1987. Street Sociology and Pavement Politics: Aspects of Youth and Student Resistance in Cape Town, 1985. *Journal of Southern African Studies* 13:303–330.

Burchell, William John. 1822–1824. *Travels in the Interior of Southern Africa,* 2 volumes. London: Longman, Hurst, Rees, Orme, Brown and Green. [Reprint, 1967. Cape Town: Struik.]

Burke, Timothy. 1990. "Nyamarira That I Love": Commoditization, Consumption, and the Social History of Soap in Zimbabwe. Paper read to the African Studies Seminar, Northwestern University, May.

Burrow, John. 1971. *Travels in the Wilds of Africa, Being the Diary of a Young Scientific Assistant Who Accompanied Sir Andrew Smith in the Expedition of 1834–1836.* [Edited by P. Kirby.] Cape Town: Balkema.

Campbell, John. 1813. *Travels in South Africa.* London: Black, Parry. [Reprint, 1974. Cape Town: Struik.]

———. 1822. *Travels in South Africa . . . Being a Narrative of a Second Journey,* 2 volumes. London: Westley. [Reprint, 1967. New York and London: Johnson Reprint Corporation.]

———. n.d. John Campbell Papers. South African Library, Cape Town.

Cancian, Frank. 1976. Social Stratification. *Annual Review of Anthropology* 5:227–248.

Carlson, Dennis G. 1984. *African Fever: A Study of British Science, Technology, and Politics in West Africa, 1787–1864.* New York: Science History Publications.

Carlyle, Thomas. 1842. *On Heroes, Hero-Worship, and the Heroic in History: Six Lectures.* New York: D. Appleton.

Cartwright, Samuel A. 1853. Philosophy of the Negro Constitution. *The New Orleans Medical and Surgical Journal* 9:195–208.

Casalis, Eugène. 1861. *The Basutos; or, Twenty-Three Years in South Africa.* London: James Nisbet.

Chadwick, Owen. 1966. *The Victorian Church,* Part 1. London: A. & C. Black.

Clapham, John H. 1926. *An Economic History of Modern Britain: The Early Railway Age, 1820–1850.* Cambridge: Cambridge University Press.

Clifford, James. 1988. *The Predicament of Culture: Twentieth-Century Ethnography, Literature, and Art.* Cambridge: Harvard University Press.

Clifford, James, and Marcus, George E. (eds.). 1986. *Writing Culture: The Poetics and Politics of Ethnography.* Berkeley: University of California Press.

Cock, Jacklyn. 1980. *Maids and Madams: A Study of the Politics of Exploitation.* Johannesburg: Ravan Press.

Coetzee, Johannes Hendrik. 1978. Formative Factors in the Origins and Growth of Afrikaner Ethnicity. In *Ethnicity in Modern Africa,* (ed.) B. du Toit. Boulder: Westview Press.

Coetzee, John M. 1988. *White Writing: On the Culture of Letters in South Africa.* New Haven: Yale University Press.

Cogan, Thomas (ed.). 1821. *The Works of the Late Professor Camper, on the Connexion Between the Science of Anatomy and the Arts of Drawing, Painting, Statuary.* London: J. Hearne.

Cohen, Abner (ed.). 1974. *Urban Ethnicity.* London: Tavistock.

Cohen, Anthony P. 1979. The Whalsey Croft: Traditional Work and Customary Identity in Modern Times. In *Social Anthropology of Work,* (ed.) S. Wallman. London: Academic Press.

Cohen, Ronald. 1978. Ethnicity: Problem and Focus in Anthropology. *Annual Review of Anthropology* 7:379–403.

Cohen, Ronald, and Middleton, John (eds.). 1970. *From Tribe to Nation in Africa: Studies in Incorporation Process.* Scranton, Pa.: Chandler.

Cohn, Bernard S. 1980. History and Anthropology: The State of Play. *Comparative Studies in Society and History* 22:198–221.

———. 1981. Anthropology and History in the 1980s: Towards a Rapprochement. *Journal of Interdisciplinary History* 12:227–252.

———. 1985. The Command of Language and the Language of Command. In *Subaltern Studies: Writings on South Asian History and Society,* Volume 4, (ed.) R. Guha. New Delhi: Oxford University Press.

———. 1987. *An Anthropologist Among the Historians and Other Essays.* New Delhi: Oxford University Press.

———. 1988. The Anthropology of a Colonial State and Its Forms of Knowledge. Paper read at Wenner-Gren conference, Tensions of Empire: Colonial Control and Visions of Rule, Mijas, Spain, November.

Collier, Jane Fishburne, and Yanagisako, Sylvia Junko. 1987. *Gender and Kinship: Essays Toward a Unified Analysis.* Stanford: Stanford University Press.

Collingwood, Robin George. 1935. *The Historical Imagination: An Inaugural Lecture.* Oxford: Clarendon Press. [Reprinted in *The Idea of History,* pp. 231–249. Oxford: Clarendon Press, 1946.]

Comaroff, Jean. 1974. Barolong Cosmology: A Study of Religious Pluralism in a Tswana Town. Ph.D. dissertation, University of London.

———. 1980. Healing and the Cultural Order: The Case of the Barolong-boo-Ratshidi of Southern Africa. *American Ethnologist* 7:637–657.

———. 1981. Healing and Cultural Transformation: The Case of the Tswana of Southern Africa. *Social Science and Medicine* 15B:367–378.

———. 1983. Symbolic Healing: Medicine as a Socio-cultural System. In *The Social History of the Bio-medical Sciences,* Volume 5, (ed.) P. Palmarini. Milan: Franco Maria Ricci Editore.

———. 1985. *Body of Power, Spirit of Resistance: The Culture and History of a South African People.* Chicago: University of Chicago Press.

———. n.d. The Diseased Heart of Africa: Medicine, Colonialism, and the Black Body. In *Analysis in Medical Anthropology,* (eds.) M. Lock and S. Lindenbaum. Dordrecht and Boston: Kluwer [in press].

Comaroff, Jean, and Comaroff, John L. 1986. Christianity and Colonialism in South Africa. *American Ethnologist* 13:1–19.

———. 1989. The Colonization of Consciousness in South Africa. *Economy and Society* 18:267–296; *infra,* Chapter 9.

———. 1990. Goodly Beasts, Beastly Goods: Cattle and Commodities in a South African Context. *American Ethnologist* 17:195–216; *infra,* Chapter 5.

———. 1991. *Of Revelation and Revolution: Christianity, Colonialism, and Consciousness in South Africa,* Volume 1. Chicago: University of Chicago Press. [Volume 2, n.d.[a]; in preparation.]

Comaroff, John L. 1973. Competition for Office and Political Processes among the Barolong boo Ratshidi. Ph.D. dissertation, University of London.

———. 1974. Chiefship in a South African Homeland: A Case Study of the Tshidi Chiefdom of Bophuthatswana. *Journal of Southern African Studies* 1:36–51.

———. 1975. Talking Politics: Oratory and Authority in a Tswana Chiefdom. In *Political Language and Oratory in Traditional Society,* (ed.) M. Bloch. London: Academic Press.

———. 1976. Tswana Transformations, 1953–75. In *The Tswana,* revised edition, I. Schapera. [First edition published in 1953.] London: International African Institute.

———. 1977. *The Structure of Agricultural Transformation in Barolong.* Gaborone: Government Printer.

———. 1978. Rules and Rulers: Political Processes in a Tswana Chiefdom. *Man* (n.s.) 13:1–20.

———. 1980. Bridewealth and the Control of Ambiguity in a Tswana Chiefdom. In *The Meaning of Marriage Payments,* (ed.) J. L. Comaroff. London and New York: Academic Press.

———. 1982. Dialectical Systems, History, and Anthropology: Units of Study and Questions of Theory. *Journal of Southern African Studies* 8:143–172.

———. 1984. The Closed Society and Its Critics: Historical Transformations in African Ethnography. *American Ethnologist* 11:571–583.

———. 1987a. *Sui Genderis:* Feminism, Kinship Theory, and Structural "Domains." In *Gender and Kinship: Essays Toward a Unified Theory,* (eds.) J. Collier and S. Yanagisako. Stanford: Stanford University Press.

———. 1987b. Of Totemism and Ethnicity: Consciousness, Practice, and the Signs of Inequality. *Ethnos* 52:301–323; *infra,* Chapter 2.

———. 1989. Images of Empire, Contests of Conscience: Models of Colonial Domination in South Africa. *American Ethnologist* 16:661–685; *infra,* Chapter 7.

———. 1990. Bourgeois Biography and Colonial Historiography: A Review Essay Dedicated to the Late Michael Crowder. *Journal of Southern African Studies* 16:550–562.

———. n.d. Class, Culture, and the Rise of Capitalism in an African Chiefdom. Ms.

Comaroff, John L. (ed.). 1973. *The Boer War Diary of Sol T. Plaatje: An African at Mafeking.* London: Macmillan.

Comaroff, John L., and Comaroff, Jean. 1981. The Management of Marriage in a Tswana Chiefdom. In *Essays on African Marriage in Southern Africa,* (eds.) E. J. Krige and J. L. Comaroff. Cape Town: Juta.

———. 1987. The Madman and the Migrant: Work and Labor in the Historical Consciousness of a South African People. *American Ethnologist* 14:191–209; *infra,* Chapter 6.

———. n.d.[b] The Long and the Short of It. Ms.; *infra,* Chapter 4.

Comaroff, John L., and Roberts, Simon A. 1977. Marriage and Extra-Marital Sexuality: The Dialectics of Legal Change Among the Kgatla. *Journal of African Law* 21:97–123.

———. 1981. *Rules and Processes: The Cultural Logic of Dispute in an African Context.* Chicago: University of Chicago Press.

Cooper, Frederick, and Stoler, Ann L. 1989. Tensions of Empire: Colonial Control and Visions of Rule. *American Ethnologist* 16:609–621.

Cope, Richard L. (ed.). 1977. *The Journals of the Rev. T. L. Hodgson, Missionary to the Seleka-Rolong and the Griquas, 1821–1831.* Johannesburg: Witwatersrand University Press.

Coquery-Vidrovitch, Catherine. 1976. The Political Economy of the African Peasantry and Modes of Production. In *The Political Economy of Contemporary Africa,* (eds.) P. Gutkind and I. Wallerstein. Beverly Hills and London: Sage.

Corrigan, Philip. 1988. The Body of Intellectuals/The Intellectuals' Body (Remarks for Roland). *Sociological Review* 36:368–380.

Corrigan, Philip and Sayer, Derek. 1985. *The Great Arch: English State Formation as Cultural Revolution.* Oxford: Basil Blackwell.

Cory, George Edward. 1919. *The Rise of South Africa,* Volume 3. London: Longmans, Green.

Crapanzano, Vincent. 1985. *Waiting: The Whites of South Africa.* New York: Random House.

Crick, Malcolm. 1976. *Explorations in Language and Meaning: Towards a Semantic Anthropology.* New York: Wiley.

Crisp, William. 1896. *The Bechuana of South Africa.* London: SPCK.

Croce, Benedetto. 1921. *History: Its Theory and Practice.* [Translated by D. Ainslie.] New York: Harcourt, Brace. [Excerpted and reprinted in *The Philosophy of History in Our Time,* (ed.) H. Meyerhoff. New York: Doubleday Anchor, 1959.]

Crowder, Michael; Parson, Jack; and Parsons, Neil Q. 1990. Legitimacy and Faction: Tswana Constitutionalism and Political Change. In *Succession to High Office in Botswana: Three Case Studies,* (ed.) J. Parson. Athens: Ohio University Center for International Studies.

Cunnison, Ian George. 1959. *The Luapula Peoples of Northern Rhodesia: Custom and History in Tribal Politics.* Manchester: Manchester University Press.

Curtin, Philip D. 1964. *The Image of Africa: British Ideas and Action, 1780–1850.* Madison: University of Wisconsin Press.

Cuvier, Georges. 1827–1836. *The Animal Kingdom,* 16 volumes. London: Geo. B. Whittaker.

Dachs, Anthony J. 1972. Missionary Imperialism: The Case of Bechuanaland. *Journal of African History* 13:647–658.

Dachs, Anthony J. (ed.). 1975. *Papers of John Mackenzie.* Johannesburg: Witwatersrand University Press.

Darnton, Robert. 1985. *The Great Cat Massacre and Other Episodes in French Cultural History.* New York: Vintage Books.

Darrow, Margaret H. 1979. French Noblewomen and the New Domesticity, 1750–1850. *Feminist Studies* 5:41-65.

Davenport, T.R.H. 1977. *South Africa: A Modern History.* Toronto: University of Toronto Press.

Davidoff, Leonore, and Hall, Catherine. 1987. *Family Fortunes: Men and Women of the English Middle Class, 1780–1850.* Chicago: University of Chicago Press.

Davis, Natalie Zemon. 1990. The Shapes of Social History. *Storia Della Storiografia* 17:28-34.

de Gruchy, John W. 1979. *The Church Struggle in South Africa.* London: SPCK.

de Heusch, Luc. 1980. Heat, Physiology, and Cosmogony: *Rites de Passage* Among the Thonga. In *Explorations in African Systems of Thought,* (eds.) I. Karp and C. Bird. Bloomington: Indiana University Press.

de Kiewiet, C. W. 1941. *A History of South Africa, Social and Economic.* Oxford: Clarendon Press.

Derrida, Jacques. 1978. *Writing and Difference.* [Translated by A. Bass.] Chicago: University of Chicago Press.

Devisch, Renaat. 1983. Space-time and Bodiliness: A Semantic-Praxiological Approach. In *New Perspektives in Belgian Anthropology, or, the Postcolonial Awakening,* (ed.) R. Pinxten. Göttingen: Herodot.

Dickens, Charles. 1853. *Bleak House.* London: Bradbury & Evans.

———. 1908a. The Niger Expedition. In *The Works of Charles Dickens,* national edition, Volume 35, *Miscellaneous Papers, Plays, and Poems.* London: Chapman & Hall. [First published in *The Examiner,* 19 August 1848.]

———. 1908b. The Noble Savage. In *The Works of Charles Dickens,* national edition, Volume 34, *Reprinted Pieces.* London: Chapman & Hall. [First published in *Household Words,* 11 June 1853.]

[Dodd, William.] 1847. *The Laboring Classes of England.* Boston: Putnam.

Dorris, Michael. 1991. Indians in Aspic. *New York Times,* Section 4, 140(24 February):17.

Douglas, Mary. 1966. *Purity and Danger: An Analysis of the Concepts of Pollution and Taboo.* London: Routledge & Kegan Paul.

———. 1970. *Natural Symbols: Explorations in Cosmology.* New York: Vintage Books.

Dumont, Jean-Paul. 1978. *The Headman and I: Ambiguity and Ambivalence in the Fieldworking Experience.* Austin: University of Texas Press.

Dumont, Louis. 1957. For a Sociology of India. *Contributions to Indian Sociology* 1:7–22.

Durkheim, Emile. 1947. *The Elementary Forms of the Religious Life: A Study in Religious Sociology.* [Translated by J. Swain.] Glencoe, Ill.: Free Press.

Durkheim, Emile, and Mauss, Marcel. 1963. *Primitive Classification.* [Translated by R. Needham.] London: Cohen & West.

du Toit, Brian M. 1978. Introduction. In *Ethnicity in Modern Africa,* (ed.) B. du Toit. Boulder: Westview Press.

Edwards, John. 1886. *Reminiscences of the Early Life and Missionary Labours of the Rev. John Edwards.* [Edited by W. Clifford Holden.] Grahamstown: T. H. Grocott.

Edwards, Roger. 1853. Report from Mabotsa, 1852. In *Report of the Missions in South Africa . . . in Connection with the London Missionary Society 1853*:31–44.

Eliade, Mircea. 1962. *The Forge and the Crucible.* [Translated by S. Corrin.] London: Rider.

———. 1964. *Shamanism: Archaic Techniques of Ecstasy.* [Translated by W. Trask.] New York: Pantheon.

Elias, Norbert. 1978. *The Civilizing Process,* Volume 1, *The History of Manners.* [Translated by E. Jephcott.] New York: Pantheon.

Ellen, Roy F. 1977. Anatomical Classification and the Semiotics of the Body. In *The Anthropology of the Body*, (ed.) J. Blacking. London: Academic Press.

Engels, Friedrich. 1968. *The Condition of the Working Class in England*. [Translated and edited from the 1844 edition by W. Henderson and W. Chaloner.] Stanford: Stanford University Press.

Epstein, Arnold Leonard (ed.). 1967. *The Craft of Social Anthropology*. London: Tavistock.

Etherington, Norman. 1978. *Preachers, Peasants, and Politics in Southeast Africa, 1835–1880: African Christian Communities in Natal, Pondoland, and Zululand*. London: Royal Historical Society.

Evans-Pritchard, Edward E. 1937. *Witchcraft, Oracles, and Magic Among the Azande*. Oxford: Clarendon Press.

———. 1940. *The Nuer: A Description of the Modes of Livelihood and Political Institutions of a Nilotic People*. Oxford: Clarendon Press.

———. 1949. *The Sanusi of Cyrenaica*. Oxford: Clarendon Press.

———. 1950. Social Anthropology: Past and Present. *Man* 50:118–124. [Reprinted in *Essays in Social Anthropology*, E. E. Evans-Pritchard. Glencoe, Ill.: Free Press, 1963.]

———. 1951. *Social Anthropology*. London: Cohen & West.

———. 1956. *Nuer Religion*. Oxford: Clarendon Press.

———. 1961. *Anthropology and History*. Manchester: Manchester University Press. [Reprinted in *Essays in Social Anthropology*, E. E. Evans-Pritchard. Glencoe, Ill.: Free Press, 1963.]

———. 1963. *Essays in Social Anthropology*. Glencoe, Ill.: Free Press.

Fabian, Johannes. 1983. *Time and the Other: How Anthropology Makes Its Object*. New York: Columbia University Press.

Fanon, Frantz. 1968. *Black Skin White Masks*. London: MacGibbon & Kee.

Farquhar, Judith. 1987. Problems of Knowledge in Contemporary Chinese Medical Discourse. *Social Science and Medicine* 24:1013–1021.

Ferguson, D. Frances. 1976. Rural/Urban Relations and Peasant Radicalism: A Preliminary Statement. *Comparative Studies in Society and History* 18:106–118.

Ferguson, James. 1985. The Bovine Mystique: Power, Property, and Livestock in Rural Lesotho. *Man* (n.s.), 20:647–674.

———. 1988. Cultural Exchange: New Developments in the Anthropology of Commodities. *Cultural Anthropology* 3:488–513.

Fernandez, James W. 1982. *Bwiti: An Ethnography of the Religious Imagination in Africa*. Princeton: Princeton University Press.

Fielder, Robin J. 1973. The Role of Cattle in the Ila Economy. *African Social Research* 15:327–361.

Fields, Karen E. 1985. *Revival and Rebellion in Colonial Central Africa*. Princeton: Princeton University Press.

Figlio, Karl. 1976. The Metaphor of Organization: An Historiographical Perspective on the Bio-Medical Sciences of the Early Nineteenth Century. *History of Science* 14:17–53.

Firth, Raymond. 1979. Work and Value: Reflections on the Ideas of Karl Marx. In *Social Anthropology of Work*, (ed.) S. Wallman. London: Academic Press.

Fogelqvist, Anders. 1986. *The Red-Dressed Zionists: Symbols of Power in a Swazi Independent Church.* Uppsala: Uppsala Research Reports in Cultural Anthropology.

Fortes, Meyer. 1949. Time and Social Structure: An Ashanti Case Study. In *Time and Social Structure: Studies Presented to A. R. Radcliffe-Brown,* (ed.) M. Fortes. Oxford: Clarendon Press.

_____. 1953a. The Structure of Unilineal Descent Groups. *American Anthropologist* 55:17–41.

_____. 1953b. *Social Anthropology at Cambridge Since 1900.* Cambridge: Cambridge University Press.

_____. 1969. *Kinship and the Social Order: The Legacy of Lewis Henry Morgan.* Chicago: Aldine.

_____. 1978. An Anthropologist's Apprenticeship. *Annual Review of Anthropology* 7:1–30.

Foster-Carter, Aidan. 1978. The Modes of Production Controversy. *New Left Review,* 107:47–77.

Foucault, Michel. 1967. *Madness and Civilization: A History of Insanity in the Age of Reason.* [Translated by R. Howard.] London: Tavistock.

_____. 1975. *The Birth of the Clinic: An Archeology of Medical Perception.* [Translated by A. Sheridan Smith.] New York: Vintage Books.

_____. 1977. *Discipline and Punish: The Birth of the Prison.* [Translated by A. Sheridan.] New York: Pantheon.

_____. 1980. *Power/Knowledge: Selected Interviews and Other Writings, 1972–1977.* [Edited by C. Gordon.] New York: Pantheon.

Fox, Robin. 1967. *Kinship and Marriage.* Harmondsworth: Penguin.

Frazier, Edward Franklin. 1957. *Black Bourgeosie.* New York: Free Press.

Fried, Morton H. 1967. *The Evolution of Political Society: An Essay in Political Anthropology.* New York: Random House.

Friedrich, Paul. 1970. Shape in Grammar. *Linguistics* 75:5–22. [Reprinted and abridged in *Symbolic Anthropology,* (eds.) J. Dolgin, D. Kemnitzer, and D. Schneider. New York: Columbia University Press, 1977.]

_____. 1979. *Language, Context, and the Imagination: Essays.* [Edited by A. Dil.] Stanford: Stanford University Press.

Fry, Peter. 1976. *Spirits of Protest: Spirit-Mediums and the Articulation of Consensus Among the Zezuru of Southern Rhodesia (Zimbabwe).* Cambridge: Cambridge University Press.

Fuller, Chris, and Parry, Jonathan. 1989. "Petulant Inconsistency"? The Intellectual Achievement of Edmund Leach. *Anthropology Today* 5:11–14.

Fussell, Paul. 1980. *Abroad: British Literary Traveling Between the Wars.* Oxford: Oxford University Press.

Gaitskell, Deborah. 1983. Housewives, Maids, or Mothers: Some Contradictions of Domesticity for Christian Women in Johannesburg, 1903–1939. *Journal of African History* 24:241–256.

Gallagher, Catherine. 1985. *The Industrial Reformation of English Fiction: Social Discourse and Narrative Form, 1832–1867.* Chicago: University of Chicago Press.

Garwood, John. 1853. *The Million-Peopled City.* [*The Rise of Urban Britain.*] London: Wertheim & Macintosh.

Gaskell, P. 1836. *Artisans and Machinery: The Moral and Physical Condition of the Manufacturing Population.* London: J. W. Parker.

Geertz, Clifford. 1973. *The Interpretation of Cultures: Selected Essays.* New York: Basic Books.

Gelfand, Michael. 1957. *Livingstone the Doctor: His Life and Travels.* Oxford: Blackwell.

Gell, Alfred. 1975. *Metamorphosis of the Cassowaries: Umeda Society, Language, and Ritual.* London: Athlone Press.

———. 1980. The Gods at Play: Vertigo and Possession in Muria Religion. *Man* (n.s.) 15:219–248.

Genovese, Eugene D. 1971. *In Red and Black: Marxian Explorations in Southern and Afro-American History.* New York: Pantheon.

———. 1972. *Roll, Jordan, Roll: The World the Slaves Made.* New York: Random House.

Giddens, Anthony. 1976. *New Rules of Sociological Method: A Positive Critique of Interpretative Sociologies.* New York: Basic Books.

Gilman, Sander L. 1985. Black Bodies, White Bodies: Toward an Iconography of Female Sexuality in Late Nineteenth-Century Art, Medicine, and Literature. *Critical Inquiry* 12:204–242.

Ginzburg, Carlo. 1980. *The Cheese and the Worms: The Cosmos of a Sixteenth-Century Miller.* [Translated by J. and A. Tedeschi.] Baltimore: Johns Hopkins University Press.

———. 1983. *The Night Battles: Witchcraft and Agrarian Cults in the Sixteenth and Seventeenth Centuries.* [Translated by J. and A. Tedeschi.] London: Routledge & Kegan Paul.

Gluckman, Max. 1963. *Order and Rebellion in Tribal Africa: Collected Essays.* Glencoe, Ill.: Free Press.

———. 1965. *Politics, Law and Ritual in Tribal Society.* Oxford: Basil Blackwell.

———. 1968. *Analysis of a Social Situation in Modern Zululand.* Manchester: Manchester University.

Gluckman, Max; Mitchell, J. Clyde; and Barnes, John A. 1949. The Village Headman in British Central Africa. *Africa* 19:89–106.

Godoy, Ricardo. 1985. Mining: Anthropological Perspectives. *Annual Review of Anthropology* 14:199–217.

Goffman, Erving. 1961. *Asylums: Essays on the Social Situation of Mental Patients and Other Inmates.* Garden City, N.Y.: Anchor Books.

Goldschmidt, Walter R. 1974. The Economics of Brideprice Among the Sebei and in East Africa. *Ethnology* 13:311–331.

Gollock, Georgina Anne. 1909. *Aunt Africa: A Family Affair.* London: Church Missionary Society.

Goody, John Rankine [Jack]. 1977. *The Domestication of the Savage Mind.* Cambridge: Cambridge University Press.

Goody, John Rankine [Jack]. (ed.). 1958. *The Developmental Cycle in Domestic Groups.* Cambridge: Cambridge University Press.

Gordon, Milton Myron. 1978. *Human Nature, Class, and Ethnicity.* New York: Oxford University Press.

Gordon, Robert J. 1977. *Mines, Masters, and Migrants: Life in a Namibian Mine Compound.* Johannesburg: Ravan Press.

———. 1978. The Celebration of Ethnicity: A "Tribal Fight" in a Namibian Mine Compound. In *Ethnicity in Modern Africa,* (ed.) B. du Toit. Boulder: Westview Press.

Gould, Stephen J. 1985. *The Flamingo's Smile: Reflections in Natural History.* New York: Norton.

Gray, Robert F. 1960. Sonjo Bride-Price and the Question of African "Wife-Purchase." *American Anthropologist* 62:34–57.

Great Britain. 1891–1892. *Bechuanaland Protectorate: Annual Report.* London: Colonial Office.

Greeley, Andrew M. 1974. *Ethnicity in the United States: A Preliminary Reconnaissance.* New York: Wiley.

Greenberg, Stanley B. 1980. *Race and State in Capitalist Development: Comparative Perspectives.* New Haven: Yale University Press.

Greenblatt, Stephen Jay. 1980. *Renaissance Self-Fashioning: From More to Shakespeare.* Chicago: University of Chicago Press.

———. 1990. *Learning to Curse: Essays in Early Modern Culture.* New York: Routledge.

Greenwood, James. 1869. *The Seven Curses of London.* London: S. Rivers.

———. 1874. *The Wilds of London.* London: Chatto & Windus.

Gregory, Christopher A. 1982. *Gifts and Commodities.* London: Academic Press.

Griaule, Marcel. 1965. *Conversations with Ogotemmêli: An Introduction to Dogon Religious Ideas.* [Translated by R. Butler and A. Richards.] London: Oxford University Press.

Grove, Richard. 1989. Scottish Missionaries, Evangelical Discourses, and the Origins of Conservation Thinking in Southern Africa, 1820–1900. *Journal of Southern African Studies* 15:163–187.

Guha, Ranajit. 1983. *Elementary Aspects of Peasant Insurgency in Colonial India.* New Delhi: Oxford University Press.

Gulbrandsen, Ørnulf. 1986. To Marry—Or Not to Marry: Marital Strategies and Sexual Relations in a Tswana Society. *Ethnos* 51:7–28.

———. 1987. *Privilege and Responsibility: On Transformations of Hierarchical Relations in a Tswana Society.* Bergen: Department of Anthropology, University of Bergen.

Gusdorf, Georges. 1980. Conditions and Limits of Autobiography. [Translated by J. Olney.] In *Autobiography: Essays Theoretical and Critical,* (ed.) J. Olney. Princeton: Princeton University Press.

Guy, Jeff. 1979. *The Destruction of the Zulu Kingdom: The Civil War in Zululand, 1879–1884.* London: Longman.

———. 1980. Ecological Factors in the Rise of Shaka and the Zulu Kingdom. In *Economy and Society in Pre-Industrial South Africa,* (eds.) S. Marks and A. Atmore. London: Longman.

———. 1987. Analysing Pre-Capitalist Societies in Southern Africa. *Journal of Southern African Studies* 14:18–37.

Guy, Jeff, and Thabane, Motlatsi. 1986. Perceptions of Mining: Labour, Mechanization, and Shaft Sinking on the South African Gold Mines. Paper read at conference, Culture and Consciousness in Southern Africa, University of Manchester, September.

Halévy, Élie. 1924. *A History of the English People in 1815.* [Translated by E. Watkin and D. Barker.] New York: Harcourt Brace.

Haley, Bruce. 1978. *The Healthy Body and Victorian Culture.* Cambridge: Harvard University Press.

Hall, Catherine. 1985. Private Persons Versus Public Someones: Class, Gender, and Politics in England, 1780–1850. In *Language, Gender, and Childhood,* (eds.) C. Steedman, C. Urwin, and V. Walkerdine. London: Routledge & Kegan Paul.

Hall, Charles. 1805. *The Effects of Civilization on the People in European States.* London: for the author and sold by T. Ostell & C. Chappel.

Hall, Stuart. 1982. The Rediscovery of "Ideology": The Return of the Repressed in Media Studies. *Culture, Society, and the Media,* (eds.) M. Gurevitch, T. Bennett, J. Curran, and J. Woollacott. London: Methuen.

Hall, Stuart; Jefferson, Tony; and Roberts, Brian (eds.). 1976. *Resistance Through Rituals: Youth Subcultures in Post-War Britain.* London: Hutchinson.

Hanna, Judith Lynne. 1977. To Dance Is Human. In *The Anthropology of the Body,* (ed.) J. Blacking. London: Academic Press.

Hannerz, Ulf. 1983. Tools of Identity and Imagination. In *Identity: Personal and Socio-Cultural: A Symposium,* (ed.) A. Jacobson-Widding. Atlantic Highlands, N.J.: Humanities Press.

Hansen, Karen Tranberg. 1989. *Distant Companions: Servants and Employers in Zambia, 1900–1985.* Ithaca: Cornell University Press.

Harlan, Rolvix. 1906. *John Alexander Dowie and the Christian Catholic Apostolic Church in Zion.* Evansville, Ind.: R. M. Antes.

Harlow, Barbara. 1986. Introduction. In *The Colonial Harem,* (ed.) Malek Alloula. Minneapolis: University of Minnesota Press.

Harris, William C. 1838. *Narrative of an Expedition into Southern Africa. . . .* Bombay: American Mission Press. [Reprint, 1967. New York: Arno Press.]

Hartley, Leslie Poles. 1956. *The Go-Between.* London: Hamish Hamilton.

Hattersley, Alan F. 1952. The Missionary in South African History. *Theoria* 4:86–88.

Hausen, Karin. 1981. Family and Role-Division: The Polarisation of Sexual Stereotypes in the Nineteenth Century. In *The German Family,* (eds.) R. Evans and W. Lee. London: Croom Helm; Totowa: Barnes & Noble.

Hay, John. 1989. Representation of the Body in Traditional China. Paper presented at the Triangle East Asia Colloquium, Raleigh, N.C., February.

Headrick, Rita. 1987. The Impact of Colonialism on Health in French Equatorial Africa, 1880–1934. Ph.D dissertation, University of Chicago.

Hebdige, Dick. 1979. *Subculture: The Meaning of Style.* London: Methuen.

———. 1988. *Hiding in the Light: On Images and Things.* London and New York: Routledge.

Hechter, Michael. 1975. *Internal Colonialism: The Celtic Fringe in British National Development, 1536–1966.* Berkeley: University of California Press.

Herskovits, Melville J. 1926. The Cattle Complex in East Africa. *American Anthropologist* 28:230–272, 361–388, 494–528, 633–664.

Hertz, Robert. 1973. The Pre-eminence of the Right Hand: A Study in Religious Polarity. In *Right and Left: Essays on Dual Symbolic Classification*, (ed.) R. Needham. Chicago: University of Chicago Press.

Hill, Christopher. 1969. *Reformation to Industrial Revolution, 1530–1780*. Harmondsworth: Penguin.

———. 1972. *The World Turned Upside Down: Radical Ideas During the English Revolution*. New York: Viking.

Hindess, Barry. 1972. The "Phenomenological" Sociology of Alfred Schutz. *Economy and Society* 1:1–27.

Hindess, Barry, and Hirst, Paul Q. 1975. *Pre-Capitalist Modes of Production*. London: Routledge & Kegan Paul.

Hobsbawm, Eric J. 1959. *Primitive Rebels: Studies in Archaic Forms of Social Movement in the Nineteenth and Twentieth Centuries*. Manchester: Manchester University Press.

———. 1962. *The Age of Revolution, 1789–1848*. New York: New American Library.

———. 1964. *Labouring Men: Studies in the History of Labour*. London: Weidenfeld & Nicholson.

———. 1990. Escaped Slaves of the Forest: A Review of *Alabi's World*, R. Price (Baltimore: Johns Hopkins University Press, 1990). *New York Review* 37(6 December):46–48.

Hobsbawm, Eric J., and Ranger, Terence O. 1983. *The Invention of Tradition*. Cambridge and New York: Cambridge University Press.

Hodgen, Margaret T. 1964. *Early Anthropology in the Sixteenth and Seventeenth Centuries*. Philadelphia: University of Pennsylvania Press.

Hollingshead, John. 1861. *Ragged London in 1861*. London: Smith, Elder.

Holquist, Michael. 1981. Introduction. In *The Dialogic Imagination: Four Essays by M. M. Bakhtin*, (ed.) M. Holquist. Austin: University of Texas Press.

Holston, James. 1989. *The Modernist City: An Anthropological Critique of Brasilia*. Chicago: University of Chicago Press.

Holub, Emil. 1881. *Seven Years in South Africa: Travels, Researches, and Hunting Adventures. . . . ,* 2 volumes. [Translated by E. Frewer.] Boston: Houghton Mifflin.

Homans, George C., and Schneider, David M. 1955. *Marriage, Authority, and Final Causes: A Study of Unilateral Cross-Cousin Marriage*. Glencoe, Ill.: Free Press.

Horton, Robin. 1967. African Traditional Thought and Western Science. *Africa* 31:50–71, 155–187.

Hubert, Henri, and Mauss, Marcel. 1964. *Sacrifice: Its Nature and Function*. [Translated by W. Halls.] London: Cohen & West.

Hugh-Jones, Christine. 1979. *From the Milk River: Spatial and Temporal Processes in Northwest Amazonia*. Cambridge: Cambridge University Press.

Hughes, Isaac. 1841. Missionary Labours Among the Batlapi. *Evangelical Magazine and Missionary Chronicle* 19:522–523.

Hume, David, 1854. *The Philosophical Works*, 4 volumes. Boston: Little, Brown.

Hunt, Nancy R. 1990. Domesticity and Colonialism in Belgian Africa: Usumbura's *Foyer Social*, 1946–1960. *Signs* 15:447–474.

Hunter, Monica. 1936. *Reaction to Conquest: Effects of Contact with Europeans on the Pondo of South Africa.* London: Oxford University Press.

Huntington, William Richard. 1974. *Religion and Social Organization of the Bara People of Madagascar.* Ann Arbor: University Microfilms International.

Hutchinson, Bertram. 1957. Some Social Consequences of Nineteenth Century Mission Activity Among the South African Bantu. *Africa* 27:160–177.

Hutchinson, Sharon E. 1988. The Nuer in Crisis: Coping with Money, War, and the State. Ph.D. dissertation, University of Chicago.

Huxley, Francis. 1977. The Body and the Play Within the Play. In *The Anthropology of the Body,* (ed.) J. Blacking. London: Academic Press.

Hymes, Dell H. (ed.). 1969. *Reinventing Anthropology.* New York: Random House.

Isaacs, Harold Robert. 1975. *Idols of the Tribe: Group Identity and Political Change.* New York: Harper & Row.

Jeal, Tim. 1973. *Livingstone.* New York: Putnam.

Jephson, Henry. 1907. *The Sanitary Evolution of London.* New York: N.Y.A. Wessels.

Johnson, Richard. 1978. Edward Thompson, Eugene Genovese, and Socialist-Humanist History. *History Workshop* 6:79–100.

———. 1979. Culture and the Historians. In *Working-Class Culture: Studies in History and Theory,* (eds.) J. Clarke, C. Critcher, and R. Johnson. London: Hutchinson.

———. 1983. *What Is Cultural Studies Anyway?* Stenciled Paper, no. 74. Birmingham: Centre for Contemporary Cultural Studies.

Johnston, Harry H. n.d. *David Livingstone.* London: Charles H. Kelly.

Jones, Coby. n.d. Leeches on Society: Bloodletting and the Economies of Blood in British Heroic Medical Practices. M.A. thesis, University of Chicago.

Kelly, Joan. 1984. *Women, History, and Theory: The Essays of Joan Kelly.* Chicago: University of Chicago Press.

Keyes, Charles F.; Kendall, Laurel; and Hardacre, Helen (eds.). n.d. *Visions of Authority in Asia.* Honolulu: University of Hawaii Press. In press.

Kinsman, Margaret. 1980. Notes on the Southern Tswana Social Formation. Paper read at the Africa Seminar, University of Cape Town.

———. 1983. "Beasts of Burden": The Subordination of Southern Tswana Women, ca. 1800–1840. *Journal of Southern African Studies* 10:39–54.

Knorr, Klaus Eugen. 1944. *British Colonial Theories, 1570–1850.* Toronto: University of Toronto Press.

Kottak, Conrad Phillip. 1980. *The Past in the Present: History, Ecology, and Cultural Variation in Highland Madagascar.* Ann Arbor: University of Michigan Press.

Krige, Eileen J. 1981. Lovedu Marriage and Social Change. In *Essays on African Marriage in Southern Africa,* (eds.) E. Krige and J. Comaroff. Cape Town: Juta.

Krige, Eileen J., and Krige, Jacob D. 1943. *The Realm of a Rain-Queen: A Study of the Pattern of Lovedu Society.* London: Oxford University Press.

Kuhn, Thomas S. 1962. *The Structure of Scientific Revolutions.* Chicago: University of Chicago Press.

Kuper, Adam. 1975a. The Social Structure of the Sotho-Speaking Peoples of Southern Africa. *Africa* 45:67–81, 139–149.

———. 1975b. Preferential Marriage and Polygyny Among the Tswana. In *Studies in African Social Anthropology,* (eds.) M. Fortes and S. Patterson. London: Academic Press.

———. 1982. *Wives for Cattle: Bridewealth and Marriage in Southern Africa.* London: Routledge & Kegan Paul.

La Fontaine, Jean S. 1972. Ritualisation of Women's Life-Crises in Bugisu. In *The Interpretation of Ritual: Essays in Honour of A. I. Richards,* (ed.) J. La Fontaine. London: Tavistock.

Lakatos, Imre, and Musgrave, Alan (eds.) 1968. *Problems in the Philosophy of Science.* Amsterdam: North-Holland Publishing Co.

Lave, Jean. 1988. *Cognition in Practice: Mind, Mathematics, and Culture in Everyday Life.* Cambridge: Cambridge University Press.

Lawrence, David Hebert. 1922. *Sons and Lovers.* New York: Modern Library.

Leach, Edmund Ronald. 1951. The Structural Implications of Matrilateral Cross-Cousin Marriage. *Journal of the Royal Anthropological Institute* 81:23–55.

———. 1954. *Political Systems of Highland Burma: A Study of Kachin Social Structure.* London: Bell.

———. 1961. *Rethinking Anthropology.* London: Athlone Press.

Leavitt, John Harold. 1985. The Language of the Gods: Discourse and Experience in a Central Himalayan Ritual. Ph.D. dissertation, University of Chicago.

Legassick, Martin C. 1969a. The Griqua, the Sotho-Tswana and the Missionaries, 1700-1840: The Politics of a Frontier Zone. Ph.D. dissertation, University of California, Los Angeles.

———. 1969b. The Sotho-Tswana Peoples Before 1800. In *African Societies in Southern Africa,* (ed.) L. Thompson. London: Heinemann.

———. 1980. The Frontier Tradition in South African Historiography. In *Economy and Society in Pre-Industrial South Africa,* (eds.) S. Marks and A. Atmore. London: Longman.

Le Goff, Jacques. 1988. *The Medieval Imagination.* [Translated by A. Goldhammer.] Chicago: University of Chicago Press.

Lenin, Vladimir Illich. 1971. Selections from *The Development of Capitalism in Russia.* In *Essential Works of Lenin,* (ed.) H. Christman. New York: Bantam.

Le Roy Ladurie, Emmanuel. 1979. *Montaillou: The Promised Land of Error.* [Translated by B. Bray.] New York: Vintage Books.

Levi-Strauss, Claude. 1963a. *Structural Anthropology.* New York: Basic Books.

———. 1963b. *Totemism.* [Translated by R. Needham.] Boston: Beacon.

———. 1969. *The Elementary Structures of Kinship.* [Translated by J. Bell, J. von Sturmer, and R. Needham.] Boston: Beacon.

———. 1972. *Tristes Tropiques.* [Translated by J. Russell.] New York: Atheneum.

———. 1976. *Structural Anthropology,* Volume 2. [Translated by M. Layton.] New York: Basic Books.

Lewis, Ioan M. (ed.). 1968. *History and Social Anthropology.* London: Tavistock.

Lichtenstein, Heinrich (M.W.C.). 1928–1930. *Travels in Southern Africa, in the Years 1803, 1804, 1805, and 1806,* 2 volumes. [Translated by A. Plumptre.] Cape Town: Van Riebeeck Society.

———. 1973. *Foundation of the Cape* (1811) and *About the Bechuanas* (1807). [Translated and edited by O. Spohr.] Cape Town: Balkema.

Lichtman, Richard. 1975. Marx's Theory of Ideology. *Socialist Revolution* 5:45–76.

Lienhardt, Godfrey. 1961. *Divinity and Experience: The Religion of the Dinka.* Oxford: Clarendon Press.

Linton, Ralph. 1924. Totemism and the A.E.F. *American Anthropologist* 26:296–300.

Lister, Margaret H. (ed.). 1949. *Journals of Andrew Geddes Bain.* Cape Town: Van Riebeeck Society.

Livingstone, David. 1843. State and Progress of the Kuruman Mission. *Evangelical Magazine and Missionary Chronicle* 8:57–58.

_____ . 1857. *Missionary Travels and Researches in South Africa.* London: Murray.

_____ . 1858. *Dr. Livingstone's Cambridge Lectures.* Cambridge: Deighton, Bell & Co.; London: Bell & Daldy.

_____ . 1861. On Fever in the Zambesi. A Note from Dr. Livingstone to Dr. M'William. Transmitted by Captain Washington, R.N., F.R.S., Hydrographer to the Admiralty. *Lancet,* 24 August.

London Missionary Society. 1830. *Report of the Directors of the London Missionary Society, May 1830.* London: Westly & Davis.

Long, Norman. 1984. *Creating Space for Change: A Perspective on the Sociology of Development.* [Inaugural Lecture for Professorship of Empirical Sociology.] Wageningen: Agricultural University.

Loudon, Joseph B. 1977. On Body Products. In *The Anthropology of the Body,* (ed.) J. Blacking. London: Academic Press.

Ludorf, Joseph D.M. 1854. Extract of a Letter from Rev. Joseph Ludorf, Thaba 'Nchu. *Wesleyan Missionary Notices—Relating to Foreign Missions* (Third Series) 12:194.

_____ . 1863. Extract of a Letter from Moshaning. *Wesleyan Missionary Notices—Relating to Foreign Missions* (Third Series) 120:203–207.

Lye, William F. 1969. The Distribution of the Sotho Peoples After the Difaqane. In *African Societies in Southern Africa,* (ed.) L. Thompson. London: Heinemann.

Lye, William F., and Murray, Colin. 1980. *Transformations on the Highveld: The Tswana and Southern Sotho.* Totowa: Barnes & Noble.

Lyons, Maryinez. 1985. From "Death Camps" to *Cordon Sanitaire:* The Development of Sleeping Sickness Policy in the Uele District of the Belgian Congo, 1903–1914. *Journal of African History* 26:69–91.

Mackenzie, John. 1871. *Ten Years North of the Orange River: A Story of Everyday Life and Work Among the South African Tribes.* Edinburgh: Edmonston & Douglas.

_____ . 1883. *Day Dawn in Dark Places: A Story of Wanderings and Work in Bechwanaland.* London: Cassell.

_____ . 1887. *Austral Africa: Losing It or Ruling It,* 2 volumes. London: Sampson Low.

Macmillan, William Miller. 1927. *The Cape Colour Question: A Historical Survey.* London: Faber & Gwyer.

_____ . 1929. *Bantu, Boer, and Briton: The Making of the South African Native Problem.* London: Faber & Gwyer.

———. 1936. Political Development, 1822–1834. In *The Cambridge History of the British Empire,* Volume 8, (eds.) A. Newton and E. Benians. Cambridge: Cambridge University Press.

Mafeje, Archie. 1971. The Ideology of Tribalism. *Journal of Modern African Studies* 9:253–262.

Mair, Lucy. 1985. Correspondence: The Cattle Complex. *Man* (n.s.) 20:743.

Maitland, Frederic William. 1936. *Selected Essays.* [Edited by H. Hazeltine, G. Lapsley, and P. Winfield.] Cambridge: Cambridge University Press.

Malinowksi, Bronislaw. 1948. *Magic, Science, and Religion and Other Essays.* Boston: Beacon Press.

Maquet, Jacques J. 1961. *The Premise of Inequality in Ruanda: A Study of Political Relations in a Central African Kingdom.* London: Oxford University Press.

Marais, Johannes Stephanus. 1939. *The Cape Coloured People, 1652–1937.* London: Longmans, Green.

Marcus, George E. 1986. Contemporary Problems of Ethnography in the Modern World System. In *Writing Culture: The Poetics and Politics of Ethnography,* (eds.) J. Clifford and G. Marcus. Berkeley: University of California Press.

Marks, Shula, and Rathbone, Richard. 1982. Introduction. In *Industrialization and Social Change in South Africa: African Class Formation, Culture, and Consciousness, 1870–1930,* (eds.) S. Marks and R. Rathbone. London and New York: Longman.

Marriott, McKim. 1976. Hindu Transactions: Diversity Without Dualism. In *Transaction and Meaning: Directions in the Anthropology of Exchange and Symbolic Behavior,* (ed.) B. Kapferer. Philadelphia: Institute for the Study of Human Issues.

Martin, Emily. 1987. *The Woman in the Body: A Cultural Analysis of Reproduction.* Boston: Beacon.

Marx, Karl. 1906. *Capital: A Critique of Political Economy.* [Edited by F. Engels.] New York: Random House.

———. 1967. *Capital: A Critique of Political Economy,* 3 volumes. New York: International Publishers.

Marx, Karl, and Engels, Friedrich. 1970. *The German Ideology.* New York: International Publishers.

Matory, James Lorand. 1986. Vessels of Power: The Dialectical Symbolism of Power in Yoruba Religion and Polity. M.A. thesis, University of Chicago.

Matthews, Zachariah K. 1945. A Short History of the Tshidi Barolong. *Fort Hare Papers* 1:9–28.

———. n.d. Fieldwork Reports. Botswana National Archives.

Mauss, Marcel. 1954. *The Gift: Forms and Functions of Exchange in Archaic Societies.* [Translated by I. Cunnison.] London: Cohen & West.

———. 1973. Techniques of the Body. [Translated by B. Brewster.] *Economy and Society* 2:70–88.

Mayhew, Henry. 1851. *London Labour and the London Poor: A Cyclopaedia of the Condition of Those That Will Work, Those That Cannot Work, and Those That Will Not Work,* Volume 1. London: G. Woodfall.

Maylam, Paul. 1980. *Rhodes, the Tswana, and the British: Colonialism, Collaboration, and Conflict in the Bechuanaland Protectorate, 1885–1899.* Westport and London: Greenwood Press.

Mazrui, Ali A. 1978. Ethnic Tensions and Political Stratification in Uganda. In *Ethnicity in Modern Africa,* (ed.) B. du Toit. Boulder: Westview Press.

McClintock, Anne. 1987. "Azikwelwa" (We Will Not Ride): Politics and Value in Black South African Poetry. *Critical Inquiry* 13:597–623.

McCloskey, Donald N. 1985. *The Rhetoric of Economics.* Madison: University of Wisconsin Press.

McCracken, Grant. 1988. *Culture and Consumption: New Approaches to the Symbolic Character of Consumer Goods and Activities.* Bloomington: Indiana University Press.

McDougall, Lorna. 1977. Symbols and Somatic Structures. In *The Anthropology of the Body,* (ed.) J. Blacking. London: Academic Press.

McGuire, Randall H. 1982. The Study of Ethnicity in Historical Archaeology. *Journal of Anthropological Archaeology* 1:159–178.

Meillassoux, Claude. 1964. *Anthropologie Économique des Gouro de Côte d'Ivoire.* Paris: Mouton.

_____. 1972. From Reproduction to Production. *Economy and Society* 1:93–105.

_____. 1981. *Maidens, Meal, and Money: Capitalism and the Domestic Community.* Cambridge: Cambridge University Press.

Meintjes, Johannes. 1973. *The Voortrekkers: The Story of the Great Trek and the Making of South Africa.* London: Cassell.

Merleau-Ponty, Maurice. 1962. *Phenomenology of Perception.* [Translated by C. Smith.] New York: Humanities Press.

_____. 1970. The Spatiality of the Lived Body and Motility. In *The Philosophy of the Body,* (ed.) S. Spicker. New York: Quadrangle.

Mill, John Stuart. 1929. *Principles of Political Economy with Some of Their Applications to Social Philosophy.* [Edited by W. Ashley.] London and New York: Longmans, Green.

_____. 1982. *Collected Works of John Stuart Mill,* Volume 6. London: Routledge & Kegan Paul.

Mills, C. Wright. 1961. *The Sociological Imagination.* New York: Grove Press.

Miner, Horace. 1956. Body Ritual Among the Nacirema. *American Anthropologist* 58:503–507.

Mitchell, J. Clyde. 1956a. *The Kalela Dance: Aspects of Social Relationships Among Urban Africans in Northern Rhodesia.* Occasional Paper no. 27. Livingstone: Rhodes-Livingstone Institute.

_____. 1956b. *The Yao Village: A Study in the Social Structure of a Nyasaland People.* Manchester: Manchester University Press.

Mitchell, W.J. Thomas. 1986. *Iconology: Image, Text, Ideology.* Chicago: University of Chicago Press.

Moerman, Michael. 1968. Being Lue: Uses and Abuses of Ethnic Identification. In *Essays on the Problem of Tribe,* (ed.) J. Helms. Proceedings of the 1967 annual spring meeting of the American Ethnological Society. Seattle: University of Washington Press.

Moffat, John S. 1886. *The Lives of Robert and Mary Moffat.* New York: Armstrong & Son.

Moffat, Mary. 1967. Letter to a Well-Wisher. *Quarterly Bulletin of the South African Library* 22:16–19.

Moffat, Robert. 1842. *Missionary Labours and Scenes in Southern Africa.* London: Snow. [Reprint, 1969. New York: Johnson Reprint Corporation.]

Molema, Silas Modiri. 1920. *The Bantu—Past and Present.* Edinburgh: W. Green & Son.

———. 1951. *Chief Moroka: His Life, His Times, His Country, and His People.* Cape Town: Methodist Publishing House.

———. 1966. *Montshiwa, 1815–1896, Barolong Chief and Patriot.* Cape Town: Struik.

———. n.d.[a] Ethnographic and Historical Notes. Mss. Johannesburg: University of the Witwatersrand.

———. n.d.[b] *A History of Methodism Among the Tshidi Barolong.* [Pamphlet.]

Monro, John. 1837. Pretences of a Bechuana Woman to Immediate Communion with the Divine Being. *Evangelical Magazine and Missionary Chronicle* (n.s.), 15:396–397.

Monthly Review. 1790. Review of *Proceedings of the Association for Promoting the Discovery of the Interior Parts of Africa* 2:60–68.

Morgan, David H.J. 1985. *The Family, Politics and Social Theory.* London: Routledge & Kegan Paul.

Muldoon, James. 1975. The Indian as Irishman. *Essex Institute Historical Collections* 3:267–289.

Muller, C.F.J. 1969. The Period of the Great Trek, 1834–1854. In *Five Hundred Years: A History of South Africa,* (ed.) C. Muller. Pretoria: Academica.

Müller, Friedrich Max. 1891. *The Science of Language,* Volume 1. New York: Scribner.

Munn, Nancy. 1977. The Spatiotemporal Transformation of Gawa Canoes. *Journal de la Société des Océanistes* 33:39–53.

———. 1986. *The Fame of Gawa: A Symbolic Study of Value Transformation in a Massim (Papua New Guinea) Society.* Cambridge and New York: Cambridge University Press.

Murphy, Robert F. 1971. *The Dialectics of Social Life: Alarms and Excursions in Anthropological Theory.* New York: Basic Books.

Murphy, Robert F., and Kasdan, Lionel. 1959. The Structure of Parallel Cousin Marriage. *American Anthropologist* 61:17–29.

———. 1967. Agnation and Endogamy: Some Further Considerations. *Southwestern Journal of Anthropology* 23:1–14.

Murray, Colin. 1980. Kinship: Continuity and Change. In *Transformations on the Highveld: The Tswana and Southern Sotho,* C. Murray and W. Lye. Totowa: Barnes & Noble.

———. 1981. *Families Divided: The Impact of Migrant Labour in Lesotho.* Cambridge: Cambridge University Press.

Nadel, Siegfried F. 1942. *A Black Byzantium: The Kingdom of Nupe in Nigeria.* London: Oxford University Press.

Nash, June. 1979. *We Eat the Mines and the Mines Eat Us: Dependency and Exploitation in Bolivian Tin Mines.* New York: Columbia University Press.

Needham, Rodney (ed.). 1962. *Structure and Sentiment: A Test Case in Social Anthropology.* Chicago: University of Chicago Press.

———. 1973. *Right and Left: Essays on Dual Symbolic Classification.* Chicago: University of Chicago Press.

Newborn, Jud. n.d. "Work Makes Free": Nazi Antisemitism and the Transformative Labor of Genocide. Ph.D. dissertation in preparation, University of Chicago.

Newton-King, Susan. 1980. The Labour Market of the Cape Colony, 1807–28. In *Economy and Society in Pre-Industrial South Africa,* (eds.) S. Marks and A. Atmore. London: Longman.

Northcott, William Cecil. 1961. *Robert Moffat: Pioneer in Africa, 1817–1870.* London: Lutterworth.

Oakley, Ann. 1974. *Woman's Work: The Housewife, Past and Present.* New York: Pantheon.

Oberg, Kalervo. 1940. The Kingdom of Ankole in Uganda. In *African Political Systems,* (eds.) M. Fortes and E. Evans-Pritchard. London: Oxford University Press.

Obeyesekere, Gananath. 1976. The Impact of Āyurvedic Ideas on the Culture and the Individual in Sri Lanka. In *Asian Medical Systems: A Comparative Study,* (ed.) C. Leslie. Berkeley: University of California Press.

Ohnuki-Tierney, Emiko. 1981. *Illness and Healing Among the Sakhalin Ainu: A Symbolic Interpretation.* Cambridge: Cambridge University Press.

Okihiro, Gary Y. 1976. Hunters, Herders, Cultivators, and Traders: Interaction and Change in the Kgalagadi, Nineteenth Century. Ph.D. dissertation, University of California, Los Angeles.

Oliver, Roland Anthony. 1952. *The Missionary Factor in East Africa.* London: Longmans, Green.

Ortner, Sherry B. 1984. Theory in Anthropology Since the Sixties. *Comparative Studies in Society and History* 26:126–166.

Orwell, George. 1934. *Burmese Days.* New York and London: Harcourt Brace Jovanovich.

Palmer, Robin, and Parsons, Neil (eds.). 1977. *The Roots of Rural Poverty in Central and Southern Africa.* Berkeley: University of California Press.

Park, Mungo. 1799. *Travels in the Interior Districts of Africa . . . in the Years 1795, 1796, and 1797.* London: W. Bulmer.

Park, Thomas (ed.). 1811. *The Poetical Works of Joseph Warton.* London: Whittingham & Rowland.

Parkin, David J. 1978. *The Cultural Definition of Political Response: Lineal Destiny Among the Luo.* London: Academic Press.

———. 1979. The Categorization of Work: Cases from Coastal Kenya. In *Social Anthropology of Work,* (ed.) S. Wallman. London: Academic Press.

Parson, Jack. 1984. *Botswana: Liberal Democracy and the Labor Reserve in Southern Africa.* Boulder: Westview Press.

Parsons, Neil Q. 1977. The Economic History of Khama's Country in Botswana, 1844–1930. In *The Roots of Rural Poverty in Central and Southern Africa,* (eds.) R. Palmer and N. Parsons. Berkeley: University of California Press.

Patterson, Orlando. 1977. *Ethnic Chauvinism: The Reactionary Impulse.* New York: Stein & Day.

Pauw, Berthold Adolf. 1960a. *Religion in a Tswana Chiefdom.* London: Oxford University Press.

————. 1960b. Some Changes in the Social Structure of the Tlhaping of the Taung Reserve. *African Studies* 19:49–76.

Pawley, Martin. 1971. *Architecture Versus Housing.* New York: Praeger.

Perkin, Harold James. 1969. *The Origins of Modern English Society, 1780–1880.* London: Routledge & Kegan Paul; Toronto: University of Toronto Press.

Peters, Pauline. 1983. Cattlemen, Borehole Syndicates, and Privatization in the Kgatleng District of Botswana: An Anthropological History of the Transformation of the Commons. Ph.D. dissertation, Boston University.

Philip, John. 1825. Report from Kuruman. *LMS Quarterly Chronicle* 3:223–224.

————. 1828. *Researches in South Africa; Illustrating the Civil, Moral, and Religious Condition of the Native Tribes,* 2 volumes. London: James Duncan. [Reprint, 1969. New York: Negro Universities Press.]

Plaatje, Solomon T. n.d.[a] Personal Notes. Centre for International and Area Studies, University of London.

————. n.d.[b] *Native Life in South Africa.* New York: The Crisis.

Porter, Roy. 1989. Preface. In *Bread of Dreams: Food and Fantasy in Early Modern Europe,* Piero Camporesi. [Translated by D. Gentilcore.] Chicago: University of Chicago Press.

Post, Ken. 1978. *Arise Ye Starvelings: The Jamaican Labour Rebellion of 1938 and Its Aftermath.* The Hague and London: Martinus Nijhoff.

Pratt, Mary Louise. 1985. Scratches on the Face of the Country; or, What Mr. Barrow Saw in the Land of the Bushmen. *Critical Inquiry* 12:119–143.

————. 1986. Fieldwork in Common Places. In *Writing Culture: The Poetics and Politics of Ethnography,* (eds.) J. Clifford and G. Marcus. Berkeley: University of California Press.

Radcliffe-Brown, Alfred R. 1950. Introduction. In *African Systems of Kinship and Marriage,* (eds.) A. Radcliffe-Brown and D. Forde. London: Oxford University Press.

————. 1957. *A Natural Science of Society.* Glencoe, Ill.: Free Press.

Ranger, Terence O. 1975. *Dance and Society in Eastern Africa, 1890–1970: The Beni Ngoma.* Berkeley: University of California Press.

————. 1978. Growing from the Roots: Reflections on Peasant Research in Central and Southern Africa. *Journal of Southern African Studies* 5:99–133.

————. 1983. The Invention of Tradition in Colonial Africa. In *The Invention of Tradition,* (eds.) E. Hobsbawm and T. Ranger. Cambridge: Cambridge University Press.

————. 1987. Taking Hold of the Land: Holy Places and Pilgrimages in Twentieth-Century Zimbabwe. *Past and Present* 117:158–194.

Read, James. 1850. Report on the Bechuana Mission. *Evangelical Magazine and Missionary Chronicle* 28:445–447.

Reed, John R. 1975. *Victorian Conventions.* Athens: Ohio University Press.

Reichard, Gladys Amanda. 1950. *Navaho Religion: A Study of Symbolism.* New York: Pantheon.

Rex, John. 1970. The Concept of Race in Sociological Theory. In *Race and Racialism*, (ed.) S. Zubaida. London: Tavistock.

Reyburn, H. A. 1933. The Missionary as Rain Maker. *The Critic* 1:146–153.

Roberts, Simon A., and Comaroff, John L. 1979. A Chief's Decision and the Devolution of Property in a Tswana Chiefdom. In *Power in Leadership*, (eds.) W. Shack and P. Cohen. Oxford: Clarendon Press.

Roe, Emery. 1980. *Development of Livestock, Agriculture, and Water Supplies in Botswana Before Independence.* Occasional Paper no. 10. Ithaca: Cornell University, Rural Development Committee.

Rosaldo, Renato. 1986. From the Door of His Tent: The Fieldworker and the Inquisitor. In *Writing Culture: The Poetics and Politics of Ethnography*, (eds.) J. Clifford and G. Marcus. Berkeley: University of California Press.

Roscoe, William. 1787. *The Wrongs of Africa, a Poem.* London: R. Faulder.

Ross, Andrew C. 1986. *John Philip, 1775–1851: Missions, Race, and Politics in South Africa.* Aberdeen: Aberdeen University Press.

Rybczynski, Witold. 1986. *Home: A Short History of an Idea.* New York: Viking Penguin.

Rymer, James M. 1844. *The White Slave: A Romance for the Nineteenth Century.* London: E. Lloyd.

Sahlins, Marshall D. 1976a. *Culture and Practical Reason.* Chicago: University of Chicago Press.

_____. 1976b. Colours and Cultures. *Semiotica* 16:1–22. [Reprinted in *Symbolic Anthropology*, (eds.) J. Dolgin, D. Kemnitzer, and D. Schneider. New York: Columbia University Press, 1977.]

_____. 1981. *Historical Metaphors and Mythical Realities: Structure in the Early History of the Sandwich Islands Kingdom.* Ann Arbor: University of Michigan Press.

_____. 1983. Other Times, Other Customs: The Anthropology of History. *American Anthropologist* 85:517–544.

_____. 1985. *Islands of History.* Chicago: University of Chicago Press.

_____. 1990. The Return of the Event, Again; With Reflections on the Beginnings of the Great Fijian War of 1843 to 1855 Between the Kingdoms of Bau and Rewa. In *Clio in Oceania*, (ed.) A. Biersack. Washington, D.C.: Smithsonian.

_____. n.d. Social Science; or, The Tragic Western Sense of Human Imperfection. Ms.

Said, Edward W. 1978. *Orientalism.* New York: Pantheon.

_____. 1989. Representing the Colonized: Anthropology's Interlocutors. *Critical Inquiry* 15:205–225.

Samarin, William J. 1984. The Linguistic World of Field Colonialism. *Language in Society* 13:435–453.

Samuel, Raphael. 1989. Heroes Below the Hooves of History. *The Independent*, no. 902 (31 August):23.

Sandilands, Alexander. 1953. *Introduction to Tswana.* Tiger Kloof: London Missionary Society.

Sangren, P. Steven. 1988. Rhetoric and the Authority of Ethnography: "Postmodernism" and the Social Reproduction of Texts. *Current Anthropology* 29:405–435.

Sansom, Basil. 1974. Traditional Economic Systems. In *The Bantu-Speaking Peoples of Southern Africa*, (ed.) W. Hammond-Tooke. London and Boston: Routledge & Kegan Paul.

———. 1976. A Signal Transaction and Its Currency. In *Transaction and Meaning: Directions in the Anthropology of Exchange and Symbolic Behavior*, (ed.) B. Kapferer. Philadelphia: Institute for the Study of Human Issues.

Schapera, Isaac. 1933. Economic Conditions in a Bechuanaland Reserve. *South African Journal of Science* 30:633–655.

———. 1934. The Old Bantu Culture. In *Western Civilization and the Natives of South Africa*, (ed.) I. Schapera. London: Routledge.

———. 1936. The Contributions of Western Civilisation to Modern Kxatla Culture. *Transactions of the Royal Society of South Africa* 24:221–252.

———. 1938. *A Handbook of Tswana Law and Custom*. London: Oxford University Press.

———. 1943. *Native Land Tenure in the Bechuanaland Protectorate*. Alice: Lovedale Press.

———. 1947. *Migrant Labour and Tribal Life*. London: Oxford University Press.

———. 1950. Kinship and Marriage Among the Tswana. In *African Systems of Kinship and Marriage*, (eds.) A. Radcliffe-Brown and D. Forde. London: Oxford University Press.

———. 1952. *The Ethnic Composition of Tswana Tribes*. London: London School of Economics.

———. 1953. *The Tswana*. London: International African Institute.

———. 1957. Marriage of Near Kin Among the Tswana. *Africa* 27:139–159.

———. 1962. Should Anthropologists Be Historians? *Journal of the Royal Anthropological Institute* 92:143–156.

———. 1963a. Kinship and Politics in Tswana History. *Journal of the Royal Anthropological Institute* 93:159–173.

———. 1963b. Agnatic Marriage in Tswana Royal Families. In *Studies in Kinship and Marriage*, (ed.) I. Schapera. Occasional Paper no. 16. London: Royal Anthropological Institute.

———. 1971a. *Rainmaking Rites of Tswana Tribes*. Leiden: Afrika-studiecentrum.

———. 1971b. *Married Life in an African Tribe*. Harmondsworth: Penguin. [First published in 1941. New York: Sheridan.]

Schapera, Isaac (ed.). 1960. *Livingstone's Private Journals, 1851–1853*. London: Chatto & Windus.

———. 1961. *Livingstone's Missionary Correspondence, 1841–1856*. London: Chatto & Windus.

———. 1974. *David Livingstone: South African Papers, 1849–1853*. Cape Town: Van Riebeeck Society.

Schapera, Isaac, and Goodwin, A.J.H. 1937. Work and Wealth. In *The Bantu-Speaking Tribes of South Africa*, (ed.) I. Schapera. Cape Town: Routledge.

Schneider, Harold K. 1964. Economics in East African Aboriginal Societies. In *Economic Transition in Africa*, (eds.) M. Herskovits and M. Harwitz. London: Routledge & Kegan Paul.

Schwimmer, Erik. 1979. The Self and the Product: Concepts of Work in Comparative Perspective. In *Social Anthropology of Work,* (ed.) S. Wallman. London: Academic Press.

Scott, James C. 1985. *Weapons of the Weak: Everyday Forms of Peasant Resistance.* New Haven: Yale University Press.

Scott, Paul. 1966. *The Jewel in the Crown.* London: Heinemann.

Seeley, Caroline F. n.d. The Reaction of Batswana to the Practice of Western Medicine. M.Phil. thesis, University of London.

Shelley, Percy Bysshe. 1882. *The Poetical Works of Percy Bysshe Shelley.* London: Reeves & Turner.

Shillington, Kevin. 1982. The Impact of Diamond Discoveries on the Kimberley Hinterland: Class Formation, Colonialism, and Resistance Among the Tlhaping of Griqualand West in the 1870s. In *Industrialization and Social Change in South Africa,* (eds.) S. Marks and R. Rathbone. London and New York: Longman.

———. 1985. *The Colonisation of the Southern Tswana, 1870–1900.* Johannesburg: Ravan Press.

———. 1987. Culture, Not History. Review of *Body of Power, Spirit of Resistance,* J. Comaroff. [Chicago: Chicago University Press, 1985.] *Journal of African History* 28:321–323.

Shorter, Aylward. 1972. Symbolism, Ritual, and History: An Examination of the Work of Victor Turner. In *The Historical Study of African Religion,* (eds.) T. Ranger and I. Kimambo. Berkeley: University of California Press.

Shweder, Richard A. 1982. The Lost Soul: A Phenomenology of Depression and a Framework for a Science of Emotions. Paper read at the annual meetings of the American Anthropological Association, Washington, D.C., December.

Sillery, Anthony. 1952. *The Bechuanaland Protectorate.* Cape Town: Oxford University Press.

———. 1971. *John Mackenzie of Bechuanaland, 1835–1899: A Study in Humanitarian Imperialism.* Cape Town: Balkema.

———. 1974. *Botswana: A Short Political History.* London: Methuen.

Simon, Edith. 1966. *The Reformation.* New York: Time-Life International.

Skinner, Elliot P. 1978. Voluntary Associations and Ethnic Competition in Ouagadougou. In *Ethnicity in Modern Africa,* (ed.) B. du Toit. Boulder: Westview Press.

Smith, Andrew. 1939. *The Diary of Dr. Andrew Smith, 1834–1836,* 2 volumes. [Edited by P. Kirby.] Cape Town: Van Riebeeck Society.

Smith, Edwin W. 1925. *Robert Moffat, One of God's Gardeners.* London: Church Missionary Society.

Smith, Michael G. 1960. *Government in Zazzau: A Study of Government in the Hausa Chiefdom of Zaria in Northern Nigeria from 1800–1950.* London: Oxford University Press.

———. 1962. History and Social Anthropology. *Journal of the Royal Anthropological Institute* 92:73–85.

Solomon, Edward S. 1855. *Two Lectures on the Native Tribes of the Interior.* Cape Town: Saul Solomon.

Sontag, Susan. 1978. *Illness as Metaphor.* New York: Farrar, Straus & Giroux.

South Africa, British Crown Colony of. 1905. *Report of the South African Native Affairs Commission, 1903–5.* Cape Town: Cape Times.

Southall, Aidan William. 1956. *Alur Society: A Study in Processes and Types of Domination.* Cambridge: W. Heffer & Sons.

Southey, Robert. 1815. *The Minor Poems of Robert Southey.* London: Longman, Hurst, Rees, Orme, and Brown.

Spicer, Edward H. 1971. Persistent Cultural Systems: A Comparative Study of Identity Systems That Can Adapt to Contrasting Environments. *Science* 174:795–800.

Spicker, Stuart F. (ed.). 1970. *The Philosophy of the Body: Rejections of Cartesian Dualism.* Chicago: Quadrangle Books.

Spitulnik, Debra. 1991. Making Money: Corporate Culture and Contestation over the "Commoditization of Airtime" in Zambian Broadcasting. Paper read at conference, Meaningful Currencies and Monetary Imaginations, Committee on African Studies, University of Chicago, March.

Spivak, Gayatri. 1988. Can the Subaltern Speak? In *Marxism and the Interpretation of Culture,* (eds.) C. Nelson and L. Grossberg. Urbana: University of Illinois Press.

Stallybrass, Peter, and White, Allon. 1986. *The Politics and Poetics of Transgression.* London: Methuen.

Stedman Jones, Gareth. 1971. *Outcast London: A Study of the Relationship Between the Classes in Victorian Society.* Oxford: Clarendon Press.

Steedman, Andrew. 1835. *Wanderings and Adventures in the Interior of Southern Africa,* 2 volumes. London: Longman.

Stocking, George W. 1987. *Victorian Anthropology.* New York: Free Press.

Stow, George William. 1905. *The Native Races of South Africa.* London: Swan Sonnenschein.

Streak, Michael. 1974. *The Afrikaner as Viewed by the English, 1795–1854.* Cape Town: Struik.

Suret-Canale, Jean. 1969. Tribes, Classes, Nations. *La Nouvelle Revue Internationale* 130:110–124.

Swanson, Maynard W. 1977. The Sanitation Syndrome: Bubonic Plague and Urban Native Policy in the Cape Colony, 1900–1909. *Journal of African History* 18:387–410.

Tambiah, Stanley J. 1968. The Magical Power of Words. *Man* (n.s.) 3:175–208.

Taussig, Michael. 1980a. *The Devil and Commodity Fetishism in South America.* Chapel Hill: University of North Carolina Press.

———. 1980b. Reification and the Consciousness of the Patient. *Social Science and Medicine* 14B:3–13.

———. 1987. *Shamanism, Colonialism, and the Wild Man: A Study in Terror and Healing.* Chicago: University of Chicago Press.

Theal, George McCall. 1891. *History of South Africa [1795–1834].* London: Swan Sonnenschein.

———. 1893. *History of South Africa [1834–1854].* London: Swan Sonnenschein.

———. 1902. *The Progress of South Africa in the Century.* London and Edinburgh: Chambers.

_____ . 1926. *History of South Africa from 1795-1872*, Volume 2. London: George Allen & Unwin.

Thomas, Keith Vivian. 1971. *Religion and the Decline of Magic*. New York: Scribner.

Thomis, Malcolm I. 1974. *The Town Labourer and the Industrial Revolution*. London: Batsford.

Thompson, Edward P. 1963. *The Making of the English Working Class*. London: Gollancz.

_____ . 1967. Time, Work-Discipline and Industrial Capitalism. *Past and Present* 38:56–97.

_____ . 1978a. Folklore, Anthropology and Social History. *Indian Historical Review* 3:247–266. [Also published as a *Studies in Labour History Pamphlet*, (ed.) J. L. Noyce. Brighton: Noyce, 1979.]

_____ . 1978b. An Open Letter to Leszek Kolakowski. In *The Poverty of Theory and Other Essays*, E. P. Thompson. New York: Monthly Review Press. [First published in the *Socialist Register*, 1973.]

Thompson, Leonard M. 1969. Co-operation and Conflict: The High Veld. In *The Oxford History of South Africa*, Volume 1, (eds.) M. Wilson and L. Thompson. Oxford: Oxford University Press.

Thorburn, David. 1990. Series Editor's Introduction. In *British Cultural Studies: An Introduction*, Graeme Turner. Media and Popular Culture, no. 7. Boston: Unwin Hyman.

Tilby, A. Wyatt. 1914. Some Missionary Pioneers in South Africa. In *United Empire: The Royal Colonial Institute Journal*, n.s. (1913) 4:190–195, (ed.) A. Colquhoun. London: Sir Isaac Pitman & Sons.

Tonna, Charlotte Elizabeth. 1844. *The Wrongs of Woman*. New York: J. S. Taylor.

Torgovnick, Marianna. 1990. *Gone Primitive: Savage Intellects, Modern Lives*. Chicago: University of Chicago Press.

Toynbee, Arnold. 1969. *Toynbee's Industrial Revolution*. New York: Augustus M. Kelley.

Trapido, Stanley. 1980. "The Friends of the Natives": Merchants, Peasants, and the Political and Ideological Structure of Liberalism in the Cape, 1854–1910. In *Economy and Society in Pre-Industrial South Africa*, (eds.) S. Marks and A. Atmore. London: Longman.

Trexler, Richard C. 1984. We Think, They Act: Clerical Readings of Missionary Theatre in Sixteenth Century Spain. In *Understanding Popular Culture*, (ed.) S. Kaplan. Berlin: Mouton.

Tristan, Flora. 1980. *Flora Tristan's London Journal*. [Translated by D. Palmer and G. Pincetl.] Boston: Charles River Books. [First published as *Promenades dans Londres*, 1840.]

Troeltsch, Ernst. 1949. *The Social Teaching of the Christian Churches*, Volume 2. [Translated by O. Wyon.] London: George Allen & Unwin.

Trollope, Anthony. 1878. *South Africa*, 2 volumes. London: Chapman & Hall.

Turner, Bryan S. 1984. *The Body and Society: Explorations in Social Theory*. Oxford: Basil Blackwell.

Turner, Ernest S. 1959. *Call the Doctor: A Social History of Medical Men*. New York: St. Martin's Press.

Turner, Graeme. 1990. *British Cultural Studies: An Introduction.* Media and Popular Culture, no. 7. Boston: Unwin Hyman.

Turner, Terence. 1980. The Social Skin. In *Not Work Alone,* (eds.) J. Cherfas and R. Lewin. Beverly Hills: Sage.

────. 1986. Review of *The Body and Society,* Bryan S. Turner. [Oxford: Basil Blackwell, 1984.] *American Journal of Sociology* 92:211–213.

────. 1990. Bodies and Antibodies: Bodiliness as Master-Schema of Person and Culture. Paper read at the annual meeting of the American Ethnological Society, Atlanta.

────. n.d. Marx's Concept of Structure and the Structure of Marx's Model of Capitalist Production: An Anthropological Re-reading of *Capital.* Ms.

Turner, Victor W. 1957. *Schism and Continuity in an African Society: A Study of Ndembu Village Life.* Manchester: Manchester University Press.

────. 1967. *The Forest of Symbols: Aspects of Ndembu Ritual.* Ithaca: Cornell University Press.

────. 1968. *The Drums of Affliction: A Study of Religious Processes Among the Ndembu of Zambia.* Oxford: Clarendon Press.

────. 1969. *The Ritual Process: Structure and Anti-structure.* Ithaca: Cornell University Press.

Uzzell, Douglas. 1974. *Susto* Revisited: Illness as a Strategic Role. *American Ethnologist* 1:369–378.

van der Veer, Peter. 1990. Review of *Tales of the Field: On Writing Ethnography,* J. Van Maanen [Chicago: University of Chicago Press, 1988]. *Man* (n.s.) 25:739.

Van Gennep, Arnold. 1960. *The Rites of Passage.* [Translated by M. Vizedom and G. Caffee.] Chicago: University of Chicago Press.

Van Onselin, Charles. 1973. Worker Consciousness in Black Miners: Southern Rhodesia, 1900–1920. *Journal of African History* 14:237–255.

────. 1976. *Chibaro: African Mine Labour in Southern Rhodesia, 1900–1933.* London: Pluto Press.

Vilakazi, Absolom. 1962. *Zulu Transformations.* Pietermaritzburg: University of Natal Press.

Volosinov, Valentin N. 1973. *Marxism and the Philosophy of Language.* [Translated by L. Matejka and I. Titunik.] New York: Seminar Press.

Vosloo, W. B., Kotzé, D. A., and Jeppe, W.J.O. 1974. *Local Government in Southern Africa.* Pretoria: Academica.

Vovelle, Michel. 1990. *Ideologies and Mentalities.* [Translated by E. O'Flaherty.] Chicago: University of Chicago Press.

Wallerstein, Immanuel. 1972. Social Conflict in Post-Independence Black Africa: The Concepts of Race and Status Group Reconsidered. In *Racial Tensions in National Identity,* (ed.) E. Campbell. Nashville: Vanderbilt University Press. [Reprinted in *The Capitalist World Economy,* I. Wallerstein. Cambridge: Cambridge University Press, 1979.]

Walter, Eugene Victor. 1969. *Terror and Resistance: A Study of Political Violence.* Oxford: Oxford University Press.

Warner, Wellman Joel. 1930. *The Wesleyan Movement in the Industrial Revolution.* London: Longmans, Green.

Warren, Kay B. 1978. *The Symbolism of Subordination: Indian Identity in a Guatemalan Town.* Austin: University of Texas Press.

Watson, Graham. 1970. *Passing for White: A Study of Racial Assimilation in a South African School.* London: Tavistock.

Weber, Max. 1958. *The Protestant Ethic and the Spirit of Capitalism.* [Translated by T. Parsons.] New York: Scribner.

_____. 1968. *Economy and Society.* New York: Bedminster Press.

Weiss, Brad. 1990. The Dreaded Nylon Tooth Extractor. Paper read to the African Studies Workshop, University of Chicago, May.

Werbner, Richard P. 1971. Local Adaptation and the Transformation of an Imperial Concession in Northeastern Botswana. *Africa* 41:32–41.

_____. 1985. The Argument of Images: From Zion to the Wilderness in African Churches. In *Theoretical Explorations in African Religion,* (eds.) W. van Binsbergen and M. Schoffeleers. London: Kegan Paul International.

White, Charles. 1799. *An Account of the Regular Gradation in Man, and in Different Animals and Vegetables. . . .* London: C. Dilly.

Whitefield, George. 1772. *The Works of the Reverend George Whitefield, M.A.,* Volume 5. London: E. & C. Dilly.

Willan, Brian. 1984. *Sol Plaatje: South African Nationalist, 1876–1932.* Berkeley: University of California Press.

Williams, Raymond. 1973. *The Country and the City.* New York: Oxford University Press.

_____. 1977. *Marxism and Literature.* London: Oxford University Press.

Willis, Paul E. 1977. *Learning to Labour: How Working Class Kids Get Working Class Jobs.* New York: Columbia University Press.

Willoughby, William Charles. 1899a. *Native Life on the Transvaal Border.* London: Simpkin, Marshall, Hamilton, Kent.

1899b. Our People: What They Are Like and How They Live. *News from Afar: LMS Magazine for Young People* (n.s.) 15:84–86.

_____. 1905. Notes on the Totemism of the Becwana. *Journal of the Royal Anthropological Institute* 35:295–314.

_____. 1909. Notes on the Initiation Ceremonies of the Becwana. *Journal of the Royal Anthropological Institute* 39:228–245.

_____. 1911. *A Paper Read Before the South African Council of the London Missionary Society at Tiger Kloof, March, 1911.* [Pamphlet.] Tiger Kloof: Tiger Kloof Native Institution.

_____. 1912. *Tiger Kloof: The London Missionary Society's Native Institution in South Africa.* London: London Missionary Society.

_____. 1928. *The Soul of the Bantu: A Sympathetic Study of the Magico-Religious Practices and Beliefs of the Bantu Tribes of Africa.* New York: Doubleday, Doran & Co.

_____. 1932. *Nature-Worship and Taboo: Further Studies in "The Soul of the Bantu."* Hartford: Hartford Seminary Press.

_____. n.d. *Letter from Africa.* [Pamphlet.] London: London Missionary Society.

Wilson, Bryan R. 1973. *Magic and the Millenium: A Sociological Study of Religious Movements of Protest Among Tribal and Third-World Peoples.* New York: Harper & Row.

Wilson, Monica. 1951. Witch Beliefs and Social Structure. *American Journal of Sociology* 56:307–313.

———. 1971. The Growth of Peasant Communities. In *The Oxford History of South Africa,* Volume 2, (eds.) M. Wilson and L. Thompson. Oxford: Oxford University Press.

———. 1976. *Missionaries: Conquerors or Servants of God?* [Pamphlet.] Address given at the opening of the South African Missionary Museum. Lovedale: South African Missionary Museum.

Wilson, William J. 1980. *The Declining Significance of Race: Blacks and Changing American Institutions,* second edition. Chicago: University of Chicago Press.

———. 1981. Shifts in the Analysis of Race and Ethnic Relations. In *The State of Sociology: Problems and Prospects,* (ed.) J. Short, Jr. Beverly Hills: Sage.

———. 1984. Race-Specific Policies and the Truly Disadvantaged. *Yale Law and Policy Review* 2:272–290.

Wolf, Eric R. 1982. *Europe and the People Without History.* Berkeley: University of California Press.

Wolpe, Harold. 1972. Capitalism and Cheap Labour-Power in South Africa: From Segregation to Apartheid. *Economy and Society* 1:425–456.

Wonderly, William L., and Nida, Eugene A. 1963. Linguistics and Christian Missions. *Anthropological Linguistics* 5:104–144.

Woolgar, Steve. 1988. Comment on "Rhetoric and the Authority of Ethnography: 'Postmodernism' and the Social Reproduction of Texts," P. S. Sangren. *Current Anthropology* 29:430–431.

Wordsworth, William. 1948. *A Guide Through the District of the Lakes in the North of England. . . .* [Facsimile of the 1835 edition.] Malvern: Tantivy Press.

Worsley, Peter M. 1968. *The Trumpet Shall Sound: A Study of "Cargo" Cults in Melanesia.* New York: Schocken.

———. 1970. The End of Anthropology? *Transactions of the Sixth World Congress of Sociology* 3:121–129.

Young, Allan A. 1978. Modes of Production of Medical Knowledge. *Medical Anthropology* 2:97–122.

Young, Crawford. 1976. *The Politics of Cultural Pluralism.* Madison: University of Wisconsin Press.

Ziervogel, D., and Mokgokong, P. C. 1985. *Groot Noord-Sotho Woordeboek/Comprehensive Northern Sotho Dictionary,* second edition. Pretoria: J. L. Van Schaik/ UNISA.

About the Book and Authors

OVER THE YEARS John and Jean Comaroff have broadened the study of culture and society with their reflections on power and meaning. In their work on Africa and colonialism they have explored some of the fundamental questions of social science, delving into the nature of history and human agency, culture and consciousness, ritual and representation. How are human differences constructed and institutionalized, transformed and (sometimes) effaced, empowered and (sometimes) resisted? How do local cultures articulate with global forms? How is the power of some people over others built, sustained, eroded, and negated? How does the social imagination take shape in novel yet collectively meaningful ways?

Addressing these questions, the essays in this volume—several never before published—work toward an "imaginative sociology," demonstrating the techniques by which social science may capture the contexts that human beings construct and inhabit. In the introduction, the authors offer their most complete statement to date on the nature of historical anthropology. Standing apart from the traditional disciplines of social history and modernist social science, their work is dedicated to discovering how human worlds are made and signified, forgotten and remade.

John Comaroff, professor of anthropology and sociology at the University of Chicago, is the author, with Simon Roberts, of *Rules and Processes: The Cultural Logic of Dispute in an African Context.* **Jean Comaroff,** professor of anthropology at the University of Chicago, is the author of *Body of Power, Spirit of Resistance: The Culture and History of a South African People.*

Index